TIME TO THINK

TIME TO THINK

The Inside Story of the
Collapse of the Tavistock's
Gender Service for Children

HANNAH BARNES

Swift

SWIFT PRESS

First published in Great Britain by Swift Press 2023

1 3 5 7 9 8 6 4 2

Copyright © Hannah Barnes 2023

The right of Hannah Barnes to be identified as the Author of this Work has been
asserted in accordance with the Copyright, Designs and Patents Act 1988.

Text design and typesetting by Tetragon, London
Printed and bound in Great Britain by CPI Group (UK) Ltd, Croydon, CRO 4YY

A CIP catalogue record for this book is available from the British Library

ISBN: 9781800751118
eISBN: 9781800751125

MIX
Paper | Supporting
responsible forestry
FSC® C171272
FSC
www.fsc.org

CONTENTS

Author's Note   ix
Gender Identity Development Service (GIDS) Timeline   xi

1   'Are we hurting children?'   1
2   The Vision   10

        Ellie   31

3   The Push for Puberty Blockers   36

        Phoebe   47

4   Early Intervention   53

        Jack   64

5   A New Era   71

        Diana and Alex   83

6   All Change   90
7   The Bombshell   111
8   How to Cope   128
9   Speed in Leeds   139

        Hannah   147

10 Raising Concerns   154
11 Scapegoats and Troublemakers   165
12 The Bell Report   179
13 Bell: The Aftermath   185

14   First Fears   201

Jacob   207

15   200 Miles up the M1…   221
16   Across the Sea   231
17   The GIDS Review and Outside Scrutiny   241
18   Regret and Redress   261
19   Data and 'Disproportionate effort'   277

Harriet   293

20   When in Doubt, Do the Right Thing   308
21   An Uncertain Future   325

CONCLUSION   345

Acknowledgements   375
Notes   377
Index   437

For my wonderful girls, who amaze me every day.
I'm so proud to be your Mum.

And for Pat, the most patient man on Earth.

AUTHOR'S NOTE

This book is based on the experiences of clinicians who have worked directly with several thousands of young people experiencing gender-related distress or questioning their gender identity. Their time at the Gender Identity Development Service (GIDS) spans more than two decades, across multiple cities. Many have not worked alongside each other, nor ever met. They are male and female, gay and straight, newly qualified and hugely experienced. Some worked at the service for a matter of months, some years, and some many years. By training they are psychologists, psychotherapists, social workers, family therapists and nurses. They are all conscientious professionals, trying to do their best for their patients.

I contacted close to 60 clinicians who have worked at GIDS in an attempt to hear as broad a range of voices as possible. Many agreed to speak to me and share their thoughts and experiences of their work. A number have spoken on the record and are named; others have spoken on the condition of anonymity, or to help inform my writing only. Where names have been changed this is indicated, but all quotations are real and accurate, recorded verbatim.

A number of governors responsible for ensuring that the NHS Trust that houses GIDS is well run have also spoken with me, along with senior clinicians working elsewhere in the Tavistock and Portman NHS Foundation Trust.

Where allegations cannot be attributed to named individuals in order to protect their anonymity, they have been double-sourced at a minimum and a right-of-reply has been given. Testimony is supported by several thousand pages of internal documentation relating to the service, alongside official reports, academic papers and legal judgments. I have also read every published Freedom of Information request relating to GIDS, as well as making some of my own.

Former GIDS service users who are identified have given permission to be so, while others have had their names changed to protect their privacy. All have provided documentation from their time at GIDS, and I am hugely grateful to them for trusting me with their stories, sharing with me their experiences and, in some instances, highly personal and sensitive information. Where clinicians have discussed clinical examples with me, all identifying information has been changed to protect patient confidentiality. I have not been privy to any identifying clinical data beyond that shared with me by the young people themselves.

Everyone interviewed for this book has either: direct experience of GIDS as a member of staff, a service user or the parent of one; raised concerns about GIDS from within the Tavistock and Portman Trust; sought to improve the service in their capacity as a governor for the Trust; or been directly involved in legal action involving GIDS.

I have conducted well over a hundred hours of interviews.

This is an area of healthcare and wider society where language is often disputed. Words and terms that are accepted at one time become outdated or even offensive at another. I have tried to use the language that was in place at the time of events being written about, and the terminology used by my contributors. I respect people's chosen pronouns throughout. I use the words 'boy' and 'girl' throughout to mean those who are at birth biologically male and those biologically female, respectively. I do this not to cause any offence to those who choose to transition, but to aid clarity.

All but two of the scores of interviews that form the basis of this book were completed before the decision to close GIDS was taken. These clinicians and former service users did not know what steps NHS England would take when they agreed to speak to me. It is a story that has been constantly evolving while I have been writing, and one in which there are, no doubt, more changes to come.

GENDER IDENTITY DEVELOPMENT SERVICE (GIDS) TIMELINE

1989 The Gender Identity Development Clinic opens at St George's Hospital, south London, under the leadership of Dr Domenico Di Ceglie.

1994 The service moves to the Tavistock and Portman Trust, north London.

May–October 2005 Dr David Taylor, medical director of the Trust, conducts a review of GIDS after concerns are raised by staff.

January 2006 Taylor's report makes a series of recommendations to strengthen the care provided.

2009 GIDS is nationally commissioned by the NHS, and Dr Polly Carmichael replaces Domenico Di Ceglie as director of the service.

February 2011 A joint team from GIDS and University College London Hospitals (UCLH) gain ethical approval for an 'Early Intervention Study' to evaluate the impact of early pubertal suppression in a selected group of young people.

2012   GIDS opens a second base in Leeds.

April 2014   GIDS rolls out 'early intervention' across the
                        service. The study's lower age limit of 12 is
                        removed as the clinic moves to a 'stage' not
                        'age' approach, allowing younger children to be
                        referred for puberty blockers.

October 2015   As referrals rise exponentially, the GIDS
                        leadership commission external consultant Femi
                        Nzegwu to advise on working practices. She
                        recommends GIDS 'take the courageous and
                        realistic action of capping the number of referrals
                        immediately'.

August 2018   Dr David Bell presents the Tavistock board with
                        a report, detailing the concerns of ten GIDS staff
                        who have shared their worries with him as staff
                        governor. He brands GIDS 'not fit for purpose'.

February 2019   Commissioned by the Trust to investigate the
                        concerns raised by Bell, medical director Dr
                        Dinesh Sinha's GIDS Review is published. The
                        Trust says it does not identify 'any immediate
                        issues in relation to patient safety or failings in
                        the overall approach taken by the Service'.

September 2020   NHS England commissions paediatrician Dr
                        Hilary Cass to conduct an independent review
                        into gender identity services for children and
                        young people.

December 2020   The High Court rules that it is 'unlikely' that
                        under-16s can give informed consent to treatment
                        with puberty blockers.

January 2021   A further report into safeguarding concerns raised by GIDS clinician Helen Roberts is submitted to senior Trust staff.

Healthcare regulator the Care Quality Commission (CQC) rates GIDS 'Inadequate', its lowest possible rating.

February 2021   The results of the Early Intervention Study are formally published. The research team 'identified no changes in psychological function, quality of life or degree of gender dysphoria' in the young people prescribed puberty blockers.

September 2021   The Central London Employment Tribunal rules that Tavistock children's safeguarding lead, Sonia Appleby, had been vilified by the Trust because she raised safeguarding concerns about GIDS.

The Court of Appeal overturns the High Court's judgment, saying that it is for doctors, not the courts, to decide on the capacity of young people to consent to medical treatment.

March 2022   Dr Hilary Cass's interim report is published, which argues that GIDS's 'single specialist provider model is not a safe or viable long-term option' for the care of young people experiencing gender incongruence or gender-related distress.

July 2022   NHS England announce that GIDS will be closed and replaced by regional centres at existing children's hospitals, with a greater focus on mental health.

1

'ARE WE HURTING CHILDREN?'

February 2017

Dr Hutchinson was seriously concerned. 'Are we hurting children?' she asked, keen to be reassured. It's the question that underpins everything she's feeling.

She was not told 'no'.

Anna Hutchinson, a senior clinical psychologist at the Gender Identity Development Service (known to everyone as GIDS), cared deeply for the hundreds of children seeking her help. They felt that the bodies they had been born with didn't match their gender identity, and many were deeply distressed. But she was desperately worried about whether the treatment GIDS could help them access – a referral for powerful drugs and the beginning of a medical pathway to physical gender transition – was ethical. Could it really be the best and only approach for *all* the young people in her care?

Hutchinson had witnessed an explosion in the number of young people seeking help from GIDS. Since 2007 it had grown from a small team that saw 50 young people each year to a nationally commissioned service treating thousands.[1] In the four years she had been there alone, the number of children referred had risen from 314 to 2,016.[2] But it wasn't just the numbers. The existing evidence base which supported the use of puberty blockers for young people was not just limited: it didn't seem to apply to the children being referred to GIDS. Whereas most of the literature on gender non-conforming children was about boys who had a lifelong sense of gender incongruence, GIDS's waiting room was overpopulated with teenage girls whose distress around their gender had only started in adolescence. Many of them were same-sex attracted – the same was true for the boys attending GIDS – and many were autistic. Their lives were complicated too. So many seemed to have other difficulties – eating disorders, self-harm, depression – or had suffered abuse or trauma. How could such different lives and presentations lead to the same answer – puberty blockers?

Dr Sarah Davidson, one of three highly experienced consultant psychologists leading the service, sat directly opposite Hutchinson in Davidson's third-floor office at the Tavistock Centre, north London. She was unable to reassure her colleague.

Their conversation was part of regular clinical supervision, during which psychologists share thoughts on clinical cases currently under their care. Over the preceding few years, these meetings had grown gradually more intense, says Hutchinson. But whenever she and Davidson came close to discussing the thorniest questions, the discussion would be derailed.

Their last supervision session of 2016 had ended badly. So much so that Dr Davidson apologised afterwards that the discussions had fallen into an 'unhelpful pattern'.[3] She, like the service as a whole, was under immense pressure. It couldn't cope with the rapidly increasing referrals and was doing its best to keep an ever-expanding waiting list under control. Hutchinson admired her supervisor. She wanted advice on the extremely complex cases that were now presenting at GIDS, and how to act in the best interests of these children.

As a member of the GIDS senior team, Hutchinson had been privy to major decisions. But she felt increasingly uncomfortable. Alongside the dramatically changed patient population, puberty blockers, she felt, were not behaving as staff had initially believed them to. Evidence from within GIDS showed blockers weren't providing time and space to think and reflect as they had been told, and as they had been telling children and their families. Some young people's health appeared to deteriorate while on the medication. And yet almost no one stopped the treatment. Hutchinson felt she was part of a service 'routinely offering an extreme medical intervention as the first-line treatment to hundreds of distressed young people who may or may not turn out to be "trans"'.[4] She says she began to think that GIDS was practising in a way that 'wasn't actually safe'. She feared she may be contributing to a medical scandal, where an NHS service was not stopping to think what else might be going on for so many of these vulnerable children. Where the normal rules of medicine and children's healthcare didn't seem to apply. Where the word 'gender' had made herself and hard-working colleagues struggle to know what was best practice.

The mental health of one of Anna Hutchinson's patients had deteriorated to such an extent that she felt they had to come off the puberty-blocking medication the service had put them forward for. She had brought this case to supervision to ask for advice.

Their mental health was about 'as bad as you could get', she explains to me. 'There were queries of sexual abuse in the family environment. It was a mess. They were so lacking in ability to function that they couldn't attend appointments with us.' Hutchinson was trying to work out what they should do. She recognised the impact that removing the medication would have, 'but equally they couldn't stay on the blocker in a safe way'. Hutchinson felt an almost overwhelming sense of responsibility: 'They're on this drug because of us; it doesn't seem to be helping with their functioning – they're not okay; there's so much going on that the gender is so low down now the pecking order of problems. But what can you actually do?' It was a difficult case that she wanted guidance on.

The second case she'd brought to discuss was similarly tough. Dr Hutchinson feared there may be sexual abuse occurring within the family of this patient, too. The school had raised concerns, not just about the young person being seen at GIDS, but also about their siblings. It wasn't clear how best to manage it. 'These were appropriate cases for supervision. I needed help with them – to think about how best to manage them,' Hutchinson explains. 'And it was after speaking about those two cases that she [Davidson] said, "Why do you bring such complex cases?"'

'What if it's not right to put young people – ten-year-olds – on puberty blockers?' Hutchinson had continued.

'It is mad,' was the reply.

Hutchinson paused. When one of the leaders of a service that helps children to access powerful, life-changing drugs comments that what they're doing is 'mad', there is clearly a very big problem. It wasn't okay just to say the work of the service was 'mad', Hutchinson thought. What were they going to do about it?*

Until its planned closure in spring 2023, the Gender Identity Development Service is the only NHS specialist service for children and young people 'presenting with difficulties with their gender identity' in England.[5] It's part of the Tavistock and Portman NHS Foundation Trust in north London. GIDS also sees, or has seen in recent years, children from Wales, Northern Ireland and Scotland, as well as young people from the Republic of Ireland. It is staffed by clinicians with a variety of professional backgrounds: predominantly psychologists, but also psychotherapists, family therapists, social workers and nurses. None of these are able to prescribe medication.

Not everyone seen at GIDS chooses to transition, whether socially, by changing their name and pronouns or the way they dress, or medically, by taking synthetic opposite-sex hormones, or surgically, once they're over the age of 17. Some children might start their transition

---

* These words and phrases are recorded verbatim in Anna Hutchinson's contemporaneous written notes. Dr Hutchinson later relayed these conversations, and wider concerns, to the Tavistock and Portman NHS Foundation Trust's medical director, during an interview in December 2018 which formed part of an official review into GIDS. A transcript of this interview was admitted into evidence during an employment tribunal against the Tavistock Trust. Dr Hutchinson also included these conversations as part of an official witness statement for the tribunal and affirmed its contents under oath. In a written response provided to the author in 2022, Dr Sarah Davidson said that she supported Dr Hutchinson 'in her day to day work and on more difficult or complex cases' and was 'always available to give her the support and guidance needed' as her supervisor. Dr Davidson said she did not recall making the comment about 'complex cases' and found it to be 'highly unlikely', given her role. She added that she did not recall a specific discussion referencing ten-year-olds and puberty blockers, but that the language recorded by Dr Hutchinson was 'not in keeping with the language I would use for any patient'. Dr Davidson did recall 'a number of discussions with Dr Hutchinson about the concept of harm and what it meant in this unique and challenging area of practice'.

at GIDS, some may wait until they attend adult gender services, and some will choose not to transition at all.

For those who do wish to pursue a medical gender transition, though, the route begins with a referral from GIDS to a hospital that houses paediatric endocrinologists – doctors who specialise in conditions relating to hormones. There they will receive a prescription for gonadotropin-releasing hormone agonists (GnRHas) – most often referred to as 'puberty blockers'. These powerful drugs are licensed by medical regulators only for use in children with precocious puberty, when children begin adolescence very young (before eight for girls, and nine for boys[6]). They are used 'off-label' – not for a condition they are licensed for – in the treatment of gender dysphoria in young people. GIDS users are most often provided with a drug called triptorelin. All puberty-blocking medications act on the pituitary gland to stop the release of the sex hormones testosterone or oestrogen. This effectively halts physical puberty, stopping the body developing secondary sex characteristics like breasts in girls, or facial hair and an Adam's apple in boys. GnRH agonists are predominantly licensed and used to treat prostate cancer in men, but they have also been used in the chemical castration of male sex offenders.[7]

It's not unusual for drugs to be used off-label, especially when administered in children. Many drugs are. But it's usually only a matter of the dose: for example, for ethical reasons, medical trials of paracetamol would have only been carried out on adults (it's very rare to test drugs on children), so their use in children at a half-dose would be considered 'off-label'. What's unusual about the use of GnRHas for use in young people with gender dysphoria is that they're used to treat a completely different condition from the one for which they have been licensed. In the process, they function in a very different way.

Once on puberty blockers, almost all (in excess of 95 per cent) young people opt to take cross-sex hormones – synthetic testosterone for those born female, oestrogen for natal males.[8] Unlike children diagnosed with precocious puberty, who later stop taking the blockers and allow their bodies to go through their natural puberty, young people with gender dysphoria don't stop taking the blocker – they do not go through the puberty of their natal sex. Yet the long-term effects of using blockers in this way are largely unknown. Even those who have been working in the field for decades concede that research in this area is poor. Dr Polly Carmichael, the head of GIDS, admitted in 2019 how 'we have struggled in the absence of such research to understand how the care we provide affects [patients] in the longer term and what choices they go on to make as they move into adulthood'.[9] Her colleague and former head of psychology for the Tavistock Trust, Dr Bernadette Wren, agreed a year later that 'studies are still few and limited in scope, at times contradictory or inconclusive on key questions' and therefore GIDS clinicians are 'concerned about overstepping what the current evidence can tell us about the safety of our interventions'.[10] The position appears to have changed little in 20 years. In 2000, Dr Wren had remarked, 'There is little evidence about the long-term effects of this intervention.'[11]

While there are studies that describe the self-reported high satisfaction of young people and their families of being on puberty blockers, and some improvement in mental health, others suggest there is evidence that puberty-blocker use can lead to changes in sexuality and sexual function, poor bone health, stunted height, low mood, tumour-like masses in the brain and, for those treated early enough who continue on to cross-sex hormones, almost certain infertility.[12] The use of cross-sex hormones can also bring an increased risk of a range of possible longer-term health complications such as blood clots and cardiovascular disease.[13]

The science is not settled, and this field of healthcare is overpopulated with small, poor-quality studies. It's often not possible to draw definitive conclusions on the benefits or harms of these treatments.[14] Many studies *claim* to show the benefits of puberty blockers to mental health, but these have all been heavily critiqued and shown to have significant methodological flaws.[15] Systematic reviews of the evidence base undertaken by national bodies have all found it wanting. England's National Institute for Health and Care Excellence (NICE) found that the quality of the evidence for using puberty-blocking drugs to treat young people struggling with their gender identity is 'very low'.[16] Existing studies were small, with few participants, and 'subject to bias and confounding'.[17] A systematic review of the clinical effectiveness and safety of cross-sex hormones also found that the evidence was of 'very low' quality.[18] 'Any potential benefits of gender-affirming hormones must be weighed against the largely unknown long-term safety profile of these treatments in children and adolescents with gender dysphoria,' it noted.[19] National health bodies in Sweden, France and Finland have all called for far greater caution in the use of puberty blockers following reviews of the evidence.[20]

Some adults opt for surgery – not available in the UK until the age of 17. GIDS itself plays no active role in surgical decisions – referrals for surgery on the NHS are made by adult gender identity clinics – and young people in their care can only start cross-sex hormones if they've been on puberty blockers for 12 months and are approaching the age of 16.

Even for the many who go on to lead happy lives as fully transitioned adults, it can be a long and challenging journey. Some data on those who transitioned decades ago (who were mostly born male) shows that the majority continue to live as trans women, although they're more likely to suffer from mental health problems.[21] Transitioning can often require several complex surgeries and a lifetime on medication. For those who go through these stages but then later regret it, or detransition and choose to reidentify with their birth sex, the decision to transition to a different gender can prove very painful.

Dr Hutchinson needed more than vague reassurances. With such a weak evidence base underpinning the work, were GIDS simply hoping for the best? If so, they were taking significant risks, she believed, with the lives of their young patients.

There is a lot of uncertainty in this field. Uncertainty over the evidence base, over the outcomes, and about whether or not medical transition will be the best option for any particular individual in the long term. Uncertainty, or lack of agreement at least, on what being trans even means. Is it something that is transitory or fixed from birth? The question was how best to respond to that uncertainty. For Hutchinson, with such serious consequences at stake, it wasn't okay to concede that so much was uncertain, and then not to manage the associated risks adequately. She accepted the argument for referring young people for puberty-blocking medication even without a strong evidence base, given the intensity of distress felt by some young people. There were consequences to not acting, just as there were for acting. But the reality for many of the young people attending GIDS, who often presented with multiple other difficulties that required urgent attention, made the decision even more complicated.

Were these young people 'well and functioning', in every other sense, Hutchinson explains, there could well be an argument in favour of medical treatment to address their gender dysphoria. These patients were 'very sure' and 'very committed' to transition. 'I'm not ever putting their identity in doubt here. I very much believe that that's what they felt they wanted at that time, and I can see why,' she says. 'But we had to see the whole picture. And when there was, possibly, sexual abuse going on at the same time, plus other complex things, I just couldn't be so casual about the risk that we were not fully understanding what was going on for these kids.'

It didn't help that Hutchinson's list of unanswered questions was getting longer and longer. Why were more teenage girls being referred to the clinic than ever before, many of them with no previous problem with their gender identity in childhood – girls who often had complex mental health problems such as depression, anxiety, eating disorders and self-harm?[22] Could the past traumas of some of these children explain why they wanted to identify as a different gender to escape from their bodies?[23] Did the increasing number of patients who appeared to experience homophobic bullying before identifying as transgender need to be explored in greater detail?[24] Was GIDS actually medicating some gay children, and some on the autistic spectrum?[25] And by what method could staff tell the difference between the patients who would benefit from treatment and those who would not? These were all profound questions, with deep ethical implications.

'We know that not all young people who identify as trans go on to live as trans adults,' Hutchinson says. 'We've always known that.' In every study in this field, poor as the evidence base is, there have always been some young people who identified as a different gender, felt intense distress surrounding this and wanted to transition, but for whom those feelings resolved. They went on to live as adults without feeling the need to change their bodies by use of hormones or surgery, and became content with the bodies and sex they were born with. These studies are small and imperfect, with methodological flaws, but, according to the NHS, showed that in 'prepubertal children (mainly boys)... the dysphoria persisted into adulthood for only 6–23%' of cases.[26] Boys in these studies were more likely to identify as gay in adulthood than as transgender. According to the fifth edition of the American Psychiatric Association's *Diagnostic and Statistical Manual of Mental Disorders* – known as the DSM-5 – rates of childhood gender dysphoria continuing into adolescence or adulthood ranged from 2 to 30 per cent for males, and 12 to 50 per cent in females.[27]

What Hutchinson wanted from the leadership of the service was an *acknowledgement* of the risks of the work: prescribing powerful drugs with largely unknown consequences to children. 'Because by not acknowledging the risks, we were kind of colluding with the idea it would work for everybody. And at that point, I think it was so clear, it wasn't going to work for everybody.' GIDS, she says, was responsible for every single young person coming through its doors. 'The ones who identify as trans for life are our patients, and we want to help them; the ones who aren't going to identify for life are equally our patients, and equally our responsibility.'

Hutchinson continues: 'It wasn't like I was saying, you mustn't give anyone the treatment. But what I was saying is we need to acknowledge it isn't going to work for everybody; that we could be getting this wrong; that people could be harmed by this treatment. And it's only through the acknowledgement of those risks, you could do anything to *minimise* those risks. At that point, by not acknowledging the risks, we weren't managing the risks at all.'

This is not a story which denies trans identities; nor that argues trans people deserve to lead anything other than happy lives, free of harassment, with access to good healthcare. This is a story about the underlying safety of an NHS service, the adequacy of the care it provides and its use of poorly evidenced treatments on some of the most vulnerable young people in society. And how so many people sat back, watched, and did nothing.

2

THE VISION

The Gender Identity Development Service was the creation of child and adolescent psychiatrist Domenico Di Ceglie. Described by his long-term colleague Dr Polly Carmichael as 'Italian, obviously, and a bit of a terrier, and also a very curious man', he wanted to, in his own words, create a service 'for children with these rare and unusual experiences' of having a gender identity that didn't seem to match the biological body they were born with.[1]

Di Ceglie was spurred on by a solitary case he'd worked with in the early 1980s, a teenager 'who was claiming that she was a boy but in a female body'. Although she spoke very little during their psychother-apy sessions, Di Ceglie felt 'there was something very profound about her sense of identity of being a boy which could not be easily explained and that was fundamental to her being.'[2]

Working as a consultant child psychiatrist in Croydon, south London, shortly afterwards, he and a couple of colleagues attempted to see all the patients who presented with gender identity problems in the area. In a borough whose population stood at around 300,000, they 'ended up with 3 or 4 cases'.[3] Despite the small numbers involved, the complexity of the cases he saw convinced Di Ceglie of the need for a specialist service.

The term 'gender identity' was coined by American psychiatrist Robert Stoller in 1964, and is generally understood to mean someone's personal sense of their own gender.[4] (For some that may not be the same as their physical sex – a trans woman, for example, is born with the physical body of a man but has a gender identity of a woman. But the concept is not without its problems; many people feel they don't have a gender identity at all.) Di Ceglie read Stoller's work, along with 'other literature on trans-sexualism', when he encountered his first case.[5] The two met in person at a 1987 conference, with Stoller apparently being 'very encouraging' of Di Ceglie's plans to start a service for children and adolescents. 'He thought that there was a real need for such a service and predicted that there would be many referrals and a lot of interesting work.'[6]

In September 1989, Di Ceglie succeeded in setting up the Gender Identity Development Clinic for children and adolescents within the Department of Child Psychiatry at St George's Hospital in south London. The name was relevant: the emphasis would be in promoting the *development* of the young person's gender identity, not changing it. Staff were to maintain an open mind as to what solution the young person might settle on in terms of managing their gender identity and to support families in reaching that solution – whether it be to transition medically, or to become reconciled with their own sex without changing their body. But Di Ceglie could see that, in some cases, by addressing other difficulties experienced by the child – things like depression, abuse or trauma – it might 'secondarily affect the gender identity development'.[7] In other words, sometimes the gender identity difficulties might resolve if other difficulties being faced were dealt with as well.

Not attempting to alter the young person's gender identity, but instead fostering 'recognition and non-judgemental acceptance of the gender identity problem' would become one of the core guiding principles of the service.[8] Others included trying to 'ameliorate associated emotional, behavioural, and relationship difficulties', encouraging 'exploration of mind–body relationship' by working with professionals with other specialities, and helping the young person and their family 'tolerate uncertainty' with their gender identity development.[9] Although they were written in the 1990s, those leading the service in later years say that these principles endured throughout: 'Those therapeutic aims still represent the core values of the service – they're

Domenico's lasting legacy,' said Bernadette Wren, a member of the GIDS Executive team from 2011 to 2020. 'He grasped that if you want to have a genuine engagement with young people you have to take very seriously what they feel and what they say.'[10]

Di Ceglie's peers were baffled. 'Originally people were saying to me, you know, what do you want to do? Who are these children?' Di Ceglie recalled, speaking in 2017. 'And then somebody said to me, "But is it that you, [by] creating a service, you are creating the problem?"' Di Ceglie reflected. 'I don't know the answer to that question, but still!' he laughed.[11] This question would grow ever more pertinent decades later.

The service in these early days was largely therapeutic: providing individual therapy, family work and group sessions. Some young people would remain in the service for years, others could be helped relatively quickly. In terms of outcomes, Di Ceglie said that only about 5 per cent of the young people seen at his clinic would 'commit themselves to a change of gender' and that '60% to 70% of all the children he sees will become homosexual'.[12] At this point in time, the small number of studies that existed supported this general picture.[13] These early findings would later appear to be forgotten as demand for GIDS grew and the clinic became busier. Alongside its therapeutic work, the clinical team also visited schools to help them understand how best to help young people struggling with their gender identity, and tried to educate other health professionals. There had been little need to 'radically change' this model over the clinic's early years, but it had been refined 'particularly with reference to physical interventions' so that some adolescents could access medication that would block their puberty.[14]

If, after extensive therapy and thorough assessment, a young person's distress in relation to their gender remained throughout puberty, they met a series of strict criteria and were around 16 years old, they could be offered medication to halt the process of their natural sex hormones being released – puberty blockers. In the 1990s little was known about how these drugs might help in the treatment for gender-related distress, and the service was cautious about recommending them. The blockers were not prescribed or administered by Di Ceglie and his colleagues themselves, but rather by paediatric endocrinologists, working alongside the gender identity team.

As the 1990s progressed, however, the Royal College of Psychiatrists established a working party to establish best practice on when, whether and how to treat young people with gender-related distress with medication. It followed a conference Di Ceglie had hosted in 1996, bringing together colleagues from around the world. There were very few professionals working with this group of children and adolescents, and it was an important moment to share ideas and experiences. A team in the Netherlands were already reporting early data that beginning the process of transitioning to another gender in late adolescence could lead to favourable outcomes in adulthood.[15] Should the UK follow suit?

A pioneer in this field, Di Ceglie co-authored the Royal College's resulting official guidelines, published in January 1998.[16] The guidelines explained that gender identity 'disorders' were 'rare and complex' in children and adolescents, more common in boys, and often associated with other difficulties. The document stressed that, when compared with adults, there was 'greater fluidity and variability in the outcome', and only a 'small proportion' of young people would go on to transition in adulthood. The majority, it said, would be gay. The first stage of any treatment, therefore, should be extensive therapy and include taking a full family history. It should focus on improving 'comorbid problems and difficulties' in the young person's life and reducing their distress caused by both these and their gender identity. The guidance advised that, if used at all, physical interventions should be staged: first puberty blockers, which are described as 'wholly reversible'; then 'partially reversible' cross-sex hormones (oestrogen and testosterone) to either feminise or masculinise the body; and, finally, 'irreversible' surgical procedures. This staged approach remains the same today.

While surgery was strictly ruled out before the age of 18, the document didn't make any age stipulations when it came to the use of puberty blockers. However, it recommended that adolescents have experience of themselves 'in the post-pubertal state of their biological sex' before starting any medications. This was considered vital to being able to provide 'properly' informed consent. The authors urged a 'cautious' approach and argued that physical interventions 'be delayed as long as it is clinically appropriate'. They also stressed the need to 'take into account adverse affects on physical growth' that might result from blocking hormones.

The guidance explained that adolescents could present with 'firmly held and strongly expressed' views on their gender identity, and that the pressure to prescribe or refer young people for these drugs could be great. However, this distress and certainty had to be understood in the context of adolescent development – a time of great fluidity. Strength of feeling 'may give a false impression of irreversibility', it explained. 'A large element of management [of the gender-related distress],' the guidance said, 'is promoting the young person's tolerance of uncertainty and resisting pressures for quick solutions.'

Professor Russell Viner (who would later become president of the Royal College of Paediatrics and Child Health, 2018–21) started providing endocrinology services to GIDS patients in 2000. At that time, using puberty blockers at all was seen as 'an advanced approach', he tells me. Other countries, such as the United States, were giving older adolescents large quantities of cross-sex hormones instead. 'The safest thing to do is to turn the hormones off,' he explains. 'But if that person wanted to transition from male to female, another option would be to give them large doses of oestrogen. But you'd have to give them really very large doses of oestrogen to suppress the body's own production of male hormones.'

There were two main reasons for making 16 the age at which blockers could be used, Professor Viner explains. First, from 16 adolescents largely have 'adult rights' to consent to treatment or refuse it. And secondly, 'from an endocrine point of view' it fitted because most people had almost completed puberty by this point. The rationale for using the blocker post 16 was 'to make it safe to introduce small doses of opposite-sex hormones if that young person wished', although GIDS and its associated endocrinologists did not do this at the time, and there was a notion, Viner says, 'that this gave them a space to think, away from the drive of their own hormones'.

The endocrinology side was linked, but kept separate to GIDS, Viner explains. 'And I think that was done for a particular reason, to emphasise the importance of the brain and the mind rather than the body.' In the United States and elsewhere, gender services could be run by endocrinologists, with the overwhelming focus being on 'fixing' the body. But he (and Dr Di Ceglie) strongly believed in the need for 'a mental-health-led service', where 'the key message' was that while there were things you could do with the body, 'mental-health treatment is the most important thing.'

In 1994, five years after the gender identity clinic had first opened its doors, it moved 11 miles north, across London, to the Portman Clinic – an old picturesque Victorian house that, together with the Tavistock Centre – a far less attractive 1960s concrete building – formed the Tavistock and Portman Trust.* It has remained part of the Trust ever since. Although referrals doubled in the space of two years, from 12 in 1994 to 24 in 1996, the service remained small, as did the knowledge base relating to this group of young people and the best way to help them.[17]

Di Ceglie's 1996 conference was written up as a book, with the help of jobbing social-science researcher David Freedman.[18] Clinicians from around the world discussed their work and patients. Eating disorders, child sexual abuse, trauma and bereavement were all mentioned as events that had preceded the development of gender-related distress in the case vignettes that featured, but proper data and analysis were hard to come by.

'The Trust said, "We don't really know a lot about what's happened to these young people, or their characteristics or anything – is it possible to do a sort of retrospective audit?"' Freedman recalls. The request came around the year 2000, and he happily accepted the challenge. Along with Di Ceglie and two others, they designed a study that would try to shed light on this patient population.

---

* There is some debate about when GIDS moved to the Tavistock and Portman Trust. Several of Domenico Di Ceglie's papers say that the move occurred in 1996, yet the Tavistock and Portman website states that the move was made in 1994. See 'The Gender Identity Development Unit is founded', Tavistock and Portman NHS Foundation Trust [website] (21 September 2020), https://100years.tavistockandportman.nhs.uk/timeline/the-gender-identity-disorder-unit-is-founded/. Elsewhere on the website, the Trust says 1996. See Glenn Gossling, 'Gender through time', Tavistock and Portman NHS Foundation Trust [website] (2020), https://100years.tavistockandportman.nhs.uk/gender-through-time/.

They went through all the case notes of the young people whom Di Ceglie and colleagues had seen since the unit had opened in 1989. And although many of the staff working back then were doing so part-time, Freedman was left with the impression that the work of the service was slow and very careful. 'My feeling was that, in those days, the service really did try to offer a non-judgmental, safe space where the child and the family could work through things,' he says. The young people, Freedman reflects, were clearly distressed, with families feeling confused and isolated. Gender identity issues were not generally discussed in society, nor known about by other professionals in healthcare, schools or elsewhere, he tells me.

Trawling through individual cases files was 'messy', but that's what they did, creating a list of measurable features that could be examined in order to produce meaningful conclusions.

'One of the things that came out of this was you couldn't predict at the beginning what the outcome would be,' he explains. Some children persisted throughout – remaining clear that they wanted to transition to the opposite gender. Others 'would come in with really a strong desire that they wanted to change gender', but later decide they no longer wanted surgery, or found 'through exploration' that they could manage the distress 'without changing their gender identity'. This didn't mean life was 'absolutely perfect' for this latter, larger group by any means, but only the minority would 'go on to transition fully or adopt an identity in the other gender'.

By the time of the audit, around 150 children and adolescents had been seen by the specialist service.[19] The very recent ones were excluded from the analysis, but the team were left with 124 patients' records to explore in order to try to establish a profile of the 'characteristics of the children and adolescents referred to the service, the source of referral and the associated clinical features'.[20] Two-thirds were boys, and on average patients had been first referred aged 11. The most common problems experienced by the children were associated with relationships, the family context and mood, the researchers noted. Fifty-seven per cent experienced difficulties with their parents or carers, 52 per cent had relationship difficulties with peers, while 42 per cent suffered from 'depression/misery'.[21]

Close to four in ten young people (38 per cent) had families which
had mental health problems; the same proportion experienced family
physical health problems. A third claimed to have been the victim of
harassment or persecution.

A closer look at the young people's family circumstances and
behaviours provides some startling findings. Over 25 per cent of those
referred to the clinic had spent time in care. That compares to a rate
of 0.67 per cent for the general children's population (2021).* The
analysis also notes that while 84 per cent had been living with their
'family of origin' at the time of referrals, this had fallen to 36 per cent
at discharge.[22] GIDS sees young people up to the age of 18. Of those
children and adolescents seen by the service at this point, 42 per cent
had experienced the loss of one or both parents through bereavement
or separation (predominantly the latter). Close to a quarter of those
aged over 12 had histories of self-harming, and the same proportion
exhibited 'inappropriately sexualised behaviour'.

The audit of cases showed that it was very rare for young people
referred to GIDS to have no associated problems. This was true of only
2.5 per cent of the sample.[23] On the other hand, about 70 per cent of
the sample had more than five 'associated features' – a long list that
includes those already mentioned as well as physical abuse, anxiety,
school attendance issues and many more. Those who were older (over
12) tended to have more of these problems.

The paper itself is unable to explain what might be going on.
Instead, it poses several alternative hypotheses. It may be that families experiencing other troubles 'find it more difficult to handle their
children's problems and thus bring their children to health care agencies more often'. Alternatively, there might be a link between family
difficulties, some of which might be traumatic for the child, and the

* The author has not been able to obtain statistics from the relevant period, it
being impossible to choose a reference year as these children had been referred
to GIDS over the space of more than a decade. However, the trend over the last
ten years has been upwards. It is likely that the proportion of children in care
during the relevant period was smaller than it currently is. See 'Main findings:
children's social care in England 2021', Gov.uk [website] (30 March 2022), https://
www.gov.uk/government/statistics/childrens-social-care-data-in-england-2021/
main-findings-childrens-social-care-in-england-2021.

development of gender identity difficulties.[24] Because either could be case, the authors stress the importance of establishing 'full histories' with young people and their families.

It's impossible to say for sure whether young people with mental health problems and traumatic pasts are more likely to adopt a trans identity, or the other way round – that the stigma and prejudice faced by trans people somehow makes the young person more vulnerable to other problems. As is common in the field, the research does not provide concrete answers. These early data were meant to be used to establish the needs of this patient group, improve service delivery and plan future research.[25] Indeed, David Freedman describes this work as the Gender Identity Development Service's 'first clinical audit'.[26]

It was also its last.*

While it provided a unique and safe space for children and their families to talk through their gender-related distress, the Gender Identity Development Unit – as it was also known – was not an integral part of the Portman Clinic.† It was based in a 'broom cupboard', according to some. 'It was such a small unit; it almost didn't figure in people's mind,' says Stanley Ruszczynski, who joined the Portman in 1997 and would go on to become the clinic director.

Despite its small size, it wasn't long before Di Ceglie's colleagues in the Portman felt unease at this new service. The model it used,

---

* Vicky Holt (a GIDS psychiatrist) and her colleagues make a note in their 2016 paper (published online in 2014) that the work 'follows on from a 2002 audit by Di Ceglie et al. conducted at the same gender identity service in London and includes a larger sample and a different focus'. While it is the case that this paper has a larger sample size – 218 – it includes only those referred in a one-year period – 2012 – rather than a comprehensive audit of the entire patient population. See Vicky Holt, Elin Skagerberg and Michael Dunsford, 'Young people with features of gender dysphoria: demographics and associated difficulties', *Clinical Child Psychology and Psychiatry* 21/1 (January 2016), 108–18, doi: 10.1177/1359104514558431.

† The name of the service tends to change and was not wholly settled until later in the 2000s. Prior to settling on the Gender Identity Development Service, it was often referred to as the Gender Identity Development Unit, but also other variations thereof.

they believed, was at odds with the core principles underpinning this world-leading provider of mental health care. The Tavistock and Portman is internationally renowned for its commitment to talking therapies, or psychotherapy. One former senior clinician described the 'parents' of the Trust as being systemic psychotherapy – which looks at the groups an individual operates in and how these shape behaviour – and psychoanalytic (or psychodynamic) psychotherapy, which builds on Freud's ideas about the subconscious and the influence this can have on our behaviour.[27]

In the late 1990s and early 2000s the Portman itself received referrals from adult transgender patients and ran groups for those who were both pre- and post-operative. Ruszczynski, who trained as a social worker but became a consultant adult psychotherapist, had worked with about half a dozen adult patients and been troubled by the cases. In particular, a couple who had attended where the husband had surgically transitioned to a woman.

'What I remember about that story was that he wanted to detransition… to go back to being a man.' The man had explained how he had woken up from gender reassignment surgery having had his genitals removed, and immediately 'knew he'd made a mistake'.

The Portman Clinic and Di Ceglie's gender identity service did not make easy bedfellows. The tension between the Gender Identity Development Unit (as it was known then) and the rest of the Portman Clinic stemmed, in large part, from the way the two viewed the relationship between the mind and the body. There was a sense that the gender service wasn't operating in line with the deep analytic thinking in practice at the Portman. Indeed, such is the standing of the psychoanalytic tradition at the Tavistock and Portman that a bronzed statue of Sigmund Freud, the founder of psychoanalysis, stands outside, observing passers-by with a neutral gaze. It's crucial to understand what the Portman Clinic in particular is and was. Stanley Ruszczynski, who was clinic director between 2005 and 2016, explains: 'We work with patients who are on the edge of society as a clinical group.' According to its website, the clinic 'offers specialist long-term help for children, young people and adults with disturbing sexual behaviours, criminality and violence'.[28]

The clinicians of the Portman Clinic, therefore, were used to people expressing their 'disturbances in their body', Ruszczynski explains. 'So, whether it's in their violence, whether it's in their self-abuse', people have a psychological structure where they use their bodies, or other people's bodies, 'to express their concern'. 'So from that point of view, somebody who comes in and says, "I want to be in a different body" – it's not that different to what we knew with our… perverse patients, and our violent patients and our… alcoholic patients, you know? They use their body to express their distress.'

That anyone might treat these young people, albeit after extensive therapy, with medication just did not make sense to some Portman Clinic clinicians. On the whole, the Trust 'does not sanction the routine use of mind-altering, brain-altering, development-altering or body-altering medications… for the treatment of mental disorders', wrote its medical director Dr David Taylor in 2006.[29] While medication wasn't ruled out, physical interventions were only used 'sparingly' and where there was a strong evidence base. This did not exist for this area of care. The Trust's preference was always for psychological and therapeutic exploration with the patient.

'At the time it really wasn't comfortable being at the Portman; we felt very marginalized,' recalls Bernadette Wren, who, prior to becoming one of the leaders of GIDS, had worked in the unit between 1997 and 2000.[30] Nonetheless, Wren acknowledges why the Portman would have reservations, saying, 'The Portman then, as now, would have been the clinic taking on as adult patients people who were among the small number voicing regret for the surgeries they had undergone.'[31]

Indeed, when trainee psychiatrist Dr Az Hakeem joined the Portman in 2000, he quickly took over the running of the two groups, and merged them. Bringing together both pre- and post-operative trans adults, he says, was 'one of the best decisions I made', and it had a huge impact on those who had not yet surgically transitioned. 'I did a survey, and I think out of the 100 patients only two did. Only 2% transitioned.'[32] Having the opportunity to talk with those who had already undergone surgery appeared to impact greatly on those considering it as an option. Hakeem acknowledges that the high regret rates he was seeing in his post-op patients – 26 per cent – is not representative of adults with gender dysphoria; they were the demographic who had been referred to his group at the Portman. But this, along with other colleagues' personal experience, certainly shaped the atmosphere in the clinic, and made them view GIDS with caution. 'Clinicians tended to build their whole understanding of trans identities on working with that group of patients,' explains Bernadette Wren. 'In GIDS, meeting very young people, we saw things differently.'[33]

In July 2002, a legal case gave Ruszczynski, Hakeem and other Portman colleagues an opportunity to voice their disquiet in public. The European Court of Human Rights ruled that transsexuals should be granted 'full legal recognition in their adopted sex, including the right to marry'.[34] In response, a group from the Portman Clinic penned letters to the *Guardian* and *Telegraph* newspapers, arguing that the decision represented a victory of 'fantasy over reality'.[35] The clinicians argued that many patients regretted their transition, while others, 'through years of psychoanalytic psychotherapy', came to a different understanding of their distress and could find ways of dealing with it 'other than by trying to alter their bodies'.[36] The letters did not go down well – either with the wider Tavistock and Portman Trust or with the trans community – but Ruszczynski and Hazeem reject the suggestion their language was harsh or demeaning. 'I would say the opposite,' explains Stanley Ruszczynski. 'We were trying to be thoughtful and considerate.' He plays down the impact, saying that because they were written by those 'bloody Portman people again', they weren't taken overly seriously.

Those within the gender identity service remember differently.

'They were unfriendly,' laughs Sue Evans, a straight-talking, chatty Londoner who joined the service around this time. A nurse by training, Evans had first met Di Ceglie in Croydon, where, she says, he was 'well thought of in child and adolescent circles in psychiatry'.

'You could sense that the two services did not sit very well with one another,' she recalls. Even clinicians who joined GIDS more than a decade after these letters were sent talk about the legacy they left. How this event soured relations between the service and the rest of the Trust. GIDS staff felt there was a lack of understanding from others about the work they were undertaking and what it was trying to achieve.

With the humiliation of the letters printed in the British national press and the growing unease of colleagues, Di Ceglie's gender service soon found itself homeless, pressured out of the Portman Clinic. After some gentle probing, Stanley Ruszczynski concedes that he and colleagues had wanted them gone. 'They didn't belong in the Portman Clinic; they didn't belong in the Trust.' Others put it in less stark terms. David Taylor, the medical director for the Tavistock and Portman Trust at the time, says 'an immunological rejection' is more accurate. The Portman was saying 'this isn't our belief system. This isn't the way we work. This goes against a deep exploration of the depths of someone's psyche and in doing so, it's destructive.'

Regardless, the Gender Identity Development Service now found itself somewhat of a physical outlier, as well as different in terms of the treatment it offered.

'And then we move, literally, to a shop along Belsize Lane,' Sue Evans recollects. 'It had a little upstairs and then little stairs that went down to the basement. And this was the clinical unit.' Patients were not seen at the shop, but this is where the service was based for over a year, and where the team would have its weekly clinical meeting every Tuesday. Young people and their families would attend the main Tavistock building, which, if it was raining, would be 'a pain in the neck', Evans says. 'You turn up with wet shoes!' No one liked being in the shop, and 'for Domenico, there's not much prestige in being the consultant of a unit that's in a children's clothes shop down the road, is there?'

Contrary to the views of former colleagues from the Portman Clinic, other clinicians working at GIDS during this time say that it was 'very psychoanalytically dominated'. The support given to children was often 'very long-term, in-depth, and very regular'. But, say others, the service always had to do its best with 'very limited resources'. The therapeutic work would be 'constrained by geography', one clinician explains, and by the simple fact that not every family wanted or would engage with regular psychoanalysis. GIDS had to work in the realm of the possible, rather than the ideal. 'It became very clear to me that you couldn't really work therapeutically with someone from Newcastle,' Sue Evans explains. 'They could come down and be assessed, but really that was… in my mind an attempt to assess and understand and explore what was going on with a view of probably referring back' to local services who could provide ongoing support. The use of local services to support the young person while GIDS worked with the gender identity issues came to be called the 'network model'. It worked best when young people could receive support locally – most often in Child and Adolescent Mental Health Services, or CAMHS, as they're most often known. But GIDS had no control over whether these local services would or did treat these children. While this was the wish, it wasn't the reality in a number of cases, and would become a far greater problem for the service in later years when referrals exploded.

Over time, Sue Evans's concerns weren't simply about geography. One 'red flag' was what she perceived as the subtle, but undue, influence of patient-support groups on GIDS's clinical practice. Evans recalls how Domenico Di Ceglie and his successor, Polly Carmichael, would regularly attend meetings of Mermaids, for example, and upon their return encourage staff to change practice.[37] It was on the advice of Mermaids, Evans says, that the GIDS team stopped including birth names on clinical letters. That might sound small, but the influence of Mermaids grew.

Mermaids is not just any old patient support group. It's a patient support group whose history is intricately intertwined with GIDS. Mermaids was set up in the mid 1990s by some parents who had attended group sessions at GIDS.[38] The GIDS groups were aimed at helping parents of children with gender identity problems not to feel so isolated, and they ran for a number of years.[39] Di Ceglie believed that a patient group like Mermaids was able to offer 'the kind of help and support that we, as professionals, cannot'. Mermaids 'contributed creatively' to the development of GIDS and in Di Ceglie's eyes was a 'complementary organization' to the service.[40]

In its early years, Mermaids' views appeared to reflect those of Di Ceglie and his service. The group's website in 2000 spoke about gender identity problems in children and adolescents being 'complex' with 'varied causes'. It noted that 'only a small proportion of cases will result in a transsexual outcome', and acknowledged that 'some gender issues can be caused by a bereavement, a dysfunctional family life, or (rarely) by abuse'. Whatever the cause, it argued – just like Di Ceglie – that children with gender identity problems were often very unhappy and needed support that was 'sympathetic and non-judgmental'.[41]

GIDS's close relationship with Mermaids was seen as such a positive by Di Ceglie that it was emphasised in the service's bid to be nationally commissioned by the NHS. Di Ceglie himself was a patron of the organisation, and, commissioners were told, the ongoing relationship with Mermaids meant 'users' views have influenced the development and organisation of the GIDS since its inception'. Furthermore, GIDS committed not just to continuing its close ties with Mermaids, but amplifying them, were its application to be successful.[*42]

Another clinician from this time recalls how the group's original leader had been 'really thoughtful and really helpful'. Their own child had experienced gender difficulties but had not gone on to transition as an adult. But over time, Mermaids became more political and harder to work with. Their position appeared to be that there was only one outcome for these children and young people – medical transition. The annual Mermaids meetings were not always pleasant, one clinician recalls. 'I didn't ever want to go… You're going to these people who are really slagging you off and saying, "Why don't you give medication, you're killing our children." It's a really extraordinary world to work in where you're working in a service… being absolutely attacked for just trying to stop and think with [children].'

Sue Evans's main concern in the mid 2000s, however, was over how quickly it appeared some of her colleagues were assessing young people and referring them for puberty blockers. There was good and

---

* Indeed, Mermaids went on to play important roles in GIDS's formal research. For example, the group officially endorsed a 2011 joint GIDS study looking at the incidence of 'gender identity disorder' in children and adolescents in the UK and Ireland. The researchers wrote: 'The London GIDS is already actively involved with Mermaids (the only UK support group for young people with GID). Mermaids is supportive of the proposed study… and of improving access to specialist services for young people with GID. They are open to greater involvement in the study and will be involved in the dissemination of study outputs.' The study is as follows: 'Investigating the burden of gender identity disorder (GID) in children and adolescents: a surveillance study of incidence, clinical presentation, co-morbidities and natural history' [HRA 11/LO/1512] (30 August 2011).

thoughtful work going on, certainly, she says. 'There were some really excellent staff,' Evans explains, 'and they all, I think, were very much working in the sort of psychotherapeutic tradition. But there were also other staff who were not.' Evans recalls questioning a colleague about a particular young person who had been approved for a referral for puberty blockers. 'I actually said to her, "Can I ask how many times you've met with the boy?" And she said, "Oh yes. Four." And I said, "What, and you're recommending him for hormones now? Four?" "Oh, he's very certain," she said.' Unlike the GIDS of 2015 onwards, there was no lengthy waiting list or intense pressure on the service to get through it. It was busy, and staff worked hard, but for Evans, there was nothing that could explain why someone would be referred for physical interventions so quickly.

The work was difficult. 'You're so wary of pathologising,' Evans explains. But the cases she saw were complex. 'I would say that every child that I assessed and worked with needed that sort of in-depth assessment and understanding and exploration... You've got to take them seriously. You've got to do good, clinical exploratory work, and develop empathy with them.' All that took time, says Evans. From her experience, there were no exceptions. 'I didn't come across simple cases. I think they were complex children.' Some had been sexually abused, she says, some were struggling with their sexuality, and some had suffered early traumas in their lives. Others were autistic or being bullied at school.

Little was known about puberty blockers, says Evans. While the idea was that 'it was safe, because it was used in precocious puberty', she felt uneasy. 'I just knew that I didn't want to take children to that [endocrinology] clinic.' Evans did not feel that these young people should be accessing medical interventions. She still thinks that under-18s should not begin medical transition. While accepting that some who identify as another gender from childhood will continue to do so, she believes that they should not transition until adulthood, 'because adolescence is about discovery and exploration and development and change'.

For a while Sue Evans had an ally at GIDS in Dr Az Hakeem, one of those from the Portman Clinic who had written a letter to the national newspapers arguing that it was 'fantasy over reality' to believe it is possible to change sex.[43] It felt good to share her concerns with someone. Hakeem had joined GIDS a couple of days a week while completing his psychiatry training. Although a qualified doctor, he didn't work with the young people directly, but instead sat in on sessions conducted by others in the team. He says GIDS didn't seem much interested in his work with adults who experienced regret – the adults that GIDS's patients might grow up to be.

Hakeem too was concerned about the influence of Mermaids, whom he describes as 'omnipresent'. 'GIDS and Mermaids were virtually inseparable,' he says. And he was highly critical of the service as a whole – more so than Evans – arguing that 'there wasn't any analytic thinking going on'. Hakeem explains that where he and GIDS founder Di Ceglie differed was in their thoughts on the role of therapy with these children. 'I don't think he believed that therapy could work. So the only way you could help them was to give them what they wanted, whereas I believed that therapy could work. And it did work with my adult patients.' Hakeem wasn't seeking to 'convert' his adult patients or influence them one way or another about whether they should transition, he says. He just wanted to encourage them to think and be equipped with all the information that was available so that they could make the best-informed decision possible. If they wished to transition, then that was entirely a matter for them.

Dr Hakeem says that his concerns were dismissed – he was a trainee, after all (albeit a trained doctor) – and that he was viewed as a 'troublemaker'. 'Everyone would sigh when I started speaking,' he recalls.

Evans says she experienced a similar reaction, and recalls a particular incident where a colleague was speaking of a young person who had lacerations to her vagina. Evans immediately asked for further details: were these major injuries or 'superficial scratches'? The colleague could not answer, Evans says. 'And I just remember I said, "But, you know, that's quite important, surely, to know that" – irrespective of gender… as a basis of risk-assessment and self-harm. But I remember two people audibly sighed in the room.'

Over several years Evans realised this was not a service she could work in. For her, 'it felt clinically something had gone wrong.' 'I used to come home and just say… "This service is not right. This is just not right. I'm really worried about some of these kids. I think they're going off [for physical interventions] too early.'"

Evans took her concerns to the Tavistock's clinical director, who commissioned Dr David Taylor – the Trust's then medical director – to investigate and write a report. Taylor is a highly respected psychiatrist who worked at the Tavistock for 30 years, leading an influential, long-term study on depression.[44] He left the Tavistock in 2011. Sue Evans was never shown Taylor's findings. The report remained hidden from the GIDS staff – and the wider public – until 2020, when it was reluctantly released following a lengthy Freedom of Information battle with the Tavistock Trust.[45]

David Taylor was thorough. He interviewed many staff: the GIDU team, those in the wider Trust, and endocrinologists at University College London Hospitals (UCLH). The endocrinologists, in particular, struck him as being conflicted. There was a 'real difficulty', he says, with the link between the psychological or psychiatric management of the young people and the endocrinological treatment. 'The endocrinologists felt they were just being used as prescribing devices. And, of course, they themselves were very unsure about whether this was a correct course of action.'

So what did a report that would remain buried for 15 years contain?

Taylor praised GIDU staff, noting that they took their work seriously and were doing all they could to help their patients, who were often very distressed. Many children referred to the service had suffered trauma, had mental health problems or had experienced 'deprived or injurious upbringings', he noted.[46] But it was clear to him that clinicians fundamentally disagreed about the best way to treat these young people. There were 'differences about the best way of translating theoretical models and clinical understanding into the most effective approaches to assessment, management and treatment'.[47] Just as would become the case in later years, clinicians did not agree on *what* exactly they were treating in young people: were they treating children distressed because they were trans, or children who identified as trans because they were distressed? Or a combination of both? It was unsurprising then that they couldn't agree on the best way to treat it.

What was perhaps most obvious to Dr Taylor was how much pressure GIDU staff were under. Pressure from multiple places and of different types. There was pressure simply from the 'demand at the door', with not enough resources to meet it. There was pressure from society, as attitudes towards gender were shifting. And this made it very difficult to 'retain impartiality'. 'Because you will be criticised. If you say what you think is impartial, someone will say you're prejudiced,' he tells me.

But above all there was pressure from patient and parent groups, a pressure that was 'quite onerous' and one that 'made it very difficult for people to have freedom of thought'. There were 'pressures upon staff to comply with the demands and expectations of patients [for puberty blockers], and sometimes of their parents, in ways that may not always be in their long-term best interest', Taylor wrote in his report. 'It is the consistent impression of a number of GIDU staff that the service was coming under pressure to recommend the prescription of drugs more often and more quickly, and that the independence of professional judgment was also coming under increasing pressure.' What's more, Taylor saw that 'clinicians will differ in their ability to resist the pressure to comply', and yet there didn't appear to be an 'overall Trust position to support' them. They didn't appear to be being supported to say 'no'.[48]

Just as today, David Taylor found that the use of puberty blockers in the treatment of gender-related distress in young people was the feature of the gender service that 'excited most controversy'. Taylor did not rule out their use, but noted that while the rationale for them 'may be valid', as far as he could tell 'they are relatively untested and un-researched'. Taylor questions whether the blockers were acting in the way that they were intended. 'Is it true that [puberty blockers] purchase time in the ways proposed? Is empirical information being gathered about what patients do with the extra months and years by which puberty is delayed?' he asked. There was not a robust evidence base underpinning the treatment. And the GIDU was not currently collecting data to try to answer some of the unanswered questions.[49]

Taylor recommended that while puberty blockers should remain available, 'Long term therapeutic inputs should be offered wherever possible'; that where clinicians maintained concerns, they should be able to decline to provide the blocker; that 'serious consideration' needed to be given to whether these young people could provide informed consent to the treatment; and that patients who did start treatment with puberty blockers should be 'followed up long-term'.[50] Indeed, thorough clinical audits of *all* service users should be undertaken by the service. Clarity was also required over where 'clinical responsibility' for these patients lay, concluded Taylor – with GIDS, who referred young people for the puberty blockers, or UCLH, who prescribed them? And when it came to finding GIDS a home in the Trust, Taylor proposed that it be hosted in the Tavistock's Adolescent Department, where 'the boundaries with other services in the Trust dealing with similar age groups can be more permeable'.[51] GIDS should be placed alongside teams dealing with eating disorders and body dysmorphic disorder in the Adolescent Directorate, he suggested.* It wasn't healthy for GIDS to be isolated, for staff or for patients.

'The overall aim', of the Tavistock's gender service for young people, Taylor wrote, 'will be an assessment and treatment service of the highest standard which also advances knowledge of the disorder and its treatment. Given that this is such a difficult and problematic area it is not an option for the Trust to provide a service that is less than the best possible.'[52]

Taylor's recommendations were largely ignored. GIDS did not become a world leader in terms of research on good healthcare for gender-questioning young people. It did not conduct regular audits of this patient group. It did not provide extensive therapy to young people prior to commencing puberty blockers. It did not follow up the patients it had referred for physical interventions, or gain data on how the 'time to think' was being used in practice. It did not follow

---

* The Tavistock and Portman Trust was made up of four clinical 'directorates' at this time. The Tavistock Clinic consisted of the 'Adolescent', 'Child and Family' and 'Adult' directorates, and then there was the Portman Clinic. Each directorate contained a number of different services. GIDS was one service. The names of these directorates have changed slightly over time – and GIDS has moved to the Children, Young Adults and Families (CYAF) Directorate, and then later to a Gender Services Division – but the broad structure of the Trust has remained.

up any of its patients. And, although it did become part of the wider Tavistock's structures, GIDS remained isolated throughout, according to the service's own staff.

Over the next decade and a half, more than a thousand children would be referred for puberty blockers, at ever younger ages.

Ellie

1994

'There are loads of different types of people in this world, and the only problem is some of them are so narrow-minded they can't get on with their lives and leave other people alone,' 11-year-old Ellie tells viewers of BBC children's television show *As Seen on TV*.

It's 1994 and Ellie says *she* is happy with the way she is. It's other people who have the problem.

Her gender non-conforming behaviour began in very early childhood. As early as she can remember. Both she and her parents recall it starting when she was around two years old. She refused to wear a dress, or anything remotely 'feminine'. 'The grandmas were really determined; I remember all the cardigans, pink cardigans, you know. I was not putting on the pink cardigan no matter what,' Ellie says, speaking in 2022.

In the film Ellie looks, and behaves, like a stereotypical boy. Short, cropped, ginger hair, baggy T-shirts and jumpers, board shorts – not a hint of pink in sight; and active – incredibly active.

'Who made the rules that a girl had to wear a dress, and nice pretty shoes, and have their hair really long and nicely done in plaits?' she asks the camera. 'And who made rules that girls have to play with dolls and boys have to play with footballs?'

Ellie knows she doesn't fit the mould of what a girl 'should' look like. She explains how some people she plays sports with think she's a boy, 'because I haven't actually told him that I'm a girl. I actually can't face it – what people are going to say.'

It doesn't sound easy.

'Sometimes I feel I'm mutated. Because when I look at myself in the mirror, I do look just like a boy. And I thought if I had long hair, then I would look really ugly. But with short hair I look just like a boy – my face just says boy. It says girl for my parents but not to me. It doesn't actually say girl to me any more.'

Her mum and dad are completely supportive. But, just prior to Ellie making this video, they thought she might benefit from talking to an expert.

'I just must have said, "I feel like a boy, or I want to be a boy or I wish I was a boy." I know that my mum says I said it,' Ellie explains to me. 'I was only distressed by other people's response to me presenting in the world that way. I was only distressed by the bullying. I was only distressed by the accusation that I wasn't a girl when I was one. I didn't mind being called a boy. But I didn't want to be bullied for it. And a lot of that came from adults.'

Ellie's parents sought a referral to the then relatively unknown Gender Identity Development Service. They wanted advice, or just an opportunity for their daughter to talk with someone who had experience of other gender non-conforming children. The service agreed that Ellie was just the type of young person they were set up to see.

Ellie met with the service's founder, Domenico Di Ceglie, for a number of one-on-one sessions over ten months.

When Ellie recollects thirty years later it's difficult for her to remember everything in detail, but she says they 'just talked'. And talked and talked and talked. Dr Di Ceglie asked gently what she was thinking and feeling about her body. She remembers replying: '"I don't like all my body. I don't like all of it. I don't like my face, and I don't like my hands. And I don't like my legs. I don't like how muscly I am." I was freckly, and I'm ginger.' Accentuating the feeling of being unlike others was the vivid difference between her and her 'brown-eyed, blonde, petite, gorgeous, slim sister'.

'I remember looking at my legs when I was little and looking at the muscle definition and the bulk on them and feeling like those aren't girls' legs,' Ellie explains, 'because I'd look at all the other girls' legs and their legs didn't look like my legs. So, I was like, they're boys' legs, then. And I want to do boy things. I knew my body was a girl's body. That was fine… I didn't want to harm it. But it just wasn't *acceptably* a girl's body, compared to the other ones around me.'

Di Ceglie listened, and then questioned. 'Why does that mean that your body isn't a girl's body?' he asked. Ellie says he told her there were all sorts of different 'girls' bodies' and that her body would change with time. 'I said that it was other people's perceptions of me that was making me feel so much disgust in my own body, or foreignness of my body. And discomfort in that.' Domenico Di Ceglie explained, in a way that Ellie as a child could understand, that if she continued to feel this way as she got older – 'if you want to be a boy and then to be a man' – there were things that GIDS could do to try to help. She remembers him explaining what transition would entail 'in detail'. There was no mention at all of puberty blockers, but they did talk about hormones and surgery. If this is what she felt she might be heading towards, he explained, she would need to continue seeing GIDS for a considerable amount of time going forward, to 'make sure that I was sure about what I wanted'.

'I understood what a transsexual was and that that was possible. I didn't know all the steps and processes to get there. But I assumed you took some sort of medicine, and I knew there was surgery as well,' she says. 'And then I knew about genitals… I expected they could be removed… This was the key point; I could never get my head around how you could make a penis out of a vagina.

'When he talked about the surgery… all I could think was that sounds really painful. That sounds really not something I want.' Di Ceglie explained that even if this was something Ellie felt she might want, surgery was 'a very long way away'. 'So having explained what is known now as phalloplasty, metoidioplasty and things, to me in a simple term that a child could understand, I sat on the ideas of it.[1] And I just said no. Just to myself. I just said, "No, that's just not gonna work."'

The other option put forward by Di Ceglie was time. Just take a bit of time to try to figure things out. That was the option that Ellie preferred. Although she was still young at the time – not even a teenager – Ellie says she doesn't know how she could have made a properly informed decision about what she wanted to do without the infor-mation on what the future might look like if she chose to transition. 'I don't know how I would have got there,' she explains.

Ellie found her time at GIDS 'really helpful'. To be able to talk openly about the feelings she had towards her body, about gender roles and, crucially, not to be judged for it. Ellie had never met or seen anyone like her, and here was someone who listened, who had knowl-edge of this area and who said, quite simply, 'This does happen, we've spoken to people who feel the same way and you're not alone.'

Ellie says that her parents' attitude towards her gender non-conformity also made an enormous difference. They allowed her to live, dress and behave how she wanted. 'I had lots of passions,' she says, most of them involving being outside and physical. The rest of her family were the same. 'It's all about role models too – not judging you and being loving and supportive.'

Ellie made the decision herself to stop seeing GIDS. It had been enormously valuable to talk through how she felt and know what options were open to her if she wanted to pursue a medical transition. For now, she was happy to take time to think.

But it was puberty that really changed things.

The boys who'd been her closest friends since childhood, and whom she had repeatedly gotten the better of at sports, suddenly grew. She talks about one friend in particular: 'We played together for years: basketball. And I beat him, and I beat him because he was just a little boy… And then one day, when we were 14, he doubled in size over-night – it felt like. He started dunking in the net, and he started taking the ball off me and he started doing all these things. And I hadn't bloody changed. But then I sort of started to go, "Oh dear," you know, that's what testosterone did.' The reality of her sex had hit her.

Quite literally at times.

'I was playing basketball at school with some boys – and I was still good. But of course, they were all big and strong, and a boy that I didn't know very well – a bit of a bully boy from the year below – we fell out over the ball. And he said, "Fuck off, you fucking he-she"… I tried to kick him in the nethers. And then he punched me. He got me in a headlock, and he punched me in the face. It must have been eight or nine times. And I got a huge black eye… and I kind of went off, you know, bruised and a bit like, "Oh dear." You know, I can't fight them any more. They're bigger and stronger than me. Those days are done.'

As unpleasant as the experience was, it was a wake-up call, Ellie says. 'I'm not a little boy, I'm not gonna be a boy, I'm not gonna be a man. And I don't want to if they behave like that. So then I started to spend more time with females and female friends and have a mixture of both [male and female]. And I developed what can only be described as one of the richest friendship groups you will ever see in your life.' She grew her hair, and even – on occasion – would wear a dress. Not often.

This was the start of being able to work things out, Ellie says. 'And then of course, I wanted to have sex!' She had had crushes on other girls, often fancying the girlfriends of the boys who were her closest friends. She couldn't say anything. She says it wasn't so much that she was embarrassed or ashamed in anyway about being attracted to girls; it was that she found the implications of being gay hard to think about. 'I knew that women together wouldn't make a baby naturally. And I was sad about it. And I still am sad about it.' So to start with she sought a male partner.

Approaching 40, Ellie has had relationships with both men and women and is bisexual. She has been in a long-term relationship with another woman for over a decade.

3

THE PUSH FOR PUBERTY BLOCKERS

As the 2000s marched on, the pressure to provide puberty blockers, which Dr David Taylor had described so vividly in his 2005 review of GIDS, became more intense. And it came from multiple quarters: the young patients themselves, who might threaten suicide, so deep was their distress; their parents, some of whom complained; and lobbies of older patients and trans adults who pressed for increased use of medication, and who pointed out that blockers could now be obtained without regulation via the internet.

This pressure to provide medication wasn't new. As far back as 1996, features appeared in the British press and on television in which teenagers questioned why 'they are having to wait so long to change their unwanted bodies'.[1] GIDS founder Domenico Di Ceglie would explain sympathetically that while the distress felt by these young people was genuine and overwhelming, they needed help in 'tolerating it'.[2] And it was necessary to have 'prolonged therapy before embarking on physical treatment'.[3] He highlighted research which he said showed that the vast majority of children who have difficulties with their gender identity grow up to become gay, not trans, and that 'it is very difficult to predict the outcome from early childhood'.[4] What's more, he explained, teenagers – even at 14 – 'cannot be totally sure at that age'.[5] Even among those over 16 who took puberty blockers, some 25 to 33 per cent did not progress to the further stage of cross-sex hormones at this time, according to Di Ceglie. 'It is difficult to know why this might be,' he mused.[6]

But demands for change grew more vociferous from the mid 2000s. Along with Mermaids, the Gender Identity Research and Education Society – GIRES – lobbied hard for GIDS to lower the age at which they'd consider treating children with puberty blockers. In fact, GIRES seemed to be the most influential group at this time. Husband and wife Bernard and Terry Reed founded GIRES in 1997, motivated by the poor treatment their trans daughter had received.[7] A year earlier they'd helped her win a lengthy industrial tribunal against her former employers. In 2008, after years of trying to make the case for early blocking of puberty, their calls intensified, and they even appeared to label British clinicians 'transphobic'.[8] Why, they argued, couldn't British clinicians be more like the Dutch? 'As far as they're concerned, a trans outcome is bad,' declared Terry Reed. 'They are hoping that during puberty the natural hormones themselves will act on the brain to "cure" these trans teenagers,' Reed argued. 'What we do know is what happens if you don't offer hormone blockers. You are stuck with unwanted secondary sex characteristics in the long term and in the short term these teenagers end up suicidal.'[9]

How would the service respond?

Although Domenico Di Ceglie was one of the early players in the field of gender medicine, it was a group based in the Netherlands who were viewed as the trailblazers for the medical treatment of children and young people experiencing gender-related distress. The Dutch had opened the first specialised gender identity clinic for young people a couple of years before the UK, in 1987, at the Utrecht University Medical Center.[10] In 2002 the service moved to the VU University Medical Center in Amsterdam and later became part of the Center of Expertise on Gender Dysphoria.

In 1998 the Dutch told the world about 'B', a 'female-to-male transsexual' who arrived at their clinic already having had her puberty blocked at 13 by a paediatric endocrinologist and who, aged 16, was requesting sex reassignment surgery.[11] This was the first known case of a young person having their puberty blocked before 16 for the purposes of treating gender-related distress. Upon arrival at the service, B saw a family therapist and had a few group sessions with other females wanting to transition. 'When no psychological obstacles remained', it was agreed cross-sex hormone treatment could start. B chose to delay this until 18, when she had finished high school, but a double mastectomy and ovariectomy (the removal of the ovaries) soon followed. One year later, the Dutch described how he now reported 'no gender dysphoria at all' and 'never felt any regrets about his decision and had never contemplated to live as a girl'.* By the time the paper was published, B had undergone a metaidoioplasty (a procedure where the clitoris is transformed into a micropenis) and was 'very satisfied with the results'.

The early papers from the Dutch team signalled not just a revolutionary approach to treatment, but also a rather curious trend found in this field of research: results are spoken about with great certainty, but they are based on very small samples, very short-term follow-ups and high rates of participants who are 'lost to follow-up' – that is, people who don't respond to researchers' invitation to participate.[12] There's also at times a somewhat selective approach taken to the use of data from previous studies.

Here's an example. The Dutch team argued that blocking puberty early (under the age of 16) can spare the young person who goes on to make a full surgical transition in adulthood 'the torment of (full) pubescent development of the "wrong" secondary sex characteristics'.[13] Existing studies, they said, show that post-operative mental health is 'primarily associated' with whether individuals could successfully 'pass... as members of their new sex', and therefore blocking puberty early would make surgery more successful later on.[14] But is that what the evidence says? In one of the papers frequently cited to justify this claim, a study of 14 patients published in 1989, the participants are all male-to female patients and none had their puberty blocked.[15] We cannot know, then, whether the findings of this study apply to females who would undergo a very different set of surgical procedures. The sample size – just 14 – is small. They represent just over half (27) of the *eligible* patients. So if the other half had taken part, that *could*

---

* The author follows the same pronoun use as the Dutch authors, who refer to B as 'she' in some parts of the paper and 'he' in the latter parts.

have radically changed the findings. Finally, the study does not only single out the ability to 'pass' as the factor in determining good post-operative mental health. It talks about several factors: social and family support are central to 'post-operative functioning', and 'urinary incontinence and the need for further surgery' also play a part. To use this study to make the case for the early blocking of puberty – especially perhaps in the case of natal females – seems a stretch. Yet it and similar studies have been influential in the development of current treatment protocols.

While reporting the success of their groundbreaking approach – based on a sample of one – the Dutch also hint at its potential risk: that lowering the age of puberty blockade might 'increase the incidence of "false positives"'.[16] It's a rather euphemistic way of saying that some young people might transition who might otherwise not have. That some would transition who, had they not embarked upon an early medical transition, would, like Ellie, have grown up to be adults comfortable in their body and sexuality.

The Dutch may have felt the need to acknowledge this risk as previous studies had shown that for the majority of young people who experienced gender dysphoria as children, this would resolve during puberty. By not allowing that full process to occur, it could be that some of those who would have come to reconcile themselves with the body they were born with would not have the opportunity to do so. Dutch clinicians also saw that some adolescents might see taking puberty blockers as a 'guarantee of sex reassignment' and would therefore be less inclined 'to engage in introspection'.[17] For the Dutch, risks were outweighed by the benefits to the minority of those who would go on to transition as adults. But, they stressed, this was an approach only for very selective patients – those with 'life-long consistent and extreme' gender identity difficulties.

B was a one-off, but the case marked the start of something. Within two years, the Dutch had rolled out a new approach to treating young people. Hormone blockers could be given from the age of 12, under certain conditions.[18] Young people had to meet the diagnostic criteria for gender identity disorder, as it was known at the time; have suffered from lifelong extreme gender dysphoria; be psychologically stable;

and live in a supportive environment.[19] And so, in 2000, what became known as 'the Dutch protocol' was born. Providing a young person met the eligibility criteria, they could receive puberty blockers at 12, followed by cross-sex hormones at 16, and surgery at 18.

Pressure grew for GIDS, and the paediatric endocrinologists who worked alongside them, to follow the Dutch example. For a while they stood their ground. 'There were external pressures,' Sue Evans recalls. 'There was international pressure; Polly [Carmichael] and Domenico [Di Ceglie] were in contact with the Dutch service in particular at that time. But at that time, that kind of [age] 16 boundary was still holding despite the pressures.' Another clinician from the time says that Di Ceglie would 'helpfully provide a space where clinicians were encouraged just to think and understand, rather than to act'. The team would discuss cases in their weekly meeting and talk about the pressure they were under. Di Ceglie would encourage clinicians not to see the answer as just 'we'll give them medication', but instead 'let's understand the distress'.

In 2005, to the disappointment of British patient groups like GIRES, rather than relax the guidance on the use of puberty blockers, the British Society of Paediatric Endocrinology and Diabetes (BSPED) issued strict and 'specific' recommendations that adolescents should have to complete puberty before receiving the blocker. Young people, it said, should be given psychological support to help them explore these pubertal changes, 'rather than to necessarily regard them as undesirable'. This would allow for more flexible thinking and the opportunity to change the course of the gender identity disorder. Puberty, it argued, was the key period for brain, physical and psychological development, and therefore 'the most likely time for change and reversibility of the Gender Dysphoria'. 'It seems neither sensible nor desirable therefore to deny the brain of any individual, the natural hormone environment at puberty.'[20]

The document is stark in relaying the potential risks to the body from blocking puberty. Growth and final adult height could be impacted, as could bone density and bone mineral content, which 'increase rapidly during adolescence and peak in the early twenties'. Without that acquisition of 'peak bone mass' these young people would be at a 'substantially' higher risk of osteoporosis. Unlike the Dutch, British endocrinologists did not see puberty blockade as 'fully reversible'. To the contrary, they insisted that 'delay or interruption of endogenous sex hormone production can have irreversible consequences'.[21]

Two of the guidelines' authors were involved with the treatment of young people attending GIDS.[22] One, Professor Russell Viner, according to *The Times*, later explained: 'I am concerned about the effects of suppressing puberty very early, particularly on the brain, which is developing extremely quickly at this age.'[23] He asked: 'if you intervene early in a young person who would otherwise change [their mind], do you reinforce their gender identity disorder? Do you remove the chance for change?'[24] Viner and his colleagues were also very alive to the 'ethical dilemmas' involved with providing 'a range of potentially harmful hormones… off-licence with no clear "medical" indication' to children. And not just ethical issues, but 'child protection concerns' too, he explained:

> Additional difficulties include frequent psychiatric comorbidity (emotional disorders, self-harm, and substance use), social deprivation, refusal to be physically examined, and use of 'black market' hormones. Further dilemmas are presented by highly active patient support groups and reports of early active hormonal treatment in other European countries.[25]

In 2005, GIRES and Mermaids organised a meeting with clinicians from gender clinics around the world to try to develop 'guidelines for endocrinological intervention' in the UK.[26] The creators of the Dutch protocol, GIDS director Domenico Di Ceglie and colleague Polly Carmichael, along with the endocrinologists who administered puberty blockers to GIDS patients, attended. So did the Harvard-based clinician Norman Spack. GIRES talked about British families 'taking their children to the USA' for puberty-blocking treatment.[27] 'The USA' in this case meant Norman Spack, who is believed to have treated a small number of British children over the next few years, including the child of Susie Green.[28] Green later became chair and then chief executive of transgender charity Mermaids. (In 2009, Green accompanied her child to Thailand, where, on their sixteenth birthday, they underwent male-to-female sex reassignment surgery.[29])

Early data from the Dutch team helped spread their protocol beyond the Netherlands, notably to Belgium and the United States.[30] In a conference paper, the Dutch researchers provided information on precise doses of cross-sex hormones that they were using, and a detailed timetable for increasing them. The conference was sponsored by Ferring Pharmaceuticals, the makers of triptorelin.

The Dutch stated that, based on observations of the 54 young people currently being treated according to the protocol, it appeared to be a 'suitable way' of treating those with gender identity difficulties. Everyone who had been administered with puberty blockers at the time of publication had 'repeatedly' said how satisfied they were. While, the Dutch argued, blocking puberty would allow adolescents to explore their gender identity with less anxiety, they noted that none had decided to stop taking the blocker.[31]

At the same time as describing the blocker as 'fully reversible', the Dutch explained how, in 'early pubertal boys', administration of the blocker followed by cross-sex hormones would leave them infertile. In older boys, whose fertility 'will regress', preservation of semen should be discussed before starting treatment. The researchers also noted how growth would be impacted by the blockers, as would bone density. The early Dutch findings suggested that while on puberty blockers young people's bone density remained unchanged. But puberty is normally a time of rapid *acceleration*. When adolescents began treatment with cross-sex hormones, 'bone density increased significantly' in both sexes, but it was unclear as to 'whether patients participating in this protocol may achieve a normal development of bone density, or will end with a decreased bone density, which is associated with a high risk of osteoporosis'.[32]

Some of those working in GIDS in the early 2000s say that 'the political pressure from activist groups was astonishing'. Sue Evans says she queried with Domenico Di Ceglie why GIDS couldn't 'just be an expert service', providing support work. She 'thought the support work for schools and families and teachers was really good, trying to reduce prejudice in the classroom and bullying'. She was stunned by his answer.

'I would swear on the Bible that he said the words, approximately: "But they wouldn't come." You know, it's having the offer of the treatment, the physical treatment... He said: "It's because we have this treatment here that people come."'

Another clinician working at the service at the time confirms they heard this too. If GIDS did not offer blockers, the service would simply not exist. Blockers were what its users wanted. That is not to say that there were not other good reasons for wanting to keep GIDS open – nowhere else offered this group of young people a space to talk through their feelings and not be judged.

For his part, Domenico Di Ceglie was open about the difficult position that GIDS found itself in when it came to offering a medical pathway.[33] He experienced 'confusion and disorientation' in trying to deal with increasing and competing pressures.[34] GIDS needed the support of the wider Tavistock and Portman Trust, which was sceptical about the use of drugs in this context, but felt it could not alienate groups like Mermaids.[35]

GIDS's existence seemed to depend upon 'a continuous process of negotiation' with 'user organizations and the wider institutions where the professional and service belong'.[36] And, as its founder and director, Di Ceglie 'felt under extreme pressure' to join one side or the other. He compares the anxiety he felt to that of Ulysses (Odysseus) having to navigate the passage between two cliffs, guarded by the two monsters Scylla and Charybdis. On the one side there was the voice of trans groups like Mermaids and GIRES, who saw physical interventions as 'the main way of reducing distress in early adolescence' and a 'lifesaving intervention in the face of suicidal and self-harming behaviour'; on the other were those of many colleagues in the Tavistock Trust and outside, who 'had the view that adolescents should only be offered psychological and social support but not the possibility of any physical intervention'. If the Trust became too unhappy, 'there was a risk that the service could be closed.' If service users were alienated, that too could have 'serious consequences for the survival and the provision of a service'.[37]

Di Ceglie admitted that it was a 'matter of conjecture what the major risk and the cost were for GIDS'. The evidence surrounding the treatment – its potential benefits and harms – did not appear to feature prominently in his thinking. The major risk, he believed, 'seemed to be the closure or reduction of the service which would have been a considerable loss for service users'. To his mind, it was his job to ensure its survival.'[38]

But it would be wrong to say that GIDS faced pressure from patient groups alone. It came also from clinical colleagues both in the UK and across the world, as well as from medical ethicists who argued that the UK's position was unethical and based on illegitimate arguments about consent.[39]

A series of professional meetings was held from 2004 onwards, at which clinical and ethical issues related to the timing of pubertal suppression in adolescents with gender dysphoria in the UK compared with other countries were discussed. The Royal College of Paediatrics and Child Health and the Royal Society of Medicine (RSM) both hosted events. 'In each meeting the Dutch, US and some UK clinicians were clear that they considered the UK service to be an outlier in not supporting pubertal suppression under 16 years,' GIDS later claimed.[40]

Some UK clinicians were becoming more vocal in their frustrations. One of them, Professor Richard Green, ex-director of the adult gender clinic at Charing Cross, argued that going through puberty in the 'wrong sex' was 'traumatic' for teenagers and would bring 'additional hardship' if they chose to live as adults of the 'opposite sex'. Many adults he had worked with had expressed their regret at not being able to transition as teenagers. Green was so disdainful of GIDS's 'conservative' approach that he organised his own conference in 2008 to rival one scheduled by the RSM.[41]

It was pressure from within the endocrinology community that proved most persuasive for those who would be responsible for prescribing the blockers, Professor Russell Viner tells me when we speak in 2022 – not patient groups. And the 2008 RSM meeting in particular was a turning point. 'There was a consensus from the adult

---

* Dr Di Ceglie politely declined to be interviewed for this book, explaining that he retired from GIDS some years ago and has reduced his work-related commitments. He directed the author towards some of his published papers which, he said, summarised his 'experience and thinking over the years'.

endocrinologists and others who were there... that this was a treatment that should be offered in the UK,' he says. This included some of the most respected and senior paediatric endocrinologists in the field, he explains.[42] Viner and Di Ceglie's peers stressed that there was a balance of risks – including the very real distress felt by young people if they did not receive treatment – but that patients and families 'had a right to have some agency'. There had been an important shift in the world of disorders of sexual differentiation, where some of these endocrinologists worked too (as did Dr Polly Carmichael) – a move 'very strongly away from operating at birth to giving people choices' later in life. Patient choice was front and foremost.

Many young people attending gender clinics, wherever in the world, are undoubtedly deeply distressed. It's argued that blocking puberty and the bodily changes accompanying it helps relieve this distress, and that the negative consequences of *not* blocking the puberty outweigh those of using a treatment with a limited evidence base. But the issue was not clear-cut. 'The Dutch data [about puberty blockers] looks promising,' GIDS clinical psychologist Dr Polly Carmichael explained in response to the criticism of GIDS from GIRES, 'but they have not been doing it for so many years that you have long-term follow-up.' In other words, there wasn't enough evidence either way about the longer-term impact of blockers on young minds and bodies. 'The question is, if you halt your own sex hormones so that your brain is not experiencing puberty, are you in some way altering the course of nature?'[43]

It is worth remembering that it wasn't just the impact of puberty blockers that was poorly understood. Within this area of healthcare, there are disagreements at the most fundamental level. Among GIDS clinicians, at least, there lacked agreement on what being trans even meant. Were young people born trans and therefore destined to become trans adults? Or could some young people have gender dysphoria which could be explained by something else, and which they might therefore grow out of, either on their own or with the help of therapy? This would become a major problem for GIDS: how could there be consensus on treatment without consensus on what was being 'treated'?

By the beginning of 2008 the British Society for Paediatric Endocrinology and Diabetes (BSPED) guidelines of 2005 were under review, and within a year or so the US, European and British endocrine societies had all issued guidance arguing that 'early intervention should happen', Professor Viner says.[44] It was seen as the 'gold standard' treatment, he says, and – others argued – it was 'unethical to withhold it'. The new BSPED position statement in 2009 acknowledged that 'rigid adherence to guidelines/protocols based on current limited evidence may not be in the best interest of some individuals'. But, at the same time, it wanted to proceed in a cautious, safe way. 'However,' it went on, 'any deviation from current practice should be made by the specialist MDT [multidisciplinary team]. Such a change in management should include comprehensive multidisciplinary assessment, informed consent, a system for monitoring outcome and ideally should be implemented as a research study.'[45]

Faced with this shifting guidance and Dutch data that 'appeared to undercut lots of our concerns', Viner explains, it seemed only sensible to proceed with research. It wasn't that his or his colleagues' concerns about the potential impact on bones or the brain had gone away, he insists, but that they needed to know more. The patient groups were 'very certain', Viner recalls, 'and we kept trying to reflect uncertainty back to them'. They found it 'very difficult to hear'. 'We're sceptics, we're scientists,' he says. They questioned whether the results were 'real' and they needed to know more.

And so, in 2011, GIDS and endocrinologists at UCLH embarked upon a research study that would allow young people aged 12 and upwards to block their puberty, provided they met certain criteria. This solution perhaps pleased no one, instead generating resentment 'in both groups' by arriving at what GIDS felt to be a middle ground. 'Some people felt that the service had gone too far in offering this physical intervention while others felt that GIDS had not responded quickly enough.'[46]

But whether it left people pleased or perturbed, what followed was certainly significant. And controversial. The NHS began medically altering the puberties of children, based on their declared identities.

Phoebe

2009

'It was the best day. I can remember the nail colour I had on and everything; what I was wearing.'

Phoebe was 15 years old when she was first seen by GIDS. That appointment, she says, was the first time she had felt validated. 'She listened to me. She listened to my story,' Phoebe explains of her clinician. There wasn't much of a waiting list back then, and after being referred by her local Child and Adolescent Mental Health Services (CAMHS), she didn't have to wait long to be seen. Phoebe had taken her mum by surprise on a trip to the doctors not long before the CAMHS referral. 'I want to be a woman,' she'd declared. Phoebe admits her mum was left feeling 'blindsided'. 'She knew I had inclinations. But she didn't realise that I was quite ready.'

Phoebe had told her parents when she was three years old that she was 'saving all my Christmas money for an operation to become a lady'. She had been one of a pair of twins – one male, one female. Her female sibling had died midway through the pregnancy. 'We think that my mum carried on producing hormones for both sets of twins,' Phoebe says. They were, and are, a loving and supportive family, but Phoebe's parents couldn't help feel worried for their child. About what would happen if they transitioned; about how society would view them. 'I see it from their point now,' Phoebe reflects as a 28-year-old adult. 'I understand when they said that my surgery wouldn't fix everything... I understand that it was more outside in society, and it is not really going to change how someone else might see me.'

The first GIDS appointment was relaxed. 'I just spoke about why I was there and what's been going on in my life… They didn't push; they weren't too invasive.' Phoebe and her family would talk about their home life – sometimes together, and sometimes in separate rooms with different clinicians – about school, and about 'people who have made our lives difficult' in the period between sessions. Bullying would often be discussed.

'I suffered some horrific abuse from a very young age,' Phoebe explains. 'I was teased and taunted for being gay.' It wasn't easy growing up in the early 2000s as a gender non-conforming boy in the west of England. 'I said to my mum, "I'm done being called gay. I'm not being bullied for something that I'm not." She was saying, "Yeah, but you can't just go into school dressed as a woman."' Phoebe would dress as a girl for parties and other events, and be seen as 'glamorous', only then to 'go into school as a boy' when Monday morning came around. But living this way became too hard. 'I was like, "Fuck 'em. They're going to bully me anyway. Why not actually be bullied for what I am?"' Phoebe's mum was terrified. But supportive.

Talking about the tough times she was having at school with GIDS staff gave her 'ventilation from life'. It was hard sometimes, and there were occasions where Phoebe had run out of the classroom in tears after friends would tell her she was 'never going to be viewed as what you think you're going to be viewed as'. But the appointments gave her an opportunity to talk about this. She thought about whether she might have been a feminine, gay boy rather than a trans woman. 'I thought about it, and I was like, no. Because it was what was down here,' she says, pointing downwards on her body. 'And I've had those inclinations from such a young age – all of the dressing up and swapping labels on toys for Christmas and things like that – it was always there.' For Phoebe, her desire to live as a woman wasn't about who she was attracted to. 'It wasn't at all sexual,' she says. It was about who she was. 'I literally used to go into the bathroom and I was repulsed. I was physically sick at times over what I saw in the mirror. I couldn't look at myself before I got in the shower.'

At 16 years old, Phoebe was given the go-ahead to go on puberty blockers.

Although she'd met with the endocrinology team after six months, by the time she started on blockers in 2011, she'd had over a year's worth of appointments at GIDS, every six weeks. There had been a delay in starting, as Phoebe was keen to look into the possibility of storing sperm in case she wanted children in the future.

It wasn't easy for Phoebe to receive her hormone-blocker injections. 'I had to go and collect them from London, because my doctor's surgery refused to prescribe them for me,' she says.

Phoebe continued to attend appointments at GIDS every six weeks, and after ten months on puberty blockers went on to the female hormone oestrogen to begin her medical transition to a trans woman. 'I was quite forthcoming with doctors about what I wanted.' And it was a big deal for Phoebe. It still is. 'I started on these really tiny little pills and it was a milestone in my head.'

It was an extraordinarily difficult time in Phoebe's life. Her mum was seriously ill, and neither she nor Phoebe's dad could come to her endocrinology appointment where they'd be discussing the oestrogen. 'I had to get the train to London for the first time by myself, and I was shitting my pants. I took the day off of school. I had a nice little All Saints dress on that I'd worked for and saved up for. And I had a little man's white shirt at the top, with a red pair of heels… And I went to the doctors.'

Soon after Phoebe had begun medically transitioning, her mum died. She's emotional when she talks about that time, but is both proud and happy that her mum saw the start of her journey. 'I got my name – Phoebe – for my sixteenth birthday present,' she says. Her GIDS clinician had helped her to get a passport in her new name. 'They helped me get a passport so I could go on holiday as a woman for my mum's last holiday. That meant a lot.'

GIDS was also hugely supportive while Phoebe grieved.

It's difficult not to see the care she received from GIDS as anything other than therapeutic, Phoebe says. 'It was so cathartic. You see what you want to see. And I saw help. I saw therapy… When someone's saying to you, "Tell me more about that"… it is therapeutic! Somebody is going to listen to you for an hour, just gab about your life – that's therapy… That is bloody brilliant.'

Phoebe says her clinicians never pushed her towards transition. She led the process throughout. And they listened. She has an enormous amount of respect and affection for those who helped her. Seeing the same person throughout her three years at GIDS made a big difference, she says. 'She really did help me navigate those really treacherous years; they were with me through school, which I think was the hardest period.'

At 18 she was discharged from the service and supported in going on to an adult gender clinic. She underwent surgery just before her twentieth birthday. 'I was really young,' she concedes. 'I was very young.' But, she says, it's the best thing she's ever done. She's thankful to the healthcare professionals who have helped make it happen. 'I do feel, like, that really, those doctors gave me my life.'

In 2021, at 28 years old, Phoebe hasn't once regretted the surgery she had almost a decade ago. But there is one thing she would change if she could.

'Before I started hormone blockers I was asked about children. I was like, "Oh my God, yeah, I'd love to be a mum."' Phoebe was asked whether she wanted to freeze her sperm. She agreed. If that was a possibility, she wanted to do it. 'Because as much as I hate what is down there, those – however long – minutes… would have made all this worth it.'

NHS fertility services local to Phoebe refused to help. The letter she received is cruel and cold in tone. It described the wish to preserve fertility as 'at odds' with her pursuit of 'gender reassignment' and therefore it would not agree to sperm storage. Furthermore, the request would not be considered because 'it does not fulfil our requirements of the welfare of any offspring that would result from the storage of this sperm in the future'. It was devastating to hear as a 16-year-old. If she wanted to pursue transition and pause the distress she was experiencing from her continuing male puberty, Phoebe would have to forgo the chance of having her own children in adulthood. 'Obviously, as a kid, I was like… I want my journey,' she says.

An NHS mental health professional has apologised for this subsequently, but it's something Phoebe's cried about in therapy. And it still affects her today. 'If I could have just had the confidence to go those few more years,' she says, she might have been able to freeze her sperm so that she could have her own biological children later in life. But, at the time, she could not see past the immediate feelings of suffering. 'It does make me quite angry.'

It's impossible not to like Phoebe. With her long, curly, dark-blonde hair, she's funny, open and entirely honest about what life is like for her as a trans woman. She's proud of what she's achieved. And her family are proud of her. 'I look in the mirror in the morning, and I smile at what has been done. I love my boobs. I love my vagina. It wasn't done for sexual reasons. It was to be comfortable with my own body.'

'I guess the problem is, like my parents said to me, "You do realise this doesn't fix everything."' Phoebe wanted her life to change, which it has. But it took her a long time to realise she couldn't control or change other people's opinions too. 'You're only in control of your business,' as she puts it. She has had relationships with men but admits that she has found it difficult. While there are men who will date trans women 'with open arms', she says, she's not necessarily sure she's found those men yet. And because life is not always easy, she wants to ensure that the process for transitioning is thorough.

'I said to my friend, I do worry that in the end it's all going to be a phase, with lots more people coming out going, "Oh no, this, this isn't what I actually wanted to do," when they've actually lived a little bit more of their life.'

'I had a really positive experience,' Phoebe repeats, but at the time she found having to wait for the different stages of transitioning frustrating and agonising. Sessions at GIDS could feel repetitive, she says, but she understands why the clinicians had to keep asking questions. They needed to make sure. 'They are only asking them for a reason.' With a little more time spent *before* transitioning, Phoebe believes, those who are now detransitioning, or having second thoughts about their transition, 'might have actually made that decision themselves without having surgery or hormone blockers'.

'I would have had the surgery at 13! But obviously *now* what I say to people is the rules are there for a reason. Detransitioning is a thing.'

She says that today, in some cases, transitioning is 'definitely' happening too quickly.

Phoebe tells me it's vital that different views are heard. Transitioning has been right for her, but she also thinks it's right that the process takes time. To try to make sure that, as much as possible, people make decisions that will turn out to be right not just now, but in many years' time.

4

EARLY INTERVENTION

The GIDS team's first attempt to get a research study off the ground was turned down.

The service – now under the leadership of Domenico Di Ceglie's long-standing colleague, consultant clinical psychologist Dr Polly Carmichael – had teamed up with endocrinologists from University College London's Institute of Child Health to submit plans for 'An evaluation of early pubertal suppression in a carefully selected group of adolescents with gender identity disorder'.[*][1] It was rejected in September 2010 on methodological grounds.

The research team wanted to examine the 'psychological, social and physical benefits and risks' in blocking sex-hormone production in a 'carefully selected group of adolescents' with gender dysphoria in early puberty.[2] But they didn't intend to use any kind of control group.

---

[*] Original documentation from the study was first obtained by Professor Michael Biggs of Oxford University, after submitting a series of Freedom of Information requests. Professor Biggs shared them with the author and her former BBC *Newsnight* colleague, Deborah Cohen, in 2019. They received further documents – including correspondence between the different Research Ethics Committees and study author Russell Viner from another source, who had also obtained these via use of the Freedom of Information Act. The original research application (exactly the same as the accepted one) was released under FOI: Tavistock and Portman NHS Foundation Trust FOI 19-20011 ('Subject: GIDS research information'), https://tavistockandportman.nhs.uk/documents/1845/FOI_19-20011_GIDS_Research_Information_with_attachments.pdf.

That is, there would be no other group of young people who were *not* in receipt of puberty blockers (or who would receive them aged 16 according to the existing guidelines) to compare results with. Without a control group, the problem for any study is that it's impossible to tell what effects may be down to the drug being administered, and what might be down to something else. According to the ethics committee reviewing the application, the study's proposed design meant 'there was no way to validate' the research.[3]

The joint GIDS/UCLH team argued that such a design was just not feasible.[4] Young people were 'very unlikely' to agree to participate if there was 'a chance they will not receive hormonal treatment', they argued.[5] The study's chief investigator, Professor Russell Viner, explained that 'less than one quarter would accept randomization', where each participant had a 50–50 chance of gaining access to puberty blockers.[6] Without going on the trial, the young person would not stand any chance of accessing the blocker at GIDS until they were 16, but Viner says that patient groups had told them that people would 'drop out of the control arm'. The team were aware this had happened in another study a decade earlier, albeit one that had wished to study the effects of GnRH analogues in the treatment of precocious puberty.[7] They thought there would be between ten and 15 participants joining the research per year, a sample size based on the GIDS caseload at the time of young people between the ages of 12 and 15 who met the eligibility criteria of the study.[8] 'If you randomise five to treatment and five to control and you lost three of them, you don't have a study… We contend that it's unethical to start an unfeasible trial,' Viner tells me. In addition, Viner also argued in the research application that these British children would go abroad if they could not access treatment here.'[9]

The design of the trial is a subject of legitimate scientific debate.[10] But for the avoidance of doubt, those assessing the application – Research

---

* Although the numbers were small, Viner explained in an interview with the author that he could see those numbers increasing and young people potentially exploited by overseas services. He explained that while this wasn't a reason to give the treatment in and of itself, it was one of the reasons they did not believe it was possible to do a randomised control trial.

Ethics Committee (REC) 1 – accepted that this kind of study couldn't be subjected to a gold-standard blinded trial: a young person would clearly know whether or not their puberty had been blocked. Instead, though, it offered alternative suggestions to the team for altering the design so that meaningful conclusions *could* be drawn. These included randomisation for a year, or a trial which compared those who immediately started the intervention with those who had a delayed start.*[11]

While there were 'some who were happy to approve the study, there was a significant number who felt that to proceed... without due consideration of alternative study design was unethical'.[12] Having been turned down, several options were open to the research team. They could appeal the decision, or submit a new proposal – preferably to the same committee – for ethical review, 'taking into account the Committee's concerns'.[13] The team opted to reapply with an unaltered protocol to a second ethics committee of their choosing – Central London REC 2.[14]

In a covering letter to this second committee, Russell Viner acknowledged that 'a randomised control trial would be the ideal way of comparing two treatment options', but repeated his view that it was not possible to have a control group.[15] There was no mention of the alternative designs suggested by the original ethics committee, but Viner pointed out that 'no other study in this area, as far as we know, uses a randomised control group or any other control group'.[16]

In February 2011, the combined GIDS/UCLH team got the green light to proceed.

UCLH and GIDS insist they always followed the correct procedures. The researchers *did* consider the comments made by the first committee and said their new application 'referenced and addressed' the original committee's concerns.[17] But they concluded that an observation study design was the only practicable option.[18] 'I might have been wrong. I absolutely recognise that these were decisions we made at the time,' Viner acknowledges in 2022. 'We have to

---

* Russell Viner told the author the research team 'absolutely' did consider alternatives, but that the year being suggested was 'the year that's probably important' in terms of pubertal development.

deal with uncertainty,' he adds. 'We felt that an uncontrolled design, even though it didn't give us causal answers, for a whole range of things provided a significant amount of information on the risks and benefits of the treatment in this very distressed, very highly selected group.'

With the study design approved, how well did the researchers present all that was known, and unknown, about puberty blockers to prospective participants? A study protocol guides the conduct and design of a study, setting out things like how many participants will be recruited, how long it will last and what outcomes will be measured. In this case, it explained that the study would run 'for about 6 years' and that recruitment of participants would stop after three years. The team envisaged that up to 15 young people would be eligible to take part each year. The people who were recruited in the third year would then have enough time to complete treatment with the hypothalamic blocker before returning to standard protocol – outside the research study. An interim report would be produced after three years, with a final report at the end of the six years.[19] The team would measure the 'benefits and risks for physical and mental health of early medical intervention', and evaluate the 'persistence and desistance of the gender identity disorder'. The 'Early Intervention Study', as it became known, sought to add to the evidence base regarding the efficacy of this treatment, with the researchers explaining that 'an improvement in mental states and overall wellbeing will support the view that the treatment is effective'.[20] The protocol also pulled together what was already known in the scientific and medical literature, setting out the potential benefits and risks of blocking puberty early in adolescence, along with the unknowns still associated with it.

The potential benefits reflected the early conclusions of the Dutch team.[21] GIDS and UCLH explained that, based on preliminary findings from the Dutch, 'it is assumed that early suppression [of puberty]... is associated with improved physical and psychological adaptation and well-being during adolescence and adulthood'; has 'a positive impact on any sex reassignment surgery in adulthood'; and is considered reversible. They say it is assumed that 'it does not have an adverse effect on either physical or psychological development'. The protocol goes on to explain that 'it is argued that reducing anxieties and conflicts associated with pubertal development allows space to explore the cross-gender identification'. These were the propositions being tested, given that 'the research evidence for this treatment is currently low'.[22]

On the flip side, the protocol also identified a number of significant risks. 'It is not clear what the long-term effects of early suppression may be on bone development, height, sex organ development, and body shape and their reversibility if treatment is stopped during pubertal development,' the protocol stated; there was a possible risk that early suppression of puberty 'may affect brain functioning and gender identity development by influencing the persistence of the GID and fixing transgender beliefs'; there could be long-term consequences of the treatment that were not yet known; and there could be 'issues regarding fertility'.[23] All concerns that had been voiced by GIDS and their endocrinology colleagues throughout the previous decade.

It's difficult to know how to take these two 'lists' together, as a number of their features appear mutually exclusive. Perhaps this simply reflected how much uncertainty was associated with the treatment at the time. But did either the protocol or the associated information sheets provided to young people and their families spell out *all* that was known – and not known – at the time?

In the case of fertility, the protocol explained that if puberty is properly blocked, adolescents cannot produce sperm or eggs. For both sexes, 'a significant period off the blockers would be required, with associated physical development, for the possibility of egg or sperm production.'[24] The information sheets given to both parents and young people say blocker treatment *could* affect fertility. But the Dutch had explained that if boys have their puberty blocked early and then proceed on to cross-sex hormones, they will certainly be left infertile.[25] Professor Viner says that adult endocrinologists had pushed back on this point at the 2008 Royal Society of Medicine conference. Young people were told, therefore, that as long as they retained their gonads – their ovaries or testes – they were likely to retain significant parts of their fertility, but probably not all of it. Young people taking part in the study, who all met Viner at least twice before starting any treatment, were also counselled about fertility and fertility preservation, though he says the latter was 'rarely taken up'.

What about the impact early blocking of puberty could have on the young person's gender identity? The protocol stated that 'it is possible that early suppression may affect brain functioning and gender identity development by influencing the persistence of the GID and fixing transgender beliefs'. In 2006, the Dutch had already reported that *none* of their first 54 young people in receipt of blockers had chosen to stop treatment.[26] By the time the protocol was submitted, the Dutch team had published data online showing that all of the first 70 young people aged 12 and upwards who had received puberty blockers had 'started cross-sex hormone treatment, the first step of actual gender reassignment'.[27] Professor Viner confirms that the team were aware of these findings and that the theory that it could be the process of puberty that changes someone's mind on their gender identity was discussed a great deal prior to the study. These explicit findings are not mentioned in either the study protocol or the information sheets.[28] Instead, they are presented via the more equivocal sentence that hormone blockers could influence 'how likely you are/they are to change your/their mind about your gender identity/their gender'. It's up for debate whether this statement accurately reflects the knowledge base that existed at the time. It is not suggested that the early blocking of puberty is in some way *responsible* for persistence – the evidence can't tell us that, largely because of the way studies have been designed. We can't infer cause and effect. But at the time that GIDS and UCLH began their own study, existing – albeit limited – data seemed to show that *all* young people taking blockers at the onset of puberty also went on to take cross-sex hormones.[29] This was not noted explicitly in the study's documentation.

Professor Viner makes two points in response. First, the Dutch team 'claimed they carefully selected their patients', he says, and that 'anybody who they thought was likely to change their mind, they were able to select out'. Viner, together with the GIDS leadership, had spent several years trying to understand more about the Dutch selection process. The UK team were clear that they would only take 'the highest-risk kids who were least likely to change their mind, who had had very

severe gender dysphoria since early childhood'. The second point Viner
makes is that much time was spent in clinic, face to face, discussing the
possibility that the blockers locked in a particular gender identity. He
says he would explicitly tell young people and their families that there
was a chance the treatment would stop them changing their minds.
Young people would also be told that there were 'unknown unknowns'
with the treatment that doctors didn't even know about yet. Viner
would impress upon the participants how small the knowledge base
was for this treatment, and that while there were theoretical risks, 'an
ethics committee has looked at these risks and thinks it's reasonable
for you… to have this treatment.'

Professor Viner acknowledges that just as it was 'theoretical' that
interrupting puberty might prevent a possible change in gender identity, it was equally true that 'blockers taking hormones out and then
giving [young people] space to think about their gender identity' was
a hypothesis. What was *real*, he says, was the anxiety and distress felt
by these young people, whose bodies were developing in ways that
they did not want. Periods were deeply distressing for those born in
a female body, he says. 'For those born in a male body, the fear that
they're suddenly going to get really large, and hairy, is huge.' Puberty
blockers could put those changes on hold. That was real. 'So,' he
explains, 'it's a real mix of reality and theory.'

There's another potential risk associated with blocking early puberty
that isn't mentioned in either the protocol or the information given
to participants: if puberty is blocked early in boys, there may not be
enough penile tissue to make a neovagina if they decide to have one
surgically constructed as an adult. While the protocol stated that
'it is argued that there is a positive impact on any sex-reassignment
surgery in adulthood', the opposite could equally be true for boys.[30]
Should families have been told this in order to be able to provide fully
informed consent? Both GIDS director Polly Carmichael and Viner
were aware of the potential issue. It had been discussed at the meeting
hosted by GIRES in 2005, which both attended. In their write up,
GIRES explained how 'undervirilised genitalia in trans girls would
provide less material to be used if vaginoplasty were eventually per-
formed. Although there are surgical means to deal this [*sic*] difficulty,

the patient and her parents or guardians should be fully informed about its implications."[31]

As we will find out, despite knowing that this was a risk for the natal boys at the start of puberty, it would take another decade before this information was *routinely* passed on to families attending GIDS.

In 2019, an official investigation into the conduct of the Early Intervention Study by the Health Research Authority (HRA) cleared the researchers of any wrongdoing. It did, however, advise that clinicians and researchers 'avoid referring to puberty suppression as providing a "breathing space" to avoid risk of misunderstanding'.[32] Instead, the purpose of the treatment should be described as being offered to children demonstrating strong and persistent gender identity dysphoria 'such that the suppression of puberty would allow subsequent cross-sex hormone treatment without the need to surgically reverse or otherwise mask the unwanted physical effects of puberty in the birth gender'. In other words, blockers were used to minimise future surgery, the HRA concluded, so should not be described as providing 'time to think'. The HRA's review was in response to a series of questions being posed to them by the BBC's *Newsnight* programme and concerns raised by members of the public.[†33] It was 'very painful' to hear

---

* Professor Viner told the author he doesn't recall bringing this up because all of the male participants in the study were at Tanner stage 3 of puberty or later. This is where the penis begins to grow and lengthen ('Puberty', NHS 111 Wales [website], https://111.wales.nhs.uk/Puberty/). All participants in the study had to be at least 12 years old, but from a physical/endocrine perspective they also had to have reached 'Tanner stage 2/3'. A Dutch paper published in 2020 – Tim C. van de Grift et al., 'Timing of puberty suppression and surgical options for transgender youth', *Pediatrics* 146/5 (2020), e20193653, doi: 10.1542/peds.2019-3653 – showed that males who had their puberty blocked at Tanner stage 2/3 were 84 times more likely to have to undergo an intestinal vaginoplasty than those who had not had their puberty blocked. Those whose puberty was blocked at Tanner stage 4/5 were ten times more likely to have to undergo this surgical procedure.
† BBC *Newsnight* aired a film about the Early Intervention Study in July 2019, after being passed original documentation relating to it and hearing concerns about its conduct. As is standard journalistic practice, the HRA – who granted ethical approval to the study and were responsible for its oversight – were given a right of reply. Their response to this was to launch their investigation. When the author and Deborah Cohen gained sight of further documentation relating to the study while writing an article for the *BMJ*, a further right of reply was sent to the HRA.

suggestions that the research team had acted improperly, Professor Viner reflects in 2022. 'If I had known what would happen later, I'm not sure I would have agreed [to lead the study],' he says.

With ethical approval granted, recruitment for the study began in April 2011, just as new information was published on the Dutch protocol.[34] An update was provided on 'B' – the first person mentioned in the clinical literature to have undergone early puberty suppression to help with their gender dysphoria – the person whose experience of puberty blockers, followed by cross-sex hormones and surgery, was deemed so successful it led to a whole new treatment approach. B was now 35 years old. He had started puberty blockers at 13, followed by testosterone at 18. He had a double mastectomy (the removal of both breasts), followed by the removal of his womb and ovaries at 20, and then further surgery aged 22 to construct a micropenis, along with testes implantation. Since even the first adolescents to have been treated by the Dutch team, according to their new protocol, were still in their early twenties, this report provided the 'first very long-term follow-up' of someone who had undergone pubertal suppression and subsequent gender reassignment.

GIDS have subsequently cited this paper when explaining the approach their Early Intervention Study took.[35] Though the service concedes that the outcomes relating to B are 'only a case study', they showed, they said, the length of time that the Dutch had been evaluating early suppression of puberty. But are B's outcomes wholly positive?

We learn that 'twenty-two years after this decision, he still is convinced that his choice to live as a man was the right one' and that the team 'did not find unfavorable medical outcomes'. The paper's abstract mentions that B had 'experienced some feelings of sadness about choices he had made in a long-lasting intimate relationship', but concludes that this first long-term follow-up of puberty suppression 'suggests that negative side effects are limited and that it can be a useful additional tool in the diagnosis and treatment of gender dysphoric adolescents'.[36]

However, a read of the whole paper reveals that in fact B was no longer satisfied with some of the genital surgery he had undergone – the metoidioplasty (using the clitoris, enlarged by testosterone treatment, to construct a micropenis). 'He did not like its size and shape and he could hardly urinate in a standing position. He was able to have orgasms, but he could not have sexual intercourse.' Despite B appearing convincingly male, we learn that he had had few stable partners and that a five-year serious relationship had ended when he chose not to live with his girlfriend. 'This made him very much regret his lack of commitment. B considered it likely that his need to distance himself from her had been related to his shame about his genital appearance and his feelings of inadequacy in sexual matters.'

How does one judge the success of a treatment pathway? The Dutch authors acknowledged that 'although gender reassignment is highly effective in relieving gender dysphoria, it is no panacea'. B's case, they wrote, shows that 'in the area of intimate relationships, it may remain difficult to find a suitable partner and overcome one's own barriers'. But they also said that pubertal suppression 'averts the despair of gender dysphoric adolescents because of their physical changes' and may make them more confident in their social interactions both in adolescence and adulthood. Both could well be true.* But should policy on such an important area of healthcare for children have been based on a single case study? To date, this is still the only long-term data available on the Dutch protocol.[37]

In July 2010, the findings from the first 70 young people to take part in the Dutch protocol were published. As well as showing that all 70 who started on the blocker went on to cross-sex hormones, the researchers said that their 'behavioral and emotional problems and depressive symptoms decreased', after taking the blockers. Moreover, 'general functioning improved significantly during puberty suppression,' the Dutch claimed.[38] This all sounded positive.

'Feelings of anxiety and anger', however, did not change. Neither did gender dysphoria and body satisfaction. In fact, for those born

---

* Having spoken directly with B, the *New York Times* reported in June 2022 that he had grown more comfortable with 'romantic and sexual relationships' and currently had a serious girlfriend. See 'The battle over gender therapy', *New York Times* (15 June 2022), https://www.nytimes.com/2022/06/15/magazine/gender-therapy.html.

female, these had worsened. Girls felt worse about their bodies after several years on the blocker. The data are also incomplete: the claims of well-being relate to the smaller number of 54 for some measures, and just 41 for others – less than 60 per cent of the total. It's not clear why this is the case. These are tentative initial findings.[39]

Between 2011 and 2014, 44 patients aged 12–15 joined the GIDS/UCLH Early Intervention Study. While this study began with admirable aims – to test the claims about what was seen as an experimental treatment in a safe research setting – GIDS, we will learn, did not wait for the data to emerge before rolling out early puberty suppression more widely. The full results would remain unpublished for almost a decade.

Jack

2011

Jack had been through a seriously tough time when he arrived at GIDS.

As a child, he was taken into care. He was fostered by relatives, but home life was abusive and there were problems with alcoholism in the household.

'When I was like three or four, I used to tell people I was going to grow up and be a boy, because I was born female,' Jack says. 'I'd never ever heard of anyone who was transgender. The only thing I'd ever heard about was people who cross-dressed, and they were always slated by people in my family. So, I thought I was some kind of weird pervert.'

Jack spent his childhood feeling confused, like a 'weird freak of nature', because he couldn't understand what exactly he was feeling, or why. He'd grown up a tomboy, mainly having boys as close friends from a very young age – 'five or six all the way up to 12'. But he knew he was 'more than a tomboy'. His best friend – another tomboy – had 'grown up to be a really beautiful young woman', but it was more than that for him. Jack had wanted to wear boys' clothes, but he also dreamt about going to school as a boy, he explains. 'I used to look at my friends who were boys and I used to dream, like, what my life would be like, if I was living in their houses… I mean, born a boy.'

But when puberty hit, Jack's foster family encouraged him not to hang out with his male friends any more. Adolescence throws the differences between the sexes into stark relief, and the idea of their adolescent female relative being in male company all the time didn't sit comfortably. 'I was accused of hooking up with them,' he explains.

From the age of 12, things went downhill. Forced to dress more femininely, not cut his hair short, abandon his friends – be more of a 'girl' – Jack's mental health suffered. He started drinking and entered a 'very, very dark place'. 'I was convinced I was going to have to be a girl forever,' he says, 'and I just started my periods and it was the worst. I was just sleeping all the time and really depressed, because I hated being myself.'

Jack became so ill, he was sectioned.

He stayed in a psychiatric hospital for close to two years.

Once in the hospital, he stopped contact with his foster family and cut his hair short once more. 'And I bought all boys clothes again, which I hadn't worn since I was 12.' He was about 15 by now. 'And I felt like myself.'

Like most teenagers, Jack started exploring his sexuality too. 'I didn't know whether I was just a lesbian. Because I'd buried it [feeling like a boy] so deep in my head from when I was a kid, I wasn't sure – if you know what I mean – so I just identified as a lesbian for a little while and in the hospital.' Jack says he caused 'a couple of safeguarding issues' in the hospital because he kissed another girl. He also kissed a boy. 'So, I think my sexuality was a bit fluid at the time.'

Jack was released from hospital into the care of a children's home. He says the staff there assumed he was a lesbian, he says, because of the way he looked – with short hair and baggy clothing that hid the feminine body underneath. And it made it him angry. 'Other than kissing a few girls when I was like 15, 16, that was it,' he says. But he felt differently once he identified at trans. 'Once I came out as trans and started dating girls that felt a lot more comfortable, because I didn't want to be a lesbian. I just knew that that wasn't right. And once I'd come out as trans and was hooking up with this girl, it was, like, a bit more natural. I felt like a man who had a girlfriend, rather than a lesbian who had a girlfriend – if that makes sense?'

Although he'd struggled to fulfil the stereotypical expectations of girls while growing up, Jack says he didn't have the language or knowledge to express what he felt when he was younger – that he was a boy. It all clicked into place after watching the British soap opera *Hollyoaks*. When he saw someone on the television who seemed just like him and identifying as trans, it just made sense.

Staff at Jack's children's home were supportive, and he found further advice online from a support group for adult trans men. Having already cut his hair short and gone back to the clothing that he'd felt comfortable in as a younger child, Jack started living life as a man, switching to boys' toilets and presenting as 'masculine'. But some changes to his routine were 'encouraged' by the reactions of others. 'I remember I was going into the girls' toilets when I was about 15, 16, and I kept getting accused of being a boy in the wrong toilets. I looked like a butch lesbian. And because I wore baggy hoodies covering my chest, they couldn't really tell if I was a girl or a boy. So they assumed I was a boy. So I stopped using the girls' toilets and went into disabled toilets for a bit. But then I kind of just gave up with that. I was like, why can't I use the boys' toilets?'

Because of his mental health problems, Jack was already under the care of the local CAMHS. At 16 years old, they referred him to GIDS.

Jack's acceptance letter from GIDS advised him that an assessment 'usually consists of four to six hour-long appointments' and that he would have to fill in some questionnaires 'looking at gender identity and general psychological functioning'. He was apprehensive about what would happen. 'I felt like they were going to accuse me of just being crazy. Because of my mental health background in the past, I was quite defensive about it.' His clinicians didn't treat him that way at all, but he didn't like being assessed by two members of staff, as was typical in GIDS at the time. 'I just felt like having two people to talk to… I felt like I was proper being judged… and I think because my background of mental health, I was quite on guard.' Jack's appointments carried on with one clinician.

He was asked about his upbringing, and when he had first thought he was trans. Jack says they felt like 'weird' therapy sessions. 'I think because I was in care, it made it really complicated for them. They didn't really, like, want to push me into any direction. And I kind of think they just thought I was a bit vulnerable.' Therapy isn't what he wanted. But because of his mental health issues he thinks GIDS wanted to err on the side of caution and 'not to take anything too fast'.

Jack's clinician never raised the prospect of puberty blockers.

Given that he was already 16 and turned 17 during his time at GIDS, it was a potential option for him. But he didn't realise. 'I was sat there under the impression the whole time that I couldn't have any treatment until I turned 18,' he recalls. 'And I remember mentioning just before I turned 18, I was like, "Oh, it's such a shame I couldn't be on [hormone blockers], because I think that would help my mental health and everything."' Instead of agreeing, Jack's clinician explained that he could have been on puberty blockers, but now that he was about to leave the service it was too late. 'And I was like, what the actual fuck? Why did you leave that till now? Honestly, I was fuming. Because my whole mindset was, right, I'll get hormones, and I'll get chest surgery, and then I'll be comfortable with who I am. And when you're waiting for that to happen, the days feel endless because you're not yourself. You're stuck in a body that isn't yours. And for them to drop that into conversation and say I could have been on hormone blockers, I was furious.'

He wasn't just angry, he felt 'heartbroken'. GIDS explained that because Jack hadn't brought up the idea of blockers himself, they couldn't be the ones 'pushing' them. Jack said that, at that time – in 2011/12 – there just wasn't the same level of information out there as there is today. It wasn't easy to know what all the options were, and 'at no point did they sit me down and explain what the process was like. They just treated it like an informal therapy session.' He understands why GIDS 'didn't want to push it down my throat or anything' and wanted him to lead the conversation, 'but they didn't educate me enough about what trans is and how the process works… honestly, it broke my heart.'

GIDS referred Jack to adult gender services at Charing Cross. He got his first appointment eight months after turning 18.

Approaching his twenty-seventh birthday, Jack is 'proper happy'.

In his early twenties, following another in-patient spell in hospital for mental health difficulties, he received a diagnosis for bipolar disorder. He takes regular medication, and with the help of his dogs, his life is now 'back on track'.

Jack has an excited, nervous energy about him. He speaks fast. Really fast. He'll talk, at times, for minutes, seemingly without pausing to take breath. He's honest, full of expression and friendly.

The team at Charing Cross Gender Identity Clinic (GIC) didn't move slowly. At his second appointment, Jack was given a prescription for testosterone. 'That's what I found so mad,' he explains. 'I was like, right, so you made me go through all that extensive stuff as a kid, but then you can just have two appointments.' He says that perhaps it was because he'd been through GIDS that the adult GIC were able to prescribe quickly, but that actually he's under the impression that it's common to get hormones on a second appointment. Jack started testosterone aged 19 and had 'top surgery' – the term used in the trans community to describe a double mastectomy and the construction of a more masculine-looking chest – a month before his twenty-first birthday. 'That,' Jack says, 'was the best day of my life, honestly.' He doesn't want to undergo any further surgery.

Whereas he'd been attracted to girls as a teenager, that has changed over time. 'I think right now I kind of identify as, like, bisexual or more towards men,' Jack explains. 'Because I've never had much interest in getting intimate with women. Other than like kissing a few girls when I was like 15, 16, that was it.' He says it's been a bit confusing being a gay trans man, and others have found it difficult to understand too – especially his nan and granddad. 'I thought I had to act straight,' he tells me. 'Does that make sense? I had to act as a straight man to be taken seriously as a trans man.' He puts this down partly to the attitude of staff in his children's home who just assumed he was 'going to be into girls... because I looked like a lesbian at first'. But he thinks his evolving sexuality may possibly have something to do with the testosterone he's taken, too. 'I think it kind of gives you a second puberty,' he says. 'And during your puberty, you kind of question everything anyway, don't you, in your mind?'

Looking back as an adult, Jack sees his time at GIDS a little differently. He admits that when he'd been under the impression that he wasn't allowed to take anything until he was 18 he hadn't really minded. It was only when he found out that something could have been given him earlier that might have helped with his distress that he was angry.

But his readmittance to hospital in his early twenties has also shaped his views on transition and whether certain safeguards should be in place. He was worried by what he saw on his psychiatric ward. 'I was like, bloody hell, is half my ward transgender? Honestly, I'm being serious.' It wasn't quite half, he clarifies, more like somewhere between 10 per cent and a third, but still, it struck him as odd.

He says that, for him, his poor mental health had always been a separate thing to his trans identity, but he wasn't sure this was the case for everyone. 'I wasn't there, like, self-harming because I was trans. I was unwell. Does that make sense? It was my bipolar. But they were, like, linking the trans stuff to mental health.' It's really hard to explain, he says, and he doesn't want to be misunderstood, or 'come across harsh'.

'I know that you're more likely to have mental health problems if you're trans… it just felt like there was too many trans people for the population in the hospital.' He says it would be the same if any group were over-represented in the same setting. It 'just seemed far too high'. And it made him think. 'I kind of wonder if in these moments of distress in people's lives – it's not that I'm saying being trans or [poor] mental health causes you to say you're trans, but that that might be the thing you think it is because you're so unwell… you might think that your life might be better if… you've got a label for the struggle you're feeling that isn't mental health, and it's part of your identity.'

What's more, he says, this hadn't been the case more than ten years before, when he was first sectioned as a teenager. 'I was the only person that the whole staff had ever heard of as being trans at the time.' To see such a shift during that time, he says felt 'too odd to be real'.

Jack says part of him is now glad that GIDS didn't rush his assessment. 'When I look back on it, I'd rather them have done that – kept me safe – because of the amount of people I've now seen who are saying they're trans when they're unwell.' He thinks it's vital that gender identity clinics have mental health professionals to make sure that people are properly supported. There need to be checks on mental health before someone transitions, he says – as long as they're done in a respectful, dignified way – even if it can feel frustrating and heartbreaking for those who will successfully transition and be happy. 'Otherwise, you end up with people regretting it, and you don't want to live your life like that. That's more traumatic to go through than just coming out as trans.'

5

A NEW ERA

By 2012, GIDS looked rather different from the service that had operated out of a broom cupboard less than a decade before. Referrals were
increasing rapidly; there was new leadership; and puberty-blocking
medication was now an option from the age of 12, albeit as part of a
research study and only if the patient met the study's entry criteria.
All young people attending GIDS would 'receive information about
this research project through a GIDS general information leaflet given
to the service users at the beginning of their contact with the service'
with those who were eligible to take part given more information.
To take part, young people had to be aged between 12 and 15, have
attended at least four appointments at GIDS over at least six months,
have demonstrated a pattern of cross-gendered behaviour throughout
childhood (defined as over five years), have had gender dysphoria that
had increased with the onset of puberty, be actively requesting the
blocker, and be able to provide informed consent. They had to have
reached Tanner stage 2/3 of pubertal development to be eligible 'from
the physical point of view'. Young people with mental health problems
'associated with serious psychiatric conditions', for example, 'psychosis,
bipolar condition, anorexia nervosa', were excluded.[1]

Having worked there part-time for years, Dr Polly Carmichael
took over the reins of GIDS from Domenico Di Ceglie in 2009.
Charming, softly spoken and encouraging to her staff, Carmichael
was the preferred candidate to take GIDS into a new era. The service

became nationally commissioned by the NHS that same year, which meant patients could now be referred from anywhere in England, and referrals – inevitably – grew: by 50 per cent per year, from 97 in 2009/10 to 314 in 2012/13, far exceeding anyone's expectations. When GIDS had applied to be a national service in 2008 it expected referrals in the financial year 2009/10 to reach 80, and anticipated that 'in the following years a limited growth is expected until a plateau is reached. It is unlikely that the number of new cases would go beyond 150 per year within the next 5 years.'[2] However, this prediction would turn out to be vastly inaccurate. There was no plateau, and within three years GIDS was receiving more than twice the predicted upper limit of referrals. Despite this unforeseen change, a business-as-usual approach was operating within the service. They didn't pause, they expanded.

Dr Carmichael built a leadership team to help steer the direction of GIDS. Dr Sarah Davidson, an energetic, confident clinician with a highly impressive record of working with the Red Cross, sat on a new 'Executive' team. She'd started at GIDS in 2006. Dr Bernadette Wren joined the team too, after returning to the service in 2011. She's described as thoughtful, highly intelligent – a calming, reassuring presence in the team. All three women were established in their careers, consultant clinical psychologists. Wren was also a trained family therapist. At all times, there was a fourth member of the Executive – a consultant psychiatrist.[3] The holder of this post changed several times over the next decade.

A second GIDS base opened in Leeds in 2012, not just to help meet demand, but to ensure that those living in the north of England didn't have to travel so far to be seen. The same year, GIDS took on junior staff for the first time in its history. A small group of trainees joined the London service – psychologists in the final year of their doctorates. One was Natasha Prescott, a tall, reflective woman who chooses her words carefully. The idea was that trainees would learn the ropes from their more senior colleagues, with plenty of opportunity to discuss cases. Dr William Crouch – an experienced clinical psychologist and psychoanalyst who joined GIDS in 2011 – ran a supervision group for the trainees. He aimed to offer some 'broadly psychoanalytical' thinking about the work that, he says, the new starters 'found very helpful'. His colleagues speak of him highly as a warm, grounded and highly competent clinician, who understood children and adolescents.

GIDS's work was understood to be specialist and complex, but the service was welcoming to those at the beginning of their careers. Hitherto it had been staffed solely by senior clinicians, generally with a lot of experience and who, in many parts of the NHS, might have been responsible for running an entire service. The trainees, though, were on a band below the entry grade for qualified psychologists. This was a big change, one of many that would occur over the next few years.

Initially, there was some scope for offering frequent appointments, as had been the case during Domenico Di Ceglie's leadership of GIDS. It was still possible to see some patients on a weekly basis in some instances. But the model underpinning how the service operated changed shortly afterwards, too. The situation where children could be seen regularly and on an ongoing basis for therapeutic support ended, and GIDS moved to a four-to-six-appointment assessment model, with less frequent appointments for those who were on treatment. Prescott recalls team members at the time 'expressing concern about the very limited opportunity for psychological work to take place because neither CAMHS nor GIDS would be offering this'.[4] Not only was weekly therapeutic engagement not feasible with the higher numbers now being referred, it was also argued that it was inequitable: those who lived further away from GIDS's clinics would not be able to attend so often.

Working at GIDS was 'crazily busy', recalls Crouch. He says the team was already one of the largest in the Tavistock, and within just a couple of years could fill the clinic's largest meeting room. He remembers that many of the young people had traumatic backgrounds and the model that was now in place – an assessment carried out over four to six appointments – was 'not enough'. 'I think you could come to a view then whether they met the criteria for gender dysphoria. But I don't think you could do what I would call "therapeutic work" in that time.'

The 'fundamental problem' was that the team could only ever carry out 'limited' psychological work with young people and families. Those attending the service, Crouch says, were generally just 'not very interested' in doing this. 'They've made a decision that there's a problem, and they have made a decision about the way it needs to be fixed and addressed.' The way it should be 'fixed and addressed' was almost always through physical interventions – puberty blockers – which were now available to young people at younger ages as part of the Early Intervention Study. The study had stipulated that it would recruit participants for three years – until 2014 – and follow them up for a further three before reporting the results.

Once blockers were an option, it inadvertently created a conflict between the GIDS clinician and the young person and, often, their family, Dr Crouch explains. He recalls a conversation that he had with many of his colleagues at the time: 'My feeling was that it pushes a kind of fundamentalist frame of mind. If you can imagine you're talking to somebody who's saying, "This is what I believe," and you're sort of invited to disagree with them. And if you question in any way, then you're a bigot, or you don't understand.' He felt that he was effectively a 'gatekeeper' to another service – the endocrinology service provided by UCLH.

This hadn't been Domenico Di Ceglie's vision, Crouch says, which had been to 'try and create space for psychological work and thinking in young people who were struggling with their gender identity'. He brings up Di Ceglie's favoured metaphor of Scylla and Charybdis, which had originally been used to describe the underlying goal of GIDS. Scylla stood for the danger of 'focusing on the workings of the mind and neglecting the reality of the body', while Charybdis represented 'a focus on the reality of the body which neglects the contribution of the mind'. Crouch says this was a 'very helpful' way of thinking about the work. But ultimately the service found itself 'too much on one side'. 'The ship's not being steered, because you're too close to one of the islands.' That island was the island of pressure groups and service users whose focus was on the need to modify the body.

Under various pressures – the numbers being referred, the demands of the young people, changes in societal attitudes and the culture of the service itself – GIDS came to have a far narrower remit, Crouch says – 'assessing whether or not young people should be put on the list to have hormone blockers' – than perhaps had been the vision put forward by its founder.

'I had no doubt that nearly all the young people I saw were very distressed,' Crouch explains. 'They needed help. But the help that they, on the whole, felt that they needed, and the help that I felt I could offer, were not the same.' And, he says, there was pressure 'not to do' the psychological work. His role, and that of others in the service, was to see whether the young person met the criteria for what was then called gender identity disorder. If they did, they would be put forward for blockers. 'We had to,' he says calmly. 'That was the sort of established pathway.' That an experienced clinician might not share their professional opinion is striking. 'It's difficult, though, isn't it?' Crouch reasons. He recalls that the research coming out of the Netherlands seemed to be suggesting that that was what should be done, that there was an established pathway, and the idea was that if young people were deemed suitable, 'they would be offered hormone blockers for a period of time until they transferred to adult services.'

That time was meant to be used to 'do some psychological work', to help the young person think about their gender and future options. 'That was the idea,' Crouch says. 'But it didn't happen because there wasn't time to do it… You didn't have time, and it wasn't what the service users wanted. And, you know, there's a lot of pressure to get the [assessment] report done and see the endocrinology team.'

'We were all sort of working in the unknown, really… what I'm saying is, as the sort of jobbing clinician in amongst it all, it's very difficult to feel that one could question this sort of established view that this is the way things should go.'

Will Crouch speaks highly of all his former GIDS colleagues. They were 'well meaning, well trained, thoughtful, intelligent' people. But, he says, while he believed there were significant differences of opinion among staff, 'I don't know what colleagues thought, or what they did… I think it'd have been very useful to have those sorts of discussions.' This was unlike his other experiences in the Tavistock, where team meetings *would* very strongly provide a sense of the way people thought about the work, and why they worked in various ways. 'I think this was probably one of the real problems,' Crouch says. 'I think if that could have been thrashed out a bit in the team, not to sort of come to some answer, but that perhaps that would have had some effect on the work that we were doing with young people.'

The difficulty at GIDS, he says, was there was 'so little time' to discuss issues properly. Team meetings were mostly 'managerial', as far as Crouch could recall. 'There was very little space to have in-depth, clinical discussions.' He contrasts this again to meetings elsewhere in the Tavistock trust, where half an hour would be set aside to talk about *one* case as an entire team.

'There wasn't much space for thinking.'

For those beginning their careers in GIDS, these were the good days. What little space there was to think would quickly become squeezed even further.

This was the service that Dr Anna Hutchinson joined at the start of 2013.

It's easy to see why Hutchinson, a driven, intelligent woman, achieved rapid promotion through her twenties. She's instantly likeable, gentle and unnervingly easy to talk to. These are precious qualities for anyone working with distressed young people.

Hutchinson began at GIDS with significant clinical experience from a number of London's leading hospitals, including at Great Ormond Street Hospital (GOSH), where she completed a number of demanding roles. It was a turbulent time in the history of the hospital, with GOSH partly implicated in the horrific death of baby Peter Connelly in August 2007. Hutchinson's experiences in these years would come to have a profound influence on her later view of GIDS.

It was Polly Carmichael who encouraged Hutchinson to move to GIDS. They'd worked together at GOSH years before and they got on. Carmichael is easy to like, her colleagues say, and inspires loyalty in those she works with. The pair had spoken about the work at GIDS, with Hutchinson remarking how fascinating it sounded. Carmichael had always made it clear that Hutchinson would be welcome, and when a role became available at the service in late 2012, therefore, it was an attractive prospect. Carmichael was generous in her offer of remuneration and intensely welcoming to her former colleague.

Just as the new trainees would learn from those more senior in the service, so would Hutchinson. In 2013 there was no formal training at GIDS for anyone joining the clinical team. There still isn't.* 'I was given an induction file with lots and lots of papers,' Hutchinson recalls. This included case vignettes from Domenico Di Ceglie's work in the 1990s and the World Professional Association for Transgender Health (WPATH) guidelines. But at GIDS, learning took place by doing. And, specifically, from observing what your colleagues did. Clinicians at GIDS tended to work in pairs to assess the young people. And the individuals making up those pairs could have different professional backgrounds. For example, a psychologist could work alongside a social worker. Typically, this assessment was completed over four to six appointments, but they could take longer in more complex cases. Hutchinson, despite her wide experience of working with distressed young people and having worked with trans adults in a sexual-health setting, had never met a child who identified as transgender before starting this job. So her first assessments were made alongside members of the Executive team – Polly Carmichael and Sarah Davidson.

Davidson was Hutchinson's supervisor. And she felt in safe hands. 'She was really warm, competent,' Hutchinson recalls of their first meeting. It was because Davidson was so impressive, so confident, that Hutchinson was able to suppress some of the unease she soon felt in the job. Although she had done a great variety of work within the mental health system, the work at GIDS, she found, was 'so outside the realms of regular clinical practice it was disorientating'. As Will Crouch says, team meetings at this time weren't generally a place where people would discuss their thoughts; there was no hint that others might be feeling the same way. But Davidson's confidence and experience provided Hutchinson with crucial reassurance. Davidson's approach, and Carmichael's, was to affirm the child in their chosen gender identity. From the outset, Hutchinson explained, the child was

---

* Those who have worked at GIDS in recent years say that formal induction sessions were eventually introduced, where people could come together and talk in groups facilitated by more experienced clinicians. But this still did not constitute formal training.

right. And so that's what Hutchinson learnt: to align with the young person and support them unconditionally.

'What struck me most about the first few cases was that they were *incredibly* complex,' she remembers. One young person claimed not just to identify as a different gender to their sex, but also to have three different alter egos, two of whom spoke in an Australian accent. It later transpired that the young person had never visited Australia. Another had experienced several previous mental health interventions, had suffered abuse and had ongoing suicidal thoughts. Hutchinson tried to employ 'best practice' with her cases: when meeting a child with a complex history she would previously have contacted the other services who had worked with them, gone through the multiple reports and compiled a meta report as part of her own assessment. That's what you do, she says. She would detail everything the young person had relayed, as well as what other professionals had said. 'And I remember taking the report to Polly and her saying, "Oh, Anna you're so brave." And I said, "Why?" And she said, "Well it's just so honest." And you know, she was praising me. And being kind.'

With each of these cases, all complex in their different ways, the recommendation was to refer the patient for puberty blockers, usually after just four sessions. 'At that point when I was working there, that was the only path that I offered them... But that was under guidance,' Hutchinson adds quickly. At the time, she explains, she was told that if the person had gender dysphoria, this was the treatment route. 'That was the protocol. You know, does this person meet diagnostic criteria for gender dysphoria? Yes. Therefore, we offer this.'

Hutchinson was uncomfortably aware that practices in the service were seriously at odds with all her previous experience of working with troubled children. 'I didn't always know *why* we were referring so quickly, but I just assumed that I didn't know enough yet,' she explains. 'We weren't being asked to give a formulation – a group of theories about why this young person is experiencing these symptoms or this distress. That wasn't what I was being invited to do... If I remember rightly, it was simply, do they meet DSM criteria?' And if they did, and they wanted the blocker? Refer them on to UCLH for the physical tests and a prescription. Young people would never receive puberty blockers at their first endocrinology appointment – that would happen at their second. The initial session was used for providing information on the potential risks and harms of the blocker and for a physical assessment, including blood tests and bone density scans.

It isn't particularly difficult to meet the clinical criteria for gender dysphoria. They're listed in the American Psychiatric Association's *Diagnostic and Statistical Manual of Mental Disorders* (DSM). It's a text of huge significance in the United States, as without a mention in the DSM, private insurers are unlikely to cover the costs related to a particular condition. The fifth edition, which replaced the old term 'gender identity disorder' (GID) with 'gender dysphoria', was published in 2013. A 'text revision' was released in 2022.[5] The use of the word 'dysphoria' rather than 'disorder' was seen as both less stigmatising, especially for children and adolescents, and a more accurate way of describing the distress that was felt by those with the condition.[6] It was meant to signify that being transgender was not a mental illness in and of itself. There's also a move away from describing someone based on their sex at birth. Instead, it is referred to as their 'assigned gender'.[7]

But the criteria are steeped in outdated gender stereotypes, and are criticised by both those in favour of faster access to medical transition for children and those who do not believe it should be available at all.[8] To obtain a diagnosis, children have to experience a 'marked incongruence' between their experienced gender and assigned (birth) gender that has lasted at least six months, 'a strong desire' to be another gender, plus a combination of other signs. These include strong preferences for dressing in clothing 'typical' of the opposite sex, and for friends of the other gender; a strong preference for toys or activities 'stereotypically used' by the other gender and rejection of those 'typically' associated with their 'assigned gender'; and a 'strong dislike of one's sexual anatomy'. These should be associated with 'significant distress' or 'impairment'.

The criteria for adolescents – those aged between 13 and 17 – (and adults) are even less rigorous.[9] They too will experience incongruence between their gender identity and 'assigned gender', lasting at least six months, along with significant distress or impairment to functioning, but then just two of a list of features, including the 'strong desire' to be rid of one's primary and/or secondary sex characteristics', a desire for the sex characteristics of the 'other gender', or a desire to be, or be treated as, the other gender.[10]

For the majority of the children and young people attending GIDS, it isn't hard to meet these conditions. It isn't difficult for many teenagers, full stop.

It wasn't just the clinical work that felt at odds with what she had known before. Anna Hutchinson was immediately struck by the influence of patient groups on GIDS – Mermaids and GIRES, specifically. 'I was used to being in a team where there was a dialogue with the patient groups that was a bit conflictual at times, where the NHS clinical team had to hold its ground a bit and say, "Well, this is why we're offering it."' That didn't seem to be happening at GIDS, she says. They weren't holding their ground, explaining why they were doing what they were, presenting the evidence base. Instead, 'I just had a real sense that the GIDS management were kind of bending over backwards to try and please.' It felt 'qualitatively really different'.*

In those early days a lot of time would be spent in meetings talking about what Mermaids were saying, or what GIRES were saying, 'and a huge amount of time was spent thinking about how to respond and how to not upset them'. Bernard Reed, the founder of GIRES, would regularly be on the phone to Polly Carmichael, Hutchinson recalls, and the GIDS Leeds team, in particular, would often bring up Mermaids. The relationship seemed 'a bit fractious' and Hutchinson suggested that it needed to be better defined and have clear limits. 'I suggested that we spoke to other services, where there was a similar relationship: where there was potential controversy in the treatment model, where there was potential conflict between certain charities or patient groups and the NHS team, because we weren't the first and we won't be the last.' It was about working in a 'morally appropriate' way, while holding

---

* Dr Polly Carmichael declined the invitation to be interviewed for this book, but in written correspondence said that she did not accept that GIDS was overly influenced by outside groups. She said she thought it 'significant' that the 'service has been criticised for its approach by advocates of a number of diverse viewpoints', including GIRES and Mermaids.

on to one's knowledge and expertise. Senior members of the team were enthusiastic about the suggestion. But it didn't happen.

Some of Hutchinson's first cases were eligible to join GIDS's Early Intervention Study. In fact, anyone who met the criteria was encouraged to join. On the whole, Hutchinson says, these were adhered to. 'But there were some cases where it was probably a bit of a grey area about the comorbid problems, and also the five years of gender dysphoria.' These could be subjective, she explains, and potentially open to interpretation. Hutchinson says her recollection is that clinicians would broach the topic with families. 'As I remember it, it was very much, "Look, your child's got distress related to their developing body; we have this medical pathway where you can have your puberty blocked, which stops the body developing; it's totally reversible, totally reversible. But what it does is it reduces that bit of distress, which allows us to explore the identity."' From her memory, it wasn't the case that everyone was coming to GIDS saying 'I really want to go on puberty blockers'. Indeed, there were instances of young people who were referred for puberty blockers who then chose not to take them. While it was Professor Viner's intention to allow only those high-risk young people who were least likely to change their minds on to the study, it's not at all clear this is what happened in practice.[*]

'Most' of those who were eligible for puberty blockers were referred to UCLH at this time, Hutchinson says. 'But I wasn't unduly worried about the blockers per se,' she adds. 'I was very much told that the blocker was to buy thinking space, time to think.' These were really distressed young people, but that distress could be reduced, at least in part, with the help of the blocker. That would allow space 'to explore what was going on for them in detail. And that made a huge amount of sense to me: that you calm down all the intensity around gender, so that you can do more broad, thoughtful work with them.' Given it was 'such a big intervention', it was implicit, Hutchinson thought, that there was 'a very large evidence base behind it'.

---

[*] In an interview with the author, Professor Russell Viner said he did not know what conversations were had in GIDS, but that when he met with patients, he was 'pretty blunt', and 'really emphasised the uncertainty' of the treatment, making sure they understood the risks.

When Hutchinson had doubts, she felt reassured by the fact that she was among such experienced colleagues. She trusted them. She liked them, and – after all – they were 'the only experts in the UK'. Hutchinson joined GIDS just after learning she was pregnant with her first child. When she left for maternity leave in September 2013, she was confused but not overly worried. She wanted to go back. Yes, there were aspects of the job and ways of working that she didn't understand yet, but, she thought, 'I can just help make that better.'

Diana and Alex

Alex was a 'super geek', Diana explains.* He was autistic and, for the first time, he was struggling at school. 'I knew he was a bit depressed and stressed,' she says, but he was doing his school examinations so it was understandable.

But when Alex came home from school one afternoon in October 2013, same as he always did, Diana wasn't expecting what happened. She casually asked him to pick something up from the floor, but he couldn't. 'He said, "I can't, I'm covered in germs." And he had his hands outstretched,' she explains.

It didn't make much sense. Alex had been showering each day when he got in from school, but Diana just thought she'd been blessed with a teenage boy with good hygiene habits. His sister hadn't thought anything was out of the ordinary either. Neither realised the showering was part of worsening obsessive–compulsive disorder, or OCD. 'He felt he was contaminated,' Diana says. 'He had his palms up, as if he was dripping with germs.' She loved her son and wanted him to get some help. She made an appointment for him to see their local doctor.

Alex had come out as gay a couple of years' earlier, and he was proud to be gay, Diana says. But she and her daughter couldn't help feeling worried for him. He'd been bullied in the past and was an easy target, she thought. At six foot three, he was a 'gentle giant', she says. He wasn't effeminate, but had always preferred female company and didn't like football. Those two facts alone had been enough for bullies to harass him at primary school.

---

* Some names and details have been changed.

Unbeknown to Diana, the bullying had continued at secondary school. Alex had told a male friend he had feelings for him, but they weren't reciprocated. He was subjected to vile homophobic slurs, his peers calling him 'gay filth', 'gay dirt' and 'gay paedo'. Some of the parents of people he'd called friends now didn't want him to be associating with their kids.

Alex didn't turn up to see the doctor.

'He said, "I couldn't get out of the shower." And I thought, "Oh crikey, this is worse than I thought,"' Diana recalls. He was referred to CAMHS to receive help for his OCD. Alex's health went downhill quickly. He couldn't return to school after the school holidays. He could barely leave the house.

Six weeks after Alex had been unable to pick something up from the floor for his mum, he was seen by CAMHS. Diana hoped this would be the help her son needed. It wasn't. 'Life really spun out of control,' she says. Alex was only a couple weeks shy of his sixteenth birthday and insisted on attending appointments alone. Reluctantly, Diana agreed. She had no idea what was being discussed, but assumed it was about how he could try to get the OCD under control.

Alongside CAMHS, Alex's school's counsellor had agreed to see him. 'I can remember it was a Thursday afternoon,' Diana says, 'and I was trying to get my son out of bed' for the appointment. 'He was like a zombie,' she remembers. 'I said, "Come on, we've to get to school for the counselling." And he yelled at me and said, "You don't understand. I'm transgender," at the top of his voice and in distress.'

Diana didn't know what he meant. It was early 2014, and she hadn't really heard the word 'transgender'. 'I was in shock. And I just said, "You're not very well," because he wasn't. He was seriously not very well. Then it all came out. "You've misgendered me since I was born,"' Alex shouted. Diana hadn't heard the word 'misgendered' either. Alex then accused her of being transphobic.

Alex explained to Diana that he'd told his CAMHS worker that he was trans. She was shocked, seriously concerned, and confused. 'I just absolutely couldn't believe what I was hearing: that he needed to go on hormones, that he was born in the wrong body. He's six foot three, wearing size 14 trainers... I felt like a juggernaut had hit me.'

Things moved quickly at CAMHS, but Alex's health was rapidly deteriorating. Just days after his birthday, CAMHS faxed through a referral to GIDS, asking that they see Alex. It was a couple of months since he'd started at the local mental health services. 'He became suicidal when he came out of his appointment and was told the wait was then 18 weeks,' Diana says. Alex had wrongly believed that his CAMHS worker would be able to give him hormones, she says, and he had obsessed over it.

Everyone Diana turned to for help with Alex's mental health affirmed him as a woman. From the moment the Tavistock referral was made, 'He was treated as if he was female,' she says. Alex was so ill that Diana was told he should be sectioned. He had calmly told the CAMHS crisis team that he would stab himself 'in the jugular vein'. Diana is in tears as she relays how ill her son was and how she tried to stay strong for her other children. Eight years on and it seems that the experience is as raw as if it happened yesterday. 'This was my child,' she says, apologising for getting upset, 'I was just in shock.' Just weeks after her openly gay son told her he was transgender, he had an appointment to see the country's top experts in gender identity.

Alex was now housebound, and not attending school. His OCD was so severe that he could not tolerate the outside world. Clinicians at CAMHS came to his home to see him. 'I had to put a plastic sheet on the floor to walk into his bedroom,' Diana says. 'He was showering, I don't know, five times a day. He developed severe IBS [irritable bowel syndrome].' Diana apologises again for being so explicit, but says that Alex's OCD was so serious that he could not clean himself adequately after going to the toilet. 'He would use literally a whole toilet roll to clean himself. And he'd be in despair, crying, and he blocked the toilet.' Alex's bathroom would become flooded 'with faeces and water', Diana explains, audibly upset. 'I'd be in tears because CAMHS is treating him as a woman and saying all this will be cured when he goes to the Tavistock.' How, she asks angrily, were the Tavistock going to deal with her son's severe OCD?

The best CAMHS could do was to give Diana 'a little booklet about some kid who was afraid of germs', she claims. 'It bore no relation to what we were going through.' CAMHS's focus was not on how they might help Alex's mental health problems, but rather on getting him to his first GIDS appointment.

It's a significant trip from Diana's home on the southern coast of England to the Tavistock in north London. Several train journeys over several hours. CAMHS tried to get Alex to focus on making the journey solo. Aware of how daunting this might be to a young man who was unable to leave his house, a psychiatrist prescribed Alex an antipsychotic drug, says Diana. He advised that Alex should self-administer if he felt 'panicky' while being in London alone. 'It began to erode my own sanity,' Diana explains. She did not understand how anyone, least of all a mental health professional, could think this was a sensible plan. 'He was so vulnerable,' she says, the emotion still perceptible. 'He couldn't touch anything without getting in the shower,' and yet here he was attempting to embark on a long journey across the country on crowded trains.

The trip was a disaster. Many hours after Alex had left their home on the south coast, he called Diana in tears. She called the police, and CAMHS. Alex managed to make it home, but he was not well. 'He walked into the house, threw up, and passed out on the bed.' It was while asleep that Diana took the opportunity to look at Alex's phone. She wasn't proud of it: she'd always respected his privacy, but she was at her wits' end. Alex was using the blogging and social media website Tumblr, she found. Using it a lot. 'And he was being groomed,' Diana claims. An older user had told her son not to worry, that everything would be fine once he had had all his surgeries. 'What the hell is going on?' she thought. She found that Alex was connected to hundreds of other young people, all of whom identified as trans.

Despite the failed attempt to make it to the Tavistock Centre for a practice run, CAMHS continued to encourage Alex to focus on his upcoming first appointment at GIDS, Diana claims. But when the time arrived, he was too ill to travel. Rather than see this as a sign that perhaps Alex was too unwell to be considering transitioning, a senior GIDS clinician said they would go to him instead. 'I said, "This is no time for him to be talking about changing his sex, because he's not functioning in any other way,"' Diana recalls. 'I kept saying that. I said that to CAMHS. I believe I phoned the Tavistock. It was insane.'

The very experienced GIDS clinician travelled several hours to see Alex. The appointment was held at the local CAMHS clinic. Diana claims the clinician welcomed her son with the words 'many transgender people go on to live full and happy lives'. 'That just set the tone,' Diana says, adding that the clinician volunteered that they could get Alex an endocrinology appointment – not right away, but further down the line. 'I can remember just thinking that's going to be seductive,' Diana says. And she was angry that the information had been 'volunteered'. Alex had not asked for it.

Diana took on the clinician. Why are you doing this? she asked. 'If he had anorexia, you wouldn't be accommodating that.' According to Diana, the clinician replied that gender dysphoria was 'totally different' to anorexia, and that there was 'no counselling' that could overcome it. The GIDS clinician explained that CAMHS would be 'dealing with the OCD' and they 'would focus on the gender', Diana says. 'I said, "But CAMHS aren't dealing with his OCD. No one's dealing with his OCD." I said I didn't think it was appropriate. And unbeknown to me, after that appointment, a second appointment had been made at GIDS... That blew my mind.'

That second appointment never happened.

Diana made her displeasure at the CAMHS team clear, telling them that affirming his gender identity was making his mental health problems worse. Her daughter had noted the same. Most of the time, Diana explains, Alex would not even come out of his room to talk to the CAMHS team gathered in his living room. If he *did* come downstairs, 'He couldn't even sit on the sofa,' Diana says. 'He would pace around the room.' Diana was furious. This was a boy who wanted to cut his penis off, she says, who saw things crawling up the walls. She believed this could not be explained by saying he was trans.

Events 'just spiralled', Diana says. 'I wasn't able to look after my own son because it made me ill as well... And I felt ashamed.' Their relationship had broken down.

A meeting was arranged for Diana, Alex, their GP, CAMHS and Alex's GIDS clinician.

Alex's GIDS clinician wrote to CAMHS beforehand, copying Diana in. The letter acknowledges Diana's 'alarm' at how severe Alex's

OCD was and how it was manifesting. They appreciated how this was the priority for her, but stressed that Alex's gender dysphoria was 'acute' and that he understood that physical treatment to confirm his identity would not solve his OCD. There was no reason in principle, the GIDS clinician wrote, that Alex's GIDS assessment could not continue alongside CAMHS's work on his OCD. But it was acknowledged that the latter was impacting on his ability to attend GIDS appointments.

When the planned 'network' meeting came around, Alex was again too unwell to attend. Diana told CAMHS and GIDS that her family was 'leaving the NHS'. Her son needed counselling and proper help for his OCD and what the NHS was offering was, in her view, neither safe nor helpful.

Alex started to see a private counsellor.

Three years after saying he was trans, and after two years of private counselling, Alex told Diana and his sister 'he was through with gender'. Diana had never been against transition per se; she just thought that it wasn't safe to consider it while Alex was so unwell. 'My son knew he desperately needed help with his OCD, and I'd termed it that if it gets helped with his OCD, he can then think about transition,' she explains. 'He knew he couldn't carry on living flooding the bathroom.'

According to Diana, Alex's trans identification had come out of the blue. Not just to her, but the entire family. Up to the point he accused her of misgendering him, Alex had been openly gay and proud to be so, Diana says. 'When you're severely bullied and you're called gay filth, gay dirt, gay paedo at school for years,' Diana says, 'it didn't take the brain of Britain to think this is a child who's so traumatised by being gay' that it might be influencing his identity. Diana believes Alex's identifying as a woman was 'an escape mechanism', a 'maladjusted reaction to being told your innate personality is that of a paedophile'.

Alex is now in his mid twenties. He is a gay man, with a boyfriend. He is secure being male, but Diana says he still has severe mental health difficulties. He spends much of his time online and their relationship is strained. But he regularly speaks with his sister and sees her a couple of times a month.

Diana still struggles to understand how any stretched NHS service would send a senior clinician several hours across the country to meet someone with mental health problems so severe that they were not attending school, and could not leave their home to attend appointments. To then raise the possibility of physical transition – arguably the most invasive option – as a way forward at the very first appointment is beyond her.

She feels desperately let down by those she turned to for help – by CAMHS and GIDS. The fact that he 'desisted' has, in Diana's eyes, showed that Alex 'didn't need anything other than time'.

Diana is a mother who loves her son, and desperately wants him to be happy and healthy. She makes one thing clear: 'I'm not anti-trans. I'm pro my son being the healthy person he is, I'm pro-health. And trans was the most unhealthy thing for my son to be.'

6

ALL CHANGE

Matt Bristow considered himself a trans ally when he joined GIDS as a trainee in autumn 2013. An openly gay man in his late twenties, he felt that trans people shared a history 'and maybe a struggle' with the LGB community. 'I was very sympathetic,' he says. Bristow thought that perhaps as a gay man he might have 'a better understanding of some trans people's experiences than a straight cis person'. 'I felt excited when I joined the service. And I was really looking forward to it,' he says.

Like everyone, Matt Bristow learnt on the job. And, like the handful of other trainees, he enjoyed the work. Although the service was busy, he says there was still an opportunity to discuss individual patients with the team when he first started at GIDS. And there was something about the atmosphere 'which kind of encouraged us to feel special'.

Dr Natasha Prescott and the other trainees from the year before were now newly qualified and Bristow worked on cases with them, as well as with senior staff. Those new to the field, and to their careers as psychologists, were still working out what they thought about it, grappling with the complexities: 'The idea of physical intervention with children does seem extreme, but... the blockers provides [*sic*] them with a much better chance of passing and having a "normal" life. And it buys them time,' one wrote.

> On the other hand, some of the young people at the service have had pretty traumatic childhoods; I can't help but wonder what impact

that might have had on their gender identities, and if transitioning to the other sex might seem as a way to reinvent themselves, to get rid of difficult pasts… This is such a dilemma.[1]

Bristow recalls that most of his assessments would be 'more on the six end' of the four-to-six-session model, and that 'there were certainly assessments that went over that'. But this could be problematic. There was an expectation to produce an assessment report after six appointments, even if the decision was that more exploratory work was needed, rather than a referral to the endocrinology clinic. 'I think in practice, that's a very difficult line to hold,' he says. 'Because young people come into the service with the expectation that they have a number of appointments, then there's a report, and then they go to endocrinology. And when the result of the assessment is that more conversations need to happen before that referral was made, it can get very tricky.'

Sometimes families and young people would be understanding of the decision, and agree, 'some strongly', that more conversations were needed. But others would become angry. 'It's one of the tensions in the work,' Bristow explains. 'On the one hand, part of the work is… to come up with an assessment report that might result in a referral. And that's kind of the gatekeeper function, I guess… And then on the other side, there's a more kind of traditionally therapeutic role, more exploring role, where you're trying to help people explore their own identity, explore meaning, think about issues that might be arising in terms of family, friends, school.' Trying to do this when the young person has a very clear idea of what their goal is, and where the GIDS clinician is seen as 'someone who's going to get in their way, or potentially deny them what they want, is very challenging'. It's a situation that takes skill to navigate, Bristow says – to build up a rapport and sense of trust, when some young people arrived at GIDS 'ready for a fight and feeling quite angry before we even said hello to them'. This dual function of the GIDS clinician – part gatekeeper, part assessor – had another effect too: it made it difficult for some young people to be honest. They 'often came into the service with the idea that if they showed any sort of sense of doubt, or uncertainty, or things weren't fitting a particular narrative, then they might lose their chance to get a referral for blockers'.

Just as Will Crouch observed, Bristow found that most young people, teenagers in particular, came to the service wanting only one thing: puberty blockers, 'and then testosterone or oestrogen as soon as it was possible.' At this point, he says, the younger children were ruled out by the Early Intervention Study's lower age limit of 12.

That would soon change. From the middle of 2014 puberty blockers became available for anyone who was eligible as standard clinical practice at GIDS. Having stressed the need to proceed with this big change in treatment with great caution, GIDS then abandoned the commitment. Going forward, young people could receive the blocker, but would not be closely monitored as part of a research study.

On top of this, not only would all those aged 12 and up who had commenced puberty be able to access physical interventions, younger children would too. The service moved from what's called an 'age' to a purely 'stage' approach, whereby access to medical interventions would be dictated by an individual child's stage of puberty – in this case Tanner stage 2^2 – not their age. Tanner stage 2 represents the beginning of physical development: the formation of breast buds in girls, and growth of the testicles in boys. Provided a child had reached this stage of puberty they could potentially be referred for puberty blockers, regardless of their age.

'Now we've done the study and the results thus far have been positive we've decided to continue with it,' Dr Polly Carmichael told the *Mail on Sunday* newspaper in 2014.[3] 'So we've decided to do "stage not age" [as the criterion] because it's obviously fairer. Twelve is an arbitrary age.' Carmichael explained that this could mean that those starting puberty 'aged nine or ten' could be considered for treatment from now on.

What was behind the decision? What were these 'results' that Carmichael was referring to?

At the time of writing, in late 2022, the current GIDS service specification states: 'The Early Intervention Clinic will continue to follow the Service's 2011 research protocol, which *following evaluation* [emphasis added], has now become established practice.'[4] When BBC

Newsnight asked for a copy of this evaluation none was forthcoming. Instead, an NHS England spokesperson said that the document was 'based on international evidence and developed with clinical experts and publicly consulted on'.[5]

It is difficult to understand how there could have been any sort of meaningful 'evaluation', given that the last participant to the study only joined in April 2014, just a month before Polly Carmichael spoke to the press.[6] The Tavistock Trust has said the move from age to stage was 'based both on international findings and on careful consideration of our own experience'.[7] When challenged, the Trust provided no concrete detail. Instead, it said, the decision to roll out early intervention and lower the potential age at which a young person could access puberty blockers was a 'clinical practice decision... shared with our commissioners'.[8]

A further enquiry to NHS England yielded greater clarity. The Tavistock, it said, had simply 'advised' the service specification text to be amended to insert the words 'following evaluation'. It 'was not intended to infer that a formal evaluation of the Early Intervention Study had been presented to NHS England for its consideration'.[9]

So, there was no *formal* evaluation. But, similarly, there could have been, at best, only very limited data for GIDS to review in terms of interim findings.

The only international findings available of this approach were from the Dutch team, and there were no data available at all on the impact of puberty blockers on those under 12. As WPATH put it in its 2012 guidelines: 'Studies evaluating this approach have only included children who were at least 12 years of age.'[10]

There are strong signs that the decision to allow younger children to be referred for puberty blockers outside a research study was taken a fair time earlier, certainly by 2013. Polly Carmichael told the *Sunday Times* in November that year that 'she planned to continue the programme indefinitely'.[11]

At this point just 23 young people had *started* treatment with hormone blockers.

Dr Natasha Prescott recalls some discussion in the GIDS team meetings about possibly extending the study and moving from age to stage, but says the decision was taken by Polly Carmichael and the Executive. 'It made no sense at the time,' she says. 'I firmly was arguing for continuing the study, extending the study. How could we not do it under a study protocol when we didn't have the data?' The decision was well intentioned: 'I think there was a real empathy for these distressed kids,' Prescott explains. And here was a potential solution to that distress. The problem with that was that part of what GIDS was trying to do as a service was to 'support families to support young people with distress'. 'Part of life and development is learning how to manage and tolerate distress, not thinking it's supposed to be taken away,' Prescott explains. The decision may have been well meaning, but 'lots of things can be well meaning, and ill-informed'.

Another clinician in the service at the time remembers differently. Andrea Walker,* a straight-talking, highly experienced social worker from the Leeds team believes the decision to roll out early intervention was based largely on two considerations: the Dutch team were doing it, and Mermaids wanted it to happen. The issue was 'becoming really political', she says. 'And if we don't do it, we're just going to become irrelevant.'

It's difficult to understand why this decision was permitted by GIDS's commissioners at NHS England. Why did they not insist on seeing some data, *some* evidence, that supported making puberty blockers more widely available, and to children so young that there were no data at all on how they might fare? Health sources tell me that 'specialist commissioning', the area of the NHS that has oversight of GIDS, encompasses more than 200 areas of treatment. GIDS slipped under the radar. That's entirely believable in an overstretched NHS, but still an astonishing admission where an experimental treatment on children is concerned.[†]

---

* Not their real name.

† Professor Russell Viner – the chief investigator of GIDS's Early Intervention Study – told the author he had 'nothing to do' with the decision to allow early puberty blockade outside a research setting. He had moved out of clinical practice in 2013 and his only involvement was with the 44 young people taking part in the research study. He added that he thought that the experience in GIDS was that patients were 'exceptionally positive' about the treatment, but explained: 'We had a couple of patients who went on and off treatment but decided to go back on. Again, lots of discussion about whether it was the right thing for them to go back on treatment.'

———

Later in 2014 the Dutch provided an update on how those who'd embarked upon their 'protocol' were faring. By now, the young people who had begun their transition with puberty blockers and cross-sex hormones had undertaken some form of gender reassignment surgery (GRS). Not only had their gender dysphoria resolved, 'but [their] well-being was in many respects comparable to peers'. Psychological functioning had 'improved steadily over time, resulting in rates of clinical problems that are indistinguishable from general population samples.' The young adults also reported a good quality of life. All very positive.[12]

The study confirmed the finding from three to four years earlier that gender dysphoria was not eased by being on puberty blockers (it got worse for girls), but only after taking cross-sex hormones or having surgery. That might sound unsurprising. After all, the young person's body hasn't begun to change while on blockers. Nonetheless, GIDS's Early Intervention Study clearly stated that this was an expectation: 'Early intervention is also associated with a reduction in the gender dysphoria experienced by these adolescents.'[13]

However, in this second follow-up study, the Dutch sample size had shrunk from 70 to 55 since the original paper in 2011 – a loss of more than 20 per cent. What's more, it revealed that one of those participants had died, following a severe bacterial infection post-gender reassignment surgery (the construction of a neovagina).[14] A mortality rate of one in 70 is noteworthy, but it didn't feature in the study's conclusions or discussion, and was simply noted as fact in one sentence in the study's methods section. It's a terrible outcome, by any objective measure. Of the 55 who *were* featured in the study, there were complete data for only 40 – just 57 per cent of the original cohort. And, as the Dutch authors pointed out, the study did not seek to evaluate the 'physical side effects of treatment'.

There are further important criticisms made of this second Dutch study. To measure how these young people felt about their bodies and gender dysphoria, they were given a set of questionnaires. Before taking puberty blockers, and again after taking them, they were asked questions relating to their birth sex; females were given questionnaires relating to the female body and female gender roles; males were given the male equivalents.[15] Birth-registered females were asked to respond to statements like 'I feel unhappy because I have to behave like a girl', 'I hate having breasts' and 'I hate menstruating because it makes me feel like a girl.' The Dutch found that the use of puberty blockers alone did not reduce gender dysphoria.[16] However, *after* surgery, those questionnaires were switched. Now, the female-born trans men were asked questions relating to a male body, and being male. They were asked to respond to statements such as 'I hate myself because I'm a boy', 'I'm unhappy if someone calls me a boy' and 'I dislike having erections'. These trans men would never respond negatively to the first two statements – they want nothing more than to be seen as male – and few, if any, had undergone phalloplasty surgery (the creation of an artificial penis). Therefore, the third question would have been redundant for most. It's been argued that simply switching these questionnaires could explain the positive results reported in terms of decreasing gender dysphoria in these young people.[17] The Dutch researchers rejected this argument, saying that while the gender dysphoria scale they administered was 'not ideal' when used after treatment, that did not imply that it '"falsely" measured the improvement in [gender dysphoria]'.[18] They stated that 'using the version of the assigned birth gender would also make no sense'. Despite their protestations, it seems impossible to know how much of the change was due to the medical interventions and how much simply to this questionnaire swap.

At the time of writing, the Dutch team have not published any further longer-term follow-ups on those who went through their protocol. Their existing studies, though, based on only 57 per cent of a cohort of 70, of whom one died due to surgical complications, comprise most of the evidence base used to justify the affirmative medical approach for gender-dysphoric youth – an approach which would become mainstream clinical practice in the Western world.

In late 2014, Dr Anna Hutchinson returned to GIDS after her maternity leave, keen finally to get stuck into the new job she'd only briefly begun. The absence of a year had brought significant change. A number of new staff had joined, enough to make it feel 'like a different team', but GIDS's activity was 'increasing faster than staffing'.[19] Space on level three of the Tavistock Centre was now scarce and some of the GIDS senior team were having to share offices. In January 2015, Anna found herself sharing her office, room 324, with a newly appointed psychotherapist, Melissa Midgen. Hutchinson recalls that Midgen, like many psychotherapists, was fiercely protective of her privacy. She wasn't interested in small talk. Inquisitive, clever and challenging, she and Hutchinson debated from the outset. It was refreshing.

Hutchinson's new responsibilities included processing referrals alongside her clinical duties. The numbers had exploded and piles of referrals sat on her desk. 'These piles were ever present and growing,' she says. 'Literally one week to the next, the pile would double... inches of paperwork that would come in over a week; and I remember the first month where we had 100... it was phenomenal. Something was happening.'

But, Hutchinson explains, 'There were no referral criteria... We were accepting everyone.' Some were appropriate. But many others were not, and these could be put at two extremes. One would be the young person who was being seen locally by CAMHS for something else, but 'just casually mentioned sexuality or gender in one appointment'. There might be a 'whole report about a child who's struggling in the world with one line about gender', but the very mention of the word 'gender' resulted in a GIDS referral. At the other end of the spectrum, you might have a young person who was so complex, with so much going on – 'gender or not' – that 'it was questionable whether an outpatients service like GIDS could deal with that level of risk'.

The rate of GIDS referrals had been increasing for years – at a rate of 50 per cent per year since 2009 – but they were now arriving at a rate of more than 100 per month. It was almost impossible to process them. Over the course of 2015/16 referrals doubled to 1,419.[20] Between 2009 and 2015, GIDS said no to just 2 per cent of those referred – a figure which included those automatically ruled out for being 18 or over.[21]

It wasn't just the raw numbers – the sex ratio of those being referred had shifted dramatically too. The number of girls (known at that time at GIDS as 'natal females', now 'birth-assigned females') seeking help had equalled the number of boys for the first time in 2011.

Previously, GIDS's caseload had been nearly three-quarters male for those referred in childhood, or two-thirds overall.[22] At first, this change was understood to be positive – a sort of balancing-out – and attributed to the fact that the girls were perhaps being better supported to seek help. But by 2015 it was clear that, in fact, something bigger was happening. There had been a complete reversal. Referrals for natal girls made up 65 per cent of the total.[23] In 2019/20 girls outnumbered boys by a ratio of six to one in some age groups, most markedly between the ages of 12 and 14.[24] The same was true in 2020/21, though GIDS don't seem to have a record of the birth-registered sex for 7 per cent of those referred (GIDS was unaware of the sex of nearly 22 per cent of young people referred in 2021/22[25]). Of those they did have details for, 68 per cent were female.[26] Moreover, the majority were girls whose gender-related distress had begun *after* the onset of puberty, during adolescence. They didn't have a history of childhood dysphoria.

And these young people had complex needs. There seemed to be increases in young people's level of risk and the severity of other mental health problems, alongside gender dysphoria. Many were self-harming; others were housebound with anxiety; some older adolescents were engaging in risky sexual behaviours. A number came from abusive families, or were living in care. It isn't that the early cases seen by GIDS were *not* complex – GIDS's early audit had shown that many of the young people attending the service had troubled backgrounds.[27] But they were so few in absolute numbers at any one time that it was more manageable. Now GIDS was seeing highly distressed young people, with multiple associated health difficulties, in the hundreds, if not thousands.

An analysis of the 218 young people referred to GIDS's London base in 2012 bears out some of the challenges: 'The associated difficulties included non-suicidal self-harm, suicidal ideation, suicide attempts, autism spectrum conditions (ASCs), attention deficit hyperactivity disorder (ADHD), symptoms of anxiety, psychosis, eating difficulties, bullying and abuse (i.e. physical, psychological/emotional, sexual abuse and neglect).' The three most common associated difficulties were bullying; low mood or depression; and self-harming – found in 47, 42 and 39 per cent of the cases, respectively. The full findings highlight just how much some of these young people were struggling. One in eight (12.3 per cent) boys had attempted suicide, the figure slightly higher for girls (13.9 per cent), with the same proportions experiencing eating disorders. More than a fifth (21.2 per cent) of girls had suffered abuse, and a tenth (11.1 per cent) of boys.[28]

These were complex, troubled young people, who had faced real difficulty in their lives. Most were experiencing gender-related distress – no one questions that – but so much else besides. Domestic violence was indicated in 9.2 per cent of cases and parental substance abuse in 7.3 per cent. As had been the case with the early referrals to GIDS, young people in care were hugely over-represented. At the time of referral, 4.1 per cent were in foster care, with a further 1 per cent in a children's home or supported accommodation – by comparison, in 2021, 0.67 per cent of children in England were living in care.[29] Some lived with extended family, rather than parents, and 1.8 per cent – while still under 18 – lived 'independently'. What's more, the GIDS team behind the paper say that these figures are likely to be an underestimate, 'as they were based on referral letters and clinician notes/reports'.[30]

In 2015/16 there were more than six times as many young people referred as featured in this paper. Young people were also no longer presenting to the service in a binary way – as a trans boy or trans girl: a growing number were non-binary – identifying neither as male nor female. Between June 2016 and February 2017, 11 per cent of a sample of those attending GIDS identified as non-binary.[31] Some of these young people would also be referred for the medical pathway. There were no studies at this time which included non-binary presentations when looking at the efficacy of pubertal suppression.

On top of this, many children were now arriving at GIDS having already undertaken a full social transition – some at primary-school age. That is, many were living as the gender they identified as, not as their birth sex, complete with changed name, appearance and pronouns. Some were as young as three or four.[32] Some clinicians say that social transition tended to 'shut down' any possibility of exploration with these children and their families. And such an early and complete social transition was *not* recommended by the pioneering Dutch team.[33] Polly Carmichael was open about the potential difficulties too. 'If a lot has been invested in living in a gender role, then, potentially, it is difficult for young people to say: "Well, actually I don't feel like that any more,"' she told the *Guardian* newspaper in September 2015.[34] While acknowledging that parents rightly want to support their children, Carmichael warned that early transition could act to close off options later on. Sometimes, she said, it becomes 'almost impossible' for young people to 'think about the reality of their physical body'.[35] 'They are living totally the gender they feel they are, but of course their body doesn't match that, and it becomes something that can't be talked about or thought about,' Carmichael said. 'Clearly, it then becomes quite difficult in terms of keeping their options open and ensuring fully informed consent for any appropriate physical interventions.'[36] There is a lack of evidence on the impact of social transition, and what limited data there are can be interpreted in different ways. A study showing that only a small proportion of children who socially transitioned later reidentified with their birth gender has been argued to show both how gender identity is stable and unlikely to change through time, and that social transition shuts down options for a child, cementing a gender identity that may change.[37] While there are opposing views on the benefits versus the harms of early social transition, it has been argued that 'it is not a neutral act, and better information is needed about outcomes'.[38]

What was abundantly clear to some at GIDS was that the young people being referred to them in swathes were not those for whom the Dutch protocol was designed, nor GIDS's own protocol from the Early Intervention Study.

In the Netherlands, those receiving puberty blockers at 12 years old, and cross-sex hormones at 16, were rigorously screened. Young people had to have experienced gender dysphoria from childhood which had worsened with the onset of puberty. They needed to be living in a supportive family setting, and, crucially, they had to be psychologically stable, with no other major mental health problems.[39] GIDS – according to almost every clinician I have spoken to – was referring young people under 16 for puberty blockers who simply did not meet these conditions.

That this was the case was openly acknowledged by those leading GIDS. 'We are not having what you might see as the ones who are in the highly regarded Dutch study,' Dr Bernadette Wren told Parliament in 2015 – the ones 'who have had lifelong GIDS [*sic*], very supportive families and very few associated difficulties. That sort of profile is a very small proportion of our young people.'[40]

In their joint written submission to the same parliamentary inquiry, Polly Carmichael and Bernadette Wren were even more explicit:

> We offer assessment and treatment not just to those young people who are identifiably resilient and for whom there is an evidence base for a likely 'successful' outcome. We have carefully extended our programme to offer physical intervention to those who have a range of psychosocial and psychiatric difficulties, including young people with autism and learning disabilities, and young people who are looked after.[41]

The leaders of GIDS said publicly that they provide physical interventions for those to whom the evidence base does not apply.

Carmichael and Wren explained that this is because they 'have felt that these young people have a right to be considered for these potentially life-enhancing treatments'. This involves 'careful liaison with local service mental health providers and Social Care, who may know these young people well and who have particular responsibilities for their well-being'.[42]

The GIDS bosses told Parliament that the service has 'no record of refusing anyone who continues to ask for physical intervention after the assessment period'. Wren repeated this in her oral evidence, saying that 'anybody who wants it' could have physical interventions.[43] 'Some young people back off from physical treatment at an early stage, but the majority who choose to undertake physical interventions stay on the programme and continue,' the pair explained.[44]

It was impossible not to notice these changes. But there were precious few opportunities to really consider what was happening. Board-meeting minutes from June 2015 are explicit: 'the number of complex cases has increased.' Several staff are quoted, and while all admit to enjoying the work, it's clear that the environment is challenging. One explains how the 'demanding' caseloads 'can feel overwhelming and a potential threat to the quality and level of work we are able to deliver'. Another, talking of her caseload of around 90 young people, says this 'can make it difficult to hold clients, their families and the professionals involved in mind'. She adds, 'We do not have the resources to offer therapy.'[45]

Polly Carmichael acknowledged in July 2015 that GIDS had reached a point where it 'would have to say enough' and that she was working on how to convey this to NHS England. The Trust's medical director at the time, Dr Rob Senior, conceded that there was a sense of 'escalating risk, not just from work pressure but also in the number of safeguarding and risk concerns that were being brought to him for advice'.[46]

The changes occurring in the demographics of young people being referred to GIDS were not unique to the UK. Colleagues in gender clinics across the Western world noticed similar patterns – especially the high numbers of teenage girls presenting whose gender-related distress seemed to have begun in adolescence.[47] But it was a paper from Finnish clinicians working at the country's only two universities involved with gender identity assessment in young people that sparked the attention of several GIDS staff.[48] The Finns had spotted just what they had – the young people coming forward weren't like those they'd heard about in the Dutch academic papers and protocol.

In the Finnish sample – which contained all those who had been assessed at the country's two gender clinics between 2011 and 2013 – more than 85 per cent were natal girls. Most had 'first presented with gender dysphoria and cross-gender identification well after the onset of puberty'. And it had arisen in the context of 'wider identify confusion'. Thirteen per cent were in care or living independently, and well over half had been 'significantly bullied at school'. But close to three-quarters of those had been bullied *before* they came to think about their gender identity. Most startling was that the fact that 75 per cent of the young people 'had been or were currently undergoing child and adolescent psychiatric treatment for reasons other than gender dysphoria when they sought referral'. These co-occurring difficulties were 'severe' and 'could seldom be considered secondary to gender dysphoria', the Finnish team wrote. 'This utterly contradicts the findings in the Dutch child and adolescent gender identity service, where two thirds of adolescent SR [sex reassignment] applicants did not have psychiatric comorbidity.'[49]

The Finns couldn't explain *why* their young people appeared to be 'psychiatrically much more disturbed than has been reported elsewhere', or why their gender dysphoria had only begun in adolescence, but knew that the findings warranted attention. If the patients weren't the same, then maybe the treatment shouldn't be the same either. 'It is important to be able to openly discuss these alternative presentations of gender dysphoria in order to find appropriate treatment options,' the Finnish team wrote. The guidelines might well need to be adjusted to take into account the needs of these adolescent girls, who would be 'very unlikely currently eligible' for medical transition. Nor might that option be 'advisable.'[50]

Unlike their Finnish counterparts, GIDS published no papers questioning whether they should reconsider the treatment on offer to young people in England. Some members of the GIDS team attempted to steer their service towards adopting change for this new cohort, but with little success. That summer Melissa Midgen raised the issue of the pros and cons of going on the blocker for 'post-pubescent natal females' with Polly Carmichael. After all, these girls had already been through puberty. Midgen wondered whether it was worth exploring the possibility that, in some cases, the service 'might be able to agree on a non-medicated pause of a year post assessment rather than having to go on the blocker prior to considering cross sex hormones'.[51] The GIDS rules stipulated that young people couldn't go straight on to cross-sex hormones, even if they were 16. Midgen's approach would have allowed more time to talk and explore with these young people who had complex histories, without it appearing punitive. The door would still be open to hormonal intervention within the same time frame.

Instead of addressing these problems head on, the solution that GIDS arrived at – to deal with the increasing referrals at least – was to recruit more staff. Across 2015 the size of the team increased from the mid twenties to the mid forties.[52] In autumn 2015, ten new staff joined in just one month.

Anastassis Spiliadis was still completing his training in family therapy when he applied for a job at GIDS in late spring 2015. Born and raised in Greece, Spiliadis is confident and cheerful, with a good sense of humour. He worked in the corporate sector, for companies like Google, before choosing this very different career. To work for the world-famous 'Tavi' was a 'fantasy', he says, and he never thought they'd take someone who was just out of training to work in their famous specialist service. They did.

Spiliadis recalls how, initially, GIDS 'didn't even have a space' in which to put him and a handful of other new recruits. As GIDS expanded, 'people were furious', he recalls. Senior people elsewhere in the Trust were asked to give up their offices to make space. They asked why they were being pushed out. GIDS eventually took over a whole floor. 'But because it was bringing in so much money they could not challenge it.'

In 2015/16, GIDS's income was 5.9 per cent of the Tavistock Trust's total.[53] Within a year, it had almost doubled to 10.4 per cent. That proportion grew further.

With a home on the third floor of the Tavistock Centre, GIDS adopted its own separate 'branding' to mark its newly acquired territory. 'I have never worked in an NHS service with a logo,' Anna Hutchinson says. Nor for a service that was constantly being filmed for documentaries, or whose leadership were often in the press.[54] That GIDS was receiving so much positive media attention was welcomed repeatedly by the leadership of the Tavistock Trust.[55]

Unlike other psychological services in which Anna Hutchinson had worked, which tried to fit their care to the individual needs of the patient, GIDS essentially provided a 'one size fits all' intervention, she says. The 'affirmative model' views the young person as the expert on themselves when it comes to gender. If anyone, of any age, self-identifies as the other gender, then they're affirmed as 'trans'. GIDS are proud to be affirmative of young people's identities, but say that this does not preclude exploration.[56] Those independently scrutinising GIDS found the affirmative approach was guiding their practice.[57]

Speaking later – in 2018 – GIDS director Polly Carmichael and number two Bernadette Wren acknowledged: 'Of course, our work is "affirmative" in many ways, in that we respect and accept completely children's sense of themselves… and in some cases, where clinically appropriate, we affirm in the most profound way by providing treatment to alter their bodies.' Yet they caveat the GIDS approach by adding: 'while accepting and respecting a child, we also hold in mind there can be no certainty about the pathway each individual will take.'[58] While it may have been 'held in mind', this didn't seem to change the way the service operated, says Anna Hutchinson. The only 'pathway' on offer was one towards physical intervention – puberty blockers. Other clinicians have told me that female adolescent onset service users would be treated differently: they would likely receive a longer assessment, or be 'held' until they could be referred to adult services. But while young people might be offered very infrequent check-up appointments, GIDS didn't provide different treatment pathways. Ongoing talking therapy, for example, was not something they could offer.

Rather than arguing that things should be slowed down with this new cohort of complex adolescents, some maintained that GIDS wasn't going fast enough. For some families, the service was too conservative – even if assessments were limited to three or four appointments. Some parents and young people took issues with 'intrusive' questions they didn't see as relevant to being referred for medical treatment.[59] Why was it necessary to ask about past trauma, for example, they ask? GIDS, they argued, pathologised trans children.[60]

Groups like Mermaids were calling for the age limit on cross-sex hormones to be lowered from 16 'all the time' and for the requirement that young people be on puberty blockers for a year first be dropped.[61] Some of the UK's parliamentarians appeared to agree with them: if anything, GIDS was too cautious.[62] Society, or parts of it at least, was calling for GIDS to move faster when it came to physical interventions, and to do so at younger ages. Bernadette Wren told Parliament in September 2015 that GIDS reviewed the question of making cross-sex hormones available at younger ages 'constantly', but explained that 'there are issues about the range of young people coming forward and the difficulty of knowing which are the children who might do really well, unless we confine [cross-sex hormones] to a vanishingly small number, which we possibly should'. Sitting next to Mermaids' chief Susie Green at the time, Wren explained that dropping the age limit would make it 'harder and harder for us to say, "No"', and that that made GIDS 'anxious'. Wren explained that GIDS questioned whether it was 'sound ethically' to allow children to make 'critical life changing decisions at 14'.[63]

Wren was explicit about the pressure Mermaids exerted on GIDS: 'I know that Susie and Mermaids would like a fast track so that young people who are already well into puberty and feel that they know that they want to move forward into physical intervention would bypass our assessment process and move straight into physical intervention,' she said. 'We feel that is not an ethical way to practise, and this is a sticking point between us and Mermaids.' Wren explained that physical interventions were not 'the royal road to perfect mental health' for many of the young people being seen at GIDS.[64]

The pressure did not go away, and in 2016 the Tavistock confirmed that it was 'highly likely' that the requirement to be on puberty blockers for a year would be scrapped, and that it was 'actively looking' at whether young people could commence cross-sex hormones at a younger age, as part of a 'research protocol'.[65] In an email exchange the following month, Mermaids' Susie Green expressed her wish for the time spent on blockers before cross-sex hormones to be reduced. Polly Carmichael replied that there could be 'flexibility' around the year requirement.[66]

It's unclear whether practice changed in response, but the age limit for cross-sex hormones was not lowered. However, GIDS did allow assessments to be completed faster. The lower limit for the number of appointments a young person had to attend to constitute an 'assessment' was reduced from four to three hour-long appointments. It's unclear how or why the decision was taken. Three sessions is referenced in the current GIDS service specification, published in April 2016.[67] The previous service specification, from 2013, had stated that 'the initial assessment phase is likely to include at least four sessions'.[68]

But sometimes a young person *would* be referred even more quickly.

The very first case that Anastassis Spiliadis saw was referred for puberty blockers after two sessions. It was a 'really complex case with a past history of trauma', he says. And there were many cues that something had happened in the past, and that perhaps the young person wanted to talk about it but was struggling to do so. However, the assessment only 'scratched the surface'. So much was 'left unexplored just because this young person was requesting medication', he says.[69]

This wasn't the only time a GIDS assessment was carried out quickly.

Dr Anna Hutchinson recalls an assessment where the young person was told they could access puberty blockers during the first appointment. The young person was bright and high-functioning, but was 'quite definitely and obviously' depressed, and struggling generally, she recalls. They didn't have a long history of problems surrounding their gender. The family were close, but seemed vulnerable, Hutchinson says, and had 'turned to us for expertise and trusted us to be experts'. Within 20 minutes of meeting this young person, a referral to UCLH for puberty blockers was offered to them by Hutchinson's co-worker. It was a decision made unilaterally and in front of the patient – there was no space for discussion. Hutchinson says she knew at the time it was 'a bit different' – it's the only case she specifically remembers from 2015 – and she thinks she made this 'very clear in the notes'. But while she saw it as 'exceptional', Hutchinson – just like Anastassis Spiliadis – didn't feel she could challenge it. 'I don't think I was on a sure enough footing with what I understood at that point to be able to say, "What the hell was that about?"'

Dr Matt Bristow remembers a very similar experience, in which, at the end of the first session, it was decided that the young person would be referred for puberty blockers. His colleague 'made the decision on her own and communicated to the young person and to their parents'.[70] He didn't challenge because his colleague was so senior.

In all these cases, they wouldn't have looked like a one-session assessment in the records. And when the Tavistock investigated the claim, it found no evidence of patients being referred after a single session. 'The assessment officially continued with big gaps between the appointments and report written in the end,' Bristow explains, but 'the decision happened at the first session and that was communicated to everyone.'[71] Hutchinson says she was asked to put the young person on the waiting list for UCLH after the first session, but 'then we completed the four sessions, which were necessary at that time... The paper trail, the explicit and obvious paper trail will look like it was following the spec.'

These are not the only instances of two-session assessments. And in all these cases I have come across, the other clinician in the assessment was GIDS Executive member Dr Sarah Davidson. Davidson denies referring or agreeing to refer a young person for puberty blockers after one appointment. 'My practice was to typically refer (where appropriate) after at least three sessions,' she said via email.

Spiliadis confirms there were other clinicians who conducted these 'speedy assessments' too, but he is referring to 'very few'.[72] These very short assessments, contrary to the NHS service specification, did not happen often but, as one senior GIDS clinician put it, they 'certainly happened'. Nor is any motive being impugned. When staff did query the speed, as Spiliadis said he did in a team meeting, the response was that the young person was experiencing 'extreme distress' and that going on the blocker was 'a way to manage it.'[73] Bristow says that the Executive team didn't want to entertain the idea that assessments were sometimes being completed in fewer than three sessions. 'The other members of the executive would say, "Oh no, no one does that in this team."'

At the time of these fast assessments, clinicians were already concerned that an assessment model whereby a decision was expected after six sessions was inadequate for some of the cases they were seeing. After just one or two, they argued, there was a far greater risk that some young people were being referred for potentially life-changing medicines, when they may have been struggling with issues such as their mental health, or past abuse or trauma.

In that first full year in the service – 2015 – Hutchinson began to feel uneasy. She tried to get GIDS director Polly Carmichael to agree to a tightening of referral criteria – something that would continue to be raised by numerous clinicians – but to no avail. By her own admission, Hutchinson was 'still learning' and still somewhat 'naive' to the patient population, but it was impossible not to worry.

Self-diagnosed adolescent trans boys – natal females – started to fill up GIDS's waiting room with similar stories, haircuts, even names – 'one after another after another'. They'd talk about their favourite trans YouTubers, many having adopted the same name, and how they aspired to be like them in the future. Given how complicated these young people appeared to be, could something else be going on that explained this, something other than them *all* being trans?

Staff found that many of their patients were not interested in exploring more deeply how they felt. Some assertively expressed their belief that even to consider that idea was transphobic, and many young people viewed the blocker as the first step towards a medical transition. Others would engage in some tentative exploratory conversations, only to grow shy again during the long months between appointments. GIDS wasn't funded to provide the psychotherapies that it was felt many of the young people needed, while desperately overstretched and underfunded local CAMHS would often refuse to become involved while patients were under the Tavistock's care.

Consequently, most of these young people would eventually proceed on to the medical pathway. There was no way they couldn't, clinicians say. If they met the diagnostic criteria for gender dysphoria, which they invariably did, then the only real *treatment* GIDS was commissioned to provide was a referral for puberty blockers. GIDS frequently describes itself as an 'assessment' service, which isn't commissioned to provide therapy.[74] However, it explicitly told parents at this time that it could offer family therapy and 'individual child psychotherapy'.[75] The service specification GIDS is guided by isn't entirely clear on that point, but in practice, clinicians say, there just wasn't the time or resources to do this anyway.[76]

Even with her doubts, Hutchinson was reassured by what she understood about the blocker. She and others were informed regularly by their seniors and the endocrinology team at UCLH who prescribed the blockers that the drugs were harmless and reversible. They gave young people time to think, they said, while not experiencing the distress of a developing body.* This was encouraging – Hutchinson felt that what many of these young people needed was more thinking all round. But it's striking that while staff say puberty blockers were spoken of as reversible within the clinic – among clinicians and with families – outside GIDS director Polly Carmichael communicated a different message. 'The blocker is said to be completely reversible, which is disingenuous because nothing's completely reversible,' she told the *Guardian* in 2015. 'It might be that the introduction of natal hormones [those you are born with] at puberty has an impact on the trajectory of gender dysphoria.' Indeed, Carmichael voiced her concern that physical interventions were perhaps being seen by some, 'unrealistically', as a panacea. 'In our experience, all the problems do not go away,' she says.[77]

It wasn't just the patients who craved a pause. GIDS was fast becoming a very difficult place to work. Junior clinicians were expected to step up to manage the ever-growing waiting list. Their caseloads were going up and up: 50, then 70, then, by 2017, 90 or 100 patients each. Work flowed into evenings and weekends. Anna Hutchinson, who by now was supervising Matt Bristow, raised the issue of junior clinicians' workloads with management. But to no avail. She had to feed back that they would just have to do it. 'I just felt awful because I knew what I was asking him to do. It was actually impossible. It wasn't just unethical and clinically risky, it was also impossible.' Clinicians fed back that they, too, were distressed, overwhelmed and confused. They also needed more time to think.

They could have had it.

---

* In the official 'Gender Identity Development Service leaflet (GIDS): information for parents' still being provided in April 2015, parents were told: 'One of the options may be to prescribe hormone blockers, which can stop the physical changes and developments associated with puberty for a limited period of time. This is considered to be a fully reversible treatment. Taking hormone blockers can allow time to think about and explore feelings about gender identity, without having to worry about the body changing in a way that is difficult to cope with.' Available via Tavistock and Portman NHS Foundation Trust FOI 21-22046 ('Subject: patient information leaflet 2015'), https://tavistockandportman.nhs.uk/documents/2585/21-22046_Patient_information_leaflet_2015.pdf.

7

THE BOMBSHELL

As a result of growing disquiet among the clinical staff and an acknowledgement of the pressure GIDS was under, in October 2015 the service's managers brought in an organisational consultant to advise on how the service could adapt to meet growing demand.

It was hoped by some that it would be easier for someone external to the service to diagnose any problems. GIDS management were perhaps 'too close to it'.[1] 'The team wasn't working particularly well,' Matt Bristow recalls. 'I think there was already at that point a sense that the numbers were really high and going even higher, and that there wasn't enough time to think. There are already concerns about is this manageable? And are we able to continue to do the same standard of work with people?'

GIDS had missed its 18-week waiting-time target for the first time the month before, despite everyone's best efforts (and the service never met that waiting target again). Perhaps a fresh pair of eyes, ones not consumed with clinical duties, could help see a way through.

Dr Femi Nzegwu, an international management consultant with over 20 years of experience, was chosen for the task. Staff completed a survey she had designed and took the opportunity to relay their concerns. 'We cannot simply survive on our wits,' one said. 'I cannot continue indefinitely with such a high personal caseload with high levels of risk and complexity… without burning out,' another pleaded. 'Too busy to stop and reflect on cases and read through current literature which is very risky in this area,' said a third.[2] Not all comments were quite so despairing, but most noted that improvements could and should be made to the way GIDS operated.

Only a minority of staff – 19 out of 55 – responded to the questionnaire which formed the basis of Nzegwu's report. There's no way of telling which roles they held – clinical or administrative. At the time GIDS listed its staff number as 32.[3] But the questionnaire was also sent to those at the endocrine clinics based at UCLH that prescribe puberty-blocking medication.

The subsequent report didn't pull its punches. It described how the GIDS team was 'facing a crisis of capacity to deliver effectively on an ever-increasing demand for its service'. It painted a picture of staff under pressure, struggling to provide the best care for patients. Staff were 'stretched beyond optimal levels of efficiency and effectiveness', the report said, and 'the current model of working is unsustainable'. Nzegwu suggested that GIDS needed to 'agree the criteria for referrals' and on 'what the service can realistically deliver' with the resources it had. She noted that caseloads were 'significant' and questioned what could be done to bring 'minimum standards' to report writing.[4]

But these were all secondary to the principal and most fundamental recommendation of all. The service needed to 'take the courageous and realistic action of capping the number of referrals immediately'.[5]

GIDS should pause. Even if for just a short period, to reshape and rethink what it could offer, and to whom.

The main recommendation was ignored.

The report's findings were shared with only a small group, during a meeting of the senior team, of which Hutchinson was a member. Everyone was there, she recalls, bar GIDS director Polly Carmichael, who was preparing for an upcoming routine inspection by the health and social care regulator, the Care Quality Commission (CQC). And for a time, it looked as though the service was going to heed the advice.

'Having this external person come in and say that was excellent,' Hutchinson says, 'because it was obvious to anybody who sat down and did the number crunching.' But it was hard for anyone in the service to say so 'without any emotional consequences, displeasing anyone or breaking the spell of the "We Can Do"'. It was hard for the Executive to admit that the service could not do what it desperately hoped to, and hard for junior clinicians who wanted to get on in their careers and didn't want to show any sign of weakness.

The recommendations were seriously considered. There was 'acceptance', Hutchinson says, that things should change. 'I remember Sarah [Davidson] and Bernadette [Wren] and everybody talking about, "Okay, well, how are we going to stop the service? How are we going to do this?"' It was acknowledged that this was a big deal, 'but there wasn't a sense that we weren't going to do it'.

Nzegwu explained that this type of action had been done by other services to get them back on their feet, and that while it wasn't common, it wasn't completely out of the ordinary either. This was hugely heartening to Hutchinson. It provided an opportunity. 'We can design the service how it needs to be designed without the constant pressure.'

The late arrival of Polly Carmichael at the meeting heralded the end of the discussion, however.

She was 'incredibly charming and positive about both the consultant and the consultant's report', Hutchinson recalls, but decided 'we're not going to do it, essentially'. And that was that. 'It was never mentioned again,' says Hutchinson. Most GIDS staff were never told about the findings, and certainly weren't shown the report itself – a source of great annoyance to some who took part. It was never even talked about among the seniors again.

It was a missed opportunity, another colleague present agreed. 'I think we could have really done a great job at making the service better,' Hutchinson says. 'We could have been the first team to maybe develop a more nuanced assessment process to acknowledge the cohort was changing, and maybe they needed different treatments. We could have sent a message out to the world, essentially, that things are changing. We need to be thoughtful. We could have changed the whole story of what was going on. Not just have been a better clinical service, but actually had an impact on global practice and society.'

There are some who say this is naive. That this is all being said with the benefit of hindsight and that it was never a realistic option. They say that it would be unthinkable and irresponsible to pause referrals.

Where would those young people go? One central aim of GIDS was to break the stigma surrounding gender non-conformity. How could it turn young people away? GIDS Executive member Bernadette Wren, who did not wish to be interviewed for this book, wrote in 2021: 'Perhaps we should have refused to carry on until more and better assistance was available. But clinical managers do not readily down tools.'[6] While not explicitly talking about the recommendation in 2015, she argued that those who work in mental health 'are used to working in impossible circumstances'. And besides, she said, 'excellent work was still continuing with many children and families'.[7]

Anna Hutchinson does not accept that it wasn't possible to agree a temporary halt. The responsible thing, she says, would have been to pause taking referrals so that GIDS could regroup. It just required 'brave leadership'. 'If our job is to look after people, then it was our job to stop if the service was not able to look after people.' Matt Bristow, for one, would have been on board with a temporary pause. 'It might have then led to a rethink at an NHS England level, thinking, "What are the resources actually needed for this?" But, by ignoring that and just continuing on and trying to do more and more and more, effectively, the message you were giving to commissioners was that this is doable.'

It's unclear whether NHS England were ever told about this report and its findings.[8] The chief executive of the Tavistock Trust, Paul Jenkins, was not aware of it until he was alerted by the BBC's reporting of its findings. Given the magnitude of the recommendations and that GIDS was his Trust's fastest-growing service, this is somewhat surprising.

However, some of Nzegwu's suggestions were acted upon. Staff were placed into smaller, regional teams and a more obvious career structure was introduced. The service began to assign a 'complexity' score to referrals, but these didn't affect the numbers accepted on to the waiting list. Referrals kept going up, and could come from almost anyone: GPs, schools, social workers, and even some charities and youth groups.[9] The main response to the report appears to be the rapid recruitment of more staff, mainly psychologists straight out of training, a suggestion put forward by NHS England, who would help in paying the bill.

Over the course of the following year – 2016/17 – the GIDS workforce doubled from around 40 to 80.[10] But rather than alleviate the pressure the service was facing, it brought additional challenges. 'At the time all these new staff started none of us had any capacity to work with them,' Dr Natasha Prescott recalls.

The *intention* had been for new, predominantly junior staff to learn on the job by being paired with senior clinicians. But, in Polly Carmichel's own words, these colleagues 'found it difficult to develop a caseload as quickly as activity had been planned'. 'There exists no formal training in this area of work and so clinicians largely learn on the job by taking on cases with existing experienced members of staff,' she explained. 'As existing staff already have full caseloads it was difficult for new staff to find experienced co-workers to work with on new cases. The impact of this factor had not been fully appreciated when we recruited the staff.'[11] Learning on the job could only work if there were other people to work with and learn from. By now, there was so little slack in the service that its basic training model couldn't work.

It's questionable if it was ever wise to attempt to staff a specialist service helping a vulnerable patient group predominantly with very junior staff. It's unclear why NHS England suggested it, and why, when it was apparent that it brought its own difficulties, an alternative solution wasn't proffered.

At the time of writing, in 2022, GIDS continues to be staffed by a large proportion of junior clinicians.

With the decision made not to pause referrals, GIDS ploughed on. But working practices became ever more fraught.

It is notable that even though the working environment was intense, difficult and highly pressured, GIDS staff acknowledge that the team was an enjoyable one to belong to. Strong individual loyalties developed and staff felt protective not just of the service, but of the Executive as individuals.

Despite the large and highly complex workload – or perhaps because of it – the team felt like a community, a family even. This was reinforced by the frequent media appearances of GIDS director Polly Carmichel, and the generous funding for staff to attend international conferences on transgender healthcare, not just across Europe but as far afield as Buenos Aires. GIDS staff had the potential to progress their careers quickly, without necessarily facing the same level of managerial or service responsibility that others would in the health service at similar grades. And they were paid comparatively well. In austerity Britain, these were benefits that most NHS employees could only dream of. According to Anna Hutchinson, in its intensity, identity and generosity, the culture of GIDS more closely resembled 'a tech start-up than the NHS'.

Nowhere was this culture more visible than on GIDS's 'away days', where dozens of admin and clinical staff would gather. These were busy, buzzy affairs, necessarily held, as the team grew, in London conference centres. The Wesley Hotel in Euston was a favourite. The stated aim of these events was to share research updates and good clinical practice. Yet it seemed at times that they functioned primarily to renew staff's commitment to the team, to pioneering new clinical practice and to supporting a deeply misunderstood minority.

It was in this atmosphere, early in 2016, that GIDS's own research team – a small group of two or three junior staff, some working on a voluntary basis – presented the early findings from the Early Intervention Study, which had begun in 2011. By now, the referring of under-16s for puberty blockers was routine clinical practice at GIDS, as, remarkably, the service had not waited for the results of the trial before rolling the treatment out.

How had the first group of young people to have had earlier access to puberty blockers fared?

The young researchers *did* describe success. They started the presentation with the findings that the children who'd had their puberty blocked reported that they were *highly* satisfied with their treatment.

Anna Hutchinson was therefore surprised when they went on to explain that the children's gender-related distress and general mental health – when based on *clinical* measures of things like self-harm, suicidal ideation and body image – had either plateaued or worsened. Surely, she thought, if the children were making good use of the 'pause' that blockers might provide, you'd expect a drop in their levels of distress? That was ostensibly the whole point of the treatment. The two sets of findings – the self-reports of satisfaction and the quantitative measures showing no improvement – were contradictory. When Dr Polly Carmichael presented these findings at an international conference at around the same time in June 2016, she presented a similar picture.[12] There had been 'no change in psychological functioning'; 'no change in self-harming thoughts or behaviours'; 'no change in gender identity or gender dysphoric feelings'; 'no change in perception on primary or secondary bodily characteristics'; but 'natal girls showed an increase in internalising problems... as reported by their parents'. This encompasses things like anxiety and depression, as well as somatic symptoms. What's more, Carmichael was explicit: 'our results have been different to the Dutch... we haven't seen any change in terms of psychological well-being.'[13] The rationale for carrying out the study had been, in part, to test the Dutch claims. Yet by now GIDS had been referring young people for puberty blockers without waiting to see whether their own data supported it.

When findings for 30 of the 44 study participants were presented to the Tavistock board in June 2015, they appeared to show even less favourable outcomes.[14] These young people had been on the blocker for one year. Researchers reported a statistically significant increase in those answering the statement 'I deliberately try to hurt or kill myself' as well as a significant increase in behavioural and emotional problems for natal girls.[15] Parents reported a significant decrease in the physical well-being of their child.[16] Why had these findings not provided pause for thought? GIDS told the BBC in 2019 that all patients were seen regularly by mental health professionals, who had concluded there was no evidence of harms that could be directly attributed to the treatment.[*17]

---

[*] Speaking to the author in 2022, Professor Russell Viner insisted that these 2015 data were 'not interim data from the study'. He says he 'knew nothing about those data' and that they were prepared 'rapidly' by a 'research assistant at the Tavistock for an internal Tavistock purpose'. Viner says these data did not match what he knew of patients in the study. When asked about the findings publicly reported by Polly Carmichael, he explained that he was not involved with the study at this point in time and only returned to help write the final paper.

While 44 children were part of the official study, by mid 2016 162 children had been referred to the early intervention clinic.[18] The youngest was eight years old, with their ninth birthday imminent.[19] The youngest person to have started on puberty blockers was ten years old. Yet GIDS appeared to have data that showed there was no impact on psychological well-being, when using more objective measures rather than self-reported satisfaction.

Anna Hutchinson was alarmed as the presentation continued in a matter-of-fact manner. Despite the idea that blockers were being administered to provide children and families with more time to think, it was becoming clear that they were all thinking in exactly the same way.

And then, in an astonishing aside, the researchers revealed that everyone in the early intervention group had at this point progressed from the blockers on to cross-sex hormones. A treatment with irreversible consequences. Every single one.

It was Hutchinson's 'holy fuck' moment. And a wake-up call for so many of her colleagues too.

'It totally exploded the idea that when we were offering the puberty blockers, we were actually offering time to think,' Hutchinson says, 'because what are the chances of 100 per cent of people, offered time to think, thinking the same thing? I mean, it looked to me like it was the opposite. And that once you're on the pathway, you stayed on the pathway, perhaps you thought less.' What's more, figures of close to 100 per cent are almost unknown in psychological research. Human beings, particularly adolescent ones, are not usually so consistent and predictable. The Early Intervention Study research team had data a year earlier that no participants had withdrawn from puberty suppression 'in the first 2 years'.[20] It doesn't appear that it was shared with the majority of GIDS staff. (Another paper published by the GIDS team in 2015 purported to show that both psychological support *and* puberty suppression were associated with improved functioning in young people with gender dysphoria.[21])

Different explanations for this 100 per cent (or close to) statistic have been proffered. Some argue that it is not surprising at all. These are trans children. Therefore they medically transition to become trans adults. End of story. Some argued that the 100 per cent persistence rate can be explained by the fact that those who took part in the Early Intervention Study were very carefully selected as the children who would be the most likely to transition as adults. It was due to the excellent GIDS assessment process that clinicians had been able to identify accurately the truly trans children from those who might change their minds and no longer identify as trans (as a proportion of children always did in every study of gender non-conforming children), in each and every case. Yet this did not sit well with some. 'That wasn't what fitted with my experience at that point,' says Anna Hutchinson. 'The Early Intervention kids that I saw right back in 2013 – they weren't particularly elaborate assessments at all.' Plus she had witnessed young people being offered the medical pathway 'after less than an hour of an assessment'.

While the persistence data being presented in a London hotel related to the Early Intervention Study alone, in which it was claimed participants had been 'highly selected', clinicians had seen from their own caseloads that very nearly all the young people who started the blocker went on to cross-sex hormones, even when they hadn't met the study's criterion of having had gender dysphoria throughout childhood. In 2016, Polly Carmichael explained to the world's leading figures in transgender healthcare that 'only two' out of the 162 children GIDS had now referred had stopped treatment.[22] Carmichael herself questioned how the blocker might be working: 'So I guess there is a question about why none, none stop once they've started on the blocker more or less,' she mused to the audience of gender clinicians.

> I guess that begs the question that either we're not putting forward enough young people for this – that there are some people that would benefit from this who are missing out on this treatment; or that in some way this treatment in and of itself may have an impact and set people on a path.[23]

Almost every GIDS clinician I have spoken with is honest and open about the fact that they simply could not predict which young people would grow up to be happy trans adults, and which would not; who would always identify as trans, and who would not. Almost every young person seen at GIDS had gender dysphoria, but there was no way of knowing the outcome. And GIDS did not, and had not followed up with its patients. Of those who changed their minds *prior* to going on puberty blockers, explains Anastassis Spiliadis, all 'were actively requesting medical and surgical interventions. And they were adamant that this was the right thing for them.' He recalls one young person in such distress, so determined to start medical interventions, that they had a panic attack during the assessment. They were screaming, 'I want my hormones.' But they later changed their mind. 'I was shocked,' Spiliadis says. 'I really didn't get it. I was certain [they] would go on hormones.'

But sitting in a hotel conference centre in central London, Hutchinson's head spun. She knew that if the blockers were actually *confirming* a trans identity, as suddenly now seemed possible, then there would have to be vulnerable children who would later realise that that wasn't the right path for them. 'I was horrified because I just suddenly thought, "Oh God, oh God."' If the service was getting this wrong, she said to herself, it was getting it wrong with some of the most vulnerable children and young people there were. Young people who already had difficulties – children who were traumatised or mistreated, autistic children, or those who might grow up to be gay.

This remarkable finding was never discussed formally as a whole group again. Even immediately after the presentation, there was little talk of it. GIDS never explored how it could be that despite their unique characters, experiences, families and beliefs, every single child had made the same decision to continue on to cross-sex hormones.

'My practice changed after that,' says Hutchinson. 'I couldn't change the system or the [service] spec, but I did tell every single person who wanted to go down the puberty-blocker pathway about this 100 per cent persistence... Informed consent means informing people about everything that you know, so I felt it was my duty to share that information with families.' Matt Bristow did the same. He and many others stopped talking about the blocker being 'fully reversible' and highlighted the unknown effects on 'social development and what pathway someone might ultimately end up on'. For parents of younger children in particular, he would list the reasons the blocker could be helpful, but also point out that 'it might crystallise an identity which is actually in the process of formation, and it might set someone on a specific path and limit down their options rather than open them up'.

It wasn't just that young people seemed to stay on the medical pathway once they had begun it; the GIDS model didn't *allow* young people time to think and explore once they were on puberty blockers. The theory had been that once the immediate distress caused by the developing body was dealt with, real thinking and exploration could take place about gender identity and what a young person wanted and felt. That made perfect sense to many. But in practice, that is not what happened. Rather than open up the opportunity to reflect, the clinical process shut it down. Once a young person was on blockers, GIDS appointments became *less* frequent, slipping to every three to six months. Some say this was down to the huge numbers of people waiting to be seen, but actually it was intended to be this way, as it was built into the service model.[24]

This was yet another way in which the GIDS model differed to the Dutch approach it was trying to emulate. 'So the idea that we were offering them more time to think was sort of being hammered at both angles,' Anna Hutchinson explains, 'both in terms of this data – this 100 per cent persistence on to cross-sex hormones – but also by then, I'd seen my patients go through the system and I realised we weren't offering them any *space* to think. So even if the blocker was buying *time* to think we weren't offering the space to do that thinking.'

Many others came to the same realisation. And it meant that the initial assessment for puberty blockers was seen by some in a whole new light. It needed to be more thorough and take far more into account. 'It felt essential that if I was going to be an ethical clinician,' Natasha Prescott explains, 'then if I didn't think that I was going to feel that it was right for this child to start cross-sex hormones, I needed to think about that *before* I put them on the blocker. Because once they're on the blocker, they've started along a path, and we saw them less frequently. So, my style of working completely shifted.'

Clinicians saw that these data had profound implications for consent. It wasn't just that families and young people needed to be told about blockers: they also needed more information on what transition might entail. 'I don't remember my supervisor having conversations with people before they went on blockers about testosterone, the limitations of surgery, the realities of transition, at all,' Prescott recalls. But given that virtually all young people would go on to cross-sex hormones, gaining consent for the blocker came to be seen as something altogether more serious. The young people concerned were potentially consenting to a set of procedures that could lead to infertility and a lifetime on medication. They needed to know what the pathway might look like. 'You couldn't do it after you put them on the blockers, you had to do it before, both in terms of exploration, but also in terms of consent,' Prescott explains.

Everything had changed. But nothing changed. While a significant number of individual clinicians started routinely telling young people and their families that treatment with puberty blockers appeared almost always to lead to cross-sex hormones, it wasn't formal policy. Matt Bristow impresses the point that even members of the Executive had begun to change their language around the blocker being 'fully reversible'. 'It wasn't that a couple of us kind of went, "Oh, my God, what are we doing?" And we then were the ones to change. It was things happening in the team where these were known about and people started to think, "This doesn't match what we've been telling people all of this time."'

Yet GIDS as a service did not adapt its practice in any meaningful way. And new clinicians who joined the team weren't told, at least initially, about the study's preliminary findings. They couldn't pass on what they didn't know.

Nearly a decade after the Early Intervention Study began, the full findings were published as a preprint in December 2020.[25] The Tavistock had failed to provide them to the High Court when asked in October 2020, only to release them the day after three judges published their view that under-16s were unlikely to be able to give informed consent to treatment with puberty blockers.[26]

The full peer-reviewed study confirmed what GIDS staff had been told four years earlier – that 98 per cent of those who started treatment with puberty blockers chose to continue on the path of medical transitioning and opt for cross-sex hormones. One of the 44 participants did not, 'due to continued uncertainty and some concerns about side-effects of cross-sex hormones'.[27]

In public at least, GIDS has never accepted that there is any link between someone starting on puberty blockers and them going on to cross-sex hormones. They argue that they are two distinct stages and that there is no evidence of causality.[28] The first assertion was rejected by the High Court in December 2020, but the Court of Appeal ruled it was not within the court's remit to have judged this.[29] The second assertion regarding causality is true. The reason there can be no claim to causality, but merely association, is because of the way that all studies have been designed – without a control group. All that can be observed is a trend – a trend that has been repeatedly observed by gender clinics across the Western world.[30] The Tavistock argues that the fact that one out of 44 participants did not commence cross-sex hormones shows that this course of treatment is not an inevitability.[31]

While the majority of participants described their personal experience of being on puberty blockers as positive, the study did not replicate the findings of the Dutch team that pioneered the use of puberty blockers in the early treatment of gender dysphoria. For these British young people, the blocker appeared to offer no psychological benefit.[32] The authors noted, 'we identified no changes in psychological function, quality of life or degree of gender dysphoria.'[33] The Dutch team's findings have never been replicated by other teams treating young people with gender-related distress.

The earlier findings presented to the Tavistock board, which showed that after a year on blockers there was a statistically significant increase in those answering the statement 'I deliberately try to hurt or kill myself', were not replicated.[34] Nor were the other statistically significant findings. Having previously found notable differences in the impact of blockers on girls and boys, the final study published data for the whole group of young people, the team saying that they tested several outcomes by sex and did not find any differences.

The researchers could not explain why there had been no change in 'overall psychological distress' or self-harm for the young people in the study, but put forward two alternative hypotheses. It could simply be that 'GnRHa treatment brought no measurable benefit nor harm to psychological function in these young people with GD [gender dysphoria]'. But it also might be that the lack of change in psychological functioning 'in an outcome that normally worsens in early adolescence may reflect a beneficial change in trajectory for that outcome' – that is to say, that treatment with puberty blockers *reduces* the normal worsening of distress young people experience through their teenage years. However, the authors conclude, 'in the absence of a control group, we cannot distinguish between these possibilities.' It's worth remembering that the original study protocol had stated that 'an improvement in mental states and overall wellbeing will support the view that the treatment is effective'.[35] By the authors' own measure, then, the early blocking of puberty in these young people was not found to be an effective treatment.

Being on puberty blockers, however, did impact physically on the participants. It adversely affected their height and bone strength relative to their peers.

GIDS currently summarises the study's findings as showing that 'puberty blockers are a well-received intervention in carefully selected patients'.[36] There is no mention of it showing that pubertal suppression led to stunted growth and that GIDS's own study showed that there is no discernible psychological benefit.

The data from the GIDS Early Intervention Study was not the only time that significant information became known to the team, but was not then routinely passed on to young people and their families. In November 2016, staff received a visit from consultant urological surgeon James Bellringer. Mr Bellringer works exclusively in male-to-female gender-reconstructive surgery. He began performing surgeries on trans women in 2000 and is widely thought of as the most experienced surgeon in this field operating in the UK.[37] He relayed in detail the difficulties that can occur for future surgeries if puberty is blocked too early in natal boys. There is not enough penile skin to perform a vaginoplasty in the safest and most effective way. Instead, a riskier procedure, with less stable results, has to be carried out.

To those listening, this was incredibly important information. Early intervention – if carried out too early on boys – could actually hinder any future surgical transition, not help it, as had been the argument from the early Dutch studies and trans support groups (who had acknowledged the potential difficulty with later surgery as far back as 2005, at a meeting attended by, among others, Polly Carmichael[38]). Families should know this, the clinicians listening felt, and be supported to make an informed decision. Almost immediately, highly experienced psychotherapist Melissa Midgen drafted an information leaflet that could be passed on to the relevant families during assessments. She had it approved for accuracy and language by both James Bellringer and Bernadette Wren, but she couldn't get the green light from GIDS director Polly Carmichael.* Six months later, in April 2017, Midgen still hadn't had a decision from Carmichael. She emailed her to request permission to share the leaflet, once again, noting that several clinicians had said that it would be helpful to have something 'on which to base a discussion with parents regarding the pros and cons of the blocker'. She did not receive a response.

Midgen's proposed short leaflet explained what feminising genital reconstruction consists of, and the preferred method used. 'In the case of creating a neo-vagina,' it said, 'the best skin available for this is the skin around the penis.'[39] There were other suitable skin types too, but where there was none available, surgeons had to use 'segments of the bowel'. And it was when they had to do this that surgeons were 'running into difficulties'. The operation itself was more 'hazardous' and more expensive. There was a risk of mucus or blood discharge and an 'unwanted smell', and in some cases corrective surgery may be required.

---

* Dr Carmichael said via email that she did not believe it was a 'fair or accurate criticism' to say that GIDS did not routinely share new information that came to light on puberty blockers with patients and their families. 'We share information about the effects of any physical intervention (including what is not known) with all young people and their families during psychosocial exploration sessions,' she stated. 'Information is also shared by endocrinologists (where the young person proceeds to that stage) prior to taking consent to treatment... GIDS is constantly adding to the evidence base and is constantly studying the latest evidence across the various specialism [sic] in this evolving field of medicine. This knowledge is then incorporated into the information sessions.'

'Perhaps most importantly it seems as though this surgery does not endure as well as previous surgeries and may well need replacement surgery after a period of time.'[40]

The leaflet explained how the Dutch team who had been offering early intervention treatment for longer than GIDS had found that '80% of those patients have insufficient suitable skin to create a functional vagina'.[41] These all needed to use segments of their bowel for surgery. The purpose of the leaflet was not to discourage treatment, or advise – it was simply to inform.

Everyone I have spoken to who saw Bellringer's presentation did, from that moment on, pass the information on to relevant patients. And I'm told that clinicians at GIDS's Leeds base were also pushing for this information to be routinely provided in assessments for the relevant children. But, just as with the data on people beginning blockers going on to cross-sex hormones, nothing was written down. The knowledge wasn't passed on to new members of staff who joined. Other clinicians who work at adult gender clinics have confirmed that not all young boys were told of this risk while at GIDS.

It wasn't until May 2019 – two and a half years later – that Midgen heard from a senior member of GIDS staff that the fertility and endocrinology team at UCLH had 'agreed to jointly write a consensus statement on the issues of EI [early intervention] and blockers and possible implications for later surgery, as well as other dilemmas the young people and their families face in relation to fertility'.[42]

It's difficult to understand why something that all agreed was so important couldn't be shared, as routine, via a proper leaflet. A leaflet that had been checked and agreed by the surgeon responsible for carrying out the procedures, and a member of the GIDS Executive. Why the reluctance to have it on paper?

'I may be wrong, but I think Polly was afraid of writing things down in case they got into Mermaids' hands,' says Anna Hutchinson. (It's why, she thinks, she also couldn't get approval to write to those whom GIDS knew they would not be able to see: those who would be too old by the time they reached the top of the service's waiting list.) Dr Alex Morris,* one of those who would always pass the information on, agrees. While she rejects the notion of being 'frightened' of Mermaids, she explains that 'anything you put on paper would be picked up, scrutinised'. Carmichael would then receive emails from Susie Green at Mermaids, or from private providers of gender care, who might accuse GIDS of scaremongering. They would take issue with 'anything that suggested there was anything dangerous, worrying', Morris says. Mermaids' view was that 'this is an increasingly normal practice, mainstream, safe thing to do, which doesn't have any significant consequences, and we should just be doing it quickly. And saving all these poor kids lots of trauma.' Having written down what had to be included in an assessment would, she said, have helped introduce more consistency across the service, though, rather than leaving it down to individual clinicians, who may or may not have been present when important new data were discussed. Clinicians who didn't know what they didn't know.

For Anastassis Spiliadis, the decision not to allow Melissa Midgen's leaflet to be rolled out for use by all clinicians was 'unethical'. 'It would change completely the way we worked, had this been published,' he says. 'We would need to acknowledge that we had done things in a wrong way in the past... and it would need to be integrated into the service protocol. So it would change everything.'

---

* Not their real name.

8

HOW TO COPE

Concerns among the GIDS team grew and solidified throughout 2016. In January Anna Hutchinson told her supervisor and the Executive that she felt 'current practice is sometimes unsafe both for staff and patients'.[1] The growing unease within the service was palpable, she says. Room 324, the office she and Melissa Midgen shared, became a place of emotional release for discontented staff. Staffers, often visibly distressed, would offload their ethical concerns about the service and their exhaustion at their workload.

At weekly staff meetings, where cases were discussed, some would express real discomfort about how the service was operating; how it was impossible to help these young people with multiple mental health challenges (among other serious problems) within the GIDS assessment approach. People would voice their concerns. Others would offer a counter view. Not everyone was worried. But these discussions could be very disturbing to those who took part and could become highly polarised. Many were struggling to square what GIDS was doing with what they knew to be safe clinical practice. After one such meeting in February 2016, Melissa Midgen wrote to the Executive team, saying that staff 'cannot sustain this level of distress and pressure within the team and maintain safe and effective practice'.[2] She explained that the team was made up of the 'best of people' but that various members 'of different persuasions and levels of experience and seniority' had found the encounter 'disturbing and unsettling'. She wrote not to level criticism, but to ask the Executive to 'consider how we can do things differently'. Polly Carmichael reassured Midgen that she was not alone in wanting to do things differently – but, fundamentally, nothing changed.[3]

In the face of a rapidly expanding team, a new cohort of more complex patients and new knowledge that a core treatment did not work in the way initially conceived, some felt completely overwhelmed. The service would discuss the difficulties they were seeing at length. But the talk would not result in action. It revealed that the GIDS Executive lacked either the ability or the will to take any meaningful action.

There were certainly things beyond the service's control.

'GIDS was just as much a victim of austerity and lack of resources' going into young people's services generally as any other outlet, one former GIDS therapist explains. Budgets for CAMHS, and youth services more widely, had been squeezed to such an extent that in many instances a young person could only receive support if they had reached crisis point.

But for GIDS to work at its best, and as intended, it relied on being able to operate in a network model, alongside other agencies like local CAMHS.[4] The idea was that for any given young person, GIDS would attend to the specific gender identity issues, while local services helped with any other difficulties they had – such as self-harming, eating problems, depression. As austerity began to bite, however, CAMHS and other services were increasingly struggling to see the young people referred to them generally. The model broke. Many CAMHS teams saw GIDS as a specialist, national service, with plenty of money. If a child had gender identity issues, GIDS should see them, not CAMHS.

Alex Morris recalls a conversation with one CAMHS psychiatrist who put the issue bluntly: 'Our commissioners have said that if the presenting issue is gender, then that's GIDS's issue and we're not funded to work with that.'

The problem was that those young people often had co-occurring difficulties that in some cases were more pressing than the gender-related distress. GIDS couldn't deal with those – but CAMHS wouldn't if GIDS was also seeing them. So the young person would fall through the cracks in terms of receiving the support they needed.

GIDS clinicians, however they view the work of the service, agree that, once referred, almost no one was turned away. GIDS would contact the referrer and explain that if risk wasn't being managed locally, they could not accept the young person on to their waiting list. More often than not the young person *would* then be referred to CAMHS. CAMHS would agree to open a case, but wouldn't actually see that young person. This often wouldn't become apparent until the young person was seen by GIDS. 'We had someone who said, "Well, we'll keep them open, if that's what you need. But we won't do anything,"' Dr Alex Morris recalls. There were some excellent CAMHS teams involved in GIDS's cases too, doing careful, thoughtful work with young people, but these were the minority. The majority were completely overwhelmed and pleased to share the load with GIDS.

Matt Bristow recalls an example which highlights just how risky this situation could be for GIDS's patients and the service as a whole. 'I remember going to network meeting with one CAMHS team, for a young person we were very concerned about, who was tying ligatures around their neck on a regular basis. And what CAMHS were able to offer them was a CBT [cognitive behaviour therapy] app. Not even regular appointments, they had an app. And I know that the clinicians there didn't feel that that was acceptable. But they didn't have any other choice because this person, who's regularly not only saying that they wanted to die, but tying a ligature around the neck, wasn't anywhere near their most risky client.'

The lack of CAMHS involvement or support for young people before they arrived at GIDS created a further problem. Left with no help whatsoever, support groups like Mermaids and GIRES stepped in to fill the gap. No blame can be attributed to very worried parents or their distressed children for seeking help when nothing else was available. But these groups are not clinicians and their personal experiences meant they held very particular views. These organisations would often use 'alarmist' rhetoric, convincing families that if their children did not receive access to medication for their distress, they would most likely take their own lives, GIDS staff say. This meant that by the time a young person *did* arrive at GIDS, their views were often so deeply entrenched as to what needed to happen – largely, puberty blockers and cross-sex hormones – that doing any kind of exploratory work became extremely difficult.

Speaking in 2015, Bernadette Wren described the wording on Mermaids' website as 'as scary as it can be'. She questioned whether it was 'helpful for [young people] to be encouraged to believe that what they feel is completely intolerable'. 'When inaccurate data and alarmist opinion are conveyed very authoritatively to families we have to wonder what the impact would be on children's understanding of the kind of person they are, and will become, and their likely fate.'[5]

Thankfully, the language does not appear to be borne out by the data, and GIDS states categorically on its website that 'suicide is extremely rare'.[6] When asked about the number of completed suicides and attempted suicides, the Tavistock have said that between 2016 and 2019/20 there were three completed suicides of GIDS patients or those on the waiting list, and six attempted suicides.[7] There was a further likely suicide between October and December 2020 of a 'young person known to GIDS'.[8] Any loss of a young person's life is one too many, and a recent study estimated, alarmingly, that 'GIDS patients were 5.5 times more likely to commit suicide than the overall population of adolescents aged 14 to 17'.[9] Some of GIDS's patients are undoubtedly very distressed. But the service also notes that 'the percentages for associated difficulties and self-harm appear to be in line with young people from the LGB population and increasing with the general population'.[10] The message that many young people identifying as trans take their own lives is one that, happily, does not appear to be true.

There is an argument from some who worked in, and indeed led, GIDS that as well as CAMHS being overburdened, GIDS's difficulty engaging other services to support young people was down to its commissioners at NHS England. 'For years, we had relied on local CAMHS teams to screen and support young people with psycho-social difficulties before referring them to GIDS, and to keep that support in place while we attended to gender concerns,' Bernadette

Wren wrote. 'But in 2016, NHS England commissioners ruled that GPs, schools and social workers could refer patients to the service directly.'[11]

But this doesn't seem to be the case. While the problem may well have been exacerbated by the increase in GIDS referrals, this wasn't a sudden change and it wasn't thrust upon them. 'All the time that I worked in GIDS from 2013 onwards, we accepted referrals from any professional,' says Anna Hutchinson. 'Many, many of us repeatedly said, "We need to tighten our referral criteria."' The previous GIDS service specification, written and agreed in 2013, clearly stated that 'referrals are accepted from a range of professionals, including CAMHS professionals, GPs, schools etc.'[12] And when it comes to insisting on CAMHS involvement, both service specifications appear remarkably similar in allowing for some wiggle room.[13]

When CAMHS *did* refuse to get involved, or the young person themselves refused to attend, GIDS would see them anyway, despite the risks involved. 'What could we do?' asks Morris. 'Because we didn't feel, I think, we could deny a service.' It was more than that, though. Clinicians say that GIDS, under Polly Carmichael's leadership, felt that the service had to be accessible to everyone. Some in NHS England recollect that the idea to allow a wide range of sources to make referrals was, initially at least, at the request of GIDS itself. Some young people might face obstinate GPs or CAMHS; restricting referrals to just these outlets would mean some who needed support would not be able to access the specialist care that GIDS could offer.

But the willingness to accept almost any and every referral seemed odd to some. While staff were being told they were a 'specialist service of national importance', Dr Matt Bristow explains, GIDS appeared to have 'the lowest bar to access out of any service'.

Could GIDS, with its monopoly on this area of healthcare for young people, really have had no influence over the service specification that dictated its practice, or its contract conditions?

Anna Hutchinson, who was in the GIDS senior team at the time, says GIDS was intricately involved in writing the service specification and contract. The service, to her surprise, she says, agreed to deliver something it could not provide. She and others had been asked to do the number crunching. The number of patients GIDS had agreed to accept under the new terms demanded many more hours than the current team could spare, given their existing workloads. 'I think what I was trying to get across was, we're not going to get on top of this,' explains another clinician. 'I think there was probably a bit of collusion in fantasy between the exec team and NHS England that if we just sort of tried hard enough and expanded the team, we would be able to get on top of it,' they add. 'And it seemed to me, and probably some others, fairly obvious that no amount of expanding was going to do that.'

One can only speculate why the leadership of a service might agree to terms they knew were impossible to meet. Only those in the room will know for sure what was said, and by whom. There was certainly an overwhelming sense that these young people needed a service. But it invites the question: what level of care could a service provide that had signed up to targets and patient numbers that just weren't deliverable? And how did staff respond?

Very differently.

Approaches to the GIDS work began to diverge hugely, depending on the individual clinician. Each took a different view on how they could best work under the pressure created by the ever-growing waiting list and the desire to get through it, and in so doing created a clinician lottery.

So busy was GIDS at this time, that sometimes staff didn't recognise families when they arrived at the clinic. One family on the receiving end of this told me they felt 'lost in the system'. They recall how at their second appointment their clinician had no notes, and had forgotten who they were and their child's name. And yet within 15 minutes, they say, their 16-year-old child – who had only identified as trans for a matter of months – was instructed on how to legally change their name and apply for a new passport. The family felt 'railroaded' and believe the clinician was unaware of how many sessions they'd attended. After the session, their child instigated a legal name change straight away, without their knowledge.

Some at GIDS tackled the problem head on. These young people needed to be seen. And that message would be delivered from supervisors and the Executive. 'Sarah Davidson was a pragmatist,' explains

Natasha Prescott. 'We had a huge waiting list. The intention was good, but the outcome wasn't. She was trying to find a way to offer a service. But that meant spreading the service more thinly.'

To some this was seen as 'decisive'. 'She wants to fix problems and make things happen,' says Alex Morris, speaking about Davidson. Davidson, Morris says, was asking the important question of '*How* are we going to make this work?' rather than saying, 'Let's have lots of meetings talking about how complicated it is.' Davidson told me that during the 15 years she worked in GIDS, the number of referrals increased markedly. 'That did, of course, create pressures in the system,' she says. 'However, safety remained our number one priority.'

Anastassis Spiliadis recalls how full-time staff were expected to hold at least 100 families on their caseload (the standard for an equivalent NHS service might be around 20 or 30), and says that he was questioned about conducting longer assessments. Clinicians saw that young people were 'in their most open exploratory phase' before starting physical interventions, one former senior clinician explained. This was why they extended assessments. 'I think the blocker shuts the young people down,' this clinician explains. 'I worried that it confirms to them something about them. It medicalizes their experiences.' As soon as GIDS said yes to puberty blockers, the exploration ended, some clinicians say. Appointments might be skipped, leaving gaps of six months between them. It could feel like young people were only there because they had to be.

Spiliadis concedes he was never pushed too hard, but he insists others were. They would be pushed to 'discharge families or to close them or to refer them on to endo[crinology] in order to free up space for new clients or patients'.

Many clinicians left. After a matter of only months in a few cases, but more often after a year or two. 'It took you quite a few months just to sort of figure out what you were doing and thinking, and then a few months to go, "Oh maybe this can change," and then a few months to look for another job,' one senior therapist explains. GIDS felt 'factory-like' and 'absolutely crazy'. Many of the young people did not seem in need of a specialist gender service at all. But because they were being seen by a gender service, it created the expectation for physical interventions. Why on earth would you wait a year and travel miles to receive therapy? this therapist asked. 'It just felt like a train to UCLH.' 'The people that I was with at that time, we all came in, we all left and everybody had various nervous breakdowns along the way.'

Some clinicians stayed but tried to keep some young people out of GIDS if they could. With referrals that were complex, but where 'you could see that it really wasn't that much about gender', this was possible, explains Natasha Prescott. She would try to meet with the local CAMHS team and the family. 'I just thought, I don't want them coming into the service. I've got to keep them out of the service, or it will just become about gender,' she says, recalling a particular case. This wasn't a viable solution, however. Setting up a meeting with other agencies takes time – the one thing that GIDS staff didn't have.

So many clinicians say that 'the numbers' dictated everything at GIDS: 'the waiting list took over the whole service,' explains Andrew Oldfield, an experienced clinician – both clinically and in terms of life.* The difficulty was how to work as ethically as possible within the constraints of the circumstances.

Some struck a balance that they were happy with and proud of.

Oldfield felt able to conduct the type of assessments he felt young people really needed. The work had done to be by someone – it might as well be him.

'We just had to go through the numbers,' he reflects, 'and we had to try to do the best we could at assessing people. I don't think I put anybody through for puberty blockers that didn't feel as though it was in some way realistic.' He says most of his assessments would be in-depth, perhaps ten or 15 sessions. 'We would delay rather than say no in many cases, because that was our position. We would say not yet; we need to do some more work. And I don't think we would say okay until we had done enough work to put it through.'

The pressure was on, he says, but as someone with a bit more experience, he felt he could practise in this way. He would affirm young people's identity, like all GIDS clinicians – acknowledging this was how they strongly felt and respecting it – but would try to explain

* Not their real name.

that adolescence was a time of huge change, and that it was *possible* they might not always feel the same. 'I often said to parents and young people, "If you choose to do this there is no guarantee that you – at 25 – are not going to think, 'Maybe I made the wrong choice.' What I want you to do is if you make the choice to do this, that you do it knowing that you've got the most information you possibly can, you're the most informed you possibly can be at this point."'

Oldfield didn't shy away from having tough conversations but says that he wasn't sure how many others were doing the same. He had a sense that some were 'surprised' when he said what he was doing. 'But you know, I wanted to be really clear that there is a risk here.' These young people had a 'right to treatment', he says. Other clinicians I have spoken with agree. He couldn't stop them being referred to endocrinology. But if they were going to go there, they needed all the information. 'I think that's the most ethical position I could find in the work. And I think the ethical edge of the work that we were doing was incredibly intense. Some people couldn't tolerate it at all. But the work had to be done.'

While finding the most ethical position he felt he could, Oldfield acknowledges repeatedly that clinical practice at GIDS was completely 'dominated by the numbers'. There could have been 'more work' on discussing sexuality with young people, he says – but numbers got in the way. Newly qualified staff who joined the service did their best, but it wasn't possible to offer them the training they needed – 'a victim of the numbers that were coming through'. There was intellectual curiosity in the team, he says, about what they were seeing, about why there were suddenly so many girls with gender-related distress, but 'the numbers were just so overwhelming for everybody' that the research couldn't happen.

Oldfield enjoyed his time at GIDS and is proud of much of the work, but he was concerned about the fact that the service was not offering much in the way of thinking space once someone had started physical interventions. 'If there was any drum that I was beating during the service, it was that this is the time we need to up the number of sessions… But again, we couldn't do that because the emphasis was on seeing the punters, getting the waiting list down.' In fact, GIDS had

no intention of seeing young people more often, its service specification suggesting that those on puberty blockers should be followed up
every three to six months.

Physical interventions at GIDS had been introduced to younger
children – initially at least – because of their supposedly crucial role in
allowing exploration of a young person's gender identity, without them
feeling distress. The 'real work' was meant to start once they had commenced treatment with the blocker. If they couldn't do any therapeutic
exploration alongside the administration of the blocker, then what was
the point of putting people on it in the first place?

For some, the implications of this were too great. They started to
draw parallels between infamous NHS scandals and GIDS's work.
In late 2016 Natasha Prescott found herself at a professional talk. At
one moment, the speaker raised events at 'Mid Staffs' – one of the
greatest health scandals in British history. Between 2005 and 2009 it
is estimated that there were at least 400 more deaths of patients than
expected at the Stafford Hospital, a district hospital run by the Mid
Staffordshire NHS hospital trust – hence 'Mid Staffs'.[14] Numerous
inquiries found that care at the hospital had been grossly inadequate.
Investigations by the Healthcare Commission and Sir Robert Francis
were littered with stories of neglect, and highlighted how a chronic
shortage of staff, inadequately trained staff, management failings and
an attempt to make financial savings had all played a part in the
breakdown of care.[15] Listening to the talk, Prescott felt she was 'over-
identifying' with the Mid Staffs nurses. 'I found myself thinking that
one way of thinking about what happened is their resources kept
diminishing, and they were trying to stretch what they had to prag-
matically be helpful. And in the process of doing so, they caused great
harm, because what they could offer wasn't safe. And I realised that
by... allowing myself to feel responsible in some way for people on the
waiting list, I'd done the same... Managing the waiting list was not my
responsibility. That should not inform my clinical work.'

These are just snapshots of the different ways that GIDS clinicians
attempted to cope with the rapidly increasing demand for the service.
Demand that couldn't be met by supply. Human beings think differently, and all were doing what they thought was best. But in practical

terms it meant that there was wide variation in practice across GIDS. A type of 'clinician lottery' emerged. For any given young person, their experience of assessment could be totally different depending on whose caseload they were assigned to. A young person could receive ten, 15, even 20 sessions before a referral to endocrinology would be considered – or they might be told that puberty blockers were the way to go within an hour or two.

These different ways of practising didn't just exist within GIDS's main London base, where all these testimonies come from, but its other sites around the country, too.

9

SPEED IN LEEDS

'I'd say 90 per cent, genuinely, were three sessions,' says Andrea Walker, a former social worker who worked at GIDS Leeds.*

The 'fourth session' would see the GIDS clinician accompanying the young person to the endocrinology clinic at Leeds General Infirmary to receive further information on puberty blockers. 'That's what took me over the edge in the end,' she says. It's impossible to verify the claim: GIDS have never placed detailed information on the length of assessments in the public domain, broken down by individual years and its different sites. It has only provided a broad average spanning many years of clinical work. Between January 2013 and December 2018, 'the average number of GIDS appointments before a young person is seen by our endocrinology team is 7.'[1]

Walker is discussing the early years of GIDS Leeds – 2013, 2014, 2015. Young people didn't just face a potential clinician lottery; according to some there was a postcode lottery, too. Mermaids, Walker says, was 'very active'. They'd even accompany some families to their assessment appointments at GIDS and sit in the waiting room as support. Just as in London, many of the young people seen were highly complex. With her background in social work, the most complicated referrals – those involving looked-after children, historical sexual abuse, self-harm – would be put on her desk. The team in Leeds at

---

* Not their real name.

the time was tiny. Walker tried her best, but it was difficult. She would try to talk about gender being a social construct, and how the young person saw themselves, 'but they weren't really there for that; they were there for the drugs.' She would try to have difficult, challenging conversations about what a medical transition might really be like, she says, and what changes to the body would take place, but it was 'soul-destroying work'. Although it was important to be honest, in order to try to gain informed consent, 'actually you're dismantling these fantasies of young people, aren't you?' she says. 'That's what I felt I was doing. I was making young people who are already really sad and vulnerable, really, really sad.' Some, but by no means all, appeared to be facing homophobia, often internal. It was 'shocking' to her that young people felt 'it's not okay to be gay' in the twenty-first century.

With some young people, Walker would try to delay and not refer for puberty blockers after three sessions. 'Some of them I did delay, and they would come back and would say the feelings are less intense. And I go, "Amazing, go away, come back in six months," you know. Some of them would get Mermaids on board.' When that happened, there'd be pressure to refer to endocrinology, she says. 'We were answering to Mermaids,' Walker states definitively.*

There were some who thrived after going on the medical pathway, Walker recollects. And she talks about them fondly and with pride. She still sees a couple from a distance and can see how well they're doing as adults. 'What I want to be really clear about is that my experience at GIDS hasn't made me feel anything negative towards the trans community. Trans people exist and are real.' She just felt that not everyone the service was seeing would continue to identify as trans forever. Her sense was that perhaps only 2 or 3 per cent would. 'And I have concerns about the assessment process. And I have concerns about that particular group of psychologists' understanding and

---

* The head of GIDS Leeds, Dr Sally Phillott, said she did not agree with this assessment. 'At that time Mermaids was an active support group that supported many of the families being seen at GIDS,' she said. 'However, no group changed the way in which clinical decisions were made or judgements exercised. We followed the NHS England service specification when referring to the endocrinology team.'

engaging in therapeutic intervention, and what that means to work with children.'

On paper, Leeds assessments looked thorough enough. But unlike the model being followed in London, sessions in the assessment phase would often take place three months apart, not every month, clinicians have told me. Having spoken to some former service users of GIDS Leeds, these long gaps were not seen as helpful. It felt like starting afresh every time.

'What they say is that we have in-depth assessments that can last up to nine months,' Walker explains. That sounds like a long time to any other psychological or social work practitioner. 'I could do a fostering form in six months. That's an in-depth piece of work... but that's meeting once or twice a week. So when as a practitioner I'm hearing a nine-month assessment, I'm thinking, "Fucking hell, you're asking all the questions that could possibly be asked." No. You've met them four times.'

Seeing young people further apart allowed GIDS Leeds to keep on top of their waiting list better, too. It meant they could open more cases at any one time. And that, according to Walker, is solely how the service was judged. Leeds was seen to be doing well, 'a bastion of good practice', because it had a shorter waiting list. Those working in London at the time also recall how 'proud' the Leeds team was that it 'didn't have a waiting list like us'.

Dr Matt Bristow frequently travelled to Leeds during this time. He says it was 'quite common for people to only have three assessment appointments' there. It was 'much more standard' than in London. 'I think that they started to develop their own ways of practising,' he explains. 'One of the reasons for me going up to Leeds, and for people from Leeds coming down to London for training days and the away days and things, was trying to join up the service. But actually, there were differences in the way that different teams operated.'

An experienced GIDS Leeds clinician recalls differently. Yes, there were large cultural differences between Leeds and London, but her personal experience was of 'snobbery from some in the London team'. The Leeds site was, she says, 'seen as a poor relation culturally and I believe some thought, intellectually'. This clinician agrees that Leeds was often 'celebrated' for its activity. They saw more cases on a daily basis. But, she says, a higher level of activity 'does not equate to shorter or shoddy assessments'.

She confirms that three-session assessments did happen, but they certainly weren't the norm. Young people were given as many sessions as they needed, she says. But she recalls one, rare example she worked on with a colleague. This young person, she says, was mature, 'at the older end', and had clearly done 'a lot of psychological work'. And they were fully socially transitioned. 'And so we did three appointments, but over two days.' This speed was a one-off, but three sessions *was* enough for some of these young people, she believes. 'If you had somebody who was really settled in a social transition, there's no social or psychological issues, sometimes… there's nothing else it can be.' If there had been cross-gender identification since early childhood which had strengthened in puberty, 'it'd be cruel to delay it any further,' this clinician says. Some cases, she insists, were 'straightforward'.

Can three sessions be enough? For some it will be, for others it won't, says Matt Bristow. 'If you're just trying to do tick-boxing and seeing if someone meets diagnostic criteria, three sessions probably is enough, because a lot of people will meet diagnostic criteria. And the question is, have they thought about the decisions and what that then means for them?… And I think it meant that the assessment was shallower. It was, I guess, more of a psycho-medical assessment, rather than a more psycho-social, emotional assessment.'

While there were cultural differences between the two teams, in 2016 GIDS's main base adopted an innovative idea developed by the Leeds team – the 'Older Adolescent Pathway'.

Faced with more referrals and a growing waiting list, it had been clear for some time that young people who were older adolescents – 16 or 17 – when referred would never get to be seen by GIDS. By the time they reached the top of the list, they would either be too old to be seen by a service for under-18s, or have only 'limited time to complete a standard assessment'.[2] Assuming they still wanted to transition or wanted the opportunity to talk about their gender identity with a professional, they would have to be referred to an adult gender clinic and begin the wait all over again.

To try to help these young people and relieve some of the pressure on the waiting list, a new pathway was designed. It aimed 'to provide a service of value to the client, with a limited time-frame available, in the context of ensuring a secure and seamless transfer to the adult service chosen by the young person'.[3] Teenagers aged 16 years and nine months or over were eligible.

The pathway had three stages. First, the young person would receive a booklet called 'All About Me'. This asked questions about 'history, development and experience of the young person's gender'.[4] Young people were also sent 'a battery of standardised questionnaires', which explored 'general wellbeing, social responsiveness, early and more recent gender history and body image'.[5] They'd then be invited to a group presentation at GIDS, along with up to fourteen others and their parents. 'It wasn't intimate,' says Dr Anna Hutchinson. The group would then split. 'I helped run one of these parent groups once,' she recalls. 'There would be the young person's group facilitated by a few psychologists and there'd be the parents' group facilitated by a few psychologists, which was mainly a presentation and then a discussion. A Q and A, quite informal.

'Then after that… they would be given the choice of coming back for a one-to-one.' This was the final stage of the pathway – a single follow-up appointment with a GIDS clinician. This, according to the full presentation on the pathway, gave the young person the opportunity to discuss any information already shared with the service, any difficulties they were currently facing, and future plans – 'i.e. further sessions at GIDS, adult services or no further service'[6] – and provide 'space to reflect'. After one face-to-face appointment under this pathway, 'this will, for some, *conclude a brief assessment* [emphasis added].' Having had a 'brief specialist assessment', young people could then go to adult services, equipped with a 'detailed report' from GIDS.[7]

The GIDS clinicians who devised the pathway hailed it a success. It resulted in a 'a reduction in the waiting list and waiting times', they said, and 'the majority of young people were satisfied'.[8]

Others described the adolescent pathway as 'fast-tracking'.

Here were young people being seen by GIDS twice – only once in a one-to-one capacity – and then being referred to adult services. Some young people who took part certainly saw it as a quicker way through the system. Theo, a female who identifies as non-binary, detailed their experience of the pathway via a series of YouTube videos.[9]

It began with a letter in July 2016. 'The letter basically says I'm too old to go to… the children's clinic, come on to this group thing… And they're gonna do like a mini assessment or something like that.' Theo didn't learn much from the presentation for young people, but was impressed by the information given to parents.

The young people were offered appointment dates there and then if they wanted to take up the offer of a one-to one appointment. This would be where GIDS would 'put together a mini assessment, you know a really small one, because they've seen us, like, twice'. The service would then make a referral to an adult clinic if that's what the young person wanted. Theo waited three weeks to be seen. The face-to-face session doesn't sound too probing. The GIDS staff went through what Theo had written on the various forms and asked about their childhood, background and mental health. Theo reveals in their videos that they have a history of self-harm and, in later social-media posts, of depression. At one point in the hour-long session, Theo says they broke down in tears. The GIDS staff responded kindly, but it was close to the end of the allotted time. 'And at the end, they sort of said, "Right, you're going to be sent to an adult clinic…" [They] said I fit all of their kind of criteria that they were looking for.'

Theo decided on the Nottingham Centre for Transgender Health. The waiting time was shorter, they say, because of the GIDS referral, and Nottingham had received Theo's 'mini assessment' before the first session. While the Nottingham clinician asked a few questions about Theo's family and childhood, it wasn't challenging. 'The easiest I've had it so far,' says Theo.

Another appointment was offered in two months' time. Theo says that again they were told that 'because of the whole Tavistock thing, he was going to try and rush it for me. And he did.' At that appointment the discussion mostly centred around testosterone: 'effects of T [testosterone], side effects, increase in libido, growth, masturbation. He gave me the consent form for T, and I signed that.'

GIDS's 'limited' assessment, which had included just one proper session with a clinician, had sped up the whole process. According to Theo, Nottingham didn't feel they needed to probe too deeply, and the time between appointments was shortened. Having a diagnosis of gender dysphoria from GIDS meant less probing in adult services, or some adult clinics at least, Anna Hutchinson says. 'The adult service was depending on and trusting that GIDS had already done a decent assessment. So rather than starting from scratch with their 18-year-olds, they would say, "Oh, this is somebody who already has the diagnosis," and then they go from there.' It has not been possible to pinpoint precisely when the Older Adolescent Pathway began. But it was certainly up and running in the summer of 2016. It was still running – in Leeds at least – in October 2018. According to GIDS's official presentation, the groups ran quarterly.[10] With up to 15 young people attending each time, and groups running in both Leeds and London, it seems reasonable to estimate that several hundred young people may have gone down this route.

Confirmation of the pathway was provided by Tavistock chief executive Paul Jenkins via email. In September 2018, a group of parents raised concerns about a number of aspects of the care that GIDS was providing, including whether it was offering a thorough assessment to *all* of the young people it was seeing. They wrote to GIDS director Polly Carmichael, copying in the entire Tavistock and Portman board. And they asked specifically about the Older Adolescent Pathway. They wanted to know 'to what extent those attending GIDS aged 16.5 years and over can be certain to receive a full assessment... Is it likely that older referrals might receive a group assessment with a single face to face appointment geared to completing a referral to the adult service?'[11]

Paul Jenkins's response a fortnight or so later attempted to reassure. 'If an assessment is not possible in the timeframe before referral to adult services, we will ensure that this is clear in the report we write,' he said. However, he then acknowledged that some adolescents are indeed receiving a different model of care. 'In Leeds referrals of older adolescents are carefully screened; some attend a one-off group session.

Others who are not considered suitable – usually on the basis of the complexity of their presentation – are not offered this.'[12]

While acknowledging the existence of the adolescent pathway, Jenkins is insistent that 'it is not fast-tracking'. A month later, in November 2018, GIDS director Polly Carmichael appeared on national television to repeat the claim. The parents' letter had been leaked to the *Observer* newspaper and the BBC's Victoria Derbyshire questioned Carmichael about it.[13] 'We absolutely don't fast-track young people,' Carmichael said. 'I just want to reassure, really, that, you know, we always precede anything with a thorough psychosocial assessment.'[14]

A clinician who worked on the Older Adolescent Pathway told me that the intention was to 'give people something when they had nothing and were at a particularly vulnerable time in life'. She questions how the report provided by GIDS could be treated as a full assessment by adult services. 'It was not a comprehensive assessment at all,' she says, and was never intended to shorten any 'assessment in adults'. Indeed, she says, some adult clinics at least were informed of the pathway and what it entailed. They should have known that these young people needed to be assessed properly.

Anna Hutchinson can empathise with these views. 'I hadn't seen it like that either when I was in the process, trying to improve this impossible system. But actually, when push comes to shove, we *were* fast-tracking them.' Hutchinson explains that she and the service as a whole, quite rightly, had been so concerned about 'distressed children languishing on a waiting list' that this pathway seemed a positive development. It was offering some kind of service. 'In a way it felt like an improvement. But in reality, when you step back, it wasn't necessarily a safe pathway at all.'

Hannah

Hannah was 15 when she came out as trans.

She was in year 10 at school and finding life generally quite tough. 'When you know something isn't quite right, you struggle to maintain a focus and... you struggle with everything else that's going on,' she explains.

Hannah grew up in a liberal family in rural southern England. They had gay friends and she 'was exposed to a lot of queer communities coming from a theatre background'. Her parents supported her when she penned them a letter saying that she was trans, but school was more difficult. 'After coming out, I couldn't go back. I dropped out fully and completely,' she says. Within 'a week or two' of her announcement, Hannah was being home-schooled.

It wasn't, Hannah says, that the school did anything particularly wrong, or that she faced severe bullying; she just says it didn't feel 'feasible' for her to return to school in a new gender. It had never been an easy environment, she explains. 'I was already quite low on the social chain at school... I wasn't really a cool person.' She says she faced some bullying, but wouldn't describe it as 'bad', and instead was largely left alone by other children. 'I was kind of so low on the social chain that it was kind of like, you know, you wouldn't even want to bully me.' Hannah laughs as she says this, but it seems an extraordinarily sad reflection. Hannah describes herself back then, in the spring of 2015, as a 'nerdy, geeky sort of kid', who cared more about getting good grades than being socially popular.

She studied at home for a few months before starting year 11, GCSE year, at a nearby college. It was a chance to begin afresh, and she attended with a new name – Hannah – dressed as a girl and using female pronouns. She studied for English and Maths GCSEs.

Prior to coming out as a trans girl, Hannah had been seen by CAMHS on at least a monthly basis since the age of six – a decade of specialist mental health help. I asked what CAMHS had been helping with. Looking back, Hannah believes her childhood difficulties can be explained by her struggles with gender identity issues; there just wasn't the language or knowledge available to see it that way at the time.

Hannah describes how there were early signs that she was trans, and not a boy. 'I did ballet dancing, and I hated sports, which was a very strong indicator of more of a feminine leaning, than a masculine leaning,' she says. She didn't have a lot of other male friends growing up and always preferred female company. It was CAMHS who referred Hannah to GIDS.

It's a long way from Hannah's home to the Tavistock Centre, and she and her parents would set off at the crack of dawn to begin the long train journey to make it in time for her GIDS appointment. Immediately, Hannah says, GIDS clinicians seemed different from other professionals she had seen. 'You felt listened to, and I think this is the key factor… [For] the first time in your life, you felt like someone understood you.' It felt 'validating'. The main goal of the GIDS assessment, Hannah explains, 'is to try and work out is this gender dysphoria or anything else?' She says she would be asked when her feelings of confusion surrounding her gender began: 'Was there anything leading up to this that may have caused it like, was this a family trauma or… different sorts of events that could have affected you to feel this way?… And they just wanted to listen to your answers.'

Sitting alongside her family, Hannah would discuss her hobbies, interests and backstory so that GIDS could try to see the 'big picture'. 'They want to know, like, your home life, you know, who do you live with? And, for me, my family was always very supportive. It was always very hands on. And I lived in a very small rural area, so there was that factor of like, how does my local area view this sort of stuff? There was a lot of that.'

She says it felt like genuine exploration, and not overly intrusive. But, she says, responding to criticism levelled by some families that the questioning is too personal, 'they have to be intrusive' to some extent. 'Sometimes it can be a bit daunting, but for me personally, like, I understood that it was all part of the process.' She says, 'You do have to have some tolerance.'

At her fourth appointment Hannah brought up the topic of puberty blockers.

Children and young people referred to GIDS are told in their acceptance letters a bit about what to expect from the service, including that an assessment usually consists of four to six hour-long appointments.[1] It's perhaps unsurprising that some young people, Hannah included, might enquire about physical interventions once they reach the fourth appointment. 'It was instigated by me. I think there's this factor of like, they never wanted to put words in your mouth,' Hannah explains. She insists that GIDS only wanted to listen to her, but she knew that blockers and cross-sex hormones were what she wanted. 'So I kind of just blurted it out. And they were like, oh okay.'

In March 2016, aged 16, and almost exactly a year after Hannah had first come out as a trans girl, she attended UCLH to be given medical information about puberty blockers. She'd been referred there after her fifth GIDS appointment. All of the information about blockers – how they worked on the body, side effects, potential risks and benefits – was provided by UCLH, not GIDS, Hannah says. After she had completed her assessment and been deemed suitable for them.

Hannah describes the information she was given about the blocker as 'very in-depth'. The team at UCLH, she says, was honest about what was known about the blocker, and what remained unknown. 'They really broke us down on all of the pros and cons of blockers to the highest degree.' Hannah and other young people attending the information session were given a lot of paperwork to take away, study and talk through with their families. She says there were warnings about 'the risk of blood clots and how different things – like if you smoke or drink alcohol – could affect the blockers'. There were a few months between appointments at UCLH to think through whether this was what Hannah really wanted, but she felt sure at her next UCLH appointment. She began taking blockers in the summer of 2016.

Hannah says she felt thoroughly supported throughout her time at GIDS. She had an entire network of professionals engaged in her care – CAMHS, her local GP, as well as the teams at GIDS and UCLH.

After 15 months on the blocker, and still under the care of GIDS, she began cross-sex hormones – oestrogen in her case. Hannah says this was approved after an 'intense discussion' at UCLH with the endocrinologists, her parents and her GIDS worker. She was asked what she thought her next steps might be.

Hannah says she hadn't asked for the meeting, but she just thought this was what happened when someone reached a certain age – she was 17 by then – and had been on the blocker for over a year. The discussion centred around how she saw herself in terms of her transition in a few years' time. 'And for me, personally, you know, I brought it up that I wanted to go on hormones.'

There was no additional assessment for this next step – the first step involving known irreversible changes. This was the case for all young people attending the service at that time. Once they had been approved for puberty blockers, it was most likely that would move on to cross-sex hormones without any further major input from GIDS. 'They kind of lightly discussed the pros and cons. But by this point, you know, you've probably done a lot of home research… and I was at a point where I was, like, very content listening to other people's stories and, you know, you surround yourself with people that are gonna help you get an understanding.'

Hannah says, for her, this process included meeting people online and attending 'queer youth groups', as well as pride events and open days offered by GIDS and other gender clinics.

Shortly after starting oestrogen, she was referred on to adult services at Charing Cross Gender Identity Clinic.

Hannah has documented her entire transition journey via YouTube.[2] As well as providing regular updates on the medication she is taking, and answering queries from other young people who may be questioning their gender identity, she also tries to be honest about the nature of some of the physical interventions involved in transitioning.

Although she's clear that she was provided with significant quantities of information about puberty blockers, Hannah has spoken about them being something of an experimental intervention. In September 2017, having been on blockers for 15 months, and just started on oestrogen, Hannah told her viewers that anyone at this point who had been on blockers was, essentially, a 'guinea pig'.[3] 'What I mean by guinea pig is that you're pretty much testing blockers,' she says. 'If you're watching this in 2017 you're probably a guinea pig… the only thing they do know for definitely [*sic*] is that they stop puberty and that your bones go a bit weird, hence why you may have a few bone density tests. The NHS know absolutely nothing about blockers!'

Hannah talks openly about the affect blockers have on someone's sex drive – it eliminates it, she says – and their potential impact on bone density. Like everyone on the blocker, she has been subjected to yearly bone density scans since starting treatment more than five years ago, with the doctors carrying them out always being 'very respectful'. How does she feel about the potential risk to her bones? 'There's a side effect with any medication,' she says. 'When you see it on paper, it can be quite frightening. But, you know, weak bones, as long as you can support that with maybe other medications or, you know, more dairy intake or whatever it is, you know, there's always extra support.' She says the regular monitoring makes her feel like she's in 'safe hands'. Hannah says that her own accretion of bone density has 'definitely slowed', but adds that 'everybody's body is different'. While she has to keep it in mind, it's 'not necessarily a worry'. 'I'm not necessarily the most outgoing, you know, rock-climbing, wall-climbing [person]; I spend my time editing video. So, of course, you know, for me, I don't necessarily need ultra-strong bones all the time.'

Tran girls continue to take puberty blockers to suppress testosterone, even when starting on oestrogen. This can only stop when they can no longer produce the male hormone, after genital surgery. Once on cross-sex hormones, however, Hannah says there are fewer concerns about bone density. Bones can begin to strengthen again.

In 2021, Hannah says she's happy with where she is in her transition and, though she hasn't ruled it out, isn't currently seeking surgery. 'I'm pretty content with who I am and what I do and how I live my life,' she says. 'Of course, you know, ideal scenario, I would be making movies all day, every day. But that's not transition-related! My struggles now are more every 22-year-old struggles: focusing on career, focusing on family and working.'

Hannah is so happy with her treatment from GIDS that, since moving on to adult services, she has acquired an active role in helping it develop. She shares a much-abridged version of her story via GIDS's official website to promote at the work of GIDS and help young people and their families know what to expect from the service.[4]

At 22, Hannah continues to have oestrogen. She wears hormone patches – rather than receive injections or take pills – which she changes, just like a sticky plaster, every Saturday and Wednesday.

Hannah's work life is almost indistinguishable from her personal trans identity. Her YouTube vlogging of her own transition journey has transformed into what she hopes will be a successful career, making trans-related video content, including at Pride events across the UK. But at the moment she receives little income from her film work. Some is done for free. She is also involved in advocacy work, trying to secure better facilities for trans people in her local area. 'My life is very full on, you know, trans-related and all things. Gender is kind of my main focus.'

Since leaving GIDS, Hannah has grown increasingly involved with the service and the wider Tavistock and Portman Trust. She's been part of the GIDS stakeholder group and is now part of the Trust-wide forum – a group that aims to reflect patient voices in the services provided.[5] The Tavistock, under the leadership of CEO Paul Jenkins, is deeply committed to ensuring that 'the trust keeps in mind the experience of patients in every aspect of its work'.[6] This view – that health services benefit when they specifically listen to their patients – is held widely across the NHS, and indeed the Health and Social Care Act 2012 places a legal duty on NHS organisations to include patients when planning or developing services.[7] This is generally known as Patient and Public Involvement (PPI).

When we speak, at the end of 2021, Hannah has just been involved with the recruitment of new clinicians to join the GIDS team.

She says she has done this at least 30 times, possibly more, over the last four or five years and for clinicians at all levels. She's allowed to question prospective GIDS staff members directly, and feed back on who she thinks might be best suited to the role.

What does she look for in a GIDS clinician? Personality, she says. Warmth, charisma and confidence. 'If you're not confident around a young person, how are they going to feel confident sharing very intimate details with you? There needs to be that level of trust and support there.' During the time she has been part of GIDS recruitment efforts, Hannah says 'times have definitely shifted'. She says there is now more education around trans issues, with the response being given by those who want to work at GIDS feeling 'more attuned towards young trans individuals' rather than 'just general young people'.

GIDS jobs interviews now begin in a different way too. 'We start off by using pronouns. That never used to happen before. You usually say, "Hi, my name is this, and this is what I do. And my pronouns are this." And, you know, to some degree it's a lot more gender-focused than it ever was.'

Hannah, like other former GIDS patients who sit on recruitment panels, is privy to all the questioning put to candidates. And while the final decision of who to hire is not down to her, she's able to provide her opinion on who is best suited to the job.

Outside recruitment for GIDS, Hannah has also had a say on how the service might be improved. She wouldn't be drawn on details, replying politely, 'I discuss it with the board. So, I won't say.' But she says that she is confident that GIDS is in 'good hands' and that 'the long goal is fantastic'. She says she feels that the 'negativity' GIDS has attracted in the media feels 'unfair'. 'I feel like sometimes the press can do a little bit of a better job talking to people... Don't go to the service direct, you know... talk to the young people under their service and see what they have to say.''*

---

* Early in 2022, Hannah told her followers on social media that she had experienced a three-week period of homelessness. The author was worried, as Hannah seemed vulnerable, and so contacted her to see if she was all right. Though it had been difficult, Hannah said she had received help and remained characteristically optimistic.

10

RAISING CONCERNS

When some clinicians thought about what was going on, they were extremely alarmed. Their concerns had grown and been cemented through 2016 into 2017. And they raised them within the service.

'I have recently had to disabuse three separate CAMHS teams about what it is we offer,' Melissa Midgen explained to the GIDS Executive. 'Unfortunately, there is an unhelpful conflation of GIDS with the "Tavistock": they could not believe that we did not offer therapy.'[1] Others had taken it as read that an institution like the Tavistock would be providing therapeutic solutions, as well as medical. They were wrong. But equally, there were some in GIDS who believed it would be wrong to 'impose therapy' on young people. 'They haven't asked for therapy. They haven't given consent for therapy,' internal meeting minutes show one clinician saying.[2]

GIDS director Polly Carmichael confirmed to the Tavistock's council of governors that the service was not offering its young patients any therapy at all. Responding to an enquiry as to what GIDS offered in terms of 'face to face counselling and psychotherapy', Carmichael 'said that the national service did not provide psychological support and that if required they would consult with the local psychotherapists to do the work through CAMHS'.[3]

The only concrete thing GIDS could offer to try to alleviate the distress felt by the young people attending the service, staff felt, was physical intervention.

And some felt 'trapped' by the clinical pathway at GIDS. Staff felt it was incumbent on them to explain why they would *not* put someone forward for puberty blockers, rather than the other way round. On occasion, if desperate parents complained about the decision not to refer their child for blockers, they would simply be assigned to a different clinician, who would refer the child anyway.

Anastassis Spiliadis was on the receiving end of two such requests in his more than four years at GIDS. Both involved extremely complex family set-ups and backgrounds, where the young person had not left their home for a number of years. 'They both wanted to go on the blocker straight away,' he says, but he and his co-worker had agreed that this would not be appropriate. 'We need to think about the whole of the person and their mental health,' he'd argued. Both families requested that different clinicians take over. 'This was accommodated straight away,' Spiliadis says, 'and they both ended up on the blocker.' Although these cases in theory would go to whoever had space in their diaries, in his experience (and others') families who complained ended up being given to 'clinicians who we all knew it was much easier to get on hormones through them, rather than other clinicians'.

It's not unusual or unreasonable to ask for a second opinion. These GIDS clinicians absolutely accepted that. And GIDS being an NHS monopoly provider was acknowledged as being difficult for parents. What concerned them was the *way* such requests were handled and that their clinical expertise did not appear to be respected by those most senior in the service. In other services, Spiliadis explains, requests for another clinician would be discussed as a team. There would be a chance to analyse and reflect on what might have happened to the therapeutic relationship. Then, if the team agreed a change of clinicians would be 'important and necessary', they would agree on how best to do that, organise a handover session and try to reflect on what had worked and what hadn't. 'There was none of that at the Tavi,' he says.

What also worried him was that some complaints and requests for a change of clinician were not coming from the families themselves, but from Susie Green at the charity Mermaids. And these would be agreed to, too. 'I remember thinking and talking to [Tavistock chief executive] Paul [Jenkins] and saying that this is really inappropriate – how come a person who's the director, or the CEO of a charity, is entitled to request a change of clinicians on behalf of a family?' Spiliadis says. Others say that while Green would contact GIDS, they didn't see her influencing clinical decisions. 'Any correspondence or any contact we received from her, you just sent it to seniors,' one clinician said.

That Green would contact GIDS on behalf of specific families is not in doubt. And the charity's serious data breach which came to light in 2019 confirmed it. It also confirmed that, such was the closeness of the relationship between GIDS and Mermaids, Polly Carmichael's line manager – Sally Hodges – agreed to 'co-ordinate' the content of GIDS's website with Mermaids so that they were 'consistent'. 'It would be valuable to think with you about the content going forward,' Hodges wrote in November 2016. In a separate email, Polly Carmichael told Susie Green it was good to be working together on a different project.[4] The service specification also allowed Mermaids to refer young people to GIDS.

Clinicians were also concerned about the levels of autism and neurodiversity they were seeing in young people referred to GIDS and wondered whether this might be impacting on their trans identification. Autistic young people tend to be more rigid in their thinking and see issues, not just gender, in a black-and-white way.[5] It wasn't that anyone thought that it was not possible to be both autistic and trans, but clinicians openly questioned whether the over-representation of autistic young people in the service warranted pause for thought and a change in practice. Some staff feared that they could perhaps be unnecessarily medicating autistic children. Less than 2 per cent of children in the UK are thought to have an autism spectrum disorder (ASD).[6] Yet, according to GIDS, 'around 35% of referred young people present with moderate to severe autistic traits.'[7]

Despite the changing demographics of the young people being referred, with very different histories prior to their trans identification or gender identity difficulties, the service was unable and not commissioned to provide more than one treatment pathway – physical transition. And while it would be the case that for *some* the solution to their gender dysphoria would be to transition, it wouldn't be for all. Some staff say that even when their clinical judgement was that it was not right to refer for puberty blockers without further exploration, there would be pressure from the GIDS Executive to do so anyway. This wasn't a universal experience, and other clinicians say they did not feel under pressure to refer for blockers, and that they were supported in their decisions not to do so.

For some staff it felt there was pressure from everyone to refer for blockers – from the GIDS leadership, outside groups like Mermaids and Gendered Intelligence, patients and their parents. There were also cases where it felt that the push for medical intervention and transition wasn't coming from the young person themselves, but rather from their family. Clinicians feared they may be seeing fabricated or induced illness (FII), a presentation previously referred to as 'Munchausen's by proxy'.

Anastassis Spiliadis recalls a case where he believes this was 'very clear'. 'The young person said that "my mum wants this for me", or "my mum wants the blocker more than I do". I mean, that was very solid evidence that something needs to happen.' The family situation was incredibly complicated. There was sexual abuse and domestic violence in the background, and the family were reluctant for others to be involved. Spiliadis and his colleague agreed that they would not be putting the young person forward for puberty blockers, given how much was going on, and 'because there was so much more to explore'.[8]

He says that despite their significant clinical concerns, Polly Carmichael suggested they refer the young person for puberty blockers.[*]

Others have relayed similar stories with similar outcomes. Not just about cases of suspected FII, but where their clinical judgement was not to refer to endocrinology, but there was pressure from the

---

[*] Anastassis Spiliadis repeated this claim in a witness statement affirmed under oath in the employment tribunal between Sonia Appleby and the Tavistock and Portman NHS Foundation Trust. He was cross-examined about various aspects of the statement. BBC *Newsnight* also broadcast the claim. When BBC *Newsnight* broadcast this allegation along with others in June 2020, the Tavistock and Portman NHS Foundation Trust responded by saying: 'GIDS is a safe and caring service which supports a wide range of children,' and: '[We] strongly refute the allegations put to us by *Newsnight*.' They did not provide any further detail on individual allegations.

Executive to do so. They were surprised by how much concern there seemed to be around not upsetting families or appearing to be punitive.

Anna Hutchinson and Natasha Prescott also recall cases where they suspected FII. Prescott explains that she would take them to supervision, 'talk about them in clinical discussion groups' and try to work with other agencies, but GIDS as a service dealt with these cases 'ineffectually'. These cases were not common. FII is rare and incredibly difficult to prove. But most clinicians I have spoken with say they suspected it in at least one or two cases that made up their large case-loads. From November 2019, GIDS formally recognised it as an issue too, as part of new safeguarding procedures, explaining how clinicians 'may become concerned about a parent/carer or other significant adult being overly-invested in the child's gender identity and being the main driving force behind the child's social and medical transition'.[9] Safeguarding is the term given to actions taken to promote the welfare of children and protect them from harm. That means protecting them from abuse and maltreatment, preventing harm, and ensuring they are cared for safely.[10] All NHS staff have a statutory responsibility to safeguard children.[11]

It was abundantly clear to some staff that things at GIDS were far more complicated than the assessment process allowed for. With some young people, the dysphoria appeared to have been immediately preceded by a traumatic event, such as the loss of a parent or a sexual assault. This wasn't being adequately taken into account by the service as a whole, some felt. 'When people were talking about cases where there had been actual sexual abuse, people found it hard to think about that in relation to gender and whether the two might be in some way linked,' Matt Bristow explains. People didn't want to look too closely at what such an experience might mean for a young person and how they relate to their body, he says. 'For example, if it was someone with a biologically female body who's being abused by a male, then I think a question to ask is whether there's some relationship between identifying as male and feeling safe.'

There were other instances that raised 'red flags', says Matt Bristow, recalling one case where a young person was being sent gifts by an adult trans woman living abroad, and the young person had told

Bristow and his co-worker that they were planning to go and live with this person. The teenager also had an 'unusual kind of profile' he says, in terms of *what* they wanted to change about their body. The GIDS pair took the case to a team meeting, explaining they did not feel the young person should be referred to UCLH for puberty blockers yet. There was too much going on. He says the response they received from the Executive was 'fairly robust, vicious' even.* They were told that it was their clinical judgement not to refer, and that was accepted, he says, 'But it was clear that they felt very differently and felt we should be referring.'

There were even young people presenting at GIDS who didn't just identify as another gender, but as another ethnicity too. 'There were several cases in the service where a young person identified as a different nationality, usually East Asian, Japanese, Korean, that sort of thing,' Bristow says. Anna Hutchinson confirms this was the case. They would have 'quite specific ideas about transitioning and then taking on this East Asian identity as well as a different gender identity', Bristow recalls. It's hard to imagine quite what must be going on for some of these young people. The fact that they also viewed themselves as a different race was sometimes pretty much parked, and they were assessed for their gender identity difficulties as if the other identity issues were not important, or an indication that perhaps this young person might be struggling more generally.

Despite the obvious complexity of all these cases – sexual abuse, trauma, potential FII – 'the answer was always the same,' says Bristow. 'That the young people eventually get put on the blocker unless they themselves say they don't want it.'

It was not that these concerned clinicians believed that no one who had suffered trauma or abuse in the past could be trans, to the contrary. But it was whether these other difficulties had been worked through.

A significant number of clinicians were also increasingly worried that sexuality, like much else, wasn't being adequately explored in assessments. 'I think there was a lot of ignorance about sexuality,' says

* This account is also given in Dr Matt Bristow's witness statement to the *Appleby v Tavistock and Portman NHS Foundation Trust* employment tribunal, which he affirmed under oath.

Anna Hutchinson. For Matt Bristow, the issue was handled so badly that he came to view the service he was working in as 'institutionally homophobic'. Homophobic comments from young people themselves, or their families, would be an almost daily occurrence, he says.

Anastassis Spiliadis is just as critical. Homophobia was 'everywhere', he says, and manifested itself in many different ways. 'It could be completely silencing people who are gay,' he says. 'It could be dismissing the reality that sexuality can play a role in how someone identifies.' He says there were many 'negative comments about gay people'. He recalls families who remarked, 'Thank God my child is trans and not gay or lesbian.' 'We had this so many times, and we're like, do we take a position as a service when this comes up? You would surely say something if someone made a racial comment to a black clinician.'

Some young people themselves would be repulsed by the fact that they were same-sex attracted. They did not identify as gay, because they did not see themselves as of their birth-registered sex. 'I had kids telling me, "When I hear the word lesbian, I cringe. I want to die"… "I'm gonna vomit if I hear the word lesbian another time,"' says Spiliadis. Some of the natal boys would feel disgusted at being attracted to other males, too, and talk about wanting to have sex the 'normal' way. But it was more striking with the natal females. A large proportion of the teenage girls seen by GIDS were same-sex attracted. 'Initially, some of them had identified as lesbian. And some of them had experienced a lot of homophobia and then started identifying as trans. It was almost like a stepping stone,' explains Spiliadis.

Clinicians would never dream of telling a young person that they weren't trans, or that they were gay instead. But where a young person had spoken explicitly about same-sex attraction or experiences, some felt it was only right to ask about this. 'I've got one young person coming to mind,' recalls Matt Bristow. He had 'experienced horrific homophobic bullying' after telling another boy he had feelings for him. This had then spread around the school. 'In talking to this young person, I could hear lots of things which pointed towards same-sex attraction, and very little which pointed towards gender dysphoria, discomfort with a body, nothing more indicative of a trans experience. And so I did say to the person that it sounds to me, listening to you, that perhaps sexuality is maybe more important to you than gender identity.' Dr Bristow suggested thinking a little more about it and talking with other people before taking steps towards a physical transition. He recalls another case where the young person began identifying as trans 'after their partner had said that they weren't gay'. This was a same-sex couple.

Clinicians says there was a 'reluctance' from the GIDS leadership to engage properly with sexuality. It was left to gay clinicians to try to help inform the rest of the team, Matt Bristow says. 'What was then thrown back at us was that we were too close to the work and that we weren't professionally distant enough.'

Many heterosexual members of staff, he says, just didn't realise that many gender non-conforming behaviours in childhood applied just as much to children who grew up to be gay, lesbian or bisexual, as to children who would grow up to be trans: things like cross-dressing, feeling different, not necessarily fitting in with other children of their own sex, or having friends predominantly of the opposite sex.[12] 'Some things which, I guess, are fairly normal for many LGB adults were read as being indicative of a trans experience,' Bristow says.

Matt Bristow came to feel that GIDS was performing 'conversion therapy for gay kids'.[13] It's a serious claim. Some clinicians have relayed how there was even a dark joke in the GIDS team that there would be no gay people left at the rate GIDS was going.[14] 'I don't think that all of the children there were gay, by any means,' Bristow tells me. 'But there were gay children there – in my view I think there were gay children – who were being pushed down another path.'

'Were people deliberately going into this field to convert gay people?' asks Anna Hutchinson. 'Absolutely not. But the fact is the outcome might be the same.' It needed thinking about. Hutchinson advises to look at the data. What little of it we have. When GIDS asked older adolescents about who they were attracted to, over 90 per cent of natal females reported that they were same-sex attracted or bisexual.[15] Just 8.5 per cent were opposite-sex attracted – attracted to males. For the natal males, 80.8 per cent reported being same-sex attracted or bisexual, and 19.2 per cent opposite-sex attracted. These percentages are high, but are from those referred in 2012. GIDS say that in their most recent statistics – from 2015 – 60 per cent of natal males were same-sex attracted or bisexual. Thirty per cent were attracted to females. The remainder 'described themselves as not being attracted to either males or females, or as asexual'.[16] For females, over half were same-sex attracted, just under 20 per cent were bisexual, and a quarter were attracted to males. GIDS make clear that these data are by no means complete.[17] We don't know what percentage of more recent referrals have been same-sex attracted.

The pioneering Dutch study tells an equally stark story about sexuality. Of the 70 young people who feature, all of whom were deemed eligible for early treatment with puberty blockers because of persistent gender dysphoria through childhood, every single one of the 33 natal females was either same-sex attracted or bisexual.[18] Not one was attracted to males. Only one natal male was solely attracted to girls, meaning that 94 per cent of the natal males were also same-sex attracted or bisexual. Based on this data, the potential 'false positives' identified early on by the Dutch team – children incorrectly thought to be trans for life and offered medical intervention – are disproportionately likely to be those children who would go on to be gay adults.

'It seems like the people traditionally known as gay or lesbian or bisexual are definitely being impacted by gender dysphoria at a much, much higher rate,' says Hutchinson.

Older studies of gender non-conforming children highlighted that the majority of young people would not medically transition but would grow up to be gay, lesbian or bisexual adults. So it seems surprising that sexuality wasn't at the forefront of GIDS clinicians' minds as a possible outcome for the young people they were seeing; indeed, Domenico Di Ceglie had repeatedly stated in the early years of the service that most children would grow up to be gay, not trans.

Some in the trans community find the suggestion that they might be gay, rather than trans, deeply offensive. It is for them to say how they identify. It's also argued that these studies which showed that many gender non-conforming children grew up to live as gay, lesbian or bisexual adults do not apply to the current cohort of children being seen at gender clinics anyway.[19] They did not have gender dysphoria, it's argued, but were simply gender non-conforming. As we have seen, the presentations and diagnostic criteria for gender dysphoria have changed. However, to throw out all research from that era would also result in dismissing the very studies which form the basis of today's gender-affirming medical care for young people.

Matt Bristow and Anastassis Spiliadis both claim that GIDS director Polly Carmichael had implied that because of their sexuality they were unable to be 'as objective as a heterosexual member of staff'.[20] Carmichael does not accept this claim.[21]

It would be wrong to assume that it was only LGB clinicians who were concerned about homophobia or inadequate exploration of young peoples' sexuality. Most people have told me that homophobia was a problem, and particularly among the adolescent girls who were presenting in huge numbers.

But there are some who feel the claims of homophobia have been overplayed. One said that this was a narrative predominantly coming from 'a number of clinicians who were gay... so they're not coming from a neutral standpoint.'

Other clinicians acknowledged that while they suspected that some young people might be gay, the world they lived in made being trans (and straight) a preferable option. It wasn't 'converting gay kids', but rather accepting reality. GIDS psychologist Dr Alex Morris gives an example of a young person who lived in a rural part of the country, with 'no liberal wokery'. They were 'somebody who you might well thought of "is this a gay young man?" and who had absolutely thought about that... and who sort of insisted, no, no, they were a woman and they wanted to live as a woman. And there was a strong sense in which in a different world in a different place, this person could have lived happily as a gay man. But they didn't live in a different world. They lived where they did, and they didn't want to move. And they were quite happy in their community and very accepted as a trans girl.'

What do you do? Morris asks. 'Are they really gay? Or are they really trans? Or is that a really unhelpful way of thinking about it? And for me, it's an unhelpful way of thinking about it.'

Were gay clinicians 'too close' to the work as it's claimed was suggested?

It's something I've asked those who were most worried. Anna Hutchinson says there's a possibility for bias in all of us. But she keeps coming back to the data. 'Statistically it was there, other people objectively measured this in the cohort.' They were not seeing something that wasn't there. 'I wouldn't say we were overly sensitive,' says Matt Bristow. 'I think we put up with hearing homophobic remarks being made on a daily basis for a number of years. And when we tried to talk about that in the team, it was kind of ignored.'

These clinicians do not take a hard-line view on medical interventions. All supported young people in going forward for puberty blockers. But clinical experience was showing them that, just as there appeared to be different pathways *into* gender dysphoria or gender incongruence, there needed to be different ways *out* if it too. And GIDS wasn't offering that. That not everyone will require medication is something that prominent LGBT charities agree with.[22]

'With every single case and family, it's important to take time to think and… and once you have exhausted all different options of managing or understanding dysphoria, the medical intervention should be the last resort, not the first-line treatment, which it is currently,' says Anastassis Spiliadis. 'The assessment leads to a medical model or nothing,' he says. Who could tolerate going away when they're so distressed? he asks. 'I wouldn't do it. I would take up the offer of something, even if it was just medication.'

But GIDS assessments were fallible. Internal emails from 2017 show that on several occasions the service referred a young person for puberty blockers only for them not to take up the chance. Some would decide that transitioning was not what they wanted, even though they'd been deemed suitable for the medical pathway.[23] Clinicians say it was impossible to differentiate those who would benefit from those who would not.

And this was why they were calling for fundamental change.

11

SCAPEGOATS AND TROUBLEMAKERS

GIDS clinicians didn't keep serious worries to themselves.

Concerns were raised again and again. There's a paper trail that shows it.

In team meetings, the most difficult questions would be asked, says Anna Hutchinson. Are we medicating traumatised children? Are we medicating autistic children? Are we medicating children who might grow up to be gay, who are disgusted by their desires, or whose parents would (consciously or not, and for reasons including the cultural and religious) prefer their offspring to be straight? It might be unbelievable to some that parents would 'prefer' a trans child to a gay child, but several clinicians confirm that, though rare, this did happen. One described a father openly weighing up what might be the 'best' outcome for their son – a gay man or a trans woman. Another has said that there were families who could not 'tolerate' their sons being gay: 'the child then sees trans as a way out of this dilemma and the family pressure the child to go along with this.'[1]

A significant number of staff say they spoke up over a period of years – sometimes one-to-one with their supervisors, sometimes with a member of the Executive, sometimes in larger team meetings and sometimes via email. One says they were even asked by a senior GIDS member of staff if they were 'transphobic' in their exit interview from the service.

There was no shortage of outlets to raise concerns, and staff took them. Many clinicians praise the way that the Executive were so approachable, and how they generally had an open-door policy. Time would be set aside every few months in what were known as 'Fifth Tuesday' meetings (held whenever there happened to be a fifth Tuesday in the month) to talk about the issues most exercising GIDS staff – consent, or 'saying "no" (or "not yet") to physical intervention', for example. It wasn't that there was no opportunity to speak up. Nor that it was discouraged.

The issue was with how it was handled.

Two things would generally happen, clinicians explain: there would be a lot of talk but no action; and those who raised issues were labelled troublemakers.

'On the one hand, there was this kind of very Tavi culture of talking about things,' Matt Bristow says. There'd be plenty of 'interesting intellectual discussion', but that's where it would end. 'There wasn't any follow-up on that,' he says. 'It felt like it was a bit of an academic debate rather than this is a clinical problem, and how do we take this forward.'

Someone would raise concerns, and someone else would move in to shut it down. Often not in aggressive way, but it would be minimised or countered. 'So sometimes I might raise something, and it would make people feel, I don't know, quite anxious or attacked,' explains Natasha Prescott. 'But then there was a real wish to protect people from horrible, unpleasant feelings, so someone would swoop in and just make it nice.' And in this way, some staff would be spared the most difficult conversations, and from really thinking through the implications of the way GIDS was working.

'There would always be the "But it's all very complex",' explains Prescott. The work *was* complicated. But simply acknowledging that it was complicated without doing anything to address it wasn't enough for some. It would be suggested that some clinicians were 'not able to hold the balance and to really, to manage both sides', says Prescott, but 'holding the balance' essentially boiled down to doing nothing – not making any changes to the way the service operated. 'There's sometimes a point where you have to take a position,' she adds. It wasn't possible to steer a course between two dangerous monsters, as GIDS founder Domenico Di Ceglie had hoped.

'Nothing changed,' Anna Hutchinson agrees. 'It was like going to confession. You'd go, you'd talk about all the worries, you'd talk about all the potential for things to go wrong. You'd talk about all the strains on people in the system, on ethics… but we still just kept doing what we were doing.'

When her supervisor had been unable to assure her that the service was not hurting children, it wasn't good enough. There was plenty of talk in GIDS about 'managing uncertainty' but this made little sense to her. 'You're supposed to live with uncertainty when a child might be being sexually abused?' she questions. 'What does that mean?' What's more, it seemed to her that 'managing uncertainty' was sometimes precisely the opposite of what the service was doing. Referring for puberty blockers was a course of action with a near certain result.

The GIDS Executive team seemed unable to explain *why* the service was doing what it was doing. Why GIDS appeared, in so many cases, to be using medication as the first-line treatment for emotional distress. The clinical team had never discussed as a group what it even understood by the word 'transgender', staff say. Are young people born trans? Does gender dysphoria necessarily equate with being transgender for life? Hutchinson realised that the answers might be too difficult for some of the staff to bear.

'There aren't any easy answers,' Bernadette Wren has said. 'You can't plausibly develop a foundational theory of gender identity in which to ground the work,' she adds.[2] Just as we have largely given up trying to understand why someone is gay, we should do the same when it comes to gender identity. Rather than try to work out *why* someone is struggling with their gender, Wren says, 'you're better off trying to help people to live well, rather than trying, probably fruitlessly, to establish the story of how they came to feel that way.'[3]

But this view felt dangerous to some GIDS staff. It felt as if the ordinary rules of medicine and safe clinical practice had been suspended. 'Differential diagnoses' – ones that suggested other factors at play – were discouraged: it was frowned upon to suggest that something other than 'being trans' – unresolved trauma, internalised homophobia, an eating disorder, perhaps – might be the difficulty that needed addressing. And even when clinicians did spend time formulating their thoughts, many young people would still end up being referred for physical interventions if that's what they wanted.[4] But why? To avoid hurting people's feelings? Most of the team had a deep fear of appearing transphobic, especially in front of colleagues who were trans. Even suggesting that someone with dysphoria might not be transgender for life felt taboo, says Anna Hutchinson. Certain words and phrases were permitted, others were not. Where it had once been the norm to talk about 'natal males and females' in relation to patients, that was now banned. 'Assigned male (or female) at birth' was now the chosen terminology. Eyebrows would be raised at those who dared speak of 'sexed bodies'. Hutchinson recalls being frowned upon for using the word 'vagina' in a team meeting. Junior staff looked on and learnt. Those who persisted in asking difficult questions were not received well.

There was a reluctance, she says, to engage with the implications of what it would mean if not every young person treated by GIDS would be trans for life. She wanted the risks to be acknowledged, and for all assessments to explain to young people that not every single one of them was going to benefit from the medical pathway; to talk to them in detail about what that might look like. 'We needed to have the conversations and we needed to acknowledge the truth of the risks we were taking.' Yet others in the team questioned whether it was right to have those conversations. 'We have to be cautious in trying to measure the impact of adverse experience,' one clinician is recorded as saying during a staff discussion on consent.[5] 'It is right to talk about it. But they also have a right not to talk about it.'

There was wide variation in practice across GIDS, perhaps none more so than between the different regional teams that had emerged following Femi Nzegwu's report. While the primary recommendation of pausing referrals and regrouping had not been accepted, the service did undergo some form of restructuring. The differences in culture and practices between teams that resulted were viewed as a 'massive' problem by some, and one that was fed back to the service's leaders, says Natasha Prescott.

As well as the talking and not acting, those who spoke out were labelled troublemakers.

'There were always scapegoats,' explains Anna Hutchinson. 'There were always people who represented the concerns of the group, and they were always driven out one way or another.'

Prescott agrees. 'I would always say things in a very thoughtful way. I'd say tricky stuff, but I would try to make it palatable. Whereas some people were just less willing, less able, and then they would get the brunt of being branded a troublemaker.'

'In the end, I became one of those people,' says Matt Bristow. 'But it happened to others, several others, where you started to get scapegoated.' The work at GIDS was not seen as the problem, he says, rather the individual speaking up was. 'And that was a pattern that kind of repeated itself over and over again.'[6]

Bristow relayed this view to the GIDS Executive via his exit interview:

On the one hand, staff are encouraged to share ideas and dilemmas. However, when this exposes some of the most challenging aspects of the work, there is a strong message given that staff should not share their thoughts or concerns. Individuals become labelled by members of the executive team as 'trouble-makers' when they have questioned the ethics 'too much' and these labels filter down through the ranks. Whether at an unconscious or a conscious level, the service then turns on the 'trouble-makers' until they leave the service. The cycle is then repeated as new individuals are invited into the 'problem' role for the service.[7]

This 'scapegoating' would manifest itself in different, often subtle, ways: conversations in corridors, being taken to one side and being told to 'tone it down a bit', not being offered the chance to do interesting projects. 'No one ever said to me, "You'll never work in the NHS," or anything like that.' says Bristow. 'But I think it felt very dangerous. It felt explosive.'

Some staff simply left the service, unable to continue working in a way that felt so risky, and fearful of the longer-term outcomes for their patients and, perhaps, their careers. But others stayed and pleaded with those leading GIDS to act and change direction. 'I am seriously worried about where this is going to lead,' Melissa Midgen wrote to the Executive in autumn 2017.[8] 'I implore you to intervene, to contain your staff, to implement meaningful treatment pathways for the changed and complex demographic and lead us, from the top down, to be the service we all deserve.' Midgen tried to impress upon the

GIDS leadership that there was not just 'disquiet' among the team, but 'extreme concern'. Speaking out in the wider team felt increasingly risky, and so it would be in private conversations that people relayed how 'mad' they felt the situation was.

Despite the pushback from colleagues, some clinicians felt a professional and moral duty to continue speaking out. 'Because I couldn't live with myself doing the work without sharing my concerns,' Matt Bristow says. 'I couldn't just put it to one side and pretend everything's okay and pretend I didn't have the concerns, just have a quiet life. It felt too worrying, it felt too important.'

'I just couldn't comfortably keep being part of a process that was, I felt, putting children at risk, but also my colleagues at risk,' explains Anna Hutchinson. Her eight years at Great Ormond Street had provided her with a schooling in child protection, and further encouraged her to raise concerns. A year after she'd joined, the cruel death of baby Peter Connelly in August 2007 shocked the country and highlighted major flaws in the system of referring at-risk children.*

A second scandal was also unfolding during Hutchinson's tenure too. Concerns had begun to be raised that the gastroenterology department was unnecessarily giving patients potentially dangerous drugs, and managing children in a 'clinically "aggressive" way that was at odds with usual medical practice'.[9]

Hutchinson managed the psychology team in gastroenterology's sister department. Ironically, she'd joined GIDS, in part, to escape a clinical culture too reliant on medical diagnosis and treatment for managing children's distress. But she'd also seen how damaging such an environment could be, not just for the patients, but for the staff working in it, too.

---

* Peter (known for two years as 'Baby P') had been seen by professionals on at least 60 occasions, including two days before he died at St Ann's clinic, run by Great Ormond Street. A year earlier, four senior consultants had warned that there was a 'very high risk' to patient safety at the clinic, but claimed that managers were 'trivialising' their concerns. Baby P's death resulted in increased awareness at GOSH about risk-taking and when cases should be referred to children's services. See also Andrew Gilligan, 'Baby P: secret reports critical of Great Ormond Street Hospital', *Telegraph* (20 November 2009), https://www.telegraph.co.uk/news/uknews/baby-p/6615338/Baby-P-secret-reports-critical-of-Great-Ormond-Street-Hospital.html.

Two of her Great Ormond Street psychology colleagues had taken their own lives. Now, several years later, alarm bells were ringing again. She relayed this to her supervisor, who understood why she might feel so worried. It was not that Hutchinson had any specific fears for her GIDS colleagues, it was more that 'it felt like an unhealthy environment'. And that 'asking people to do things they can't achieve' isn't good for them. 'People break sometimes, and you have to be mindful of your colleagues as well as your patients.'

Faced with no discernible action from the Executive, staff began to look for other ways to raise their concerns, to other people who might listen – and act.

'Are you worried about anything?' the poster asked. 'We've got a Speak Up Champion.'

Anna Hutchinson took a picture of the poster with her phone. She didn't do anything with it for a long time. 'But after the supervisory relationship to my mind had broken down as a place to voice concerns, I thought maybe that was the next place to go.'

'Freedom to Speak Up Guardians' were introduced to all NHS trusts following the Mid Staffs scandal, which was understood to have been caused, in large part, because of a culture that ignored or silenced staff concerns. The role was introduced in an attempt to avoid another situation in which senior clinicians and managers failed to listen to what they were being told and to act upon it if required.[10] At this time, the Tavistock's Freedom to Speak Up Guardian was Gill Rusbridger, head of social work for the Trust. Her line manager was chief executive Paul Jenkins.

'I remember going and saying, "I am not whistle-blowing,"' Hutchinson smiles. Why was she so vehement about that? 'Because I was terrified. You know? Everybody in the NHS knows that we say the right things about whistle-blowers, but it's tribal, isn't it? Anybody who speaks out against a system that they're part of inevitably is going to have a hard time.'

Rusbridger was caring. She was interested in how the Trust could care for Hutchinson, who was pregnant with her second child. But she didn't tackle the concerns head on. 'It was very much focused on looking after me, as opposed to the patients,' reflects Hutchinson.

'There was a little bit of me, I think, that hoped as I told her how bad I thought it was and the risks that were being taken, that she would say, "Anna I know you're not a whistle-blower, but I have to act on this." I think I was hoping that somebody would take it off my shoulders.' Hutchinson desperately wanted someone to say that everything was fine, to explain why clinical practice was as it was, and that no one was being hurt. But they never did.

Coincidentally, just days before Hutchinson met with Gill Rusbridger, the Trust had received a visit from the National Freedom to Speak Up Guardian. Rusbridger commented how she'd been 'delighted' to 'discuss best practice for developing an open and honest culture, where staff can speak out about any concerns about unsafe patient care'.[11]

Unbeknown to Hutchinson at the time, Matt Bristow, Anastassis Spiliadis and Melissa Midgen also went to see Gill Rusbridger in 2017. At least one other did too, but there may have been more.

Hutchinson was advised by Rusbridger to take her concerns to another senior figure in the Trust – to the director of 'quality and patient experience'. Louise Lyon sat on the Tavistock and Portman's board. 'She was really senior, and she definitely had a role in making sure everything was safe and functioning well.' Over spring and summer 2017, Hutchinson met with Lyon three times, on each occasion trying to impress how worried she was about practices in GIDS. 'I think in the third meeting, she started looking a bit anxious.' Hutchinson remembers Lyon saying that she needed to act on what she was hearing. Others also sought out the ear of Lyon. She listened, acknowledged that the concerns were serious, but it was unclear to all of those involved what action resulted.

It needs to be noted that concerns were not confined to those who are named here.'

Four additional clinicians, whose identities are not known, also took their concerns outside GIDS in autumn 2017. This time to Sonia Appleby, the children's safeguarding lead for the Tavistock Trust. They told Appleby of 'challenges regarding Mermaids, rogue medics and the political expectations of the national service'.[12] Staff reported that they felt 'coerced into not reporting safeguarding issues, and to do so is "transphobic"'; that they had a 'lack of confidence in Children's Social

Care'; and that they feared that the service was seeing children who saw 'being transgender as a less oppressive option than acknowledging they are gay'.[13]

Appleby heard how staff were worried that some young children were 'being actively encouraged to be transgender without effective scrutiny of their circumstances' and that there was a 'lack of a team position regarding the clinical management of gender issues and what to do when there are safeguarding concerns whatever the genesis'.[14] Staff claimed that 'team meetings are fraught events' and made 'specific allegations that Polly [Carmichael] is unwilling to listen to these concerns'.[15]

At the time, clinical staff at GIDS's main London base, including the Executive team, numbered around 40.[16] Combined with those who sought out Gill Rusbridger and Louise Lyon, it meant that a quarter of GIDS staff, outside the Executive leadership team, were raising concerns at this time.

Although staff didn't know it then, Sonia Appleby would continue to raise their concerns for years to come.

Even after having raised concerns repeatedly with seemingly no action, Hutchinson says the situation didn't feel completely helpless. There were attempts at getting sexual orientation on the agenda a bit more, and 'people were really working hard to try and make it better'. The service was certainly not functioning well, she says, but there was a feeling that if she could just articulate her fears in a different way, perhaps the Executive would 'get it' – 'They'd understand it and we could improve the service and make it safer.'

She'd had a series of heated meetings with her supervisor Sarah Davidson and at one point been told that if she was unhappy in any way it might be best if she found another job, she says.* Now, heavily

---

* Anna Hutchinson included this claim in a witness statement supplied to the employment tribunal between Sonia Appleby and the Tavistock and Portman NHS Foundation Trust. The statement was affirmed under oath, but Hutchinson was not questioned. Hutchinson also has a contemporaneous written note of the encounter. Dr Davidson said the following in an email response: 'I recall, towards the end of her time at GIDS that Dr Hutchinson was not happy in her role. I was her supervisor. When we discussed her future, I would have noted that one of her options was to explore different roles.'

pregnant with her second child, Hutchinson knew this might be her last chance to reiterate her concerns to the service chiefs. 'I felt it was last-chance saloon, really,' she says. 'And I knew I wanted to push a bit harder than I had before.' Her next stop was Bernadette Wren, a voice who many in GIDS turned to when they needed reassurance about what they were doing, and who many speak about with respect. They had often discussed the complexity of the work together but Hutchinson 'was probably more frank' than she'd been before. 'And I was basically saying, "What are we doing?"' Hutchinson says that she and Wren acknowledged that lesbian, gay and bisexual outcomes were likely for gender non-conforming children. 'I said, "We need to be honest about this."' It was imperative that the service explore sexual identity development as well as gender identity development given that fact, she argued.

Hutchinson reads from her contemporaneous note of the conversation: 'and she said, "Polly won't keep it in mind all the time, her head is full of too much stuff. We need to be realistic." That's the quote from that meeting.'[17] It was incomprehensible to Hutchinson, 'acknowledging that we might be medicating a cohort who possibly don't need medicating'. She pushed the point. 'I think I just said, "We can't keep doing this." And that's when she said to me, 'Well, what do you want me to do about it, Anna?" To Hutchinson, it seemed like those at the top of the service felt just as stuck as she did. As she recalls it, that was the end of the conversation. 'I kind of lost my faith a bit at that point.'

Finally, in September 2017, Anna Hutchinson went to see her long-standing colleague, service lead Polly Carmichael. Hutchinson told her she was worried. She was concerned the clinicians in the service were 'at risk of confirmation bias' in their assessments, explaining that thinking had become too narrow and being trans was seen as the only outcome for these young people. She told her boss, 'I think we might be diagnosing and medicating kids who may not benefit from it in the long run.' Carmichael reminded Hutchinson that GIDS was doing a much better job than private providers, but this didn't feel good enough to Anna Hutchinson. 'Oh, Anna, you can't think like that,' Carmichael had proffered, characteristically kindly, in an attempt to alleviate the fear, 'you'll go mad!' 'And I said, "But Polly, I do think like that." And it was a bit awkward. Then we wrapped up the conversation, and I went on mat leave.'

Hutchinson had by now almost lost all hope. But there was still part of her that clung on. 'I thought if somebody grabs this, there is still so much potential to make this service safer and better. And I wanted to be part of that.'

Dr Natasha Prescott left GIDS in February 2018.

It was a difficult decision, she told the Trust at the time, and she had 'very conflicted feelings' about it.[18] But after more than five years she felt she could no longer stay. Her practice had changed dramatically as she learnt more and saw more young people. She'd started undertaking longer assessments – longer than the four-to-six-session model – but 'recognised that this approach was at odds with the pressures to assess quickly'.[19]

Prescott had been a trainee when she joined GIDS in 2012. 'I was an inexperienced member of staff,' she tells me. 'I did some work that I regret.' She is brutally honest, and takes responsibility for her work, admitting that at the beginning of her time at GIDS she wrote 'those awful assessments'. It's upsetting to 'own what you've done', she explains, but she learnt how to do the GIDS work properly by doing it. And doing it properly is more difficult. 'It's nicer and easier to give the person what they want,' Prescott explains. 'You have to be challenging and they don't always like you for it.'

While Prescott accepts that she did some work she is not proud of, she learnt, and 'once I learnt, I changed'. She tried to change GIDS too. 'And when I realised that I wasn't going to have any success, that's when I [left].' The service, she says, did not seem to learn. And this was what was so upsetting. 'It's okay that I did things that I look back and think are not okay, providing that's then a basis on which we learn,' she explains, 'not for someone else to come along and do the same thing as me and learn through the same process. That's not just ignorant, that's harmful.' This point is made repeatedly by former GIDS staff: the service seemed to 'forget' what had gone before. Whether that was the fact that adolescence was a time of fluidity; that many young people with gender-related distress would grow up to be gay or bisexual adults; or that puberty blockers almost always seemed to lead to cross-sex hormones. It seemed that the knowledge learnt from years of experience was not retained in the service or passed on to new clinicians who joined.

There was a 'choice point', Prescott says: she could stay, work towards the next promotion and develop her career – which would mean 'letting go of some things and shutting up' – or, she says bluntly, 'I could be congruent with my values. And get out.'

On her way out, Natasha Prescott relayed her concerns very clearly to the Trust, via her exit interview. She described the benefit of longer assessments 'to develop a therapeutic relationship' with a young person and to 'really engage in the dilemmas of commencing physical interventions, which have profound medical implications... and lack a substantial evidence base'.[20] She acknowledged that this lengthier and more thorough exploration was not 'a feasible service model', with the numbers of young people being referred. But, she believed, the '4–6 session assessment framework' was 'insufficient for building a relationship and doing the necessary work' with particularly the 'adolescent assigned at birth females' with often 'longstanding co-occurring difficulties' who had come to dominate referrals to GIDS.[21]

Prescott explained that those who worked in the service for many years saw that significant issues had gone 'unexplored' prior to young people starting puberty blockers – disclosures of sexual abuse and homophobic bullying, for example. They had seen that a 'significant proportion' of young people's lives had not improved while on blockers or cross-sex hormones, and 'she became increasingly worried about the work she or other services had not undertaken before irreversible interventions were commenced'. By the time Prescott left GIDS, 'she was heavily leaning towards the view that medical interventions were too readily available and that they were not suitable at the current time for the majority of young people she was assessing'. None of this is to say that Prescott was against physical interventions for some young people. She was not. The operative word is *some*. She was concerned that the GIDS model had not adapted to consider the changing nature of referrals it was seeing. She told the Tavistock, too, that 'there is increasing concern that gender affirmative therapy, if applied unthinkingly, is reparative therapy against gay individuals, i.e. by making them straight'.[22]

Just as Dr Prescott relayed these words, a small group of gay, lesbian and bisexual GIDS clinicians met with Ruth – now Baroness – Hunt, then chief executive of the UK's largest LGBT charity, Stonewall. The group had invited her to hear more about the work of GIDS, and share some of their views on the relationship between sexuality and gender identity. Anastassis Spiliadis was among those in the informal meeting. He says it was 'a really good, really fruitful discussion', and he speaks highly of Hunt. Spiliadis claims that Hunt acknowledged that perhaps more needed to be done to promote identities like butch lesbians, who tended to be 'invisible', and says that she listened to the concerns of frontline clinicians. There was agreement that GIDS would try to collaborate on this with Stonewall, Spiliadis says, but nothing more came of it. Hunt stepped down from the charity in 2019.

Those who voiced their worries about the work at GIDS could find their lives difficult not only *within* the service, but as a result of outside groups too. Having written a favourable review in an academic journal of a book whose 'central contention is that transgender children *don't exist*', GIDS psychotherapist Melissa Midgen found herself targeted by Gendered Intelligence and Mermaids, both of whom are criticised in the book.[23] Midgen expressed her view that, as things currently stand, 'we do not have sufficient evidence or understanding to know whether there are children born into the world intrinsically "trans", in "the wrong body" as it were'. Midgen sets out her view clearly. We know that there are many happy and successful trans adults, she says, and that it is 'logical to infer that some of the children and young people we see in Gids will grow into adults whose gender dysphoria is such that the only reasonable "solution" or treatment is a social role transition followed by medical intervention'. But, she adds, 'the complexity of presentation of the children seen at Gids… suggest[s] that for many of them at least there are reasons for their body dysphoria other than an inborn "trans" nature.' While some will grow up to be trans adults, others will not. 'It is both my experience, and the argument posited throughout this book, that the current socio-cultural situation is one which has permitted an inflation of the idea, and that we are indeed co-creating the very notion of the "trans kid",' writes Midgen, explaining that 'many scores of hours' had gone into the formation of her 'thoughts, ideas, concerns and dilemmas' on the subject.[24]

Following publication of the review in a specialist publication for fellow psychotherapists, chief executive of trans-led organisation Gendered Intelligence, Jay Stewart, wrote to Polly Carmichael, asking to know what steps had been taken to address the 'inappropriateness of the review'. He said he hoped that Carmichael would prevent Melissa Midgen from making any further comments in the public domain and that she (Carmichael) would have issued a public statement apologising for the review. Stewart advised that the fact of a member of the GIDS team expressing such views made him question the current relationship between Gendered Intelligence and GIDS. But Carmichael was wholly supportive of her colleague Melissa Midgen over the review.

Several months later, Mermaids mentioned the book review and Melissa Midgen in a written submission to Parliament. The charity stated that GIDS had members of staff 'who are openly unsupportive of TNB CYP [trans and non-binary children and young people]'. There was in fact nothing in Melissa Midgen's book review that suggested that she was unsupportive of the young people in her care, or that she was not trying to do the best for them and their individual circumstances. Mermaids asked that 'a thorough audit' be carried out of the views of GIDS's staff, 'to ensure every TNB child is dealt with in a respectful and supportive way'. The charity went further, arguing that training should be given to ensure all staff had 'a correct approach' to gender issues.[25]

On this occasion, GIDS neither submitted evidence to an inquiry concerning its own area of work, nor sought to publicly defend its staff whose reputations had been attacked. But the service did not heed Mermaids' demands.[26]

12

THE BELL REPORT

When Melissa Midgen went to see Dr David Bell in the summer of 2017 it was not her intention to be a whistle-blower. It was just that she, Hutchinson and others felt that, though concerns were frequently being raised and listened to on one level, no action ever followed. Perhaps someone outside GIDS, committed to the Trust's values and with extensive clinical experience, needed to be made aware of staff's worries.

Having raised their concerns within the service and now to various senior figures in the Trust, for the first time staff found someone who would not only listen, but try to do something about it.

Dr David Bell was a consultant adult psychiatrist at the Trust. A former director of postgraduate training at the Tavistock and president of the British Psychoanalytical Society, he is described by some as the most senior psychoanalyst at the Tavistock at that time. He was also the staff representative on the Trust's council of governors. Staff governors are elected by their peers to represent Trust staff and ensure they have a say in how services are run. More generally, the role of the council of governors in an NHS trust is to 'challenge the board of directors and hold the non-executive directors to account for the performance of the board'. The governors must question and challenge the board and make sure the Trust is running 'effectively and smoothly'.[1]

Bell explains that he'd had a 'constant peculiar feeling that there was something going on' at GIDS for a number of years. But nothing more than that. He says it was impossible not to notice how much and how quickly the service had grown. And he had a sense that no one in the Trust wanted to talk about the work that GIDS did in any detail.

But he hadn't anticipated what Melissa Midgen might say. Bell listened carefully. His fears had been confirmed, he says. 'I felt all my worries were now borne out, now had a proper form and articulation, which they didn't really have before. And I was very concerned.' Dr Bell enquired whether others felt the same. They did. And they also took the opportunity to speak to him.

For some, it was the first time they'd felt properly heard. 'It was the first time anybody had said to me, "Yeah, you've got a really good point," and "Yes, it does matter if we get it wrong,"' says Anna Hutchinson. Her concerns weren't minimised. Over the next 11 months, ten GIDS clinicians went to meet Bell, some on several occasions, to share their anxieties about the service – again, about a quarter of those directly working with children and young people. At each meeting, Bell took detailed notes, initially unsure of how he might use them.

Bell was shocked by what he heard. He found himself on a 'very rapid learning curve' – he was used to working with adults and had never worked with young people with gender identity difficulties, but he believed what he was hearing. He had no reason not to, he says. 'They all brought very similar preoccupations,' Bell explains, 'some people emphasising one thing more than another, but in terms of the main preoccupations that they brought, they were similar. And they most certainly did not have a rehearsed quality… It wasn't like that at all.' Some staff, but not all, were 'extremely distressed', he says. 'One person wasn't sleeping… because they kept thinking about the children they put on the [medical] pathway and felt that they'd done damage.' He felt 'disturbed' by what he was hearing, he says, and 'that this was all part of something called the Tavistock'.

What's more, he was struck by the fact that these clinicians felt afraid. 'Nine of the ten didn't come to speak to me in my office,' Bell explains. Instead, they met him off-site. He says some staff 'felt they were under surveillance'. There was plenty for Bell to be alarmed about, he says. Not just what the clinicians were relaying about the functioning of GIDS, and how anxious they were about speaking out, but also the fact that they had raised their concerns with other senior figures in the Trust before him. 'I was very shocked by that,' he says. 'What if someone had said in a hospital that they had strong reasons to believe that some of their children were being given the wrong medical treatment, by staff who worked too much under pressure? This would be explosive. And if you said that to a manager, or Speak Up Guardian, there'd be an inquiry.' The only reason he can see for the concerns not being investigated is what he saw as a 'pressure within the institution to not think – which everyone was influenced by'.

The more he heard, the more he felt compelled to do something. 'I can remember having tea with my wife,' Bell recalls, 'and saying I don't know what to do. But I think I've got to take this on.' He decided he would use his notes to compile a report that would be shared with colleagues on the council of governors. 'And I remember her saying that she'd support me in that, but did I really understand how big this was going to be? And what I was taking on?'

He didn't.

Bell confided in a few long-standing colleagues and governors too. 'I said, "Look, this is like toxic waste. You take the lid off this, Dave, you're gonna get enmeshed in something,"' says Marcus Evans, who was just about to retire from the Tavistock after more than three decades working at the Trust. 'I knew it would be trouble,' he adds. Marcus Evans is married to Sue Evans, who'd raised concerns about GIDS's practices back in 2005. He knew just how 'troubled' she had been by what she'd seen, and how seemingly nothing had changed after she'd spoken out. Marilyn Miller, who worked with Bell on the council of governors, was also made aware that GIDS staff had gone to him with concerns.

In July 2018, David Bell informed the Tavistock's chief executive and chair that he would be writing a report on GIDS. He submitted it a month later.

The report featured many of the concerns that some GIDS staff had felt and expressed for years. And it did not pull its punches. Across its 54 pages, it described the lack of a coherent clinical model underpinning the service, argued that GIDS had come to adopt an 'excessively affirmative attitude' to gender identity, combined with 'an inability to stand up to the pressure of a highly politicised external world', and asserted that many of the children were 'well rehearsed' in what to say during assessments 'in order to get the results they want'.[2]

But, predominantly, David Bell's report relayed clinicians' concerns about whether the care GIDS was providing was always safe. And if it wasn't, that the consequences for their patients might be dire.

Bell made it clear that plenty of senior figures in the Tavistock Trust had heard these worries before. He personally spoke with both Gill Rusbridger and Louise Lyon, who, he says, 'agreed that the concerns needed to be escalated'. What's more, according to Bell, the Trust's then medical director – Dr Rob Senior – had conceded that there was a need to change both the service model and the leadership of the service.[3]

'There is a repeated pattern of raising concerns… but nothing changing,' one GIDS staff member told Bell. Another explained that it was not that there was no opportunity to speak, or that it was discouraged even, but it would never result in action. 'Nothing *ever* happens,' they said. 'We are told: "We need to understand we are doing our best"… "We are doing this far better than anyone else."'[4]

Bell heard that 11 people had left in the last six months alone because they had ethical concerns.[5]

Staff told David Bell that 'those who begin to understand the difficulties and start to question, very often leave'. They are somehow 'evacuated by the system', one clinician explained. 'If staff say they are stressed then they are told "you are weak, incompetent."'[6]

'All clinicians described a pressure upon them to process referrals rapidly,' Bell wrote.[7] They stressed the highly complex nature of their cases, and the high levels of distress of those in their care. Clinicians told Bell that GIDS's service users were some of the most vulnerable, traumatised children they had ever worked with.

A small number of children, clinicians claimed, were pushed by parents to pursue a trans identity, rather than come out as gay. There were fears, more widely, that in some instances the family seemed more invested in transition than the young person themselves. Bell was told that young people had even described feeling 'let down' by the assessment process, with one quoted as saying, 'I came here [to] be able to help me tell MY story... but instead you just went along with what the family said.'[8] Bell makes a point of saying that almost everyone had raised the issue of homophobia in the service.

Staff explained how GIDS had taken on large numbers of psychologists with 'very little clinical experience' to try to cope with the rapid rise in referrals. Such inexperienced clinicians, it was feared, would not have the authority to stand up to the considerable pressure coming from families and others to refer for physical interventions. Ultimately, the pressure of work resulted in an inadequate clinical service, staff said. Caseloads could be astronomical – as high as 140 – and this meant that it was impossible to hold individual families in mind. Some explained why they'd had to leave GIDS. 'I could not go on like this,' one said. 'I could not live with myself given the poor treatment the children were obtaining,' said another.[9]

The report also revealed how many had been alarmed to learn from GIDS's own data that virtually all young people who started treatment with puberty blockers appeared to move on to cross-sex hormones. Some staff felt the implications this might have for future fertility were 'played down'. What's more, staff told Bell that they felt that puberty blockers did not always appear to be helping the young person, that some became 'more depressed' after starting the medication, but that this was sometimes dealt with by simply adjusting the dose, rather than further exploration as to what might be behind the feelings.

Bell's report paints a picture of a climate of fear, in what was meant to be a care setting. 'I was very troubled when it became clear to me that directors of the service were endeavouring to find out who the staff were,' he wrote.'[10]

---

* Polly Carmichael has rejected this summary, insisting that she was concerned about the contents of the report and the serious issues raised, not in who might have contributed. This, in turn, was challenged by a former senior GIDS member of staff in testimony given under oath in employment tribunal proceedings: Hannah Barnes, 'after the DB report I was approached by Polly to ask if I knew who had spoken to him. I didn't and I didn't myself. And there was a real focus on who'd taken part rather than the issues raised in that report' [Twitter post] (17 June 2021), https://twitter.com/hannahsbee/status/1405564012868276231.

Dr Bell was also explicit about what had hitherto been unspoken: the pivotal role GIDS played in maintaining the financial viability of the Tavistock Trust.

GIDS's rapid expansion meant it made a significant contribution to the Trust's total income. The proportion grew from 5.9 per cent in 2015/16 to 13.5 per cent in 2018/19 – the financial year Bell's report was published.[11] In the same year, a permanent contract was signed for the Tavistock to deliver the adult gender service at Charing Cross GIC too (it had taken over on an interim basis the year before[12]). Together, the gender services constituted 21.8 per cent of the Trust's total income. They were vital. 'I think the fair thing to say would be that the loss of that income will be very highly significant,' Bell explains. 'And in the current climate of constant cuts would have huge implications for the continuation of the Tavistock as we know it.'

What's more, the income from GIDS was guaranteed. The service wasn't competing with anyone else. In an NHS which has faced extensive cuts, where individual Trusts have constantly to bid for services and income is precarious, a national contract like the one GIDS had with NHS England was 'gold dust'. Bell argued that knowledge of GIDS's economic importance had made it difficult for those with legitimate criticisms to raise them.

Dr Bell was no less devastating in his conclusions. He branded GIDS 'not fit for purpose'.[13]

Children's needs were being met in a 'woefully inadequate manner', he said, something that could only be improved by a radical rethink of GIDS's whole approach. Without this, Bell wrote, not only would children be put at risk, but so would 'the whole reputation of the Trust'.[14]

He concluded with a vivid warning to those leading the Trust: 'It needs to be borne in mind that these concerns have been raised widely and in the event of any future incident or enquiry we will be very vulnerable if we have not shown that these concerns have been addressed in an appropriate, adequate and properly monitored manner.'[15]

13

BELL: THE AFTERMATH

To say that the findings of David Bell's report did not go down well would be an understatement. It marked the beginning of real media scrutiny of GIDS and set in motion a chain of events in which Bell found himself at war with the most senior figures in a Trust to which he had dedicated his professional adult life.

There is much claim and counterclaim surrounding what happened in the weeks and months following Dr Bell submitting his report to the two men at the top of the Tavistock: CEO Paul Jenkins and chair Paul Burstow (the former Liberal Democrat health minister). The report was quickly shared with GIDS director Polly Carmichael, who disseminated it among her senior team. The dispute was over who else should be able to see it and how it should be responded to.

Bell intended to share his report with his colleagues on the council of governors. He'd made this clear early on. After all, he had been approached by GIDS staff in his capacity as staff governor, and therefore it was only right and proper that the council of governors should be the forum in which to discuss it. Furthermore, Bell argued, it was the council's job to hold the board to account. Tavistock chairman Paul Burstow disagreed. While the council had an important role in holding the board to account, it was not its job to review the serious issues raised in Bell's report. Both Burstow and Jenkins recognised the seriousness of the issues raised, Burstow explained to governors, but argued that the best course of action was for GIDS to be reviewed by the Trust's new medical director, Dr Dinesh Sinha. Professor Burstow insisted that Bell's report raised significant and far-reaching issues about GIDS, but this was ultimately a matter for the board to consider once the review had reported back.

Bell was instructed not to share his report. He was informed that the Trust had taken legal advice which supported this decision, and that given the Trust's duty of care to GIDS staff it would be wrong for it to be circulated. To disseminate the report to the council of governors, it was argued, would likely be strongly challenged by senior GIDS staff and there was a risk to confidentiality and of compromising the proposed review.

Bell disagreed, and opinion among his fellow governors was split. Some agreed with Paul Burstow's judgement. Others opposed the plan. Vehemently, in some cases. 'Dr Bell's report absolutely should have gone to council first,' says Marilyn Miller, and been thoroughly discussed. The appropriate action, in her mind, was to have approached the concerns with the 'open attitude of scientific enquiry' that the Tavistock was famous for. But it was more than that. She felt that the Trust's management was prioritising a duty of care to the managers of GIDS, over the duty of care to those who had spoken out. 'They went to Dave as a governor, because everything else failed,' Miller explains. They had not felt listened to by the GIDS management. And this fundamental point was being missed. The Trust had a duty of care to *all* its staff, she says, not just those leading GIDS. 'I was thinking about patients,' says Miller, too. Where was the consideration of their needs? But she was also thinking more widely about the Trust and the dangers the situation posed. Miller had trained and worked at the Tavistock for many years before she became a governor. She cared 'very greatly' about it and its future. She feared that by not handling the concerns properly it could put GIDS and the national contract at risk, something that would be a disaster for the Trust. The reputation of the Tavistock was on the line.

Miller also felt cutting the council of governors out of the process amounted to a 'lack of due process'. A feature of all NHS foundation trusts is that the chair of the board is also chair of the council of governors. In this instance that was problematic. David Bell's report,

Miller says, questioned not just GIDS, but the role of the board too. It was vital that the governors be able to provide oversight. But, she says, it wasn't particularly appreciated when governors questioned the actions of the board. 'Our job was about accountability,' Miller says, about knocking on doors and asking questions, but when she and Bell had done so previously (on plans for relocation of the Tavistock and completely unrelated to GIDS) it had not been welcomed and had led to friction between the council and the board.

The Trust leadership saw that David Bell had fulfilled his role and should play no further part going forward. He was not given permission to be involved in the review into GIDS, or to address the board or the council directly about what he had heard. Bell sought his own legal advice and shared his report anyway. 'The legal opinion that I was given was not only *can* I send it, but I had an *obligation* to send it. That is, if there was ever an inquiry, and I had this report, and I didn't give it to the governors, I would be in breach of my duty.'

Life for David Bell became more difficult.

Told he was to have no involvement in the medical director's review, Bell nonetheless wanted to ensure that the process was robust. When he heard that Dinesh Sinha had emailed the GIDS team on 16 October (2018), inviting 'nominations of 4–5 staff representatives, who will be willing to be interviewed for the purpose of the review', Bell was less than impressed.[1] He took it upon himself to write to the whole GIDS team telling them that the review was being carried out as a result of 'very serious concerns' being raised to the council of governors – perhaps not knowing that Polly Carmichael had informed them of this already. He wrote that if *anyone* had concerns they wished to raise with the review, they should do so and know that they could do so anonymously.

Bell's intervention was not viewed kindly. He received a letter to his home address from CEO Paul Jenkins, suggesting that he had been guilty of bullying and harassment. He was informed that his emails to the GIDS team had caused great anxiety and were a cause of distress and upset. He was ordered not to talk to anyone in GIDS, not to interfere with the review into the service, and not to speak to Sonia Appleby – the Tavistock's safeguarding lead for children. Bell wrote back, vehemently rejecting any allegation of bullying or harassment, and pointing out that GIDS staff had sought him out to discuss their concerns. He felt a duty of care to them and wanted to ensure that any review into their claims was robust, but he had been shut out of the process. He insisted that he had simply carried out his professional duties when compiling his report, and that its contents were a protected disclosure under whistle-blowing law. He agreed to accept the instructions from Jenkins, however. The review had been widened following his intervention, and he had no further reason to contact anyone.

Bell's relationship with the Trust deteriorated further, and he remained concerned about GIDS and how the Trust responded to those concerns. In early 2020 procedures were set up for disciplinary action to be taken against him. 'One of the allegations against me was I had disobeyed an instruction that I could not speak on anything that wasn't to do with my employ in the Trust.' He believes this was motivated by his speaking out at a public event for those who had detransitioned and for writing a foreword for a book containing criticism of GIDS.[2] A copy of the book was later removed from the Tavistock library after complaints were made.[*] Bell's lawyers told him he could 'ignore' the Trust's instruction, 'because it was not legal'.

The threat of disciplinary action hung over David Bell until his retirement in January 2021. 'It was sad to be ending it that way,' he says, 'but I think the main sadness was my distress at the loss of the Tavistock traditions, and an incompetent management who'd let this happen.' He has no regrets. 'It sounds like a rather arrogant thing to say, but when you feel so sure that you're right, and you're on the right side, it gives you a real feeling of strength.'

Some have suggested that David Bell was 'not a neutral sounding board'; that he'd always been somewhat sceptical about the work

---

[*]   Such was the Trust's sensitivity over criticism of GIDS, and this book in particular, that even an email sent advising staff that they could buy it more cheaply from the publisher than from Amazon landed former Portman clinic director Stanley Ruszczynski with the threat of disciplinary action and a note on his HR file. His offence? Abuse of the Trust's email policy.

GIDS was doing and how influential it was becoming within the Tavistock at the expense of psychoanalysis; and that he did not believe that young people should embark upon medical transition.[3] But Bell does not appear to have been motivated to write his report by anything other than genuine concern about what he was hearing. Even if these things are true, it does not mean his report didn't reflect what staff working in GIDS had told him. Those whom I have spoken to who shared their thoughts with Bell say he relayed them accurately.

But within the Tavistock and Portman Trust, the picture was very different.

Dr Bell had made himself unpopular. He remembers an encounter with one colleague, who asked, 'What are you doing, Dave? Do you realise the implications of this? Do you want to see the Tavistock go down? If the Tavistock closes the GIDS service, this could be the end.' Bell was unapologetic in his reply. 'I said to this very senior colleague, "*That* – I'm sorry to say – is not my problem. It's the Trust that decided to invest in this, it's the Trust who decided to put too many of its eggs in one basket"... I said, "I don't have any trouble. I don't sweat over whether I'm doing the right thing. I just think of those children."'

It is true that Bell's report did include some of his own views and analysis. GIDS Executive member Bernadette Wren is quoted as saying that he 'kind of ran away with it and wrote a report that was full of his own criticisms'. He used 'very, very extreme language, implying senior staff were harming children', she said.[4] There are no names in his report, but Bell does argue that the way GIDS was working might be putting young people at risk. This is what GIDS staff had told him. Others have said the report would have been better received had the language been toned down a little. It's been described to me as both 'prosy' and 'polemical' by several figures outside of GIDS, but those same people acknowledge that Bell made an impact. And they don't question the truthfulness of the testimonies contained in the report.

'In retrospect I think I can see why it wasn't received very well,' says Anna Hutchinson. 'It wasn't tentative. But everything until then had been tentative, and everything had been so tentative that it almost lost its edge.' At least Bell's report cut through, she says, because nothing else had.

It does seem that objections to Bell's report were more about how he had gone about writing it and the tone used, rather than the content. Indeed, in an email to the most senior GIDS staff in which she shares David Bell's report, Polly Carmichael says: 'I don't think there are any issues of which we are not aware and which have not been raised in some form within the team.'[5] Carmichael apologises for sending it, as she herself had found it 'difficult to read'.[*]

Carmichael has said she was troubled by the report's 'divisive tone'. In her view the Bell report was 'not constructive or balanced', and was disrespectful to the young people being cared for by GIDS.[6] It would also be 'deeply upsetting' to GIDS staff, 'some of whom identify as gender diverse.'[7]

The rest of the GIDS team – those still seeing hundreds of children and young people – were never shown Bell's report. Dr David Burrows, a junior psychologist in the team, who is very positive about the service, says he was vocal about that particular decision.[†] 'I thought it was outrageous how they [the GIDS management] handled it,' he says. 'I just thought they were treating us like children. It's such a bad way to manage a team.' Burrows understands that management would have been concerned about the report being leaked, 'and that there were possible moles or something in the service, but it made everyone feel quite suspicious.'

When the existence of the report was made public in November 2018 by the *Observer*, the Tavistock Trust responded by questioning the motives of the staff who'd spoken to Bell.[8] The Trust was concerned by the 'tone and manner in which allegations have been made'. They revealed, the Trust argued, 'a negative attitude to gender dysphoria and gender identity which does not reflect the views or the approach of the Trust or GIDS'.[9] For some of the clinicians who'd contributed to Bell's report this confirmed what they'd been saying all along: that if you

---

[*] The appendices containing the verbatim quote from GIDS staff who spoke to David Bell – which run to more pages than the main findings – were not shared, as they hadn't been forwarded to Carmichael at this point.

[†] Not their real name.

raised concerns, you would face accusations of transphobia. Although the word itself wasn't used, they believe that this is what the Trust's response was saying.

Later, in February 2019, when some of Dr Bell's findings were leaked to the *Sunday Times*, 'the media publicity only increased ill feeling.'[10] The Trust responded to the leak by saying that Dr Bell had 'no expertise in this field' and claimed that the report 'presented hypothetical vignettes rather than actual case studies'.[11] This was untrue. The messenger was being shot.

Some were appalled by the statement and ended their formal relationship with the Trust.

Marcus Evans had only become a governor in September 2018, after a lengthy clinical career at the Tavistock, including 20 years at management level. GIDS immediately came across his radar. He knew concerns had been raised with David Bell and he'd been copied in to correspondence from a concerned group of parents. He also knew that concerns about GIDS went back years. Evans was not given permission to see Bell's report initially. He was told it would be circulated as a background document when governors got to read the findings from the official review into GIDS, conducted by the Tavistock's medical director Dinesh Sinha.

Sinha's report, completed in February 2019, accepted many of the concerns outlined by Bell. It agreed that caseloads were 'excessive', with staff feeling pressured to see lots of patients, and there were concerns about 'how to address particularly complex presentations'. While some staff felt comfortable in extending assessments for young people beyond six sessions, 'several interviewees felt a sense of implicit pressure from seniors to maintain throughput and keep to the frame rather than extend, due to the pressure of the waiting list.'[12]

Sinha said he had 'seen and heard evidence suggestive of variance in practice' among the GIDS staff group, and that 'there were examples given where certain seniors in the service were reported, as doing fewer assessment sessions before coming to their conclusions'. Sinha stated that it was 'freely acknowledged that this was not meant to be a psychological therapy service'.[13]

Sinha described the GIDS leadership as 'being unable to act' and noted that he had been told that patients who complained were reallocated to other staff members. When it came to physical interventions, he explained that evidence provided by GIDS appeared to support 'the shift in impact of using hormone blockers, in that a majority of young people then went on to have cross-sex hormones' and that some clinicians were concerned about this.[14]

On the issue of consent for these medical treatments, Sinha described the appearance of significant shortfalls. There was a 'lack of uniform process' and 'no mandatory need for gaining signed consent from young people and their families at GIDS'. Sinha acknowledged some clinicians' concerns over whether all young people could truly understand 'issues such as fertility and its impact on their adult lives' before embarking on medical treatment with puberty blockers and cross-sex hormones. It was an area that 'needs to be enhanced', he said.[15]

Perhaps most importantly, Sinha accepted that clinicians had raised concerns over a lengthy period, but that senior staff had failed to act:

> It was clear from the description of chronology of events that senior staff both within the service and within the directorate had been independently aware about the various concerns for some length of time, including questions raised about the model by some staff, staffing pressures within the service including from the waiting list, managing referrals safely and adequately, safeguarding issues within this population of young people and management of concerns both from young people, their families and staff.[16]

The Tavistock's medical director also noted that implementing change at GIDS may have been hampered by fearing 'a backlash from one of the external groups'.[17]

While the official review into concerns raised about GIDS confirmed a fair amount of what David Bell set out in his report, there were some oddities. Sinha described 'repeated concerns from a minority of clinicians about being subject to bullying, when they repeatedly brought up concerns' – seemingly acknowledging that staff felt they were punished, or 'scapegoated', for speaking up. And yet he also said that 'there were no consistent reports of... shutting down of discussion'.[18]

Safeguarding was barely mentioned, other than to say that practice in this area had recently improved with the appointment of a 'safeguarding lead' within GIDS. Sinha recommended that 'safeguarding concerns and practices need to be evidenced through quarterly audits', both statements suggesting perhaps that concerns were not being properly recorded hitherto and there was room for improvement, but there is no detail.[19]

Most curious is that although the report acknowledged a number of serious concerns, they were not fully reflected in its findings, and it is perhaps surprising that the Tavistock and Portman NHS Foundation Trust stated publicly that 'none of the concerns around safety or safeguarding [highlighted by Dr Bell] were upheld by our Medical Director'.[20] Tavistock chief executive Paul Jenkins said that the review did not identify 'any immediate issues in relation to patient safety or failings in the overall approach taken by the Service in responding to the needs of the young people and families who access its support'.[21] But at many points in the report he appeared to be doing precisely that – questioning whether the overall approach by GIDS was responding to the needs of all the young people coming through its doors.

The February 2019 meeting at which Sinha's report was first shared was 'long' and 'bruising', Marcus Evans recalls. He questioned why the service didn't appear to have a model and why it was so detached from other departments in the Trust. But his major concern was about the lack of any data in the review document. 'I used to produce reports for the commissioners all the time – they love the statistics,' Evans explains. Yet the document produced by Sinha contained 'no data at all'. It was striking, he says, that there was 'nothing about ethnicity, age, length of stay, outcomes, nothing'. When it came to data on the outcomes of those who'd been seen by GIDS, Evans says he was told there were none. '[Sinha] said, "No, we just don't collect it."' Evans found this 'absolutely extraordinary'. Sinha's report did not contain a single statistic or piece of data.

There were other aspects of the review that Evans felt had been conducted well, however, and after lengthy discussion, to his 'shame', he says, he voted to support the report. Evans says he 'felt bad doing it' – to his mind, the report hadn't tackled the underlying question of how best to help this group of children and young people. 'And I had a really sleepless night,' he recalls, 'feeling guilty about the fact I've sort of gone along with it. And then I had my reprieve.'

The reprieve was the Trust's response to the leak in the *Sunday Times*.[22] 'I thought, well, there's my evidence – not that actually I needed any.' Evans believed the Trust had 'no interest' in taking the concerns raised about GIDS seriously: 'They just wanted to shut the whole thing down.' Bell, 'probably the trust's most senior clinician', had been badly treated too.*

Evans tendered his resignation immediately. I asked him why he hadn't asked questions about GIDS himself in the years between Sue Evans raising concerns and David Bell's report. 'Everybody's protecting their patch,' he answers, honestly. 'I didn't get involved with GIDS, because I'm fighting for the survival of the things that matter for me.' When resources are scarce, people fight for their own service. They don't question what's going on elsewhere in case that might impact them in some way. 'Everybody's got their weak points,' Evans adds.

For others on the council of governors, the public response to the leak would prove to be just the beginning of a sustained attempt to glean answers from the Tavistock Trust about how GIDS was operating, what data lay behind its work, and whether the same pathway was suitable for all the young people it was seeing.

———

* Tavistock and Portman CEO Paul Jenkins declined to be interviewed for this book. Responding to request for comment, he said he did not accept that the Trust did not adequately address the serious concerns raised about GIDS. 'It is a feature of grievance and complaints procedures generally… that not all concerns will be resolved to the satisfaction of all parties involved,' he said. Jenkins cited Sinha's review as evidence that the Trust took concerns seriously, and stressed that following his report, 'action has been taken to strengthen elements of practice', including safeguarding policies and procedures for gaining consent for those referred for physical interventions.

When Dr Juliet Singer applied to be a governor, she had no preconceptions of GIDS. She'd sought advice from the service on a young person she was working with at Camden CAMHS, also part of the Tavistock and Portman Trust, and been told GIDS was an assessment service, 'not a treatment service'. But, if anything, she was in awe of the Tavistock and its world-leading reputation for mental health services. Towards the end of her six-month stint in CAMHS, Singer stumbled across a leaflet about becoming a governor. A trained doctor, specialising in child and adolescent psychiatry, Singer had taken an 18-year break from medicine to make documentaries. She returned to the field in 2017, keen to get up to speed again with how the NHS functioned. Becoming a governor, she thought, would provide an interesting and new perspective. 'I had no knowledge at all of what I was about to walk into,' she says.

Elected in November 2018, her first meeting as a governor discussed David Bell's report and the review of GIDS that was now underway. Immediately she started asking questions. She was concerned by what she was hearing, but one thing leapt out: the huge increase in girls identifying as trans. 'I remember saying, "What I really think we need to find out or what we need to understand is why on earth so many girls are wanting to change their gender"... And I remember Paul Jenkins saying, "Yes, we need to do some research."' Singer felt reassured initially. She says now that she had a 'naive confidence' that data on GIDS's patients 'would all be there, really well recorded'. It wouldn't take long for her to realise it wasn't.

Alarm bells started ringing even before her second meeting came about. While away on holiday she read the *Sunday Times* article on David Bell's report and the Trust's response to it. She was 'furious'. 'I felt like it [the Tavistock's statement to the press] was unnecessarily aggressive,' Singer says. 'I didn't believe what they said was true, either.' For ten GIDS staff to have gone to Bell and been afraid to do so within the Tavistock building pointed to 'really significant levels of concern'. 'My anger was about what it made the Tavistock appear like, which was thoughtless and defensive, and not taking these clinicians' concerns seriously,' she explains. On the one hand the Trust appeared to be pursuing a sensible approach to the report by getting the medical director to conduct a review, but on the other it was undermining the credentials of the report's author. The two didn't marry up. Singer was so angry she emailed the Trust's leadership. She had only been in post for a few months. 'You just think these kids are suffering and struggling, and I'm not seeing a path by which we're going to learn more information to help them.'

Singer recalls the council of governors being given the opportunity to be involved in the development of the *GIDS Review Action Plan* that followed the review, and she took the chance.[23] She met with GIDS boss Polly Carmichael, Tavistock CEO Paul Jenkins and several other governors and non-executive directors.

Immediately, she asked why GIDS thought it was seeing so many teenage girls. This had been a preoccupation among many GIDS staff, too, but a question the service had struggled to answer. The 'reasons are not fully explicable', GIDS said.[24] Perhaps the increase is 'due mostly to the greater tolerance of gender-diverse expression in westernised society' or perhaps a male status is 'still regarded as preferable'.[25] When asked publicly why three-quarters of referrals to GIDS were female, a representative of the Tavistock Trust said they simply didn't know.[26] But clinicians like Anna Hutchinson and Melissa Midgen have posited that 'there are multiple, interweaving factors bearing down on girls and young women' that help explain why so many are experiencing gender-related distress.[27] They say they have witnessed a 'toxic collision of factors: a world telling these children they are "wrong"; they are not doing girlhood (or boyhood) correctly', girls struggling with their emerging sexuality, and girls who 'struggle in puberty because it is uncomfortable, weird and unpredictable (particularly heightened if they happen to be on the autistic spectrum)'.[28]

A mother of a teenager herself, Juliet Singer had been thinking about what girls were experiencing in their lives – reports of celebrity child sexual abuse, easy access to pornography – and what impact that might be having on how someone relates to their body: 'what it's like for boys who are learning about sex through watching quite hardcore porn, and what it's like for girls having their first intimate experience with boys who are versed in porn'. 'I raised this as a conversation in this meeting,' Singer recalls, explaining that to change a service you need to understand its population. 'And then Polly Carmichael says, "Oh, you're critical."' Singer didn't know what this meant at the time.

She now understands it was a reference to being 'gender-critical' – a belief that biological sex is real, important and immutable, and not to be conflated with gender identity. 'But that was her response. It wasn't "Yes, this is something we've been really worried about. And this is something we're trying to understand."'

Singer says she 'lost faith' at that point. 'My view was always, you can't keep this discussion inside the clinic. If this is an issue that's related to the wider society, then we've got to start having conversations that involve the wider society.' Having only been in the job a matter of months, Juliet Singer was disillusioned, but didn't quit. 'I stayed because I couldn't walk away. I didn't have hope that as a governor I could change things, but at the same time… I wanted to keep trying.'

It wasn't just a spluttering of governors, and a sizeable number of GIDS staff, who were worried. Concern came from all quarters.

It's striking how much respect is held for Dr Bell by colleagues across the Trust, both as a person and as a clinician. 'If there's one thing I could say about him,' explains one senior staff member, 'he's a man of integrity. So, for me, this person was being maligned and being made out to be something that I didn't recognise.' Many in the Tavistock and Portman NHS Trust, outside GIDS, were gobsmacked at the way David Bell – and the very serious staff concerns contained within his report – were being handled. Following the Trust's initial public statement in November 2018, a group of more than a dozen of the most senior clinicians from the Tavistock's adult and forensics services, including the Portman Clinic, wrote to CEO Paul Jenkins. They felt that the statement given to the press, criticising the 'tone and manner' in which GIDS staff had raised concerns and stating that these revealed a 'negative attitude' to gender identity, put the reputation of the Tavistock Trust itself at risk.[29] It made staff and students from *all* departments question whether they could ask questions or raise worries without fear of being publicly criticised. The group of clinicians, some of the most senior in their specialist fields, believed that the public statements of the Trust revealed a reluctance to discuss GIDS and any concerns around the way it was working. And they questioned whether GIDS's contribution to the Trust's income was impacting on the ability to tackle the concerns in a more open and constructive way.

While this group of Tavistock and Portman staff were alarmed, they also made it clear they wanted to help. The Trust, after all, had significant expertise that might be of benefit to GIDS: expertise in autism, trauma and significant mental health difficulties.[30] If there were difficulties in the service, could others be called upon to assist in any way? They suggested that an external voice be added to the review being undertaken by the Trust's medical director, perhaps someone with a legal background, and they called for open discussion of David Bell's report and the issues raised within it. Staff accepted that there may be issues with tone and some of its conclusions, but there had to be a way of producing some of the report's key points in a way that would allow them to be openly debated and tackled. Failure to do so would result in permanent reputational harm to the Trust and its board, they argued.

The group met with Paul Jenkins and Tavistock chair Paul Burstow in March 2019.

'There were two concerns, really. One was the fact that we hadn't been able to have a proper dialogue internally... And then the second concern was the GIDS service itself,' recalls one of the senior clinicians who was there. The meeting 'went nowhere', they add. Colleagues were met with a 'totally defensive' attitude' from the Trust's chief executive. 'By the end of the meeting, Paul Jenkins's face was purple. He was so angry. I've never seen a man change colour quite so vividly.' It was pointed out to Jenkins that while he was understandably angry about leaks to the press, he had to question *why* some had felt the need to do so. This had happened on 'his watch'. 'It's happened because people haven't felt able to discuss things within the Trust,' suggested clinicians.

Those who were present say nothing constructive came from the meeting. 'I don't have any recollection of any fears being assuaged,' said one. 'There was just total denial,' says another – 'a culture of total denial that there were any issues' with GIDS. 'If you had any criticism to make at all you were someone with "negative views",' one says. Or it was suggested that criticism of GIDS was criticism of individual staff members. These Tavistock staff outside GIDS had a lot of respect for those leading the service. They had known them for many years. One clinician says: 'This is not a service run by incompetent people; it's an under-resourced service that isn't given the time needed to properly assess patients coming through their doors.'

Paul Burstow, clinicians recall, was calmer. 'He suggested a further meeting, and that further meeting never took place.'

But GIDS was discussed in various other forums in the Trust, says Stanley Ruszczynski, who was clinical director of the Portman Clinic at the time. He recalls at least two meetings, both well attended, where attempts were made to talk about GIDS, the concerns raised by staff to David Bell, and how best to move forward. 'But they never got anywhere,' he says.

Not everyone shared the concerns that Ruszczynski and other senior staff held about GIDS, and the way the Trust did not appear to want to discuss and address concerns openly: 'There are some people that are supportive [of GIDS], and there's some people that are sort of neutral,' Ruszczynski says. But he believes well over half of the Tavistock and Portman staff outside GIDS had questions about how the service was being run.

It seems odd that one response to the serious concerns being raised by GIDS staff was a concerted effort to grow the service, along with the adult gender services at Charing Cross. This was listed as an objective of the 2018/19 'Strategic Plan and Operational Plan'.[31] Several senior Tavistock figures were well aware of the difficulties GIDS was facing at this time. The Trust continued in its aim of growing gender services the following year too, in its 'Operational Plan' for 2019/20.[32] Its two gender services accounted for 21 per cent of the Trust's income, the plan noted, but it admitted that it struggled to fill vacant staff positions in them.[33] Even setting aside the concerns expressed by GIDS staff about safety, safeguarding and clinical practice at the service, it was noted that GIDS had experienced a 'fourth consecutive year of exponential growth' for referrals and its waiting list had grown. There's an acknowledgement that 'the service is focusing on remodelling and quality improvement to ensure those on the waiting list are seen as promptly as possible, while maintaining a safe service for those currently open to GIDs'.[34]

It is curious to want to grow a service that is struggling both to recruit staff and to keep up with the demand it already faces. But, if measured by the proportion of the Trust's income gender services contribute, the strategy was a success. Just a year later, in the draft 'Operational Plan' for 2020/21, gender services for children and adults were said to make up 28 per cent of the Tavistock's income.[35] It was a 'ridiculous' strategy, says a former experienced clinician from GIDS Leeds. 'It should have been regionalised. I don't think that you should grow a beast of a gender service... I wasn't aware it was part of our strategic plan. I always thought they... just weren't thinking about it.' But at the same time she sensed 'that GIDS was propping up a lot of the other stuff that wasn't lucrative in the Trust. And that's why they wanted to hold on to it.'

The Trust insists it took the concerns raised by Bell's report very seriously. As soon as the chair and chief executive had read it they commissioned a review of GIDS to look at the issues raised. The process was thorough, the Trust argues, and did not substantiate the criticism levelled at GIDS in the report. It was important that the Trust made this clear to the public when responding to leaks to the British media. None of the concerns around 'safety or safeguarding' were upheld by a review of GIDS undertaken by the Tavistock's medical director, the Trust said in response to the leaks to the *Sunday Times*.[36]

Some of those who'd spoken to medical director Dinesh Sinha were surprised by the statement. They knew what they had told him, and their remarks did not appear to be reflected in the resulting report. It would take more than a year before BBC *Newsnight* broadcast some of what was relayed during that review, and for the Trust's assertion that the review did not find 'any immediate issues in relation to patient safety or failings in the overall approach' to be openly challenged by some of those who took part.[37]

14

FIRST FEARS

May 2019, House of Lords, London

Dr Anna Hutchinson sat on an uncomfortable chair at the back of a
stuffy House of Lords committee room nestled deep inside the Palace
of Westminster. Following an hour or so of presentations on the topic
of the 'ethics of transgender healthcare', a question-and-answer session
was taking place.[1] Those who had given presentations or addressed
the meeting sat around a horseshoe-shaped table, as is characteristic
when parliamentary committees take evidence. Those observing were
squashed close together in rows at one end of the room. There were
doctors, lawyers, parents of young people with gender identity difficulties and a small number of journalists.

Sue Evans, the psychoanalytic psychotherapist who had worked
at GIDS in the early 2000s, introduced herself from the side of
the room. 'I used to work many years ago in the Gender Identity
Development Unit at the Tavistock; it was a traumatic experience,
I have to tell you.' Hutchinson's ears pricked up. She'd been sitting,
listening and observing silently throughout, but this caught her off
guard. 'And I resigned,' Sue Evans continued, 'because I wasn't happy
with it… I did try to whistle-blow when I was there and there was
an inquiry, but…' Evans changed the subject without finishing her
sentence.

This was extraordinary to Hutchinson. 'Who is she?' she thought.

'I've never met her before.' But before she could think through what she'd just heard, the meeting moved on.

A parent spoke of their concern that their child might be on a 'one-way conveyor belt' to puberty blockers if they were seen by GIDS, a claim rebutted by the Tavistock's robust director of communications, Laure Thomas, who had been standing at the back of the hot, airless room throughout. 'It's not a conveyor belt,' she insisted, but explained that GIDS was an assessment service. Thomas tried to impress upon the audience that GIDS was, in fact, more cautious than some of those gathered had made out, insisting that all young people had to have at least four appointments before being referred for puberty blockers. NHS England stipulated that GIDS assessments were generally between four and six sessions, she said. Unfortunately, this wasn't true. 'Three and six,' Anna Hutchinson interrupted. Four, Thomas insisted. Three, corrected Hutchinson, before Sue Evans interjected.* Evans hadn't intended to speak that day at all, she says. But when Thomas, who was not a clinician at GIDS, spoke, Evans could not help herself. 'In that moment, I just had to say "No, I'm sorry, I worked there years ago, and even back then I saw [rushed assessments] happen."'

Thomas insisted that, on average, most young people had far more appointments than the minimum and that fewer than 50 per cent went on to physical interventions. She also explained, correctly, that when compared to practices in other countries – the United States in particular – GIDS was far more cautious.

The meeting wrapped up and moved to a nearby pub. Hutchinson was trying to process what she had heard only an hour or so earlier. 'I couldn't believe it,' she says. 'We honestly thought we were the first people to have thought, "Maybe there's more going on here? And actually, if there is more going on here, then people are being put at risk"… And then we found out other people had thought exactly the same more than ten years before and there'd been another review, and no one had ever told us.'

---

* Hutchinson was correct. She'd been working in GIDS at a senior level when the service specification was written. It states that the initial assessment will 'typically be over three to six meetings depending on the individual'. The official minimum had been reduced from four to three.

Evans and Hutchinson talked at the pub. 'We just stood, and we just shared some of what had gone on,' Evans recalls. 'And it was just so good to have that moment... because she felt as strongly about what had gone on [as I had] and, obviously, it was by now ten times worse.' Being married to Marcus Evans, who'd resigned as a governor of the Tavistock when he didn't believe the concerns raised by GIDS staff in David Bell's report were being taken seriously enough, Sue Evans knew about the report, but not who had taken part. 'Anna went, "Yeah, I'm one of them."' Later that night the two exchanged text messages. It had been good to talk. 'We kind of both said it was really cathartic for us,' Evans recalls.

The House of Lords meeting also marked the very beginnings of what would become a landmark legal case against GIDS, questioning the use of puberty blockers in children and young people. Also listening to proceedings that afternoon was Paul Conrathe, a solicitor who was involved in another case, defending a former police officer accused of posting transphobic tweets.[2] Evans recalls having a conversation with Conrathe after the event, where he offered to arrange a meeting 'to have a think about' what any future legal challenge might look like. 'I think that was how it started to develop,' Evans says. Parents present at the meeting also introduced her to 'Mrs A', who would become a complainant in the case. She says the House of Lords meeting had been like 'a horror show' to her. Although she'd known about David Bell's report, Sue Evans had managed to remove herself from thinking too much about GIDS for more than decade. But learning what was happening in the United States – where children as young as 13 were receiving double mastectomies[3] – and how things could go in the UK, she felt there had to be some kind of action. To her nothing had worked – there had been no meaningful changes at GIDS following her concerns, David Bell's report or Marcus Evans's resignation. She wondered whether change to clinical practice could only come through the courts.

Events moved quickly. In just five months, Sue Evans went from breaking a 13-year silence on her time working at GIDS to announcing her intention to take legal action against the Trust, along with 'Mrs A' – the mother of a teenage girl on the GIDS waiting list.[4]

They argued that young people could not give informed consent to treatment with puberty blockers. Evans would later be replaced as a claimant by former GIDS patient Keira Bell.

Having listened to proceedings in the House of Lords that afternoon, I wanted to find out more about the 'inquiry' into GIDS that Sue Evans had mentioned. When had it taken place? Who carried it out? What did it conclude?

No one had a copy of it, it seemed. And Evans herself had never seen it. After resisting for 15 months, in August 2020 the Information Commissioner's Office (ICO) ruled that it was in the public interest for the Tavistock to disclose the document, saying that patients, prospective patients and their families should be able to see this information.[5]

When I first received and read Dr David Taylor's report it was immediately striking how similar the concerns contained in it were to those being made by GIDS staff more than a decade later. Clinicians grappled with the same issues.

The recommendations Taylor made in January 2006 were – in his own words – 'not rocket science'.[6] 'They're about core values of clinical practice,' he said, 'taking a complex problem seriously, just as you would do in any other branch of medicine.' There would 'very likely' be 'no single, obvious treatment of choice', he had concluded, but rather a combination of 'thorough assessment followed by a variety of therapeutic options'.[7] For those who maintained a wish to medically transition, puberty blockers should still be available, Taylor had said. After therapy. And after they had been given all of the information that was known. And all patients should be followed up.

As he explains now, 'The basic stance of the report was, if we're going to do this, let's do it properly.' Doing it 'properly', he says, would have meant allowing the service to grow, properly resourcing it and, crucially, having 'research as an essential component in it'.

Taylor was aware that his recommendations would not be popular. Doing things properly might also mean fewer referrals – in the short term at least. 'It is likely that some of the improvements to the service will be resisted by some of the patients hitherto referred to it and by some among the patients' organisations even while they are to their long-term benefit,' he wrote. 'This may reduce referral rates and the risk attached to this needs to be estimated.'[8]

Speaking to BBC *Newsnight* in 2020, Taylor was explicit. 'If you try to set out to please or comply with someone, whether you're a parent or a clinician, then you won't be helping them.' It is vital for clinicians to keep an independent perspective, he added. 'Therefore, there will be some people who will say "I don't want this", and that is perfectly their prerogative.' But, he says, 'I do think that maybe the service as it developed to some extent lost its compass in those respects.'[9]

When, in 2019, Sue Evans finally got to see the report she had in part prompted, she had mixed feelings. 'I was surprised at the level of detail,' she says. But she was deeply upset that David Taylor's recommendations had not been acted upon, particularly the need to follow up with patients and monitor outcomes. She believes that this is 'unforgivable' when the treatment is so significant, and Evans is emotional when talking about it. 'Medicine is experimental,' she accepts. 'To develop anything new, you take risks with people's health and their lives.' But it has to be done safely. For GIDS not to have followed up the impact of the intervention it was referring a sizeable proportion of its patients for is 'terrible', she says. 'It's the most serious thing.'

Speaking to me in 2021, Taylor admits that he had no expectation that his recommendations would be acted upon. 'I knew when I formulated those recommendations that they were the right thing. I had no doubt about that,' he says. 'But I also knew they wouldn't follow it.' Why? He cites many reasons. For one, it was not in the nature of the Tavistock, he says. What he was proposing would require change from the Trust's leadership and Domenico Di Ceglie, and 'they thought they knew a better way'. What he was proposing would be difficult and potentially make them unpopular. 'If you propose thoughtful, reasonable things, you will be – as well as appreciated – you'll also be opposed. It's difficult.' Perhaps, Taylor muses, the Trust decided 'tactically and strategically, there were more important things'.

The Tavistock and Portman NHS Foundation Trust told BBC *Newsnight* that David Taylor's report was 'not relevant to the circumstances and issues faced by the GIDS service today'.[10] Some of those who worked in GIDS or sat on the Tavistock's council of governors beg to differ. Taylor's report was hugely relevant, they say. 'The concerns were exactly the same concerns,' says Anna Hutchinson. She believes Taylor's review was 'robust', and that had it been implemented it would have transformed the service that she joined in 2013. For her, it was evidence that another opportunity for GIDS to change direction, to think about whether children and young people could be better cared for, had gone begging.

Jacob

Jacob has never really seen himself as a girl.

'Even when I was like a toddler, I would go by names from male characters I saw on TV,' he says. 'I would say, "My name's Jack-Jack," or Indiana from Indiana Jones or Harry from Harry Potter.'

Jacob's mum, Michelle, agrees.* From the age of three Jacob would take his younger brother's clothes and wear them. 'And Jacob's favourite thing was the backwards hat and an Indiana Jones T-shirt.' Even at preschool, he hadn't liked answering to the female name he'd been given at birth, Michelle remembers.

Jacob started presenting as a boy at school from Year 1, he says, aged five or six. 'I wore a hat, because I didn't want to show my long hair, and when we went swimming, I'd wear trunks.'

When Jacob was seven, Michelle went to her GP for advice. Jacob's desire to be a boy was increasing, not going away. She'd read about something called gender dysphoria online, but didn't know much about it. She thought that Jacob's behaviour seemed 'a little bit more than just tomboy behaviour', she says. Jacob wanted to *be* a boy, Michelle explains, and 'used to describe thinking as a boy'. The GP listened and sent Michelle away. 'She said, "Look, go away for two years. Come back when Jacob's nine and then we'll talk about it again."'

That's exactly what Michelle did. At nine years old, Jacob still wanted to be a boy. He used the boys' toilets at his junior school and continued to choose boys' names to be referred to. This time the GP agreed that what Jacob was experiencing seemed more than just being

---

* Names have been changed.

a tomboy. The GP was aware that there was a specialist gender clinic for children at the Tavistock in London, but referred Jacob to his local CAMHS first so that they could explore if there was anything that might be influencing Jacob's behaviour.

Michelle thought CAMHS did a good job. The psychotherapist Jacob saw talked about all sorts of things – not just gender. 'They talked about relationships at home, relationships with friends at school,' Michelle says. And they talked about an 'incident' that occurred, which, Michelle explains, 'could have exacerbated the issue with being a bit more anti-female'. She doesn't go into any more detail because Jacob doesn't want her to. But the implication is that something happened to Jacob that might make him feel uncomfortable towards his female body.

CAMHS also discussed Jacob's parents' divorce and how that had made him feel. He'd been about five when the split happened, but Michelle describes her ex as 'very sexist'. He'd get their sons doing what he saw as 'very masculine jobs', Michelle explains, but get the girls – Jacob and his sister – to 'tidy up and clean things'. CAMHS explored both this family background and the 'incident' with Jacob but felt when it came to his continuing desire to be a boy, he needed to be seen by experts. CAMHS referred him to GIDS, noting in their referral letter that Jacob had 'persistent ideas about wishing to be seen and treated as a "boy"'.

Jacob and Michelle had their first appointment at GIDS in 2014. Jacob was 11 years old. That same month, GIDS's Early Intervention Study recruited its final participant, having reached the end of its first three years.

By now, all Jacob's school friends knew him 'as a guy'. But it was a confusing time. 'Being trans,' he explains to me, 'is like you have moments where you feel like yourself, you feel like the person you should have been,' but his feelings changed a lot. 'There were moments where I felt very, very low' about being trans. 'I wanted to create a new person to go with how I actually feel,' he says. But there were other moments when 'it wasn't really something that mattered as much' as things going on in everyday life: starting a new school or other life events. 'But it was always there. It wasn't something that went away.'

When Jacob arrived for his first GIDS appointment, he says he was at the beginning of his 'lowest point'. Puberty had started, and while Jacob hadn't had a period yet, he was frightened. 'It feels wrong,' he explains to me. 'That's not what should be happening; that isn't the right type of puberty; that's not the one you should be experiencing. And then it's the fear. You start overthinking about what it's like to have periods, what it's like to have breast tissue, and it becomes more scary than anything else.'

Jacob had a good group of friends at school, who accepted him for who he was. They saw him as a boy, called him by the name he'd chosen and thought little of it. These were the people he relied on and with whom he felt most himself. 'But then you have moments where that kind of is pushed aside by the fact that you weren't born properly, if that makes sense?' he says. 'Boys thought I was weird,' he says. 'They didn't like hanging around with someone who wasn't a real boy.' But girls were more accepting. 'So you end up living your entire life in a no man's land, where you're not really a girl but you're not a boy. You don't fit in with either side... If I hang around with the boys, I have this, like, envious jealousy towards them. Because for me, I want that so badly... But it's not a reality. And... when you hang around with the girls, you feel like you're in the wrong place.'

Neither Jacob nor Michelle knew anything about puberty blockers when they arrived at GIDS. They'd never heard of them and weren't asking for them.

'I think it was my first, maybe second appointment with Tavistock, and they were the ones who brought up hormone blockers,' Jacob recalls.

A lot of the things that had been discussed at CAMHS – the distressing 'incident', Jacob's parents' divorce – weren't really spoken about at GIDS, Michelle says. There was next to no exploration of Jacob's broader life. The sole focus was on gender identity. How Jacob saw himself, where he saw himself in the future, and what he wanted from GIDS. It felt strange to Michelle to ask this of an 11-year-old child. Both she and Jacob say that the clinicians were keen to promise an outcome that would make Jacob 'happy'. But Jacob describes himself repeatedly, even at the age of 11 or 12, as 'a realist'. 'Jacob's very much, "Well, this is the gender I was born and no surgery or drugs or anything is ever going to change the biology. It's very much putting a cloak over it,'" Michelle says. 'I admire Jacob for that because by being a realist – although it does make Jacob very unhappy – it does mean that Jacob has a kind of very logical understanding about being gender-dysphoric or transgender. And the Tavistock actually got frustrated with Jacob about that.'

Jacob did not even speak in some of the GIDS appointments. He felt unable. 'I had pretty bad anxiety,' he explains, 'so I couldn't, like, talk to them properly. To me, they were strangers.' When the conversation turned to puberty blockers, he didn't feel able to talk to his two clinicians about 'more personal stuff'. Michelle would do most of the talking. Not in an overly pushy-parent way, but because Jacob couldn't. He would tell Michelle what he wanted to say on the train ride from home to the Tavistock, so that she could then pass this on to the GIDS workers. 'And so she would say, "Well, Jacob's feeling really bad about herself' at the moment,'" experiencing body-image problems 'because of all of the anxiety about having to go through girl puberty', Jacob says. Michelle asked the GIDS team if there was any kind of therapy or therapeutic intervention that could help ease Jacob's distress, that would mean that puberty wouldn't be as bad as he feared. Jacob and Michelle say they were told no. There wasn't. But Jacob says the GIDS clinicians explained that 'there's this thing called hormone blockers. And they're basically like a full stop at the end of the sentence. They'll stop your puberty for as long as you need it to be stopped. And then as soon as you get old enough, you can go on testosterone.' Jacob relays the words as if he can remember the conversation as though it were yesterday.

Jacob was pleased when he heard about puberty blockers. He was a realist, but these sounded great. 'I was relying on the so-called experts to give me information,' he says, and they had given him this option. 'A cure is how they sold it to me.' He was told not to worry. Puberty blockers were 'completely reversible' and wouldn't harm his body. 'It basically stops your female hormones,' the GIDS clinicians had said, adding 'it doesn't make you gain weight'.

_____

* This is a verbatim quote.

'After the conversation we had with them, I was like, I want to do it,' Jacob explains. 'I am scared. I don't want to go through puberty, I can't go through puberty. I really don't want to. And then my mum's like, "Okay, well, I really want to do some more research about [the blockers]."' Jacob couldn't wait for Michelle to do the research. He wanted the blockers immediately. 'I actually ended up pushing my mum to just sign the consent forms,' he says. 'I was the one pushing my mum to push my dad to sign the consent forms, because the way it was sold to me was like an answer to all my worries.'

To Michelle it seemed that the message coming from GIDS was less of a sales pitch, but more 'Why else are you here?' 'I know that's awful to say,' she says, 'but that is how I felt. Unless you're there for them to be a vehicle to send you to the UCLH to get the drugs, I felt that their view was, well, what's the point?' She understood why young people were so keen on a 'miracle cure', as she puts it. 'I think from their perspective, they're living in a body that they don't feel comfortable in and obviously they'd want to do anything to fix that situation. And I really did feel that GIDS did play upon that.'

Michelle was surprised too. When she'd first sought help years earlier from her GP, she'd been told that GIDS were the experts. They'd be the ones to talk through what all the options were for Jacob. 'But that fundamental word, "options" – I really didn't feel that that was really covered. They offered one solution. One. There is *an* option – which [is] you go on blockers, and then you go on testosterone, and then you have an operation,' Michelle claims. Less invasive options, like Jacob continuing to dress in the gender he preferred, weren't discussed.

Although she was concerned, Michelle says she felt she was in an almost impossible situation. 'As a parent, you feel like you have to be so careful what you say because one of them is a social worker,' she says, referring to the people assessing her child at GIDS. It would never have been GIDS's intention to make parents feel uncomfortable – GIDS clinicians simply have a variety of professional backgrounds. But it did impact on Michelle. Michelle says she felt like she didn't have much of a choice, 'that that was the route that they were taking with Jacob'. She didn't feel she could say she wasn't sure.

Ultimately, Michelle trusted the experts. 'I'm quite an enquiring mind,' she says, 'but you think that they're doctors and psychologists, and they kind of know what they're talking about… we felt like they knew what they were talking about. And we thought that we were doing the right thing to help Jacob, really.'

It wasn't just the medical pathway that Michelle felt was being pushed. She says the family were asked whether they'd thought about changing Jacob's name by deed poll. 'And then the next minute, we've just done it,' she says.

After four appointments spread over just four months, Jacob was referred to UCLH to commence treatment with the blocker. He had just turned 12. The assessment report written by his two GIDS clinicians stated that 'hormone blockers can provide young people with the opportunity to explore and experiment with their identities without the anxiety and challenges associated with ongoing pubertal development'. It added, 'It is considered to be a fully reversible treatment.'

Jacob arguably did not meet the criteria of the Early Intervention Study, or early intervention more generally, which had now been rolled out as standard practice at GIDS. Jacob had not actively been requesting blockers. Technically, by the time his assessment report and referral were written, he had been at GIDS for six months – as stipulated by the study – but his four appointments had taken place over just four months.[1] He had no contact with the service outside of those.

Like all GIDS patients on the medical pathway, Jacob continued to be seen by the service, albeit infrequently. Appointments would be every four months, then every six months. He would have liked to have been seen more often. Meetings were spaced so far apart that an issue he might have raised at the previous meeting could have changed or resolved itself by the next, he explains, but it would then be brought up again. 'You never get a chance to actually move on,' Jacob says.

Jacob's mum Michelle says that the trans-led support group Gendered Intelligence was talked about 'all the time' throughout Jacob's time at GIDS. The group listed GIDS Executive member Sarah Davidson as part of its team for a time and also, according to Anastassis Spiliadis, once worked alongside GIDS clinicians to deliver official training on gender diversity to other health professionals.[2] Bernadette Wren has also spoken publicly of GIDS's relationship with Gendered Intelligence.[3]

Jacob was encouraged to look at the group's website and do some research. But this baffled Michelle. 'To me, if you've got someone that's working for the NHS, why are they pushing a charity?' she asks. Jacob was given a leaflet for Mermaids too, but it was Gendered Intelligence that was talked about more. Michelle felt that to point young people towards certain resources and 'like-minded people' was 'pushing an agenda'. At the time of writing in 2022, young people are still directed towards Gendered Intelligence and their resources on several pages of the GIDS website.[4]

The influence of these outside groups – Mermaids and Gendered Intelligence – was also felt at GIDS 'Family Days'. Neither Jacob nor Michelle speaks favourably of the events, Michelle branding them 'chaos' and lacking any kind of structure or boundaries. Jacob did not like the fact that the sessions for young people attending GIDS were invariably led by trans adults from either Gendered Intelligence or Mermaids. These adults had often not been through GIDS themselves, Jacobs says, and they were only interested in hearing about positive stories. 'I couldn't discuss my way of thinking,' he says, because those facilitating the discussion only chose people who were like them – fully sold on medical transition and its merits, Jacob recalls. It's understandable that GIDS would want to try to show that many who transition are happy. But to Jacob there was no diversity of opinion allowed or presented. No other ways of seeing what 'being trans' could mean.

The GIDS appointments and Family Days were a sideshow, however. Life for Jacob was immensely difficult. Being on the blockers was not living up to what he had been promised.

The puberty blockers prescribed to Jacob by UCLH slowed down his puberty, he says, but they didn't stop it. 'I still got showings,' Jacob says, referring to spots of blood. 'And I still got breast-tissue development.'

The response from the endocrinology team at UCLH was to adjust the dose of medication Jacob was on. It didn't work. Each time a higher dose of triptorelin – the drug predominantly given to the young people attending GIDS – was tried, Jacob still 'broke through'.

'I was on the highest-level dose of a completely experimental drug they'd only used twice,' he says. When upping the dose or changing the drug didn't work, they say, endocrinologists at UCLH gave Jacob beta blockers – medication that slows the heart down – alongside the puberty blockers in the hope that this would help.[5] Michelle says she was told that this was to see whether they could get the hormone blocker to move more slowly around Jacob's body, something that – combined with the higher dose of the blocker – might 'stop the breakthrough'. 'To be honest,' she says, 'that's an experiment.'

And one that seemed dangerous.

Jacob collapsed at school. Just 14 years old, he was left lying on the floor behind a locked toilet door for 40 minutes before someone found him. 'I rang up UCLH and I was not happy,' Michelle recalls. 'And I said to them, "I'm not doing this – the beta blockers – any more. If you want to carry on with the blockers with Jacob, you need to find a way of doing it without putting Jacob at risk"... I said there's no way you should be messing around experimenting with these things with my child.'

The puberty blockers affected Jacob in other ways he wasn't anticipating, and which he says he hadn't been told about before starting treatment. He experienced a range of intense and unpleasant side effects, as he tried different doses. 'On one of them I had really bad insomnia. And another one, I had really bad anger problems.' The anger didn't feel normal. 'I actually broke my knuckle while I was on the blocker,' from punching something, he says.

Then there was the depression. 'Your mood goes like it's a roller coaster,' he explains. 'There are moments when you're euphorically happy. And the next day, you crash really bad and you are exhausted. And then you're really, really depressed, like, suicidal depressed.' Jacob says he had felt depressed before starting on puberty blockers and had experienced anxiety. These had made him 'feel low' but nothing compared to his temperament on the blocker. Jacob's physical health suffered too. He gained 'tons of weight', so much so that he got stretch marks.

Then there was the problem with Jacob's bones. They kept breaking.

'I'd never ever broken a bone before I started the blockers,' Jacob tells me. 'On the blockers I broke my wrist twice, my knuckles, my toe.

It really ruins your bone density.' Four broken bones in just a few years. Jacob was advised to take vitamin D. His blood work showed that he was 'incredibly deficient'.

As Jacob's health deteriorated and his puberty continued to 'break through', he grew increasingly distressed. Like any other person experiencing medical problems he wanted to be able to talk to his doctors in privacy, but he didn't feel he was given that basic right. Every time Jacob and Michelle would attend appointments at UCLH, someone from GIDS would sit in. They wouldn't have minded so much if it were Jacob's own clinicians, but that's not how the arrangement works. GIDS clinicians are rota'd to attend the endocrine clinic at UCLH. It means that on any given day there's a chance the young people attending might be their own patients, but the likelihood is that they won't be. But the agreement between GIDS and UCLH is that someone from GIDS must attend all endocrine-clinic appointments at UCLH. For Jacob, it meant that every time he and Michelle made the trip to London to talk about the medical problems he was encountering while on the blocker, a different member of GIDS staff would sit in each time. 'It's awful,' Jacob says. 'These were private medical discussions about things that I was already self-conscious about. And I had to talk about them in front of a stranger.'

After more than four years on the blocker, Jacob felt worse than he ever had before the medication. While his friends were getting their first boyfriends and girlfriends, experiencing their first kisses and sexual experiences, he felt nothing. 'You have no desire, no drive whatsoever,' he says. 'You don't even feel attracted to people.' While sitting his GCSE exams he felt he was 'being left behind'. Emotionally, he felt years younger than his peers. Michelle noticed it too. And physically, Jacob had stopped growing. Her child was not developing in the way he should.

'I was desperate for it to work,' Jacob says. But the puberty blockers weren't working. And he'd been told by his doctors that even when he went on to testosterone, he would have to continue taking blockers. 'They told me that I would have to be on the blocker for the rest of my life if I decided to take testosterone, and I was like – excuse my language – I was like, screw that.'

At the beginning of 2019, Jacob had had enough. He told his mum, Michelle, 'I'm not doing this any more.'

Jacob took his last injection of puberty blockers in January 2019. He had started on them aged 12, and had been receiving regular injections for more than four years. They hadn't been the 'magic bullet' he and his family had been promised.

His decision to walk away from UCLH and GIDS wasn't planned really, but he'd had enough. A number of factors combined. There was the news that even when Jacob went on to testosterone, as GIDS had talked about from his initial assessment at the age of 11, he would still have to take blockers to suppress his naturally occurring oestrogen. He could not face the prospect of his health problems – both physical and mental – continuing indefinitely.

Then there was the challenge from Jacob's siblings. 'You've been on the blocker for so long,' they said. 'How do you even know that you're trans? How do you even know that you have these feelings?' Jacob knew these questions were coming from a place of love. His brothers and sister thought he should come off the blockers because they were 'ruining' his body. Michelle remembers Jacob's response. 'I don't know. I just know that's how I feel,' he said, 'and I dream as a boy.'

And finally, there was what happened at UCLH. Jacob was 16 and feeling 'very body-conscious', Michelle explains. He wanted to have a private conversation with his doctors, without a GIDS member of staff present. On one occasion, the request was agreed to, but Michelle and Jacob say they were told, 'If this happens again, you won't be allowed to be seen without a representative from GIDS in there.' Those were the rules, and they had to adhere to them.

Jacob claims they were told that there were many others who could take his place if he was unhappy.

Jacob never went back to GIDS. A year later, in March 2020, Jacob's GP received a letter informing them that he had been discharged.

The improvement to Jacob's health was immediate when he stopped the blockers. 'I felt so much better in terms of mood. I could sleep better. I grew quite soon after I stopped them.'

His identity didn't change.

In 2022, more than three years after stopping puberty blockers, Jacob is 19 and still trans. He uses a male name and male pronouns, and dresses in a way that he says is typically male. His passport and driving licence say male. But he's not on any medication. He hasn't chosen to take testosterone and has no plans to. 'I'm quite content with just being me at the moment,' he says. 'To be honest, I think I'm gonna be like that for the rest of my life. I'm just all right with what I'm doing at the moment, which is nothing. I'm happy dressing as a boy, I'm happy saying that I'm a "he". And even if people don't really believe it… it doesn't really bother me.' As he gets ready to start university, Jacob tells me he wants to leave the experience at GIDS behind, and 'live my life'.

But he's angry about the five years he was at GIDS. He says he was 'sold a lie'. Jacob uses the word 'sold' dozens of times over the several hours that we speak. He says it's the only accurate way he can describe how he feels.

GIDS clinicians 'raced at 100 miles an hour', Jacob says. 'There had only been four appointments, and they had already been discussing hormone-replacement therapy, already discussing the operations you could have. Always talking about hormone blockers. For me they were complete strangers, and they were selling me false hope.'

Michelle is angry too. Watching Jacob go through so much pain was 'shocking'. All she wanted was for her child to be safe, healthy and happy, but she didn't know how to help him. 'It felt like they were abusing my child, and I felt helpless to stop it,' Michelle says, explaining that she hates to put it this way, but it's how she feels. 'And I actually felt like if I did speak up and say anything, that I was the one that was being judged. Because why would I think like that? Surely, I should be doing everything I can for Jacob to follow his pathway?'

Michelle is left with unanswered questions. 'They're happy to dish out drugs without knowing those answers,' she says. GIDS had talked about the blocker providing young people 'with the opportunity to explore and experiment with their identities without the anxiety and challenges associated with ongoing pubertal development', Michelle says, so why weren't the ongoing meetings with Jacob about doing that 'exploring'? They weren't. Instead, it felt more like 'you get on the train, and you continue to testosterone', Michelle says. She is understanding about the fact that GIDS clinicians might not have known everything there was to know about the blocker and its impact at that time, but says that should have been reflected. She questions why the blocker was talked about with such certainty. 'It shocked me that they're pushing for the kids to go on [them],' Michelle says. 'It did feel like that.'

Michelle would have liked it if they had been better supported as a family, too. It would have been useful, she says, to have someone to talk to and 'not feel judged'. Someone independent, perhaps, who she could honestly air her worries with. It would have helped Jacob's brothers and sister too, who also struggled to deal with what their sibling was going through.

What Jacob wanted was for someone to be more truthful with him. Someone to explain what going through puberty might be like. Someone to prepare him for what challenges might lie ahead if he continued to identify as male. And someone to acknowledge that the medical pathway might not be the *only* way to live a happy trans life. The Tavistock does not have the capability 'of offering anything other than giving you the drugs', Jacob claims. 'I honestly don't think that they have the slightest clue about what it actually means to be trans.'

Jacob absolutely believes that puberty blockers should be available to young people. For some people, he says, that will be the 'only option'. And for those people the blocker must be fully explained, he says, complete with all the side effects and unknowns. 'But I think that there is a spectrum,' he says. Not everyone has to 'go the full nine yards to be trans like the Tavistock suggests. I honestly do not think that's how it works.' Plenty of people, just like him, are 'going to the Tavistock as children not really knowing where they stand and being offered permanent solutions', Jacob believes. 'And I think that that is wrong.' 'All I wanted was guidance,' Jacob continues. 'How to use bathrooms when you're comfortable enough to use the boys' toilets, how to explain yourself when you have relationships (if that's what you want),' explaining being trans to family. 'I was needing that. But that's not what I was given. I was given miracle cures and false hope and then I was told to put up with it, and if you're not willing to, then leave. And that is what happened.'

It's difficult talking to Jacob and Michelle. The experience of more than four years on puberty blockers and frequent visits to both the Tavistock and UCLH have clearly taken their toll. They both regret, and possibly resent, all the time spent focusing on Jacob's gender identity. Michelle says the more Jacob's gender identity was concentrated on – 'and it was talked about all the time' – the more it became the only focal point in life.

'I would have preferred Jacob to spend all of that time at school,' Michelle says. 'Every day that we had to go the Tavistock, or the UCLH or to CAMHS or to the doctor, was school time.' 'When I left [GIDS] and I actually got a chance to do proper work and proper revision… my grades got increasingly better,' Jacob says.

How is Jacob now?

He still feels left behind when he compares himself to his friends and his siblings. It's like 'playing catch-up', he says, 'but it's that you can't really catch up because you're so far behind.' It's 'weird', he says. 'I still haven't had my first kiss and I'm almost 19.' But he does not have any sexual feelings at all. 'I still don't feel attracted to people,' Jacob says, and he doesn't know if that is something that will ever come back.

The claim always made about puberty blockers is that they are physically reversible at least, and as soon as you stop, normal puberty resumes. This is based on their use in the treatment of precocious puberty, where treatment is generally discontinued as soon as a child reaches ten or 11.[6] When used in the treatment of gender dysphoria, so few young people come off puberty blockers that we really don't know what happens.

With Jacob, his growth resumed quickly, he and Michelle agree. But resumption of puberty was much slower. It took more than two years for Jacob to start having periods. They didn't begin until a few weeks before his eighteenth birthday. Even now, more than three years after coming off the blocker, Jacob's periods are sporadic and there are many months between them.

These 'data' are not being recorded anywhere, however. Since deciding to come off puberty blockers in February 2019, no one from GIDS or UCLH has been in touch to see how Jacob is, or to offer monitoring of any kind. Michelle finds this astonishing. She cannot understand how Jacob could have been on a drug for more than four years, experienced known adverse side effects, and been offered no follow-up. Both GIDS and UCLH have 'absolutely no idea how Jacob is and more importantly how both having blockers and subsequently coming off them has affected him', Michelle says. And Jacob does not know either.

'It is one of the biggest regrets in my life is that I went on blockers,' Jacob tells me. 'I went on the blockers because I was petrified of the possibility of puberty.' He says GIDS should have prepared him better for that and 'not just given me this drug'.

'I was a child,' Jacob says. 'And I still don't know how it's affected me properly. I still don't know the full damage that it could have done to my body. And that is just a scary fact.'

15

200 MILES UP THE M1...

July 2019

Dr Kirsty Entwistle sat on a bench on a cobbled street in northern Portugal, her phone held tightly to her ear. It was the middle of summer and she had been speaking with Anna Hutchinson for what seemed like hours.

Hutchinson, at home in her garden in south London, had read Entwistle's 2,700-word open letter to GIDS director Polly Carmichael just days before, and had been trying to take it in. The two women had never met, or even known the other existed. Unlike Hutchinson and other London-based GIDS staff – many of whom had now left the service due to concerns with the work – Kirsty Entwistle had been working at GIDS's smaller Leeds site. Yet here she was, expressing the exact same concerns.

Entwistle had not held back in her published account.

'I think it is a problem that GIDS clinicians are making decisions that will have a major impact on children and young people's bodies and on their lives... without a robust evidence base,' she wrote.[1]

Entwistle described how traumatised, deprived and sexually or physically abused children were referred for puberty blockers without their pasts being properly explored; how she was 'shocked by the complexity of referrals'; how some young people being assessed did not even have some of their 'most basic needs met'; how staff who raised concerns about the safety of children were labelled 'transphobic'; how it was 'highly unlikely' that any child attending GIDS would be told that they were *not* transgender; and how the London leadership had failed adequately to take on board the concerns raised by numerous clinicians.[2]

She rejected the claim that GIDS held the 'middle ground' in a 'polarised' debate. 'I don't think GIDS holds the middle ground at all,' she said. In her view, it was 'more closely aligned with the affirmative model', which unquestioningly accepts that a child is transgender if they say so and that medical interventions are often a necessary next step. She urged Polly Carmichael to listen to the concerns of her staff, take action against those who make 'false accusations of transphobia', for GIDS to stop referring to puberty blockers as 'fully reversible' and to 'better protect children and young people by ensuring that every child at least has a comprehensive psychosocial assessment before the medical pathway is considered'.[3]

'I saw the letter and, wow! I thought she was phenomenally brave,' Anna Hutchinson says. There had certainly been discussions in the London-based GIDS team that Leeds assessments might be faster on average than London ones, and, in fact, when Kirsty Entwistle joined GIDS in 2017, the Leeds team referred more young children – those under 15 – for puberty blockers than their London counterparts, quite something given the larger size of the London team and the fact it saw more young people.[4] I've been told that GIDS Leeds completed about a third of the workload. But Hutchinson had had no idea that colleagues in Leeds shared her concerns. Kirsty Entwistle's letter was yet more confirmation that there was nothing unique about Hutchinson and her London colleagues being worried. Rather, there was something in the nature of this work, where potentially life-changing medications are used to treat a condition in children with no physical illness, that brings out feelings of deep unease.

As the pair talked, Entwistle remembers saying that she wished someone from the outside could try to answer the question 'Is this ethical?' For the arguments to be heard in court, even, where they 'could be dealt with really rationally with all the emotion taken out of things'.

That opportunity would soon come.*

Originally from Manchester, Kirsty Entwistle joined the GIDS Leeds team in October 2017, excited about securing a job at the prestigious Tavistock. She'd been taught by some of its best and most respected thinkers for her doctorate. When a job came up that would allow her to be closer to friends and family and yet still work for the eminent Tavistock, she says, 'I couldn't believe my luck.' 'I went to the Tavistock thinking that I was going to be working in this amazing place with lots of really amazing thinking.' It didn't happen. Things started to go wrong, Entwistle says, 'almost instantly'.

By her own admission, Dr Entwistle was 'naive' about this field when she took the job at GIDS. 'I didn't know anything about the whole conflict over it,' she says, so was taken aback with the response she received when she admitted that she didn't think that she personally had a gender identity. She remembers saying to a small group of colleagues that she was trying to work out what gender identity *is*. 'I said, "I don't have a gender identity, I'm just female."' This was immediately branded as 'transphobic'. It may sound small, but this early accusation of transphobia and the shutting down of thinking had a profound impact on Entwistle. 'Just being called transphobic, it doesn't sound like you should be so anxious about it, but I just instantly felt completely anxious.' Others present mostly kept quiet; another said it wasn't okay to say things like that. 'I just felt completely trapped,' she says.

This early experience made Entwistle feel that GIDS might not have been what she thought she had been signing up for. 'I felt tricked, because in my interview I talked… a lot about psychodynamic theory, and they were like, you know, this is great, this is great. And then I get there and then instantly… smackdown.'

'Confusing' is the word that Entwistle uses a lot to describe her GIDS experience. 'Mad' is the other. Like other clinicians, she found most of her colleagues nice people to work with. 'There was a lot of

---

* Dr Entwistle was later a witness in judicial review proceedings against the Tavistock and Portman NHS Foundation Trust.

laughter and light-heartedness,' she says, and on the whole 'people were very friendly'. She liked them. The clinic was nice too, a 'fancy Victorian building' nestled among lawyers' offices, round a leafy square in central Leeds. The walls were plastered with colourful paintings done by GIDS patients. But she couldn't square the atmosphere with the clinical work. Within a matter of weeks she felt 'there's no thinking going on here'. She worked on a couple of cases with the colleague who had branded her 'transphobic' and was concerned.[*]

In one, Entwistle says a young person's interest in a popular children's toy was seen by her colleague as an indication that the child was transgender. Dr Entwistle strongly felt 'that should not be a sign of anything' and certainly shouldn't be used to make a clinical decision about whether to refer for puberty blockers. There was trauma in this child's childhood. And they were being 'relentlessly bullied', subject to vile homophobic slurs. Yet her colleague, she says, indicated to this young person at the second session that they would be referred to endocrinology services.

The level of homophobia she witnessed generally across her case-load shocked Entwistle. She says it wasn't discussed in the team, and there was no training on how to talk about sexuality with young people. She recalls listening to young people and feeling strongly that they would grow up to be lesbian or gay, but being unable to voice this. Like many adults who have spent significant amounts of time in metropolitan cities she was surprised to find that homophobic bullying was not a 'thing of the past'. Even more surprising, she says, was the language used by the young people themselves – 'old fashioned slurs' that she hadn't heard since the 1980s.

In another case with the same colleague, a young person was doing well in life and 'presented as being happy'.[5] There was no visible

---

[*] Dr Entwistle also provided details of these cases in a witness statement provided in support of an employment tribunal brought by Sonia Appleby, the children's safeguarding lead of the Tavistock and Portman NHS Foundation Trust. The Trust chose not to challenge its contents in questioning and Entwistle affirmed the contents of the statement under oath. A letter that Entwistle wrote to the Tavistock's Speak Up Guardian, Gill Rusbridger, dated 29 July 2019, sets out further concerns.

distress, Entwistle recalls, and she describes there being 'lots of laughter and chatter between the three of them'.[6] In both cases, Entwistle felt her colleague was 'too quick to recommend the medical pathway and I did not believe there was a current clinical need for puberty blockers in either case'.[7]

Entwistle raised her concerns with her supervisor and the head of the GIDS Leeds service. Instead of tackling the issues head on, she says, an agreement was made that Entwistle and this particular colleague would not work together again on future cases, 'as our approaches were incompatible'.[8] Entwistle would continue with one case, and her colleague the other. The response was 'inept', Entwistle says, and 'merely served to avoid addressing' the real issues.[9] In her mind, the problem facing the head of the service was simple: either there was a genuinely transphobic member of staff in Kirsty Entwistle, or some children were being put on puberty blockers for no clinical reason. The solution arrived at – to split the cases and no longer put the two clinicians together – addressed neither.*

The head of GIDS Leeds, Dr Sally Phillott, advised Entwistle that she could speak to another consultant in the Tavistock, outside of GIDS, to try to help relieve some of the distress and confusion she was feeling. 'So, I rang [the consultant]. And... talking to her was like, this is what I was expecting from the Tavistock – somebody who is really thinking.' Looking back, Entwistle says the several conversations she had with this person were incredibly helpful. But at the time she felt 'ashamed' at having shared such raw emotions. At one point she describes almost 'howling' down the phone. The senior Tavistock clinician listened as Entwistle described her concerns about the work, and how she had had nightmares relating to it. 'She encouraged me to leave.'

After leaving her post, Entwistle told the Tavistock Trust's Speak Up Guardian, Gill Rusbridger, that she believed 'people feel unable to speak freely for fear of being labelled transphobic... and that this

---

* Dr Sally Phillott, the head of GIDS Leeds, said that for reasons of confidentiality it was 'not appropriate to comment on individual cases or staff'. 'What I can say is that I believe that such issues were dealt with seriously and sensitively, in line with Trust policies, with the best interests of patients and their families in mind,' she added.

has an impact on the care of young people at GIDS'.[10] Clinicians in Leeds, she says, weren't able to use meetings as a space to think freely about what 'might be driving a young person's distress and gender dysphoria apart from transgenderism without fear of being labelled transphobic'.[11] She says she had witnessed others being branded as transphobes, just as she had been.

Just as her colleagues in London had noted, Entwistle saw that different clinicians behaved very differently to one another in assessments. Sometimes more junior members of staff felt 'obliged' to go along with the decisions of the senior clinician. In other instances, it felt like 'the blind leading the blind'. Entwistle says there would often be two entry-level clinicians working together with complex young people, both with only a matter of a few months' experience. Entwistle says that she and colleagues would often feel 'baffled' but constrained by the assessment model GIDS was working to. 'We just kind of felt like we had to resolve something or come to some kind of conclusion within six sessions, because that was one of the guidelines you're working to.' She was unaware that some clinicians in London had by now started trying to extend assessments beyond six appointments, believing that more exploratory work was needed before any informed decision about what to do next could be taken.

She felt similarly uncomfortable referring some of the older teenagers to adult services. It felt like 'passing the buck', she says. 'I knew on some level this is totally irresponsible: to see a kid for two, three, four sessions, and then make a referral to adult services; give them a diagnosis and send them off.'

The work felt 'unethical' to Entwistle. She says she wasn't the only one who felt this way either. The young people presenting to the service had such complicated backgrounds that it was 'impossible' to carry out an adequate assessment in this time. 'Even though as a new starter I was meant to be taking on low- to medium-complexity cases I would say that the vast majority of children on my caseload had had traumatic experiences.'[12] Entwistle's caseload included children with parents who'd been long-term psychiatric patients, families where the mother had accused the father of rape, a number of children who had only 'minimal verbal communication skills', and 'many' who had witnessed domestic violence. Three per cent were families where a parent was a registered sex offender. 'That seems above average,' she reasons. 'So that needs to be audited. Does everybody have... sex-offending parents on their caseload?'[13]

To put that figure into some context, in 2018 there were 58,637 registered sex offenders in England and Wales, the vast majority of whom are male.[14] The total male population aged 18 to 65 was more than 18 million.[15] That gives a male adult offending rate of 0.3 per cent – less than ten times that seen in this snapshot of GIDS families. It's not a perfect comparison by any means, but one would not expect to see this rate in Entwistle's caseload.

The reaction in the GIDS Leeds team to Entwistle's letter is interesting. 'At first I thought, "Wow, that's brave. Credit to her,"' one former colleague told me, before explaining a sudden shift in sentiment. The team was upset, she said. 'I think people felt a bit let down. But also, I think people felt as though she'd sort of put discussions that were felt to be confidential for the team out into a public arena, which didn't feel right.' This Leeds clinician said the letter created a 'backlash' against the service, which they then couldn't respond to. But she recognised the behaviour Entwistle had identified in the one colleague, saying that 'there was bullish behaviour' and that they were 'difficult to challenge', to work with and manage. 'This clinician did have strong ideological beliefs, and this created tensions within the team and in co-working pairs,' she said. Ensuring that Entwistle and this colleague didn't work cases together was the only real solution, she said, because clinically they 'operated completely differently'. Several clinicians have insisted that there are inevitably professional differences of opinion within any children's mental health service. GIDS, they say, is not unique. But it seems extraordinary that a clinical service contained staff who held such different views, and who approached the work so differently that they could not work together. There are clear implications for GIDS's service users.

This experienced Leeds clinician also recognised the complexity of Entwistle's caseload. Is the objection, then, more that the concerns were made public, rather than that they weren't valid? Partly, it seems. But this clinician also feels as though 'everything's been amplified' when it comes to those who are critical of GIDS. She didn't agree that the majority of cases were about mental health and trauma. 'We would be seeing it now in terms of detransitioning; we're not seeing it,' she says. 'And I think that young people need to be given more credit for knowing who they are.'

Kirsty Entwistle doesn't believe she gave accurate information on puberty blockers to the families she saw at GIDS.

And she feels 'awful' about it.

She had no idea that GIDS's own data indicated that almost everyone who started on puberty blockers went on to take cross-sex hormones. She hadn't been told this by anyone in the service. Nor was she made aware of the surgical problems that can result later for boys if puberty is blocked too early.

She recalls several families in which one parent was distraught at being told their child was being referred for puberty blockers. 'On one occasion I watched a mother sob after I informed her that her young teenager had "consented" to my colleague's offer of puberty blockers. The child's father, a man with a bad temper who made me feel uncomfortable, was pleased. Going along with it, and seeing that mother cry because she knew she couldn't object, will always be a stain on my conscience.'[16]

Entwistle remembers talking to the parents in these circumstances: 'I was saying… "It's just to buy some time, you know, give time to think without their body changing," and selling this whole "buying time" line, because that's what I'd been told,' Entwistle remembers. 'I wasn't giving accurate information to these parents.'

In retrospect she regrets having agreed to these referrals.

'What I did – or rather what I failed to do – at GIDS was wrong and I'm ashamed of it and wish I could go back in time and do the right thing.'[17]

This was a large part of Entwistle's motivation for writing the open letter to GIDS director Polly Carmichael. She wanted to say sorry. Sorry for not being able to be more forceful at the time.

But a previous professional experience also had a profound effect, which stirred her to speak out.

Like Anna Hutchinson, Entwistle had worked with medically and emotionally vulnerable children before joining GIDS. While she was a junior, entry-level clinician at GIDS, she had the best-part of 15 years' previous experience working with young people.

Entwistle's first job after graduating with her first degree was in a private children's home in Rochdale. It was 2003. 'We were just support workers. You know, we didn't have any proper training... And we were working with some of the most disturbed kids that you could imagine.' It was a home for young people deemed risky to themselves and to others. Soon after starting the job, a 12-year-old girl arrived at the home. She'd been in a secure unit beforehand, because she was running away all the time. Not long after she'd arrived in Rochdale, the same thing happened. The situation 'deteriorated into chaos'. The girl would run away frequently, and sometimes be missing for weeks. 'And she'd come back. And she'd be in a terrible state,' Entwistle remembers.

This young girl was being groomed. When she went missing, she was having sex with grown men. As soon as she left the home, there would be 'some predatory man' waiting in a car to pick her up. Kirsty Entwistle, barely an adult herself, was her key worker. 'And I remember saying, "How do you feel after you've had sex with these men?" and she turned around and she just said, "I want to kill them."' Entwistle knew the girl needed help. But CAMHS wouldn't be flexible when she wouldn't turn up for appointments. And the police spoke about the girl with contempt. 'Nobody helped us,' Entwistle reflects sadly.

But, she says, the episode taught her that sometimes, for very complicated reasons, children can want something that might harm them. This young girl repeatedly said she *wanted* to go and meet these men. Men who were subjecting her to horrific abuse. Entwistle's job was 'to stand in front of the door', and stop that happening. She would be kicked, punched, screamed at and spat at in the process. Sometimes, she says, something has happened to children 'that makes them want something so badly that is harmful to them'.

To be clear, Entwistle makes no comparison between the widespread sexual grooming of young girls at children's homes in northern England and practices at GIDS. The point she is making is that it is not easy to say no to a child in distress, desperate for something they believe will help them feel better. But sometimes, adults must.

'The other thing is, we had no idea… that this… was a systemic thing… we just thought we had this particular kid who was doing this.' The country would later learn that the sexual abuse of vulnerable young girls in care by older men was widespread. And a stain on the national conscience. Not just in Rochdale, but in Rotherham and across England.[18] Some men went to prison for the crimes, but certainly not all those who were guilty of them.[19]

Kirsty Entwistle had written to several people about her experience at the children's home, 'and nobody was interested'. 'They didn't even write back to me. And so, I guess that was why I kind of thought I need to write the letter [about GIDS]. Because it's not going to arrive on a plate – the chance to talk about this – you've just got to go and do it.'

'I just thought I'm going to be stuck with this. The same way that I feel stuck with what happened in Rochdale… I'm just sorry, you know, and this is what I think.'

16

ACROSS THE SEA

April 2019, Dublin, Ireland

Dr Paul Moran wanted his concerns about GIDS's assessments of Irish teenagers on the record.

Concerns that he and his colleagues at the adult National Gender Service felt were growing. They'd met with staff at Ireland's largest paediatric hospital – Children's Health Ireland at Crumlin (known simply as Crumlin to most) – a month earlier, but the meeting's record he'd received didn't correspond to the discussion they'd had. These minutes, he typed forcefully on his keyboard, 'do not reflect in any way the meeting which took place'.[1]

The main focus, he explained in his email, was what he believed to be the 'current unsafe service at Crumlin'.[2]

Ireland did not have, and – at the time of writing – still does not have, its own facility to help gender-questioning young people. Acknowledging the gap in provision, the country's Health Service Executive (HSE) turned to the Tavistock for help. At first the arrangement was low-key. GIDS began seeing Irish children in 2012 under the 'Treatment Abroad Scheme' (TAS).[3] This covers the cost of medical treatment in another EU or European Economic Area (EEA) country, or Switzerland, when it's not available in Ireland.[4] Irish youngsters would fly over from Dublin to London and be assessed by the GIDS team. The numbers were initially tiny, with just one patient referred for care in 2011/12, three the following year and four in 2013/14.[5]

But these soon increased dramatically, doubling to eight in 2014/15 and then catapulting to 27 a year later.[6] This reflected what GIDS had seen among its English referrals, and although the numbers themselves were small, Irish referrals increased sevenfold in the space of two years. It was agreed, therefore, that rather than dozens of children flying across the Irish Sea to London once a month for appointments at the Tavistock Centre, GIDS's clinicians would come to them. Monthly clinics at Crumlin began around 2015. Endocrinology services, if needed, were supplied by a paediatric endocrinologist at the hospital. Curiously, despite the 'treatment' now not taking place 'abroad', it remained funded by the TAS.

Initially, the arrangement didn't draw much attention. The numbers were small, and it took time for those assessed by GIDS to be old enough to migrate across to the adult service, based at St Columcille's Hospital in Loughlinstown, half an hour away. It was only when enough of those who had first been referred to GIDS in 2015 became old enough to have their care moved across – several years later – that Paul Moran and others started to sense that all was not well.

Consultant psychiatrist Dr Paul Moran is a details man. He takes his work seriously and communicates his concerns clearly. He's been supporting transgender adults for close to 30 years. The same is true of his colleague, consultant endocrinologist Professor Donal O'Shea, who speaks honestly about the difficulties in their work. The pair had both spent time in London in the 1990s working in this field – Moran at Guy's Hospital, O'Shea at Charing Cross Gender Identity Clinic. They say they've helped hundreds of people transition successfully. 'For people who are ready, have a clear, stable understanding of their gender, social supports, and are physically and mentally healthy, I see it as a fantastic thing,' says Moran. Similarly, O'Shea says that some of the very best outcomes he sees are in his trans patients.

But both men have also seen the consequences of poor assessment prior to transitioning. It's a decision taken for life, explains Moran, and so 'it's far better to transition well, than transition quickly'.

Returning to Ireland from London in the early 2000s, the pair worked together to treat a handful of trans patients each year. 'And then, by 2010, 2011, it was very clear we were not able to cope with the numbers that were coming at us, and we needed a formal service,' O'Shea states. They pitched their idea for a national gender service, and eventually received funding for it around 2016. But this was only after they'd seen the devastating impact of some shoddy work done by others.

'We were seeing very haphazard referrals from Irish psychologists operating mainly in the private sector, where somebody was going along, saying, "I think I have gender dysphoria," and there wasn't really an assessment being carried out,' O'Shea says. 'We began to see more and more disasters,' Moran explains. Extremely poor mental health and regret, and several patients took their own lives. They were receiving hormones from Loughlinstown but had been assessed before that by private therapists. Moran says all these cases 'had big red flags, easily visible', that would have been picked up by 'any proper assessment'.

The pair developed a new service, initially without any money coming from the HSE. 'We realised this was unsafe and we needed to develop a proper system. Instead of troubleshooting problems *after* the event, we needed to assess people *before* they start hormones – identify who was ready; and for those who weren't ready, what needed to be done to make transition safe,' Moran explains. The gender service that resulted put in place a robust assessment with a psychiatrist prior to any hormonal interventions being given. This kind of model, which includes a mental health assessment, attracts criticism from some in the trans community for being excessively cautious, outdated and pathologizing.[7] 'Our service is trashed online for being conservative and blocking,' O'Shea admits, but O'Shea and Moran insist their approach has dramatically improved outcomes for trans people. 'The remarkable drop off in adverse outcomes was spectacular when we introduced more thorough assessment,' Moran says. There have been no suicides in recent years, he says.

Their previous experience of the potentially devastating conse-quences of inadequate assessment prior to transitioning meant alarm bells rang when they saw the reports accompanying patients, who'd been seen by GIDS, move across to their adult service.

When it was just a couple of young people migrating across to Loughlinstown, their care initially continued without additional review. O'Shea explains that he hadn't seen any difficulty with the arrangement – after all, they'd been assessed by the world-leading Tavistock. He was happy to continue their prescriptions for puberty blockers or cross-sex hormones. O'Shea had worked with patients assessed by GIDS in the 1990s and recalled that back then they carried out 'very good assessments and recommendations'.

But 25 years or so later, things felt different. 'The endocrinologists started noticing that these people were experiencing a lot of problems. A lot of them weren't ready for this,' says Paul Moran. 'Generally, what would happen is the endocrinologist would contact me saying, "Listen I've got this kid here, we took him over from Crumlin and he looks very unwell, depressed, or he's self-harming, will you take a look?"… That's when we started to notice there's a problem here with the assessments.'

The first thing Moran wanted to do with any patient was to go through their records. But in many instances, he says, Crumlin didn't hold any records for the young people who'd been assessed by GIDS. The Tavistock would then be asked for them, but they 'generally refused on the ground they didn't have patient's permission to send records'. It was a mess.

When he did get to see *some* assessment reports, it brought little comfort. Moran immediately voiced his concerns with endocrinologist Donal O'Shea. O'Shea saw a four-page assessment on Tavistock headed paper – it seemed thorough. 'But when you actually look at the assessment it was four pages of words,' he says. 'It was describing an upbringing; it was saying the individual wants to [transition]. But it wasn't forming an opinion.'

The assessment reports were littered with 'red flags' that hadn't been highlighted. 'The social situation was so chaotic that the idea that you would just jump in with hormones and start treating, without social-work input, without liaising with the school, the key worker, you know, it was clearly potty.' Several children had been in and out of care, had no family support for transition or had severe autism. A number weren't attending school. There were cases where there was physical abuse in the family, alcohol and drug misuse – both by family members and sometimes by the young person themselves – and 'certainly a lot of homophobia', O'Shea says. Some files referenced 'allegations of sexual abuse' too, according to Paul Moran. But they then did not show whether this had been explored or any conclusion reached. The Tavistock reports might say 'it's a complicated situation', Moran explains, 'but there seemed to be a big rush to commence treatment'.

Irish referrals to GIDS mirrored what was seen more generally: they increased rapidly; young people often seemed to present with multiple co-occurring difficulties; and they were overwhelmingly female. Of 51 active Irish cases being seen by GIDS in February 2018, 33 (65 per cent) were female.[8] In 2019, girls made up 80 per cent of those referred from Ireland.[9] Between 2011 and 2021, 238 young people in Ireland were referred to GIDS.

It wasn't that the GIDS assessments had been too short – the young people had been seen a fair number of times. But, Moran insists, they lacked depth, thought and clarity. In some cases, it was unclear as to how a young person had come to start on blockers or cross-sex hormones. Many reports, he says, spoke about the young person's feelings about themselves but lacked a history of the child's development. 'There was certainly very little about their mental health, nothing about psychosexual issues,' and very little about how the gender identity issues had developed over time. When reports identified clear difficulties in the person's life, there'd be no recommendations on how to alleviate them, Moran says.

Some patients had barely left their homes, such was the state of their mental health. 'You could have a patient who they would have seen who was bedroom-bound, not attending school, clearly mentally unwell; they'd started on hormones, but there'd be no looking at the functional problem. So, we get to see the patient four years later, and they haven't left the house for years. But they were taking their hormones religiously. Lots like that.'

GIDS director Dr Carmichael says she does not accept this criticism of the service, and stated that 'GIDS has never received any direct complaint or concern from the Irish National Gender Service about the quality of treatment of any referrals'. She said that all children referred to GIDS from Ireland have to undergo a psychiatric assessment in local services beforehand.

Paul Moran first voiced his concerns with the Irish health authorities in the summer of 2018. Irish newspapers later reported them.[10] He and Donal O'Shea had set up a series of meetings with clinicians at Crumlin. The adult team acknowledged that 'it wasn't fair to Crumlin to be trying to deal with this endocrinologically'. Donal O'Shea says the children's hospital 'needed a system where they would be able to stand over the assessments' that had been carried out by an outside team. He and Moran felt that Crumlin needed to have its own assessment team, including mental health experts. Then arrangements could be put in place to ensure a seamless move from youth services to the national gender clinic. This never happened. Despite several attempts, Crumlin has not been able to recruit an adolescent psychiatrist and, at the time of writing, has no permanent paediatric endocrinologist on staff.[11]

But back in 2018 this was the aim. And at a meeting that summer, Moran voiced his worries about what they were seeing. 'I spoke to the meeting saying, "I have grave concerns about patients we're seeing, assessed by Tavistock."' At the beginning of 2019, details of David Bell's report containing the concerns of GIDS staff hit Ireland, along with news of clinicians resigning from the service. 'We said, "Okay, this confirms what we've been thinking."' Donal O'Shea shared his past experiences of the poor outcomes than can result from poor assessments with Irish healthcare bosses – of having to talk to the mother of a young adult who had taken their own life. 'I've sat down and apologised where we've done harm and where, based on inadequate assessments, I have started treatments and sent people forward for surgery who clearly shouldn't have gone down either route,' he says.

In early 2019, a colleague at the National Gender Service conducted an audit of 18 referrals of young people assessed by GIDS. I have seen a redacted copy of that document. In seven cases there appeared to be no assessment report supplied at all. Ten young people had serious mental health problems (including self-harm, depression, suicidality and eating disorders), were autistic or had incredibly difficult life circumstances alongside their gender identity issues. In seven, the reports were unclear.

A further meeting was arranged for March 2019. A member of staff from Crumlin took notes. It was these minutes that Paul Moran objected to so strongly.

Sitting in the hospital's boardroom, the psychiatrist expressed his concerns that the service being provided to young people was 'unsafe'; that there appeared to be 'no documentary record of assessments for most patients being treated at Crumlin Hospital', and where there *were* assessment reports, they were 'inadequate for the purpose of treatment'.[12] He asked questions too. How many patients were being assessed by the Tavistock? What proportion of those patients did they have records for? Moran says Crumlin were unable to provide satisfactory answers.

Of those young people who'd been assessed by GIDS and were now on either puberty blockers or cross-sex hormones, some appeared to be doing well, but others were not. It wasn't clear to the adult team who should be receiving treatment, and who should not. Paul Moran called for the assessment service provided by GIDS to be 'terminated with immediate effect'.[13] Why did he feel the need to 'correct' the minutes of that meeting? It was with a view to the future, he says: 'To have it on record that we did speak about the concerns; we did say that the service should be discontinued for these reasons; so that in the future we could not be accused of having sat idly by.'

The HSE have told the Irish press that these concerns were 'not representative of the many clinicians who refer to the Tavistock'.[14] And according to Crumlin's clinical director at the time, the concerns expressed by Paul Moran, Donal O'Shea and their colleagues were not shared by staff at Crumlin working with the young people assessed by GIDS.[15] Instead, they were mostly concerned with making sure these patients could make a safe transition to adult services. Moran wanted that too, but the service currently in place for those young people was 'unsafe and substandard', he said, and incompatible with the adult service at Loughlinstown. He and others were not prepared to continue treatment on the basis of Tavistock assessments. But it was difficult to know what the best way forward would be.

Moran explained to Crumlin's clinical director about the problems they'd experienced years before, when people had started to transition medically without having been properly assessed. The situation they faced now, he said was potentially worse. 'Even with poor assessment, the odds of incorrect treatment are much reduced in the adult cohort than in teens (meaning, a bigger percentage of regrets etc.),' he wrote in an email, explaining that adolescence tends to be a time of great change. 'The adult legacy cases, being over 18, were also able to make informed consent about these life-changing treatments (and in cases of regret, this has been an important issue).' He issued a stark warning: 'For these reasons, it is likely we will encounter significant levels of regret and other adverse outcomes in the Crumlin legacy group over the years to come which will be difficult to defend.'[16]

Unable to reach an agreed solution with either those responsible for the clinical governance of Crumlin children's hospital or those at the HSE in Ireland, in late 2019 the team at the national gender clinic made a decision: new treatments would not be started by those who had been assessed by GIDS without a fresh assessment. Treatment that had started would not be withdrawn – the team recognised that putting someone back could be damaging – but generally young people would need to be assessed again before moving on to the next stage of their medical or surgical transition. It was not a blanket policy – where it was clear that a young person was doing well, a further assessment wouldn't be needed. And there are some who fit this description, O'Shea acknowledges. But they are the minority. 'There are then degrees of complexity in the other 80 per cent,' O'Shea says. They might be there 'sitting mute beside a pushy parent' or accompanied by a key worker. 'And there's flags that mean you need to move very carefully before you run down a road of surgery or further hormones.'

Both men fear for what might unfold for the Irish children who have gone through GIDS. Right now, it's unclear. 'There is a chance it'll be fine. There's a chance it will be a disaster,' O'Shea reflects.

'What we're seeing with that group that are coming through, is some are a disaster and are going through an assessment with us and pausing. You know, just give it more time to work things out.' Some have stopped their treatment altogether, and many others have chosen not to start. 'A lot of the patients are not taking the hormones even after they're prescribed, and I say a lot – a significant percentage.'

It's worth saying again that doctors Paul Moran and Donal O'Shea have been helping adults transition for more than two decades. They care greatly about their work and believe that a successful gender transition is one of the best things they have witnessed in their medical careers. 'But equally, some of the worst outcomes I've seen in my career have been [transition] done badly,' O'Shea explains. Where it's happened 'too quickly', or 'in a person where it isn't gender dysphoria – it's a sense of not belonging', then 'that's the disaster'.

Paul Moran says that he and his colleagues are already seeing former GIDS patients who were 'clearly not ready or suitable at the time they were started' on medical interventions. There have been missed opportunities to help improve the lives of these young people, he says. He recalls a patient who had been referred for puberty blockers by GIDS, despite their life circumstances being chaotic. 'They had dropped out of school, were involved with drug taking, lots of underage sex, the child had been in and out of care… So it was a complete disaster at the time the Tavistock started them on blockers.' Moran says that GIDS's thinking in relation to the person was 'woolly' – a sense that going on puberty blockers was some kind of 'halfway treatment' while the young person worked issues out; that they wouldn't undergo any permanent masculinisation or feminisation. But this person stayed on the blocker for years – and that's 'dangerous for their bone health', says Moran. When this person wanted a referral for surgery, 'they were still in chaos'. But 'the conversation we had about surgery was the opportunity to engage with this person about other issues', Moran explains. He managed to get them to engage in a rehabilitation programme for their substance misuse and help secure a better housing situation. 'We achieved in a relatively short period of time a very big shift of wellness and development. And I thought, "This could have been done six years ago."'

Paul Moran is most worried for those born female, whose gender difficulties began in their teenage years, once puberty had hit, who have made up the bulk of referrals to GIDS in the last five to seven years. 'We're going to see the fallout of these people. And many of the people who feel they're doing okay at the moment – it's only in the mid to late twenties that the real regrets start.'

The funding arrangement between the HSE and the Tavistock and Portman NHS Foundation Trust was due to end in January 2021.[17] But while GIDS clinicians are no longer flying to Dublin, the HSE are still paying for Irish children to be seen by GIDS in England. There is no paediatric gender service in Ireland.[18] At the time of writing in 2022 young people from Ireland continue to be referred to GIDS. Even after GIDS's planned closure was announced in July 2022, the HSE remained committed to referring Irish young people.[19] It is, however, 'exploring the availability of the service in other EU jurisdictions'.[20]

Consultant endocrinologist Donal O'Shea describes the situation facing Irish youth today as 'awful'. While he hopes that any harm to former GIDS patients will be limited 'because we're not going to be acting on inadequate assessments', he is worried. 'Unless we get the assessment of our children with gender issues right, then inevitably the system is going to cause them harm: either by not assessing them at all and helping them to progress when they need to progress on their gender journey, or by assessing inadequately and recommending treatments that will ultimately cause them harm.'

Donal O'Shea and Paul Moran voiced their concerns repeatedly. Their starting point in conversations, explains Donal O'Shea, was always 'We've got to make sure we don't do harm here'. They faced, in O'Shea's words, a 'kind of institutional laziness' in response. A hope that 'if we ignore it, it will go away'. It was not that they were not listened to. 'I think it's worse than that, actually,' O'Shea explains. 'I think that they listened, chose to ignore, and chose to push down a route that would cause them the least – I'm gonna say – hassle, distress, trouble.'

17

THE GIDS REVIEW AND OUTSIDE SCRUTINY

Many staff left the service in the months following the publication of the GIDS Review in March 2019. Between April 2019 and February 2020, 16 people resigned, including Anastassis Spiliadis and Anna Hutchinson.[1] It cannot be said that all resignations were linked to the review, but for some Dinesh Sinha's report and his recommendations were the final straw.

By the time Spiliadis was interviewed by Sinha, he had been raising concerns in the service for close to four years. He'd spoken to Gill Rusbridger, the Trust's Speak Up Guardian, more than a year earlier, and saw the review as the perfect opportunity to convey all that he was worried about. He hoped that someone would act. 'I was very positive that he would do something,' Spiliadis says. 'I spoke to Dinesh only when I realised that nothing happened with what I had shared, or what I had told Gill Rusbridger.'

Some staff who were no longer at GIDS, like Matt Bristow, also contributed to the review. Bristow had left the Trust in May 2018. 'I was broken by the service,' he says. He'd been asked to do 'too much', carrying a caseload of 140 families. He was shocked to see years later that Polly Carmichael had applied the label 'vulnerable' to him.[2] 'It took quite a while to heal, and to kind of get back on an even keel. But it wasn't me being vulnerable. It was a toxic environment that was just asking impossible things of staff,' Bristow says. By the end, he 'felt exhausted and anxious. And traumatised.' Despite the experience,

Bristow cared deeply for the young people being seen by GIDS. When the official review was launched, he was 'hopeful that something good might come out of it', he says.

Anna Hutchinson took part in the GIDS Review with the same sense of last-ditch hope. She had not returned to the service from her maternity leave yet, and there was still part of her that felt that if only someone could tackle the significant issues GIDS was facing, she would want to be part of that better, safer service. 'I hoped that this was an objective, clever outsider who would be able to see things clearly,' she says. Indeed, that's why chief executive Paul Jenkins decided that Sinha was the right candidate for the task. He had only joined the Tavistock a month before being asked to carry out the review into GIDS.

Prior to her interview with the Trust's medical director, Hutchinson spent hours pulling her thoughts together into a carefully worded document, evidencing everything she was saying, including providing Sinha with copies of her contemporaneous handwritten notes.[3] 'I'd been fobbed off so many times,' she says. 'I was desperately trying to be assertive: "You've got to listen to these concerns, they are serious,"' Hutchinson explains, 'but also, "I'm not mad and I'm not bad. And here is my evidence."'

This document clearly and forcefully outlined Hutchinson's many long-standing worries: the speed of referral for medical interventions, the disproportionate number of children who were autistic, were same-sex attracted or had suffered trauma, the service's poor handling of sexuality, and the 'two defining changes to the knowledge base in the past 5–10 years'. These, she explained, were the increase in the number of girls coming forward, and the fact that 'the puberty blocker was not performing as we all believed it to be'. They weren't providing time and space to think and reflect. 'Sadly, GIDS chose not to pause for thought,' she wrote. 'I believe that they are now routinely offering an extreme medical intervention as the first line treatment to hundreds of distressed young people who may or [may] not turn out to be "trans" (however that might be defined.) This is potentially scandalous in its negligence and scale.'[4]

Hutchinson described how the Executive team 'value pragmatism and "getting on with things"'. How raising of concerns would be taken as personal criticism, and how she had witnessed a somewhat unconventional management style – something others have spoken of too – whereby members of the Executive could be in tears or 'shouting at each other in meetings'.[5] 'Thinking' in GIDS, she said, was often only 'performative'. It didn't result in action. Hutchinson was honest about her own failings too, conceding that she had participated in clinical work which she now regretted. 'With an individual caseload the size of a small primary school I simply didn't have the energy or resources to do enough thinking at times.'[6]

At the start of her face-to-face interview for the GIDS Review, Dinesh Sinha told Anna Hutchinson he hadn't read the document.

It's unclear whether he did or did not. Speaking under oath in 2021, Dr Sinha later said that he read everything that was given to him from those he interviewed as part of his review into GIDS.[7] But having been told he had not read her document, Hutchinson outlined all her concerns and set out her attempts to raise them with the GIDS Executive and others in the Trust.

And so did a number of her colleagues.

They challenged the approach taken by GIDS on numerous occasions.

Anastassis Spiliadis told Sinha that, in his view, GIDS operated according to a 'business model'. That the response to young people (and the increase in referrals) was driven by what resources were available, as opposed to clinical need. Sinha sought to clarify: 'So you are saying that in your understanding the frame of the assessment has been set with resources in mind rather than the clinical presentation.' Yes, replied Spiliadis.[8]

GIDS's assessment model was directly questioned by several staff. 'We were told three to six sessions, but the pressure was always to do it [in] less,' Matt Bristow told Dinesh Sinha.[9] 'One of the weaknesses is that in the protocol it specifies that it is between three to six sessions, when from a clinical-needs point of view, many clinicians in the service argue that this does not suffice for such big decisions around how to manage gender dysphoria,' Spiliadis explained.[10]

GIDS offered only one 'treatment', staff said – a referral for physical interventions. And this was highly problematic. 'How does that affect the family and the service user?' Sinha asks Anna Hutchinson.

'I think it means that things are not interrogated properly and a lot is ignored really,' she replied.[11]

Sinha was told by multiple clinicians that in GIDS there was no way of saying no to the medical pathway. 'The reality is that if a family keeps insisting on [puberty blockers], we have very little space to say no,' stressed Spiliadis. This was the case 'even if my clinical judgement is that I feel[,] for this young person and family, it is not the right time,' he explained.[12] Other clinicians voiced the same concerns. They are not being quoted to protect their anonymity.

On consent, clinicians were also assertive with Sinha and stressed that existing processes were not safe.

Sinha was told by at least half a dozen GIDS staff that they felt that various aspects of the service were unsafe, that exploration was not possible, that concerns were shut down, and that safeguarding was inadequate. In other words, the service was failing to protect children from harm and make sure they were safe.

Dinesh Sinha asked several clinicians directly whether they thought GIDS was safe. Each time the answer was the same. No.

Were referrals managed in a 'safe and adequate' way? 'No, I do not think it was safe in terms of self-harm,' Bristow replied.[13] 'Do you think the safeguarding practices are safe and adequate for the service? Because you seem to suggest they are not,' Sinha asked Anna Hutchinson. 'No, they are not,' she responded.[14] 'In all of my previous work, if you had a concern, you refer them on, you tell people, you talk about it. And that did not happen.'[15]

Hutchinson and Spiliadis told Dinesh Sinha that even in the most complex of cases, referrals to social services would be discouraged.

Anastassis Spiliadis gave this example to the Tavistock's medical director:

I had the case with a mother, sexually abused for years... throughout her childhood and adult life, she had been presenting with PTSD-like symptoms in the session and I was seeing the young person with another colleague and the young person has not communicated any distress in relation to gender. The ideas were all coming from mum... I had very clear concerns about this.[16]

He brought this up in supervision and with the social workers in the team. 'They told me we cannot do anything, we cannot refer, we cannot do anything.'

GIDS has argued that it wouldn't be up to the service to make a referral to social services – this would be down to others involved with the young person: perhaps a CAMHS clinician or a school. But this wasn't Hutchinson's or others' experience. People are used to the concept of 'referring up', she said. 'I remember one case, for example, where I did make a safeguarding referral but the referring CAMHS clinician knew about the safeguarding concerns but literally referred it to us to get us to deal with it... it is pushed back on us.'[17]

GIDS was undoubtedly in a difficult position. 'Care needs to be taken not to escalate issues too early, potentially doing more harm by damaging the therapeutic relationship with the young person and their family,' Carmichael has said.[18] 'These issues require lots of thought and discussion in GIDS as to what is a safeguarding issue and what is not and whether the threshold for referral has been reached. It is very nuanced and really challenging work.'[19] All agree the work was challenging. For some clinicians though, that threshold – on balance – was often too high.

Not only was Dinesh Sinha told that various aspects of GIDS's practice felt unsafe, and that there were too few safeguarding referrals, multiple clinicians claimed that when staff raised concerns, they were 'scapegoated' or shut down.

'I know I am not the only person in team [sic] who felt that there was a level of bullying and scapegoating by certain individual members of staff,' Matt Bristow tells Sinha.[20] 'People who would raise concerns[,] they will get shut down and then they would leave,' he adds.[21] Anastassis Spiliadis also confirmed that he felt 'silenced'.[22]

Many clinicians told Sinha of the homophobia they witnessed: how

---

* Some of the transcripts of the interviews are very poor. Clinicians were told that they would have a chance to review their transcripts and make any changes which would improve accuracy, or remove identifying material if they had chosen to speak anonymously. However, Anastassis Spiliadis only received his transcript back to review after Dinesh Sinha presented his findings. The author has heard the same from others too.

young people appeared to be experiencing internalised homophobia and how some families would make openly homophobic comments. GIDS clinicians had told Sinha that some parents appeared to prefer the idea that their child was transgender and straight than that they were gay, and were pushing them towards transition.

On top of all of this, Sinha heard that staff had been actively discouraged from seeking help and advice from the Trust's children's safeguarding lead, Sonia Appleby.

'I know that Polly feels she does not like Sonia's scrutiny. I think that is odd. She is the Trust safeguarding lead,' one clinician told Sinha.[23] Another explained how taking cases to Sonia Appleby was 'incredibly helpful' but felt that 'going outside the team is somehow to you know errm, not being a traitor, but like we are exposing something.'[24]

Anastassis Spiliadis was most explicit. 'People were not encouraged actually to talk to the safeguarding team outside the GIDS safeguarding team.'[25] GIDS had appointed its own designated safeguarding person in September 2018, he says, 'but up until then there was a very clear message actually from senior management about being really cautious about how we talk to the safeguarding team at the Tavi and specifically Sonia Appleby.'[26]

What was that about? Dinesh Sinha asks him. 'I think there is a message from Polly that... She thinks that Sonia Appleby has a very clear agenda about GIDS and she thinks we are not on top of the safeguarding concerns in GIDS.'[27]

These three named GIDS clinicians – Anastassis Spiliadis, Matt Bristow and Anna Hutchinson – were not the only ones who relayed serious concerns to Dinesh Sinha. I have read a number of other transcripts with clinicians expressing similar sentiments, telling Dr Sinha that the service as it was currently operating was not safe and, in some instances, categorically stating their belief that children were being harmed.

Not all staff would have been critical of GIDS. And even the most critical acknowledged that good work was also taking place. It is also true that some clinicians working in GIDS at that time viewed the service in an extremely positive light. David Burrows, a junior psychologist at GIDS, tells me that 'it was a really brilliant place'. 'When you're working with these young people and families and actually seeing the amazing progress they can make in themselves over the assessment period, that was hugely rewarding.' When it came to the 'shutting down' of concerned colleagues, it was not something he says he saw. He did not feel that he wouldn't have been able to raise concerns if he was worried – he just wasn't worried.

It is not disputed then that Dinesh Sinha heard evidence that may have contradicted the material quoted above. Multiple interviewees told Dr Sinha that they did not see any problems with GIDS's safeguarding practices. 'The clinicians always have the best interests of the young person and if they feel that the young person was at risk of being harmed they would raise the concerns,' said one.[28] GIDS director Polly Carmichael rejected the allegation that GIDS as a service 'ignored or suppressed' the concerns raised in David Bell's report, telling Sinha that if she could be accused of anything, 'it would be being too open'.[29] Several junior GIDS staff said that they had been supported in raising safeguarding concerns and had sought advice from outside the GIDS team without issue.[30]

But, given that at least a third of the GIDS frontline staff interviewed highlighted significant issues that questioned the service's underlying safety, it is hard to see how the conclusion drawn by Tavistock chief executive Paul Jenkins – that the review did not identify any 'failings in the overall approach taken by the Service in responding to the needs of the young people and families who access its support' – is accurate.[31]

Dinesh Sinha wrote in the introduction to his findings: 'Where I have encountered conflicting evidence, I have sought to make findings based on the balance of information from interviews and evidence.'[32] But it is unclear why the serious ethical and safety concerns of a sizeable proportion of GIDS staff do not appear to be fully reflected in his report or the resulting *GIDS Review Action Plan*. Perhaps 'on balance' he did not believe them, or was more persuaded by the views of others. But when people raise concerns about the safety and safeguarding of children, is it really something that comes down to how *many* raised those concerns, and how many share them?

Whatever the reason for this lack of acknowledgement, it was a huge disappointment to some. Yet another person had heard their concerns and not acted in the way they had hoped. 'It felt like a whitewash,' says Matt Bristow. 'It felt like it was it was a predetermined kind of outcome.'

Hutchinson was shocked too when she read Dinesh Sinha's report. 'If you actually read the report, he acknowledges a large number of concerns, significant concerns,' she explains, 'and then at the end, he says, "Oh, there's no safeguarding issues." How can you conclude that? You've said all of this, and then you concluded it's fine.'

On sexuality too, Sinha's conclusions seemed baffling. He mentioned the word 'homophobia' only once, writing: 'there seemed no particular concerns held by a majority of interviewees around there being a lack of sufficient openness to hearing about the experience of homophobia by clinical staff within face-to-face clinical meetings.'[33] This may well have been the case – that the *majority* did not voice concerns. But, again, the concerns voiced by a sizeable minority had been serious. Several gay members of staff claimed that they had been bullied and that they felt GIDS was homophobic. They felt sexuality was poorly understood by many of their colleagues.

It was at this point that Hutchinson knew she would not and could not return to GIDS: 'Because it wasn't going to change, and I couldn't work in that system any more.' She says she felt 'totally disillusioned'. 'I honestly thought that you'd go higher up the hierarchy and eventually somebody would stop this,' she says.

Initially, Hutchinson did nothing herself. Each time there was disappointment with the way either the Tavistock Trust or GIDS dealt with concerns, it felt like a blow. And it took a little time to recover. But a comment made at the House of Lords meeting in May 2019 spurred her back into action. The Tavistock's director of communications, Laure Thomas, had been asked about the *GIDS Review Action Plan* and what would be implemented as a result. Thomas said that it was difficult for the Trust if staff had safeguarding concerns but didn't raise them in the right way, at the time. To choose this as the *only* element of the plan to mention publicly felt strange to Hutchinson, especially when she knew that people's concerns had now gone to the Tavistock's medical director himself.

Anna Hutchinson wrote to the two men at the very top of the Tavistock – chief executive Paul Jenkins and chair Paul Burstow. She wanted to address the point about raising concerns head on, writing: 'If staff did not share their concerns in the correct manner initially then there should surely be some interest as to why this might be the case, without assuming this is only a problem in these staff members?... The main issue must surely be whether any of these concerns were related to child protection,' she wrote. 'I believe that you have a responsibility to act on them if they are.' She explained that she had spoken to some colleagues and believed that 'a number of very specific, potentially child protection level, concerns were shared with Dr Sinha during the review process'.[34]

Both men replied the same day, Paul Burstow initially, who explained that he would discuss the concerns with Jenkins and ask him to provide 'a fuller response'. He added that the review had led the Trust to commission a review into its 'freedom to speak up arrangements to ensure we maximise the opportunities for people to raise concerns in a safe space.'[35] Paul Jenkins promised to respond 'more fully in the next couple of days'.[36]

Tavistock CEO Jenkins did not address Hutchinson's concerns in his next reply, nor confirm whether the concerns raised were being 'properly investigated' as she had asked.[37] Over several emails, neither Jenkins nor Burstow confirmed whether they had read all of the transcripts from the review.

Anna Hutchinson ended the conversation on 15 July 2019. She said: 'as a matter of record I would like it noted that I am not reassured.'[38] She remarked that she found it 'baffling' that at no point had either man asked what concerns she had been privy to, 'given that I have informed you that they may be significant', and potentially child-protection concerns. She had discharged her professional duty 'to report concerns to those with the responsibility for managing them', she added.[39]

'That's when I think I changed as a human being,' Hutchinson reflects. 'I just think I became a bit more cynical, I guess.' She had gone from believing that positive change could be made and that there was the goodwill to do that, 'to believing that this was a system that knew that it was taking risks with children's well-being but was not going to do anything about it.'

Paul Jenkins appeared on BBC Radio 4's *Today* programme a week after Anna Hutchinson had ended their email exchange. He was there to respond to the open letter that Dr Kirsty Entwistle had posted about her experience of GIDS Leeds. She had raised concerns about the standard of care being provided, the lack of a thorough evidence base underpinning the use of puberty blockers to treat gender dysphoria, and how concerns were responded to by the GIDS management.

Jenkins told the BBC's Justin Webb that with respect to puberty blockers, 'as we know today, those treatments are fully reversible.' He also said that the issues raised by Entwistle had not been raised within the Tavistock itself. 'If those issues were raised with me, and I think one of the disappointments here is that those issues were not raised in the organisation, then yes, we would [take action] if that was justified.'[40] It was striking to many who heard it, not least Hutchinson, who had been in an email exchange about significant safeguarding concerns with Jenkins just days before.

Matt Bristow was also surprised to hear the Tavistock chief executive's claims, when GIDS's own website at the time said that 'the long-term effects regarding bone health and cardiovascular risks are still unknown'. What's more, he said, while GIDS clinicians had once used the phrase 'fully reversible', they had long since stopped doing so on the advice of their medical colleagues.[41]

A group of senior Tavistock Trust clinicians wrote directly to Paul Jenkins to express their dismay – it was another attempt to voice their concern about how the Trust seemed to be dealing with criticism of GIDS. They pointed out that it was not possible to make such a categorical statement about the reversibility of puberty blockers, and that this was unsupported by the medical literature. They were also alarmed to hear their CEO claim that concerns had not been raised by GIDS staff internally, when it was clear they had.

———

Anna Hutchinson kept trying to get someone in the Tavistock not just to acknowledge the concerns, but to act on them.

Later that year she was invited to meet with two more senior figures – Dr Sally Hodges, the Trust's clinical chief operating officer and former director of the Children, Young Adults and Families (CYAF) directorate – a role in which she was Polly Carmichael's line manager – and Ailsa Swarbrick, who had been appointed to the new position of divisional director of gender services following the GIDS Review. Melissa Midgen had met with Hodges first and was heartened by how seriously she had taken her concerns. She encouraged them to speak to her former GIDS 'room-mate', too.

Hodges told Hutchinson via email that the more they heard, the more they were worried about the junior staff in GIDS.[42] Hodges acknowledged the frustration felt by GIDS clinicians in getting their concerns heard and explained that it had also been 'frustrating from a management perspective to get access to staff to hear about what has been happening'.[43]

Hodges and Swarbrick listened to Anna Hutchinson in her private practice room in central London. She wasn't tentative with them, and talked them through years' worth of supervision notes, and other documents which detailed her concerns.[44] The meeting ended on good terms, Hodges assuring Hutchinson that while it would take time to change, she hoped it would be visible soon.

Here were two of the most senior figures in the Tavistock Trust accepting that there were problems at GIDS – after the Review had concluded. Hodges conceded that the Trust had been too slow to act. But Hutchinson was not hopeful. She did not doubt their sincerity, but the action promised seemed to be little more than enacting the *GIDS Review Action Plan*, which, in her mind, had not addressed the fundamental issues that she and several colleagues had raised.

In June 2020, BBC *Newsnight* broadcast some of what GIDS clinicians had told Dinesh Sinha during the GIDS Review.[45] We read scores of pages of official transcripts of interviews that had taken place as part of the review. Responding to the BBC, the Tavistock said that GIDS was a 'safe and caring service which supports a wide range of children'.[46] It said that safeguarding was of the 'utmost importance to the Trust' and that it stood by the 2019 review of GIDS. It was 'confident that it fairly addressed the issues raised' and said it strongly denied the allegations put to them by *Newsnight*.

Newsnight showed some of the transcripts it had seen to the Children's Commissioner for England and contacted the healthcare regulator, the CQC.[47] Both were interested in speaking to those who had worked at GIDS. The CQC encouraged anyone with specific safeguarding or safety concerns to contact them directly.

Change quickly followed the broadcast, as clinicians' concerns reached a wider audience. But, inside the Tavistock, unease grew. And outside, scrutiny increased.

Juliet Singer had become concerned about GIDS almost immediately upon becoming a governor at the Tavistock in 2018. She was worried by the testimony in David Bell's report, and at the way the Trust had responded to media leaks surrounding it. But she'd been assured by the Trust's leadership that the issues raised had been thoroughly investigated by medical director Dinesh Sinha and had not been upheld. *Newsnight*'s film had thrown that into doubt.

Singer and several governors met with Paul Jenkins and Paul Burstow in the days that followed. 'I was worried that we weren't really getting to the nuts and the bolts,' she explains. She questioned whether Sinha's report had sufficiently represented the concerns expressed to him. In short, she didn't trust what she'd been told, and asked to see the transcripts for herself. She could not shake the feeling that 'there was something going really badly wrong'. She and others provided multiple reassurances: they would read the transcripts in an office on the Tavistock's premises; they would not take them away, or be given copies. The request was declined.

Paul Jenkins insisted that he and the Tavistock board remained satisfied with the way the review had been carried out and that concerns raised had been dealt with robustly. There had been oversight of the process from a non-executive director and a governor. Both were 'provided with the transcripts and gave assurance to the Trust Board and Council that the Review Report is a fair and accurate reflection of the matters raised', he said.[48] He said 31 interviews had been conducted with staff from a range of backgrounds, but omitted to say that six of these were outside GIDS, and four were members of the GIDS Executive.

Paul Jenkins argued that the interview transcripts couldn't be shared because some individuals had wanted to contribute to the review on an anonymous basis. This argument surprises some of those staff who did participate anonymously. It's the opposite of what they wanted. 'I wanted my transcript to be read,' explains Anna Hutchinson. 'I was trying to get so much into it because I thought, like we were told, it would be read. We were told it would form part of the report.' Indeed, those who contributed were sent (or were meant to be sent) their transcripts to be reviewed before the review was published – so that they could remove any information that might be too identifying.

Paul Jenkins told Juliet Singer that 'it is not helpful, in my view, to reopen the arguments around the Review'.[49] Not helpful for whom? she wondered.

Singer remained unsatisfied and told the Tavistock chief executive so. She wondered what evidence the board had been given for it to form the view that it was 'satisfied'. She questioned how Dinesh Sinha's report fairly reflected the concerns raised when extracts of the transcripts broadcast by *Newsnight* 'gave specific reports of breaches of guidelines by senior staff, in terms of number of consultations before progression to medication, and in terms of discouraging access to the safeguarding office'. She asked what investigations had taken place to examine these alleged breaches. While she understood the wish not to reopen the GIDS Review, it was necessary to do so, she said, so that the council of governors could 'satisfy themselves of the adequacy of practices pursued, both in GIDS and indeed in the Review itself'. She too wanted both GIDS and the wider Tavistock to move forward in a constructive way, addressing the issues acknowledged in the service. But this was 'only possible if there is more openness and candour' from the Trust's management than they had currently shown.[50]

'We are not able to have confidence in the actions the Trust is taking, since we are being denied the information from which to assess this,' Singer wrote. 'Underlying what the Trust has said throughout, and reiterated in your letter to us, seems to be a decision that no specific fault whatever should be admitted by the Trust, not even within its own governance structures.'[51]

A stalemate ensued. The council of governors was not granted permission to read the transcripts, and some remained unconvinced that the GIDS Review accurately reflected the testimony it had heard.

It wasn't the only time Singer had questioned the Trust's willingness to share information. When, in May 2020, the NHS updated its official guidance on the use of puberty blockers to treat gender dysphoria in young people, the Tavistock had not felt it necessary to communicate it to patients. Whereas the NHS had previously said that the effects of the treatment were 'considered to be fully reversible', the new guidance sounded a note of caution. 'Little is known about the long-term side effects of hormone or puberty blockers in children with gender dysphoria,' it said. 'Although GIDS advises this is a physically reversible treatment if stopped, it is not known what the psychological effects may be.' The NHS also said that it was 'not known whether hormone blockers affect the development of the teenage brain or children's bones'.[52]

To some these changes seemed significant.[53] The official NHS guidance now acknowledged that much was unknown about the treatment. Juliet Singer asked the Trust's management how it was going to respond to the update.[54] Was it going to contact the young people under the care of GIDS who were currently receiving the treatment? 'I was trying to put across the point that if I were a young person on it, or a parent with a young person on it, I would think this was really important,' Singer says. She thought that GIDS, and the Trust, would have wanted their patients 'to have the opportunity to have a discussion with a clinician about it'.

GIDS would not be contacting patients or updating its website, Tavistock CEO Paul Jenkins confirmed several months later. NHS England had told the Trust that this was 'a routine change to their website', he said, and 'while there is a shift in tone', it did not represent a change in guidelines, nor the service specification which GIDS worked to. Any potential risks of physical interventions, Jenkins explained, were covered by colleagues responsible for prescribing the blockers at either UCLH or Leeds General Infirmary. The Trust believed the wording on GIDS's website was already adequate. This stated (then and at the time of writing): 'The blocker is a physically reversible intervention: if the young person stops taking the blocker their body will continue to develop as it was previously. However, we don't know the full psychological effects of the blocker or whether it alters the course of adolescent brain development.'[55]

Senior clinicians in the Trust have told me it was 'flabbergasting' that GIDS didn't update its own website or issue a statement acknowledging the NHS. Like Juliet Singer, they believed there was an ethical duty to tell people.

Outside the Tavistock, there were important developments taking place in the autumn of 2020.

In September, NHS England announced that Dr Hilary Cass – one of the UK's leading paediatricians – would undertake an independent review into gender identity services for children and young people. The review's remit would be wide-ranging, with a 'focus on how care can be improved for children and young people'.[56] This provided great reassurance to Juliet Singer: 'I suppose that I had a sense of relief that it was being taken really seriously by certain people in the NHS.'

The following month, October 2020, the CQC inspected GIDS. The inspection was undertaken 'due to concerns reported to CQC by healthcare professionals and the Children's Commissioner for England', the regulator said. Those concerns had been passed to the Children's Commissioner by BBC *Newsnight* and 'related to clinical practice, safeguarding procedures, and assessments of capacity and consent to treatment'.[57]

A team of inspectors visited GIDS's main London base and its smaller Leeds site and rated the service 'inadequate'. Inadequate is the CQC's lowest safety rating. It means that a service is 'performing badly' and that the regulator has taken action against the organisation running it.[58]

The report, published the following January, is a damning read.

The CQC's inspection supported much of what Hutchinson, Spiliadis, Prescott, Midgen, Bristow and numerous others had been saying for years. The regulator acknowledged that some assessments consisted of 'two or three sessions' – remembering that two was in breach of the NHS England service specification GIDS is supposed to follow. The regulator noted that GIDS did not always adequately manage risk; that consent did not appear to be recorded routinely; and that some staff 'felt unable to raise concerns without fear of retribution'.[59]

The CQC acknowledged that caseloads were high and could be 'stressful and difficult to manage'. One member of staff had a caseload of over 100. Staff at GIDS were found to 'not always assess and manage risk well', with many young people receiving care or on the waiting list being vulnerable and at risk of self-harm. The CQC reviewed 29 care records, noting that 'the recording of risk and of plans to manage these risks varied considerably'.[60]

Some patient records demonstrated good practice, but others contained only 'limited information'. The CQC gave the following example to highlight this: 'one record had very little information about risks, despite the referral letter stating that the young person had frequent suicidal thoughts and had previously harmed themselves by cutting.'[61]

Assessments of young people were 'unstructured, inconsistent and poorly recorded'. The CQC found that 'there was no clear rationale for clinical decision making', with assessments varying greatly between clinicians. Assessments had 'no standard questions for staff to explore with young people', and 'most records of assessment sessions were simply descriptions of conversations that had taken place' between the clinician and the young person and their family. 'Whilst the criteria for considering referring young people for administration of hormone blockers was set out in the service specification, we saw no reference to this on any patient records,' the CQC said. Care records 'were not completed in a consistent or structured manner. This meant that many records did not demonstrate good practice.'[62]

In a sample of records of young people referred for puberty blockers, the CQC found that more than half referred to autistic spectrum disorder (ASD) or attention deficit hyperactivity disorder (ADHD). Yet, the regulator noted, GIDS generally did not record how many patients had a diagnosis or a suspected diagnosis of ASD. 'Records did not demonstrate consideration of the relationship between autistic spectrum disorder and gender dysphoria' or that the needs of autistic patients had been 'fully investigated', something so many clinicians had been concerned about. The CQC said that while 'staff were experienced and qualified and had the right skills and knowledge to meet the primary needs of the patient group', they 'did not necessarily have the skills or experience to meet the needs of young people with complex needs'.[63]

The process for gaining consent to puberty-blocking treatment and assessing capacity was also criticised. 'The records of young people who began medical treatment before January 2020 did not include a record of their capacity, competency and consent,' the report said. Again, the CQC did find good practice – something concerned clinicians had always said – but this was the exception rather than the rule. 'Staff's approach to enabling young people to make their own decisions was unstructured and inconsistent although there was some evidence of good practice,' the inspectors noted. 'However, whilst staff demonstrated their work on helping young people to understand information about treatment, there were very few details on the records of staff engaging in the more difficult task of supporting young people weigh-up the foreseeable risks and consequences.'[64]

Consent procedures were meant to have been tightened up following the GIDS Review and publication of the *GIDS Review Action Plan* in March 2019. Dinesh Sinha had identified this as an area requiring improvement. Prior to January 2020 there had been no standard procedures for recording 'consent, capacity and competency'. When GIDS carried out audits of compliance with their procedure for consent and capacity in March and September 2020 – a year after the review – these still came back wanting. The March audit reviewed ten records of young people referred for hormone blockers and 'only three contained a completed consent form and checklist for referral'. Furthermore, the CQC 'found no evidence that staff had completed an assessment after the documentation was found to be missing'. The regulator explained that 'this meant that staff had still not assessed the capacity and competency of young people receiving treatment, despite being aware that they had not done so'. The September audit showed improvement, but still found 10 per cent did not have a complete set of referral documents.[65]

The CQC raised concerns that a number of young people who were receiving hormone blockers had not been fully assessed for competency and capacity as their treatment started before the introduction of the new consent protocol. The regulator 'asked the trust to review this'.[66]

It also expressed grave concern about those waiting to be seen by GIDS, noting that over 4,600 young people were on the GIDS waiting list. Some had been waiting for over two years for their first appointment. The regulator insisted waiting times and the service provided overall must improve.

'The service was not consistently well-led,' the CQC argued, rating the leadership inadequate. Along with feeling fearful of raising concerns, 'staff did not always feel respected, supported and valued.' This wasn't how all GIDS staff felt, and the CQC heard from those who felt positive and proud about working there. But some said that the 'high caseloads and constant external scrutiny meant they worked under relentless pressure'.[67]

The CQC raised the *GIDS Review Action Plan* from March 2019 – the result of the Trust's internal review. It noted that while improvements had been made in some areas, 'there were still many areas where improvements had not been consistent'. There was still wide variation in practice between clinicians, the CQC noted, and, just as Dinesh Sinha had been told, and David Bell before him, in late 2020 the healthcare regulator found that some assessments were completed over just two sessions. Indeed, assessments ranged from 'two or three sessions to over 25 sessions, with some young people receiving more than 50 sessions'.[68]

Despite the criticism levelled at the service, its leadership and the processes it followed – or didn't – staff were found to treat the young people in their care with 'compassion and kindness'. On the measure of whether the service was caring, it was rated 'good'. Staff 'understood the individual needs of young people' and supported them 'to understand and manage their care'. Feedback from young people and parents receiving care and treatment from GIDS was 'overwhelmingly positive'.[69]

The Tavistock Trust agreed 'with the CQC that the growth in referrals has exceeded the capacity of the service'. It apologised to patients and their families for the length of time they were waiting to be seen and 'very much' accepted 'the need for improvements in our assessments, systems and processes'.[70]

Some GIDS staff welcomed the CQC's report. 'I'd have been really surprised and bitterly disappointed had the outcome been anything else,' says Liam McConnell,* a family therapist working in the service at the time. 'In my view it's a failing service.'

McConnell didn't experience the CQC's report as an attack on GIDS staff, but plenty of others did. Many were upset. 'I think they felt it was a reflection on their work as individuals, whereas I didn't. I felt it was a comment on the organisation,' he says, explaining that the vast majority of his colleagues were 'very concerned and hard-working' and wanted 'to do their best by the young people they work with and their families'.

Another former senior member of GIDS staff echoes these sentiments. They welcomed the fact that the CQC had heard that the management was inadequate, but said it was 'galling' that the CQC hadn't seen some more of the good work, 'as well as the bad stuff'. 'I want it recorded that staff worked so hard to do what was asked of them,' they say.

Within days of the CQC branding the Tavistock's Gender Identity Development Service inadequate, it was announced that the GIDS Executive would be officially 'disbanded'.[71] Bernadette Wren had already retired from GIDS in 2020. The remaining figures of Polly Carmichael, Sarah Davidson and Rebecca McLaren would remain in the service, but 'have roles in workstreams and projects relevant to their skills and experience'.[72] Davidson had tendered her resignation shortly before publication of the CQC's report.

Director for gender Ailsa Swarbrick would chair a new 'Interim GIDS Management Board'. This in turn would be accountable to a

---

* Not their real name.

new 'GIDS Oversight Committee' to be chaired by Tavistock CEO Paul Jenkins. Polly Carmichael would remain GIDS service director and 'have a place on the GIDS Interim Management Board'.[73]

Despite receiving the lowest possible rating from the healthcare regulator – for the management of its waiting list and its leadership in particular – there was no change at the top. Sources within the NHS tell me internal discussions were held about Jenkins's future, but he was not asked to step down. It is hard to see why leadership change was not insisted upon.

18

REGRET AND REDRESS

November 2019, Manchester, England

Two hundred or so people were gathered in a church hall on a cold Saturday in November. They were there to listen to a group of young women they'd neither met nor heard of.

A local feminist group, Make More Noise, had organised the event to help with the launch of a new – but ultimately short-lived – support group for detransitioned people: those who have undergone a medical or surgical gender transition but then chosen to revert to their natal sex. The organisers were surprised. Tickets had sold out, and some attendees had flown in from overseas to take part.

Anna Hutchinson had agreed to take part in a panel discussion of medics and therapists. It was the end of a busy week, which had seen her speak out openly in the media for the first time. She had featured in a BBC radio documentary and a film about detransitioning.[1]

When Hutchinson spoke to the Tavistock's medical director for the review into GIDS, she was brutally honest about her concerns. But she also didn't want to be right. 'Let's pray that I am wrong,' she had said, 'because if I am not wrong very many vulnerable children have been very poorly treated and will be left with, potentially, a lifetime of damage here.'[2]

But since handing her notice in six months earlier, word had got out that some GIDS clinicians were concerned, and a very informal group of worried medical professionals across the world had formed. Would she be open to working with young people who had detransitioned, Anna Hutchinson was asked? She was. But up to this point her fear that GIDS had not helped all the young people it saw had been theoretical. She wanted to talk to someone with experience of detransitioning before seeing anyone in a professional capacity. 'That was one of the most painful conversations,' Hutchinson recalls. This young woman had little respect for professionals – which was fair, Hutchinson acknowledges, because 'she'd been totally shafted by the respect of the professionals involved in her care'. 'And so she was able to turn around and be quite challenging, which is good. And I was prepared to be challenged.' The young woman was blunt: 'I can understand why children make these mistakes, but you? You are adults.'

Hutchinson believed that the stories of those who detransition deserved to be told. 'Because it absolutely represents the dangers, doesn't it?' she says. 'And it represents a failure to our patients. These kids' experiences represent the lack of thinking at time one, that has put them in this position at time two.'

Back at the Manchester conference, the floor was handed to a group of six young women to share their stories.[3] All had undergone a gender transition: some had socially transitioned, changing their name, clothing and pronouns; some had regularly injected testosterone; and some had transitioned surgically, having their breasts removed or undergoing a hysterectomy. All were aged 23 or younger.

One had been a GIDS patient. The others, some from outside the UK, had attended gender clinics in Western Europe, or had begun transitioning as young adults. Most of the young women were quiet and nervous; the audience, which included both current and past GIDS staff, had to lean forward in their seats, straining to hear what impact transition had had on these young lives.

'I regret all of it,' said one who had undergone a double mastectomy and hysterectomy. 'I wish someone would have been there to tell me not to get castrated at 21,' she added.[4]

'It didn't make sense for me to keep on altering my body,' another explained. 'When I was 16… I never considered that I could be interested in my [long-term] health.'[5]

Another didn't regret her surgery but pleaded for a different way to treat gender dysphoria. 'I was experiencing a lot of hate towards my breasts and now I don't have them anymore… and the hate is gone of course. But it helped with the symptom and not with the underlying problems.'[6]

Some in the audience listened and cried. They had been responsible for treating young women just like this.

'It was upsetting,' says Anna Hutchinson. 'Their stories are almost unbelievable… One of them had had her womb and ovaries removed. And then, while recovering from that surgery, they were handed flyers advertising phalloplasty,' she recalls. 'One of them had had the most devastating eating disorder before they were operated on.' None of the young women were exclusively opposite-sex attracted.

Not all those who spoke that day wished to be recorded. Before the panels started, two others addressed the room. One was a young, unassuming woman named Keira Bell. She quietly shared her story, out of the spotlight.

With her deep voice – a permanent legacy of years taking the male hormone testosterone – the 22-year-old spoke softly, but with determination. Bell had first been seen at GIDS in January 2013, around the time that Hutchinson was meeting her first patients there. Bell was 15 years old at the time. After three appointments, during which the now 16-year-old described how she wanted to be a boy, she was judged a suitable candidate for puberty blockers. Twelve months later, she started taking testosterone. Three years after that, aged 20, she underwent a double mastectomy, removing both her breasts to make her body more closely resemble that of the man she craved to be. She told those gathered in Manchester that she now deeply regretted her transition.

Just two months after speaking to a room of 200 in a church hall, Keira Bell was prepared to share her story with the world.

In January 2020, Bell replaced Sue Evans as the lead claimant in a legal challenge against GIDS's practices.[7] Bell argued that the approach taken by GIDS was unlawful because the risks of puberty-blocking medication are not adequately explained – in part because they are not fully known – and that children cannot give informed consent to the treatment. She said that the clinicians who put her on to the medical path to transitioning did not adequately explore the reasons she felt the way she did about her female body.[8] They didn't investigate her difficult childhood – being brought up by a mum struggling with alcoholism, or the chaotic living conditions she faced while attending her appointments. Around the time she was approved for testosterone she had been kicked out by her father and was living in a youth hostel.[9]

In retrospect, she said, what she needed was therapy: someone to ask why she felt the way she did about her body and how she might reconcile being female with the need not to be stereotypically 'feminine'; and to reassure her that her attraction to other women was not something she needed to be ashamed of.

'What was really going on was that I was a girl insecure in my body who had experienced parental abandonment, felt alienated from my peers, suffered from anxiety and depression, and struggled with my sexual orientation,' she said. 'I was an unhappy girl who needed help. Instead, I was treated like an experiment.'[10]

How much does GIDS know about how many of its patients either desisted – that is, stopped identifying as trans before starting a medical transition – or detransitioned?

Next to nothing.

Discussion about this was discouraged, says Anastassis Spiliadis. Even though it was obvious that some young people who had been insistent on medical transition changed their minds, he says that GIDS didn't even like the words 'desist' or 'detransition' to be used in the service.

'I was in a service where no one had ever asked the question: how many of the people that we see actually changed their mind?' Spiliadis says. 'Not in terms of just the blocker but in terms of their identification.' He expected a therapeutic service to be curious about this, so he and his colleague Anna Churcher Clarke decided to write an academic paper about what they were seeing.[11] 'And even when we wrote the paper, they were like, "You should not publish it." Polly was telling us, "You shouldn't publish it, because it's a red flag, and people will think that we are transphobic.'" Spiliadis told Dinesh Sinha about the experience during his interview for the GIDS Review. He claimed that senior management had been resistant to publishing the paper 'because they felt that this would challenge what we do as a service affirming people's gender narratives'.[12] But this changed as soon as the review was announced. Bernadette Wren approached him, he says, asking whether GIDS could use the paper 'as evidence that the Service is not silencing clinicians'.[13]

'Only Bernadette Wren was supportive of us publishing it,' Spiliadis says, and she 'managed to convince Polly'. But only if some of the language was changed. The word 'desistance' was not to be used. Spiliadis says he was told it was 'provocative'. 'And she would want us to use the term "assigned male or female at birth", whereas we had used "natal male" or "natal female".' He says he was 'negative' initially, and wanted to refuse the request, but the pair agreed to compromise. Those searching for any evidence of young people desisting while at GIDS would not easily find their paper in a search 'because we had used "discontinued their identification" or "changed their mind",' Spiliadis explains. And instead of using 'assigned sex', the paper used 'male-bodied and female-bodied'. This felt important to Spiliadis, 'because it's the reality of the body. You can't say that this is transphobic.'

Fifteen per cent of young people in his sample changed their minds about wanting to transition, Spiliadis says. But, he adds, this was just a snapshot in time and a very small group. 'All of these people who changed their mind, they were actively requesting medical and surgical interventions. And they were adamant that this was the right thing for them,' he says. What did these young people who changed their minds have in common? 'Longer assessment,' Spiliadis explains. 'Most of them longer than the three to six sessions that the service specification said or suggested.' When young people had more time to think and talk through all that was going on for them, some came to the understanding that their gender identity wasn't what was causing them most difficulty. Once other difficulties had been thought through, some were less distressed by their sex. Many of the young people were on the autistic spectrum, and 'many of them had a history of bullying in early childhood and primary school'. They had experienced homophobia too. 'These were some of the key themes that came up when analysing the data.' From this point on, Spiliadis talked openly with all the young people he saw about the possibility that they might change their minds.

What about service-wide figures? Unbeknown to Spiliadis, GIDS had publicly confirmed in 2016 that it would collect data on the number of young people they saw who changed their minds or who stopped medical treatment. 'We are currently setting up a database that will collect data of young people that have chosen to cease physical interventions / de-transition,' the Trust said.[14] Plans were still under-way in summer 2017, the Tavistock explaining that 'we are only at the early stages of setting up the data base [*sic*] to collect this information', and so it would take 'at least another year or two to be able to publish something' on the numbers choosing to stop treatment.[15]

By September 2019 the plans had been ditched. The database had not been set up. 'There are currently no plans in place to set up such a database, owing to the complexity and multiplicity of the choices young people make,' the Tavistock said.[16] What was the reason? It appeared that it would be too time-consuming. 'While information is recorded in patient notes on the choices people make with regards to physical intervention, this is not done in a collatable format,' the Trust said.[17] Yet three years earlier it had said the project was underway, and there had been a willingness to put in the hours to get the data.

GIDS could not or would not reveal how many patients had chosen to cease physical interventions, but said they could confirm that some young people did come off hormone-blocking treatment and for a number of reasons, including to preserve fertility, or a change in gender identity.[18] The Tavistock added that the numbers stopping hormone treatment were 'very small' and 'not necessarily an indication of the young person no longer identifying as trans'.[19] However, by this time, in 2019, GIDS had been notified of young people who had detransitioned. Meeting minutes from July 2018 note: 'One young person on testosterone for a year has just been in touch to say "I'm not trans any more". Yet they are quite virilised.'[20]

Responses to questions asked by Tavistock governors about detransition were no more fruitful. Following BBC *Newsnight*'s coverage of the topic in November 2019, Tavistock chief executive Paul Jenkins was questioned about what the Trust knew about its patients. Meeting minutes show Jenkins emphasising that 'it was unclear whether the individuals had used the Trust's services or another gender identity service'.[21]

Governors continued to ask questions, but their concerns were minimised by both Paul Jenkins and Paul Burstow. Tavistock chair Burstow said there was 'need to be clear' that published data 'indicates that the incidence of people wishing to detransition after treatment to be [*sic*] or expressing regret about treatment to be generally very low'.[22]

'One of the real concerns that governors had was about [GIDS's] follow-up,' explains Juliet Singer. She says that once those running the service realised people were detransitioning, she'd expect their response to be, 'Let's speak to them and find out what went wrong,' because, she says, 'Obviously something did go wrong. They went through a procedure that they've changed their minds about with long-lasting impact. This is a terrible outcome for those people.' Singer says this is what science and medicine is all about: we need to be constantly checking that we are offering the right treatment, to the right people, and find out what the possible harms are. 'Detransitioners could be really helpful for us to understand more about the patients that are coming through the clinic.'

In an email, Paul Jenkins pointed governors towards a paper presented by the Charing Cross Gender Identity Clinic 'which suggests that the numbers are small and that a common reason for de-transition is lack of social acceptance'. He acknowledged, however, that 'a small number' of GIDS patients who have started physical treatments 'have decided to change path either whilst with the service or in adult services'. He stressed GIDS will 'always support young people either in the service or if contact is made after they have been discharged', and said that the Trust was 'keen to learn more about this important issue'.[23]

Like all research in the field of trans medicine, the data on detransition are poor. The only honest answer to the question 'how many people detransition?' is that we don't know.

Some argue that detransition is very rare and that the proportion of people who change their minds or regret transition is less than 1 per cent.[24] But the studies this figure is derived from are methodologically flawed.[25] Some, like the one cited by Tavistock CEO Paul Jenkins, looked only at patients who were *currently* being seen in adult gender identity clinics, during a one-year period. It is unlikely that many who no longer identify as trans and have stopped treatment would be current patients at a gender identity clinic. Indeed, a later study which asked people this specific question found that less than a quarter had informed their clinicians that they had detransitioned.[26]

In addition, many studies are old and do not reflect the changes in young people presenting at gender clinics around the Western world. They predate the widespread use of puberty blockers and the increase in females seeking treatment. A study by the Dutch team, which shows low levels of regret, for example, looks at adult patients only, and does not include anyone who began their medical transition under the age of 16.[27]

It's also argued that regret often relates to dissatisfaction with surgery, not transition per se. But some of the studies used to make the claim look only at those who were born male and underwent genital surgery several decades ago.[28] Concentrating solely on surgical regret automatically excludes those who have taken cross-sex hormones but not undergone surgery too. A large Swedish study claiming a 2.2 per cent regret rate is based solely on the number who had received 'a new legal gender between 1960 and 2010, who then applied for reversal to the original sex'.[29]

More recent studies, which are beginning to reflect those who have transitioned in the last decade or so, have suggested different findings. Although they are still far from perfect, there are now several studies which suggest a higher rate of detransition than previously thought.

In the UK, data from GIDS itself suggest that a little over 5 per cent stopped treatment with either puberty blockers or cross-sex hormones 'and reverted to identifying with their birth gender' while still under the care of the service.[30] Of the nine people who detransitioned after cross-sex hormones, all but one were female. A further 3 per cent chose not to start treatment with puberty blockers after attending the endocrine clinics at UCLH or Leeds Children's Hospital. UCLH's lead paediatrician, Gary Butler, notes: 'This of course may be an underestimate' – as not all patients could be reached. What's more, these data relate solely to those who detransitioned or desisted while still under GIDS's care. It does not capture those who may have changed their minds after leaving GIDS.

A study of those discharged from an adult gender clinic in southwest England between 1 September 2017 and 31 August 2018 flagged 'twenty-one sets of notes out of the 175... as potential cases of detransitioning for consensus discussion'. Several were excluded – for example, two had stopped taking hormones but 'did not revert to their original gender role'. However, close to 7 per cent (6.9 per cent) of cases 'were agreed by all authors to meet the case definition for detransitioning. Regret was specifically documented in two cases.'[31]

GPs undertaking an audit of patient records to try to look at how to improve care for their trans and gender non-conforming patients found that a fifth – eight patients out of 41 – had voluntarily stopped taking hormones. 'These patients had been on treatment for a mean of five years (range 17 months–10 years). Four transmen had comments in the records that related to a change in gender identity or detransitioning (4/41, 9.8%).' None of these patients had undertaken surgery as part of their transition, but had taken testosterone. The other four continued to identify as trans, though one, 'who had experienced orchidectomy [removal of the testicles]', had a record of regret.'[32]

Others have attempted to look at the reasons *why* people have detransitioned. These studies challenge the narrative that detransition tends to be driven by a lack of acceptance from family or society, or because of surgical regret. In the first exploratory study authored by a detransitioned person, 45 per cent of those questioned felt that they were not properly informed about the treatments they underwent before undergoing them, while 33 per cent felt only partly informed. The most common reason for detransitioning – 70 per cent – was realising that their gender dysphoria was related to issues other than being transgender.[33]

Similarly, Lisa Littman found that while discrimination played a part for a sizeable proportion of those who chose to detransition – 23 per cent – it was outweighed by other factors.[34] Sixty per cent had become more comfortable identifying as their natal sex, while close to half (49 per cent) had concerns about potential medical complications from transitioning. Thirty-nine per cent came to the view that their gender dysphoria was 'caused by something specific such as trauma, abuse, or a mental health condition', while 23 per cent said that homophobia or difficulty accepting themselves as lesbian, gay or bisexual had been a reason for transition and subsequent detransition.[35]

The data we have are small and limited. Some studies used online surveys, with self-selected samples, rather than complete data sets.[36] There are difficulties with these methods. But the picture emerging from more recent studies that have attempted to look at detransition or regret, and which include those who transitioned in the last decade or so, appears to be of a much higher rate of detransition than previously acknowledged. While we may not ever know the true number, we do know for sure that there are some young people who started their transition at GIDS who have detransitioned and identify again as their birth sex. Some are seeking help from therapists.[37] But there are others who express their anger and regret at what has happened, but know that the changes they have made to their bodies are so great it is impossible to live again as the sex they were born as. Keira Bell has shared her story with the world, but some of those who seem most unhappy with their treatment at GIDS are speaking out only online. They do not wish to share their stories with journalists, and their privacy should be respected. But their existence should not be discounted or ignored.

On 7 October 2020, Keira Bell's case against the Tavistock and Portman NHS Foundation Trust began at the Royal Courts of Justice in London. Restrictions due to the Covid-19 pandemic meant only those directly involved with the case were granted access to the court hearing the proceedings (journalists and others had to watch via video link in separate court rooms). Keira Bell sat next to Stephanie Davies-Arai, who was an 'intervener' in the case. 'We held hands tightly,' Davies-Arai recalls.

Davies-Arai had closely followed events at GIDS for years and founded the organisation Transgender Trend in 2015. She was awarded the British Empire Medal for services to children in June 2022.[38] An experienced feminist campaigner, Davies-Arai was worried about the increase in young people, particularly girls, identifying as trans. She called for quality, evidence-based research to help explain the changing population seeking help from gender clinics across the world. While she had a constructive relationship with GIDS in the early days, it broke down when she began to criticise openly some of the service's practices and ask awkward questions about the work it undertook.

Davies-Arai joined the court case to make a cultural argument in relation to consent. 'I wanted to put it in context, how these girls – mostly girls – arrived at the clinic with a set of beliefs,' she says. That set of beliefs was 'that they were really boys'. She argues that GIDS wasn't providing 'other information that would help these girls understand themselves and conceptualise those feelings in any other way'.

Jeremy Hyam QC, representing Keira Bell and Mrs A – the mother of an autistic child on the GIDS waiting list – challenged the evidence base underpinning the use of puberty blockers to address gender dysphoria, branding the drugs – in this context – 'experimental', and argued that there could be no 'age-appropriate discussion' of the possible consequences of blocking puberty on future fertility or sexual function. It is a 'fairy tale' to believe otherwise, and 'an affront to common sense'.[39]

Sections of Keira Bell's written witness statement were provided to those listening to the court proceedings. 'I am a twenty-two-year-old woman left with no breasts, a deep voice, body hair, a beard, affected sexual function and who knows what else that has not yet been discovered,' she explained. 'I made a brash decision as a teenager (as a lot of teenagers do) trying to find confidence and happiness, except now the rest of my life will be negatively affected,' she said. 'I cannot reverse any of the physical, mental or legal changes that I went through. Transitioning was a very temporary, superficial fix for a very complex identity issue.'[40]

Lawyers for the Tavistock and Portman Trust insisted that the suggestion that children could not give informed consent was 'a radical proposition' that went against long-standing medical practice – so-called Gillick competency.[41]

The Tavistock argued that GIDS practised according to a service specification set by NHS England, delivered in line with 'emerging evidence for best practice', and relevant national and international guidelines. The Trust insisted that treatment with puberty blockers 'is not viewed as a pre-cursor for the prescribing of cross-sex hormones' but rather that these are two 'separate and distinct treatment processes'.[42]

Across two days of legal argument the room of assembled press and observers was largely silent. But there was an audible gasp at one stage. Questioned how it was possible to have an age-appropriate discussion about the loss of orgasm with a young person who has never had one, the Tavistock's QC remarked that 'many adults are happily asexual'.[43] The judge jumped in: but it could not be assumed that a given ten-year-old would be one of those people?[44] That was why there was an ongoing dialogue, came the reply. Plus, the majority of young people starting on puberty blockers are not so young, but are 15 or older, explained Fenella Morris QC.

The three High Court judges agreed with Keira Bell: children under 16 with gender dysphoria are unlikely to be able to give informed consent to treatment with puberty-blocking drugs.[45]

The court did not make comment on the 'benefits or disbenefits' of treating children with gender dysphoria with puberty blockers but argued that it is right to describe their use in this context as 'experimental'.[46] The judges noted that much of the evidence for the use of puberty blockers was taken from the treatment of precocious puberty – a 'different condition' from gender dysphoria, and one where blockers 'are used in a very different way'.[47]

Having weighed up the evidence before them, the High Court was also unpersuaded by the Tavistock's claim that puberty blockers and cross-sex hormones were entirely separate stages of treatment. 'In our view this does not reflect the reality,' the judges said. 'The evidence shows that the vast majority of children who take [puberty blockers] move on to take cross-sex hormones,' and that these are part of 'one clinical pathway'.[48]

NHS England acted immediately, halting all new GIDS referrals for puberty blockers, 'unless a "best interests" order has been made by the Court for the individual in question'.[49]

GIDS was also required to carry out a 'full clinical review' of all current cases of children under 16 who were already on blockers. If clinicians believed that continuing treatment with puberty blockers was in the young person's best interests, they also had to apply to the court 'for final determination of that individual's needs'.[50] If GIDS clinicians concluded that it wasn't appropriate to make such an application, then arrangements must be made for 'puberty blockers to be withdrawn within a clinically appropriate timeframe and within safe clinical arrangements'.[51]

GIDS and the management of the Tavistock were in a state of 'complete and utter shock', a senior clinician tells me.

There had seemingly been no expectation that the judges would side with Keira Bell. The GIDS leadership had appeared confident throughout. 'As someone working there at the time, my sense was that there was a great deal of surprise. It felt as if the organisation was very ill-prepared for that outcome,' says family therapist Liam McConnell. It did not appear that the prospect of losing had even been considered. Indeed, Paul Jenkins had thought that the judicial review and CQC inspection would present opportunities for GIDS and the Trust to move on from the upheaval of David Bell's report, the GIDS Review and the leak of its transcripts to the media, and general critical scrutiny of the service.

'I think quite a few of us thought, why didn't GIDS plan for this in advance? Why didn't they have a plan B?' says McConnell. Clinicians were furious at how the Tavistock had gone to court 'so ill-prepared', and staff were angry that they'd been left to deal with distressed and confused families, equipped with no information to pass on. They felt 'left in the lurch to answer families', McConnell explains. 'I think virtually all my colleagues had people who were extremely distressed and very angry, and we didn't have the information to give them.' There were young people who had been told they could go on to puberty blockers who were now left in limbo. They wanted to know what was going to happen, McConnell says, 'and we weren't able to answer any of those questions'.

The anger of GIDS staff was genuine. But there were other feelings too, McConnell says. Some GIDS clinicians were relieved. 'I can recall some of my colleagues saying things like, "Well, that's taken a bit of the pressure off." It was a different sort of pressure, because you obviously got very angry, distressed families, but equally, I think people were in a position of doing assessments and saying to families, "Really sorry we don't know, but currently we can't recommend you go for the medical pathway, because it doesn't exist at the moment."'

'If the government had swooped in and said, "We're just going to ban the use of hormone blockers for this purpose," I think most of us, many of us, would have gone, "Okay, we'll crack on with the work,"' agrees Dr Alex Morris, who had left GIDS by the time of the judicial review. 'Because in all sorts of ways, I think blockers became a focal point that was a distraction from getting into what's actually helpful for people.' She knows that some of her former colleagues would disagree, but from her perspective 'a blanket prohibition under a certain age would in a way have been helpful to us at GIDS from the point of view of doing useful therapeutic work... I wouldn't want to be the person making that decision, but had someone done it, I think probably a good chunk of the staff at GIDS wouldn't have lamented it.'

For a few months GIDS was in a state of paralysis. But other legal developments in 2021 further changed the way the service was allowed to operate.

The GIDS medical pathway was formally reintroduced in August 2021, following another court case that March.[52] This ruled that parents could consent to treatment with puberty blockers on behalf of their child, and that there was no 'general rule that puberty blockers should be placed in a special category by which parents are unable in law to give consent'.[53] Mrs Justice Lieven, who had also ruled in the Keira Bell judicial review, stated:

> The factors identified in Bell, which I fully agree with, do not justify removing the parental right to consent. The gravity of the decision to consent to PBs is very great, but it is no more enormous than

consenting to a child being allowed to die. Equally, the essentially experimental nature of PBs should give any parent pause for thought, but parents can and do routinely consent on their child's behalf to experimental treatment, sometimes with considerable, including life-changing, potential side-effects.[54]

However, Justice Lieven repeated her view that 'the use of PBs for children with Gender Dysphoria raises unique and highly controversial ethical issues', and noted that 'it may well be that, given the particular issues involved, additional safeguards should be built into the clinical decision making'.[55]

The Tavistock successfully overturned the initial judicial review judgment in September 2021.

The Court of Appeal held that it was not appropriate for the Divisional Court to have provided either generalised guidance about the likelihood of young people being able to provide informed consent at given ages, or definitive statements, especially in areas of medicine which are controversial, and in which there isn't medical consensus.[56] The original High Court ruling had said that in most cases those who took blockers went on to further interventions like cross-sex hormones and surgery and, like the NHS, that the long-term impact of the blockers was also unknown.[57] 'We think that it would have been better to avoid controversial factual findings,' the Court of Appeal said.[58]

The Court of Appeal agreed with the Tavistock Trust that it is for doctors, not the courts, to decide on the capacity of young people to consent to medical treatment.[59] The judgment explained that while there are 'strongly held contrary views', the High Court's original declaration 'would require the clinicians to suspend or at least to temper their clinical judgement and defer to what amounts to the clinical judgement of the court'. While the earlier guidance was 'driven by the very best of intentions', there was nothing unique about puberty blockers that meant that the Gillick principle ('that it was for doctors and not judges to decide on the capacity of a person under 16 to consent to medical treatment') should not apply, the Court of Appeal judged.[60]

The Court of Appeal made clear that it wasn't for them to judge whether 'treatment for gender dysphoria is a wise or unwise course'.[61]

These were decisions for the NHS, the medical profession and its regulators, government and Parliament.

Concluding the judgment, the Court of Appeal insisted that clinicians should 'take great care before recommending treatment to a child and be astute to ensure that the consent obtained from both child and parents is properly informed by the advantages and disadvantages of the proposed course of treatment.'[62] 'Clinicians will be alive to the possibility of regulatory or civil action where, in individual cases, the issue can be tested,' it added. While the CQC inspector found that consent had not always been adequately obtained, the fact that GIDS had 'fallen short of the standard expected in its application of the service specification does not affect the lawfulness of that specification'.[63]

The legal challenge over puberty blockers in England appears to be over. In April 2022, Keira Bell's attempt to the take the case to the UK Supreme Court was rejected on the grounds that 'the application does not raise an arguable point of law'.

But practices at GIDS were left permanently changed. In August 2021 NHS England established an external panel – the Multi-Professional Review Group (MPRG) – to review each proposed referral for children under 16 for puberty blockers to ensure that procedures for assessment and for informed consent had been properly followed by GIDS. This remained, and is still in place at the time of writing. It will remain so even after the planned closure of GIDS, until a new treatment protocol is agreed.[64]

The judicial review brought the eyes of the world on to GIDS, allowing those not originally privy to its practice to form an opinion. And, as we shall see, it revealed just how little a service operating for 30 years knew or recorded about its often vulnerable and highly distressed patients.

19

DATA AND 'DISPROPORTIONATE EFFORT'

Although the judicial review against the Tavistock ultimately failed, the successful appeal did nothing to address the question of data. Or the lack of it.

The initial proceedings and judgment throw into sharp focus how a clinical service that had been running for thirty years, referring young people for medical treatments about which little is known (in terms of long-term side effects at least), had collected next to no data.[1]

The High Court expressed its 'surprise' at GIDS's inability to provide data, remarking on it on three occasions. GIDS could not say how many people had been referred for puberty-blocking medication between 2011 and 2020, nor the age distribution for those referred. The judges noted their surprise 'that such data was not collated in previous years given the young age of the patient group, the experimental nature of the treatment and the profound impact that it has'.[2]

GIDS did not have data on the number of young people referred for puberty blockers who had an autism diagnosis. 'Again, we have found this lack of data analysis – and the apparent lack of investigation of this issue – surprising,' the judges noted.[3]

And GIDS said that it did not have 'any data recording the proportion of those on puberty blockers who progress to cross-sex hormones'.[4] 'We find it surprising that GIDS did not obtain full data showing the figures and the proportion of those on puberty blockers who remain within GIDS and move on to cross-sex hormones,' the judges said.

GIDS had not provided the results from its Early Intervention Study of 44 young people to the court either, explaining that it was in the peer-review process. The judges pointed out that this would not impact the data involved, but these were still not supplied. The results of the study were finally published in a (non-peer-reviewed) preprint the day after the initial judgment was handed down in December 2020.[5] This paper showed that 98 per cent of those who had commenced puberty blockers started cross-sex hormones while they were still being seen at GIDS. Of the many hundreds who commenced puberty blockers outside this research study – from 2014 onwards – GIDS reported that they could not say how many had followed the same trajectory.

The lack of data stunned some of those who worked in GIDS. They couldn't understand how the service could not provide the data the court had asked for. 'It took the wind out of me,' one senior staff member at the time tells me. And made them furious. The Executive had found time to write papers about 'postmodernist, high-level theoretical ideas and stuff', they explain, but the service was not following up the children and young people it had cared for. GIDS could not even tell the High Court how many of the young people put on blockers were autistic, they say, in despair. 'We don't fucking care about post-structuralist ideas; in the end so many of us were saying we want to know some numbers, some actual numbers. How many?'

'There was a research team and that was well staffed and funded,' the clinician explains. It looked as though GIDS was collecting as much information as it could. Briefings would be given at regular away days, they say. 'It wasn't obvious that no meaningful data was being collected.' Dr Anna Hutchinson agrees. 'I assumed they were following up when I was there. The research team were always giving out questionnaires. It was a central part of how we worked,' she says.

Dr Juliet Singer was not surprised. The judicial review 'must have been embarrassing' for the Tavistock, she thought. 'How could it not be, to be so publicly shamed?' But she had been asking questions about data and GIDS as soon as she'd been elected a governor in November 2018, and had received no adequate answers.

'I mean, we were aware of the lack of data. And we were aware of their position that [GIDS] held themselves as experts. And it was always difficult for me to understand how they could hold both those bits in their mind at the same time – because how can you be an expert on something without data?' Singer says. 'How can you be experts when we don't know the impact of the treatment, the side effects and the long-term effects? And we don't know any of the outcomes. Without all of that, what are you expert in?'

Singer was left unsatisfied, having met with both Paul Jenkins and Paul Burstow in the summer of 2020, before the judicial review. 'The absence of such past data seems to have been a serious failing, given that treatments recommended by GIDS can have life-changing consequences for the Service's clients,' she noted. But what was being done to rectify it? How did GIDS assess co-morbidities, she asked? What extra work was carried out in cases where autism was suspected? Surely audits could have taken place of basic information like the number of assessment appointments, co-occurring difficulties, common themes and family backgrounds, she noted, as this would be captured in patients' notes. What information was available to GIDS on the referrals it had received in the past, Singer pressed, and what was the service doing to understand the 'present outcomes of its work'?[6]

Paul Jenkins acknowledged that the 'the issue of data on outcomes is a significant one and is an area where, with hindsight, it would have been helpful if we had a more robust historic dataset'.[7]

However, to create such a data set retrospectively 'is not easy', he says, 'without disproportionate effort'.[8]

It meant GIDS would not try to learn about what had happened to its patients, many of whom were vulnerable, had suffered trauma, abuse and bullying, and had undergone significant novel medical interventions.

Singer 'felt sick' reading the response.

It was 'uncaring', she says. Disproportionate to whom, she wondered? To the girls who had been coming through GIDS's doors in the thousands? 'These are people who may have been better served with other types of treatments. The numbers are massive. It's new; it's different. Everything should be done to try and understand it,' Juliet Singer insists. 'At what point does it become proportionate in his mind?'

Singer felt it wasn't simply that the Tavistock didn't view learning more about how patients at GIDS had fared as a priority – it was more than that. 'It's like they're actively not wanting to find out,' she says. She argues, too, that the research GIDS *has* embarked on, with the help of more than £1.3 million, covers those aged under 14 only and over a period of just two years.[9] It will still leave many gaps in our knowledge, particularly on the cohort of teenage girls being referred in growing numbers, Singer says.

GIDS supplied the High Court with data from just one year – the year before the judicial review – 2019/20.* Analyses were carried out of patients referred to endocrinology services by GIDS for puberty blockers and, separately, of those who were discharged from GIDS that year.[10]

The first analysis showed that 161 children were referred by GIDS for puberty blockers. Three were ten or 11 years old, while 95 (59 per cent) were under the age of 16.[11]

The second set of data needs a bit more unpicking. This was an analysis of a random sample of patients discharged from GIDS. It was not a random sample of *all* GIDS patients. Those who have been discharged are likely to be those who have decided they do not wish to be assessed at GIDS any longer, or those who are now too old to remain under its care. Some will have 'aged out' before ever being seen by GIDS and will receive treatment in adult services.[12]

This analysis showed that 16 per cent of discharged patients had accessed puberty blockers during their time with GIDS, with 55 per cent of them subsequently being approved for cross-sex hormones during their time with GIDS.[13] This does not mean that only half of those who began puberty blockers continued on to cross-sex hormones. It just means that *while they were at GIDS* half began taking cross-sex hormones.

Nearly a quarter – 23 per cent – of patients were discharged without ever having been seen. They had not been assessed by GIDS and

* The service didn't have historic data. It was only in March 2019 that GIDS introduced a new data field to patient clinical records which would allow for quick searching of those who had been referred for physical interventions.

therefore it would not have been possible to refer them to endocrinology.[14] What's more, 69 per cent transferred to adult gender services when they left GIDS, presumably to either start or continue a medical transition.[15] The fact that such a small proportion were referred to endocrinology while at GIDS may well be a reflection of how old they were by the time they'd got there – a legacy of the service's lengthy waiting list.

But the data GIDS have made public don't paint the full picture. The Trust's council of governors were provided with a little more information. They learnt that the 16 per cent figure rises to 26 per cent when patients who were never seen or only received one appointment before referral to adult services were removed. The governors were also shown data that confirmed that two patients were referred to endocrinology after only two appointments. The Trust was satisfied they had been appropriately assessed.

Having denied that two-session assessments ever took place, a random sample of GIDS patients from a single year found that they did, a finding also made on another sample of patients by the inspectors from the CQC.[16]

Discharge data is not representative of the whole GIDS population, as, importantly, those who commence treatment with the blocker must remain in the service up to the age of 18 so that they can be monitored. Those who are on the blocker or cross-sex hormones but who are not approaching 18 are unlikely to be picked up by this analysis. We do not even know if the discharge data from 2019/20 was representative of other years. It seemed wrong, therefore, to argue, as chief executive Paul Jenkins did on BBC Radio 4's *Today* programme, that this piece of analysis on this particular sample illustrated evidence of the 'cautious' approach taken by GIDS overall.

None of the clinicians I have spoken to recognise the 16 per cent figure. It was always acknowledged to be higher than that, they say, but getting accurate data was always difficult and something the service struggled with. Some staff argue that 16 per cent is so low that, if true, young people simply would not be coming to the service.

It's also at odds with what GIDS has stated repeatedly in various forums over the years immediately leading up to the judicial review.

GIDS personnel have frequently said that around 40 to 45 per cent of young people seen by the service are referred for puberty blockers.[17] Although this is rightfully described as a 'minority', it's a sizeable one.[18]

Where does that figure come from? And what does it actually mean?

Like many statistics provided by GIDS, it's an average. It applies to all children and young people assessed by the service – from the very youngest (three years old) to the very oldest (17 years old). Those at both ends are very unlikely to be referred for physical interventions, as the younger ones are not eligible, and the older ones will often wait to go straight on to cross-sex hormones in adult services. But what is going on in the middle – for those who would actually be eligible, given their age and stage of puberty?

In a 2018 paper co-authored by GIDS director Polly Carmichael, GIDS Executive member Bernadette Wren, UCLH lead paediatric endocrinologist Gary Butler and researcher Nastasja De Graaf, the oft-cited 40 per cent figure is mentioned.[19] 'Following psychosocial assessment at the GIDS, on average 38–40 per cent of all clients attend the joint endocrine clinics, although this varies across the age range.'[20] Readers are then presented with the following graph, which explains that figure:

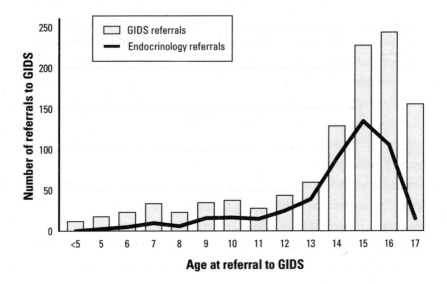

The x-axis – the horizontal one – is the age of referral to GIDS, not the age of referral to endocrinology. The data being shown are the 'numbers of young people presenting to the Gender Identity Development Service (GIDS) between 2010 and 2013 by age at initial referral (bars) and the proportion who had been referred on to the paediatric endocrinology clinics by 2017 (line)'.[21]

One can see immediately that the proportion of those referred for blockers changes dramatically depending on the age at which they were referred to GIDS. The low levels of referrals to endocrinology for those first seen at GIDS in childhood could be explained in a number of ways. On the one hand, someone who was aged five, say, at referral in 2013 would be only nine years old in 2017, and would most likely be ineligible for puberty blockers. The same reasoning would apply to many of the younger children. It could also be, as GIDS has often pointed out, that gender dysphoria in younger children tends to resolve in the majority of cases.

The Tavistock were asked for the data behind the graph – the actual numbers behind the plotted points. The Trust said that it did not hold the data. This was because 'the lead author for this paper was from a different institution and the person in our Trust who had collated this data did so for her PhD and has now left the Trust'.[22] The lead author is Gary Butler, based at UCLH, of whom the same request was made. UCLH too said that they did not hold the data, stating: 'The data in relation to the above request is not held at UCLH. We would respectfully refer you back to the Tavistock and Portman NHS Foundation Trust, as NHS England have commissioned them to provide a Gender Identity Development Service (GIDS) for Children and Adolescents.'[23]

Neither organisation involved in referring and prescribing puberty blockers off-label to children will say that it has the data behind their own published papers.

The Tavistock's response was challenged. Could it really be the case that a PhD researcher had taken the time to analyse data that belonged to GIDS – important data at that, pertaining to a key treatment pathway for its patients – and that the service had not retained it in any shape or form? The Trust's head of communications carried out an internal review of the FOI request and concluded that the Trust had made efforts to locate the data, including 'discussions with Dr Polly Carmichael, but unfortunately we have not been able to locate the information'.[24]

Without access to the data, I have resorted to attempting to derive the numbers behind the graph by measuring the intervals, lengths of bars and the position of the line. While imperfect, this did allow me to arrive at GIDS's average of 38–40 per cent. As can be seen just by looking, it shows that those seen by GIDS at the beginning of or during puberty were far more likely to be referred for puberty blockers than not. Of those first referred to GIDS aged 11 to 15, the majority went on to be referred for puberty blockers, the highest proportion appearing to be those aged 14. Around 70 per cent of young people referred (and seen) by GIDS at 14 were referred to endocrinology.[25]

The idea that the 40 per cent figure masks wide variation was supported by comments made by Polly Carmichael in 2017. 'We found that about 42 per cent of all referrals coming to the service decide to undertake physical treatments at some point,' she told fellow mental health professionals. That compared to 'about 25 per cent of young people before the age of 12'.[26] The same point was made by a senior GIDS clinician speaking at a conference for British gender identity experts in 2019.[27] Around 40 to 45 per cent of GIDS patients were referred to endocrinology, she said. But when one looked at those referred to GIDS prepubertally, it was more like 20 to 25 per cent. Taking the lowest of both those ranges, it would necessarily mean that the majority, approximately 60 per cent, of those referred to GIDS as adolescents experiencing puberty were then referred on for medical treatments.[28]

It is worth noting that the data provided above are for those first referred to GIDS between 2010 and 2013. The service did not provide puberty blockers to those under 16 (other than to the 44 young people in the Early Intervention Study) until 2014. I have been unable to find any updated statistics at all. UCLH told me that the data provided in the 2018 paper above was 'the most up to date information and the latest complete analysis from when the service was commissioned in 2009'.[29]

The statement that only a 'minority' of those seen by GIDS are referred for physical interventions has been challenged as misleading by some clinicians, too. 'That less than 50% will receive hormone treatment via the child and adolescent service *itself* is plausible,' Dr Matt Bristow argued on Twitter. However, 'many more' went on to receive hormones from adult services. 'I regularly had conversations with older adolescents about whether they wanted to wait for adult services where they might be able to start testosterone/oestrogen directly without going on the blocker, as under the adolescent protocol,' he said. 'Many trans boys who'd completed puberty chose to wait for adult services to get testosterone.' Some opted to stop their periods in the meantime, by taking the contraceptive pill.[30]

Former GIDS family therapist Anastassis Spiliadis recalls that even for clinicians in the service, it was impossible to get reliable data on the proportion of young people being referred for physical interventions. He was responsible for delivering training on working with young gender non-conforming people, but noticed that the numbers being provided by the research team kept changing. 'I realised that every six months… the percentages of the people going on medical interventions were different. One time it was 20. The other one was 40.' It did not make sense to him that it could be fluctuating so dramatically. He says he spoke to the research team and then realised 'that it was not a representative percentage or number'. In the end, Spiliadis says, Polly Carmichael advised him to stop using these percentages when delivering training, 'because she acknowledged that it was not representative'. Spiliadis felt that this was a basic question that the service should be able to answer – how many people go on to medical interventions – 'and basically we're told that we shouldn't be answering that question'.

---

* In a paper published in July 2022 (Gary Butler et al., 'Discharge outcome analysis of 1089 transgender young people referred to paediatric endocrine clinics in England 2008–2021', *Archives of Disease in Childhood* (18 July 2022), doi: 10.1136/archdischild-2022-324302), it was claimed that 'currently, around 21% of young people referred to the GIDS go forward to the endocrine clinic to consider hormone treatments'.

Any figures put into the public domain had to go through the Tavistock's communications team first for approval, clinicians say – even if staff were delivering teaching or going to see a CAMHS team. Similarly, all Freedom of Information requests relating to the work of GIDS or Charing Cross GIC had to be cleared by the communications team before they were sent.[31]

What about the overall number of young people who have been referred for puberty blockers by GIDS?

This question has been asked repeatedly of the Tavistock Trust, including by me. More often than not they have not answered, saying either that they do not hold the data or that they do not hold it in a way that is easily searchable and that it would therefore take too long to find.[32] It seems surprising that it took GIDS until March 2019 to introduce a new data field to patient clinical records which would allow for quick searching of those who had been referred for physical interventions. By this point the service had been running for 30 years.

Occasionally, the Tavistock has provided answers to this question. In October 2017, for example, the Trust said that 1,261 young people had been referred to endocrinology services.[33]

In other answers the Tavistock has provided some data on the younger patients it sees – those aged under 15 – who are referred to the 'early intervention endocrine clinic'. Between 2014 and 2018, 302 children aged 14 or under were referred to endocrinology services.[34] A further 48 children under the age of 15 were referred for physical interventions in 2019.[35] In 2022, the Trust said that 354 children had consented at UCLH and Leeds Teaching Hospitals Trust to accessing puberty blockers as part of the 'early intervention' cohort between 2012 and 2021.[36] This suggests that the referral of younger children for physical intervention slowed dramatically in more recent years, from a rate of roughly 50 to 60 per year between 2014 and 2019, to just one or two children from 2020 onwards.

In April 2022, UCLH informed me that between 1 April 2010 and 31 December 2021 it had issued prescriptions of puberty blockers to 1,415 patients, but this included the same young people being counted in multiple years.[37] The Trust did not provide me with the information broken down by sex or age of patient at time of prescription as I had asked. Upon appeal, UCLH sent the age and sex breakdowns from 1 April 2019 onwards only, but not the relevant totals.[38] I requested this information again and received it.[39] Curiously, despite females far out-numbering males in GIDS's caseload, UCLH issued more prescription to those 'assigned male at birth' in 2020, 2021 and 2022.[40] After several attempts, spanning six months, UCLH could not provide me with the number of *individual* patients to whom they had prescribed puberty blockers. However, in an unexpected email from UCLH, ten months after my initial request, I was provided with the number of *new* pre-scriptions for puberty blockers issued between April 2019 and August 2022 only. From April 2019 to December, 29 young people began treatment with blockers at UCLH, 24 in 2020, 9 in 2021 (during a large proportion of which new referrals were on hold because of legal action), and 14 in 2022.[41] This marks an apparent change in practice. Both legal action and additional oversight from the MPRG (and perhaps media scrutiny too) appear to have dramatically impacted on the numbers being referred by GIDS for physical interventions. Other GIDS/UCLH data suggest that in some years well in excess of 100 children will have been referred.[42]

I put the same questions to Leeds Teaching Hospitals NHS Trust, but they said the request would require a manual review of patient notes and this would exceed the cost limits set out in the Freedom of Information Act.[43] When I narrowed down my request, it was declined again. The Trust said they were planning on publishing the data at 'some future date' that was not defined.[44] All involved with referring for or prescribing puberty blockers seem coy about sharing the data. It is difficult to know why this may be. The data are there – albeit contained in patient records. Outcomes for 1,089 patients referred to UCLH and Leeds and discharged before 2021 were published in July 2022, but hitherto the three NHS trusts involved seem not to have taken it upon themselves to do much to look, share or collate data on their patients.[45]

'But what about outcome?' GIDS founder Domenico Di Ceglie asked – in 2002. 'What has happened to children and teenagers, some of whom have attended our service for years? What kind of life do they have? What memories do they have of their contact with our service?

We know little about this, except in an anecdotal way. It is now time that we start to find out.'[46]

But they didn't find out.

There have been two attempts to follow up GIDS patients' outcomes, both by doctoral students. Neither produced statistically significant findings, or represented a comprehensive audit of how GIDS's former patients have fared.

The first, in 2007, tried to contact everyone over 18 who had attended GIDS since it opened in 1989, but ended up with just 14 participants, including Ellie, who we met earlier. From the limited sample it had, the research appeared to back the conclusions of previous studies, which had seen 'childhood GID [gender identity disorder] as an indicator of either later homosexuality or genuine cross-gender identification'.[47] Six were classified as 'transsexuals', with four having undergone surgery. 'The most common outcome was the absence of gender dysphoria with a co-occurring bisexual/homosexual sexual orientation,' the author, Hitomi Nakamura noted. Four of the fourteen were 'exclusively heterosexual'.[48]

The second study, in 2018, had a narrow target sample – GIDS patients who had been referred to the Charing Cross Gender Identity Clinic between 2011 and 2016.[49] Seventy-two people responded – a little over a fifth of those eligible. Doctoral researcher Lorna Hobbs stated that 'participants were generally satisfied with their intervention decisions and the decision-making process', but that it was very difficult to draw meaningful conclusions.[50] The follow-up was short-term, and these young adults were at very different stages of their transition. Participants had varying experiences of GIDS and adult gender services. Many spoke of how distressing it had been to wait so long to be seen at both and said that access to medical treatments was too slow. Some felt the assessment process at GIDS to be too intrusive, while others would have liked more therapeutic input. One person wrote: 'I was pressured at the child services [*sic*] to take hormone blockers but I didn't want to due to my own research on the side effects.'[51] Two people could be described as 'detransitioners', though Hobbs does not use the word.

The 2022 paper on the outcomes of those seen by UCLH and Leeds is arguably the best data we have. It represents the *first* attempt to analyse what has happened to young people referred for medical interventions (we don't know anything about those who were not). It said that 1,151 young people were referred from GIDS – 827 to UCLH and 324 to the Leeds Children's Hospital – and had now been discharged.'[52] Of these, 91.7 per cent continued identifying as gender variant, and 86.8 per cent were discharged to NHS adult gender identity clinics (GICs).[53] The youngest child to be referred was seven years old. They later sought treatment privately. Jacob's history is not accurately reflected – there is no female-born 12-year-old who stopped treatment but remained trans in the data. As we learnt in Chapter 18, 5.3 per cent stopped treatment either with puberty blockers or cross-sex hormones. A further 2.9 per cent stopped identifying as gender-variant after being seen in the endocrine clinic but before starting blockers, and 27 young people were referred to the endocrine clinic but did not attend. It is not known what happened to them.

Overall, then, GIDS knows little about what has happened to its patients over the last 30 years.

It has never tracked what has happened to them or conducted long-term follow-up studies, though I understand that some young people are now asked to provide their consent to be followed up in the future. Professor Russell Viner confirmed that there is consent to conduct a long-term follow-up of the first 44 young people to receive puberty blockers under the age of 16. When asked, the Tavistock was unable to answer the questions of how many young people in its care decided to preserve their fertility prior to medical transition, how many patients go on to adult gender services, or how many leave GIDS after receiving talking therapies only.[54]

We also don't know how common bone problems are for those who, like Jacob, start treatment with puberty blockers at a young age and remain on them for several years. It would not appear that UCLH or Leeds General Infirmary is collecting such data, even though the impact of the accrual of bone mineral density has always been seen as a potential risk.

---

* There are more young people who have been referred but are still under the care of GIDS and are therefore not picked up by this analysis.

Everyone referred for puberty blockers by GIDS and monitored by UCLH or Leeds has yearly bone mineral density scans. But there have been calls from UCLH to make these less frequent. A 2019 academic paper questioned whether it was necessary to have yearly scans, pointing out that they 'can be a large expense to service providers'.[55] The paper reported that 'there was no significant change' in overall bone mineral density for this group of young people. It stated that 'bone mass accrual resumes' when cross-sex hormones are introduced, but acknowledged that the full extent varies.[56] It is not known whether young people who commence cross-sex hormones after pubertal suppression will reach their *peak* bone mineral density.

The findings have been criticised. The fact that there is no significant change in bone density should be worrying, claim other endocrinologists. Puberty is usually a time of rapid bone-mass accrual. For it to stay static 'should be of great concern to any practitioner using this medication'.[57]

The UCLH paediatric endocrinology team also suggested that 'it may be clinically inappropriate' to compare the bone mineral density of children who have had their puberty blocked with those of the same age who have not. 'We suggest that reference ranges may need to be re-defined for this select patient cohort.'[58] When Oxford professor Michael Biggs analysed the data for some of the young people contained in the paper, he found that when compared to their non-puberty-blocked peers, their bone density was very low. 'Up to a third of patients had abnormally low bone density, in the lowest 2.3% of the distribution for their sex and age,' and, 'A few patients recorded extremely low values, in the lowest 0.13% of the distribution.' Biggs argues that, given these findings, the recommendations of the UCLH team are 'surprisingly complacent'.[59]

Here in the UK, I have spoken to a senior physician who is worried about what he has seen: a young adult transitioning from female to male, who has been on puberty blockers, and who now has osteoporosis. This doctor, with decades of experience, has never previously seen osteoporosis in an otherwise healthy young man. What worries him is not simply the osteoporosis, but that the young person does not seem to be concerned about it. 'The only thing that mattered was transition,' the doctor explains. 'If osteoporosis doesn't matter to someone receiving puberty blockers, then they probably shouldn't be receiving them,' he says.

'My case is not a one-off,' he adds. 'There are others with cases like mine,' but doctors are 'quite wary of speaking out'.

In preparation for this book, some very senior figures in GIDS suggested to me that it is 'naive' to think that they could have done more in collecting data and analysing outcomes, especially over the longer term. They explain that it costs money to do research. GIDS didn't have it, and – until recently at least – no one was throwing millions of pounds at them to do the studies. And, they say, they didn't have the time. 'All we could do was see the patients.' They bristle when I point out that a handful of former GIDS patients are now online, expressing regret about the changes they have made to their bodies – changes which began at GIDS. And they are defensive when it's suggested that GIDS may have missed an opportunity to add to the evidence base. But they do acknowledge that long-term data is needed: ten years at least, not a year or two. They also point out that the Tavistock is not an institution that could support them in that. The Trust does not have a decent grounding in conducting proper research, they said. Others agree. Dr David Taylor had called in his 2006 report for the Trust to turn GIDS into a 'an assessment and treatment service of the highest standard', with research as an 'essential component' of it.[60] But, he says, without investment at a Trust-wide level, GIDS couldn't do this. He would have liked to see the Tavistock invest in a research institute or form partnerships to conduct research, like other NHS trusts have done so successfully. Without a strong research ethos, GIDS struggled.

And where have those overseeing GIDS been? What responsibility should NHS England take for not insisting on proper outcome data from GIDS? A senior clinician told me they now 'feel like an idiot' when they think about GIDS's Early Intervention Study. It 'hasn't really contributed anything' to advancing the evidence base for the use of puberty blockers to treat gender dysphoria, they say. But where does the buck stop, they ask? With the leadership of the Tavistock? With NHS England? 'The most powerful stakeholders in that situation might have said, "You've done a trial; let's have a look at the findings."

Why didn't that happen? Did they not care? I just think sometimes maybe there's been this constant trap around this being so special and unique, and they're doing this thing that nobody else understands. And that created this cloak of mystery, really.'

This senior clinician asked why GIDS has not been held to account by its commissioners at NHS England? There were requirements to provide data as part of the contract, they say. If these were not being provided, why wasn't it insisted upon?

I do not know the answers to these questions. Perhaps, as some have suggested, it was down to numbers. 'When there were 50 kids a year, it seemed more acceptable not to have the evidence,' one former GIDS clinician muses. But this does not adequately explain why neither GIDS nor their commissioners invested in making sure they collected data on their patients and the medical interventions they were referring them for. GIDS has had thousands of young people on its books since at least 2015. It appears that no one knows what has happened to them.*

---

* Dr Hilary Cass, who is undertaking an independent review of gender services for children and young people for NHS England, is trying to find out. To help, the UK government has changed the law to allow the team working with her access to the medical records of those who have attended GIDS between 2009 and 2020 and who have a Gender Recognition Certificate. The Cass Review team explain that this legal change will allow them to conduct as thorough a follow-up of the many thousands of young people assessed by GIDS as possible. While they could have conducted their research without these health data, which were protected under the Gender Recognition Act (thought to apply to a maximum of 754 people), the team say they 'were not prepared to do this because this might have excluded people with some of the most favourable outcome and hence bias the findings'. See the following links for more detail: Sajid Javid, 'Health update: statement made on 30 June 2022 (UIN HCWS170)', Parliament.uk [website], https://questions-statements.parliament.uk/written-statements/detail/2022-06-30/hcws170; 'The Gender Recognition (Disclosure of Information) (England) Order 2022', Legislation.gov.uk [website] (30 June 2022), https://www.legislation.gov.uk/uksi/2022/742/contents/made; 'The Gender Recognition (Disclosure of Information) (England) Order 2022: equality impact assessment', Gov.uk [website], https://www.gov.uk/government/publications/the-gender-recognition-disclosure-of-information-england-order-2022-equality-impact-assessment/the-gender-recognition-disclosure-of-information-england-order-2022-equality-impact-assessment; 'Research programme', Cass Review [website], https://cass.independent-review.uk/research/.

Harriet

When Harriet* said she wanted to be known as Ollie, it took the school just a day to accommodate the change. Fifteen-year-old Ollie, a trans boy, was now a pupil at an all-girls' school.

He wasn't the only one. Ollie had a couple of non-binary friends, who identified neither as male nor female (he had first identified as non-binary, too), and there were a handful of trans-identified teenagers in the year below. Between 2 and 3 per cent of years 10 and 11, the last two years of senior school, identified as trans. Ollie was also dating another trans boy, 'which gave us both quite a popularity boost'.

Ollie's family were 'incredibly supportive'. They were confused, but wanted him to be happy. His mum 'saw that I'd become much more confident and comfortable in myself and so she saw it as a very positive change. She's always been my biggest supporter.' Immediately after coming out Ollie experienced a 'honeymoon period with great mental health', he explains. 'I felt freed of keeping the biggest secret of my life and had a healthy relationship.' Being trans seemed like the answer to everything: 'why I'd felt so strange, why I'd felt like I couldn't relate to most people. There's a whole list of things I felt like I could now explain – sexuality crises, discomfort with being in a single-sex school, hating hot weather, holidays, because I had to change the clothes I wore, not knowing how to interact with my family, hating large social situations.'

The immediate few years before coming out as trans had been difficult. While still identifying as female, Ollie had dated a girl. They were

---

* Names have been changed to provide anonymity.

both around 12 or 13. 'She was terrified of others at our girls' school finding out we were together, so I was barely allowed to speak to her in person… She was concerned about what her friends and family would think. I just felt invisible, like I was living a double life.'

Ollie was also self-harming and experiencing suicidal thoughts. As Harriet, he was referred to CAMHS but 'never received a response or any help'. He later found out that his GP had received a letter back, 'saying something like the demand for services was too high and that my symptoms were not severe enough to be seen'. Without a 'real coping strategy' things got worse, and Ollie was 'frequently suicidal'. Despite what Ollie calls a 'track record of depression, anxiety and suicidal ideation', he did not receive any mental-health help either before or while being seen at GIDS.

In 2017, after a nine-month wait, Ollie was first seen by GIDS. He was 16 – soon to be 17 – and it had been a year since he'd come out as trans, and had been using a male name and male pronouns. He'd started college as a young man but felt 'incredibly insecure' about it. He 'saw medically transitioning as a solution'.

Sitting in jeans, a T-shirt and a hoodie, Ollie knew what he wanted from GIDS: testosterone and then 'top surgery'. 'I was asked if I wanted puberty blockers, but I said I didn't find them necessary as I thought I was finished with puberty.' This came up at the first appointment, the clinicians 'talking about the standard procedure GIDS had and how I'd like to progress with them'. Ollie hadn't brought up blockers. In fact, he'd been trying to avoid it. He was 'worried they might want me to take them as a prerequisite to testosterone'. When the service explained that he *would* have to go on puberty blockers first, it seemed a bit, well, pointless. There was nothing to block. He'd started his periods when he was still at primary school. Ollie made it clear to GIDS: 'I didn't want any kind of medical intervention unless it was to transition… I remember being frustrated that Tavistock likely wouldn't be able to offer me testosterone or top surgery and feeling like I was waiting for nothing.'

GIDS does refer young people for cross-sex hormones at 16, but only if they have been on the blocker for 12 months beforehand. No young person can be referred for cross-sex hormones by GIDS without previously having been treated with the blocker.

Despite his disappointment, Ollie stuck with the GIDS assessment process. He knew it would result in a quicker referral to adult gender services than if he was referred directly. An assessment by GIDS and subsequent referral to a gender identity clinic would still be his fastest route to hormones on the NHS. 'If you were referred by GIDS, you could be bumped up the waiting list as the assessment was already complete,' he says.

Ollie was offered puberty blockers twice across the five appointments he had at GIDS, declining both times. He recalls them being spoken about 'quite casually'. 'As far as I remember they were described as fully reversible, no negative effects were mentioned. Just like a pause button.' The second time blockers came up Ollie was asked if he was 'still sure' he didn't want a referral. This time it was more in reference to the 'heavy and painful periods' he always experienced. Puberty blockers could stop the periods. He declined, also turning down the contraceptive pill to bring about the same effect. 'I think it was less that the blocker was being pushed on me, but more that they had a kind of road map for patients there (blockers then hormones) so there was nothing else they could offer me. And perhaps they didn't know how to deal with someone who wasn't interested in their road map at all.'

There was little substantive discussion about the testosterone that Ollie so desired and he was 'very quickly bored'. 'I started to see the appointments as a waste of time, or just a stepping stone towards the adult GIC, the promised land of hormone therapy and mastectomies,' he tells me. 'The [sessions] themselves I remember as having much less discussion about gender identity than I'd expected,' he says. He talked about school performance, future plans and fertility, but there was limited discussion on mental health or on sex or sexuality. With a separate clinician, Ollie's parents talked through his early development and the fertility issues they had experienced years before. But mostly the family would all be in the room together.

Ollie recalls that fertility was discussed at each of the five appointments that made up his GIDS assessment. He found it frustrating. He told the clinicians he was 'sure' he wouldn't have his own biological children, but they encouraged him to look into freezing his eggs and to research adoption. 'I was told to ask my GP for a referral to local fertility services and was warned about the risks of infertility with taking testosterone,' he says.

He was also asked about his body. Specifically, what he didn't like about it. 'One of the things I'm quoted as saying is that I was uncomfortable with my weight as I felt it accentuated my hips,' Ollie says. 'There wasn't in-depth questioning of why I felt the way I did; saying that I was uncomfortable with my body was enough. As far as I remember there wasn't much, if any, discussion of secondary sex characteristics aside from my hips. If they'd asked, they'd have found out I was uncomfortable with my breasts since they developed in primary school.' Ollie found it almost impossible to talk in any intimate detail about his body as his parents were often sitting alongside him. And although they are a close family, very few teenagers want to discuss their body in front of their parents. He doesn't recall discussing the binding of his breasts, something he'd been doing every day for well over a year by the time he was seen by GIDS. Binding, he says, 'made the hatred of my breasts much worse, not to mention the breathing difficulty and lasting chest pain'.

Overall, Ollie felt 'babied' and that the assessment hadn't been 'planned or tailored at all to me'. 'It felt like they had no idea how to assess someone on the verge of being eligible for adult services. One session I was given a sheet of paper and a tub of crayons, and was gently prompted to draw a 'gender timeline', with different-coloured crayons representing my 'different identities' since birth… I still kind of can't believe they asked a 16/17-year-old to do that.'

He felt that the questions you would, or should, ask of someone on the cusp of adulthood – about sex, relationships, sexuality – just weren't posed. 'They didn't ask much about my friends,' he says, 'who were all suffering with eating disorders.' Ollie had explained he had 'a lot of friends also identifying as non-binary', but it wasn't discussed further. He told the clinicians about his experience of dating a girl in the years before, something they later referred to in his assessment report as a 'sexuality crises between the ages of ten and 13'. Ollie's boyfriend – another trans boy – was also being seen and assessed by GIDS at the same time. This wasn't an uncommon occurrence at the service, and little was made of it. It seemingly wasn't explored why two female-bodied young people might identify as gay men rather than lesbians.

After a five-session assessment spread over seven months, Ollie got what he wanted – a referral to the adult gender identity clinic in Nottingham. And despite fears of having to wait for years to be seen, he was delighted to be offered an appointment after 15 months. He was now finally in a place where his medical transition could begin.

Ollie was approved for testosterone at his first appointment at Nottingham GIC – formally known as the Nottingham Centre for Transgender Health. He was 18 and says the GIDS assessment report was taken 'as gospel' by the doctor he saw.

'The guy that I saw was quite senior,' Ollie says, and simply commented 'so you had your assessment'. He asked Ollie a few lifestyle questions, about alcohol and recreational drug use, but there were no further probing questions. Ollie just needed a blood test. 'I got the letter in the post to say I could take it [testosterone], and then I was on it the next month.'

Ollie was also told at that first appointment that the minimum time between starting testosterone and having surgery was six months. 'Exactly six months after I started, I had the appointment to get the top-surgery referral.' As was allowed under both the NHS and the World Professional Association for Transgender Health (WPATH) guidelines, only one signature was needed for chest surgery – whether that's reconstruction for trans women or double mastectomies for trans men – and Ollie's doctor happily signed off the procedure.[1]

In January 2020, aged 19, Ollie underwent a double mastectomy. There were some complications – some significant swelling on one side – and Ollie had to travel long distances, not just for the surgery itself, but for an immediate post-op check-up too. 'I had never had surgery of *any* kind before,' Ollie says, 'and, you know, I read all the posts, I looked at lots of pictures, I was prepared for it to look horrible. And, you know, probably be in pain.' But Ollie wasn't prepared for what happened the night of the procedure. 'I woke up, freaking out. I couldn't breathe. I think I was just panicking. I had to have two nurses come in in the middle of the night in the hospital and try and calm me down.' This wasn't the last time this happened. The site became infected and again Ollie had to go to A & E. Antibiotics cleared up the infection and the swelling eventually came down, but the aftermath of the surgery wasn't easy. Thankfully, they were relatively short-lived, and he did eventually heal well.

It wasn't long after having his breasts removed that Ollie started to have doubts. Doubts about being trans. The complications from the double mastectomy were 'a little bit traumatic', but Ollie's health was also deteriorating more generally. The testosterone he'd been taking for close to two years had 'really negatively' affected his health. He was frequently getting painful urinary infections because of vaginal atrophy, caused by the testosterone. When women don't have enough oestrogen, it causes the vaginal walls to thin. This can make sex painful, cause burning during urination and cause urinary tract infections.[2] Ollie's GP 'had also started refusing to do blood tests on behalf of the GIC'. His blood hadn't been checked for hormone levels in over a year, and this was frightening as well as dangerous. Several trans adults have relayed a similar story to me – of how some GPs do not feel comfortable being involved in their ongoing care and have refused to administer prescriptions of hormones or provide blood checks.

But it was more than this. Ollie didn't decide to detransition because of poor health. He knew he wasn't a man. What's more he knew he was a woman attracted to other women. He stopped taking testosterone in November 2020 and identified once more as female.

Ollie is now Harriet again.

No one at GIDS had discussed surgery with Harriet, despite her being clear from the start that that was what she wanted: testosterone, and then top surgery. She says she was told 'you can talk about that at adult services'. 'I think the assumption that they had was that wherever I was going next would kind of go more into it.' There was some 'light discussion about testosterone' but no proper conversation about what medical and surgical transition might entail. Neither the GIDS team nor Nottingham sought to ask how she saw herself when she was old. 'Because if they'd asked, they would have had quite a depressing answer – that I probably couldn't picture myself being old.'

The first time Harriet received any proper medical information on testosterone and its impact on the female body was at her first Nottingham appointment. The same appointment where she was approved to start taking it. 'When I had to sign and say, "Yes, I agree to this because it's off-label."' At GIDS they had touched on some of the cosmetic effects – Harriet recalls 'balding, acne, face shape, voice and body shape' all being mentioned. But she sees these as 'superficial'. 'I don't remember discussing things like atrophy, cardiovascular risks, cancer risks or likely needing a hysterectomy until I went to Nottingham GIC.'

Harriet liked some aspects of being on testosterone. 'I was definitely excited. And nervous.' She remembers recording voice updates like so many other young trans men do online, monitoring how her female voice dropped in pitch to sound masculine. The changes to her voice, she says, were 'very quick', with a noticeable difference after just a month or two. She didn't like the weight gain. 'Some of that was muscle, but a lot of it wasn't,' she says. She struggled with this, having always had a difficult relationship with food. But it was the rapid hair growth that startled her. 'I remember the first genuinely negative feeling I had was some really dark hairs started like growing here,' she says, pointing to the tops of her shoulders. 'Just like a patch. And I remember looking at it being like, I do not like that.'

When we speak, Harriet has been off testosterone for over a year. She is smiling and friendly, intelligent and laid-back. Very down to earth. Her face is unmistakably feminine. And while she says she has to shave regularly because of the time spent on testosterone – daily if she is going out – there isn't any stubble visible. 'I "pass" as a woman in person now, from what I can tell,' she says, 'but my voice is so deep that it would never pass over the phone. Even this is the first time I've used the name [Harriet] again with anyone – I still struggle saying it.'

It's hard trying to go back. Her colleagues try to 'avoid pronouns completely' when referring to her and, strangely, this seems to be what the few people who are aware of her detransition seem to find most difficult – they don't know what pronouns to use. No one has been unkind, but telling people she has detransitioned has certainly been different to coming out as trans, she says. 'Definitely no celebrations from anyone this time!' Harriet laughs. 'I'm not concerned by what people think, but I feel alienated. I'm scared for the future, and I worry I won't be able to get things like the sex marker on my passport corrected. My exam certificates were all replaced or in my other name.' Harriet believes she will face some 'friction' about her voice, and possibly her chest, but doesn't regret her decision to detransition. 'It does feel a bit like waking up from a nightmare or regaining control of my mind after someone else took over. Emotionally I'm pretty exhausted, but I'm physically much healthier, and I care much less about what people think of me.'

Unlike most who detransition, Harriet *has* been back to her gender clinic. She felt extremely nervous in doing so, but she returned to Nottingham in early 2022, more than a year after she had begun detransitioning. She mostly wanted help with administrative matters – how to go about changing her name back on important documents and NHS health records. She doesn't have a Gender Recognition Certificate (GRC) but is grateful because, at the time of writing, there is no mechanism in place for their reversal.

British detransitioners who have obtained a GRC when transitioning currently cannot legally return to their natal sex. This is for several reasons. They cannot obtain a new GRC because, under the current system, to obtain a certificate a person must have a diagnosis of gender dysphoria – a marked incongruence between their gender identity and birth sex.[3] By definition, those who detransition do not have gender dysphoria and therefore cannot get a new certificate. The current 'statutory declaration' which forms part of the process of legally changing gender identity also commits the individual to retaining the change for their lifetime. However, there have been calls from Parliament to amend the wording 'to permit people who have legally changed their gender identity to reverse their decision'.[4]

Harriet was pleasantly surprised by the meeting at Nottingham. 'I kind of hyped it up in my head to be this terrifying thing. And it was just a nice chat with a nurse.' Although the nurse was kind to Harriet, she explained that there wasn't anything more the GIC could do for her. Harriet wondered whether some problems she'd been having with her periods might have been down to stopping testosterone. Unlikely, she was told. She spoke to the nurse about concerns over both hair loss in some places and excessive growth in others. 'And they're like, "Yeah, we can't do anything about that."'

Harriet's doctor at Nottingham Centre for Transgender Health is a big deal in trans healthcare.

Professor Walter Bouman was president of WPATH (2020–22). He did not respond to my request for comment or answer any questions relating to Harriet's case or the care offered by the Nottingham GIC: whether it was common practice to approve cross-sex hormones after a first appointment; whether he was satisfied that Harriet had undergone an extensive assessment prior to referral for surgery or whether he saw the GIDS assessment as fulfilling that task; whether he had personally been informed by colleagues in Nottingham of Harriet's decision to detransition, given that she had attended in 2022 to seek help; and whether the clinic generally kept a record of its former patients who chose the same path.

In his role as an experienced clinician working with trans patients, Bouman was a witness in support of Dr Helen Webberley in her medical misconduct hearing at the Medical Practitioners Tribunal Service (MPTS).[5] The case was brought after concerns were raised with the General Medical Council (GMC) by, among others, UCLH endocrinologist Gary Butler. He was relaying the worries of several GIDS clinicians about the care Webberley and her company GenderGP were providing to young trans-identifying patients who were also being seen at the service or on the GIDS waiting list. Webberley was found to be competent to provide treatment, and 'could properly be described as a GP with special interest in gender dysphoria', but to have failed to provide adequate follow-up care to two young people prescribed testosterone. She was also found not to have discussed the risks to fertility directly with an 11-year-old before prescribing puberty blockers.[6] Helen Webberley says she discussed fertility options with his mum 'until she was happy, and that she [the mum] had discussed this with him'.[7] At the time of writing, Webberley has lodged an appeal with the High Court challenging the verdict of 'serious misconduct' and a two-month suspension from practising handed down by the tribunal. The GMC will be defending the appeal, which is listed for 14 March 2023. Her medical licence is on hold while the proceedings are active.

In a separate, unrelated hearing, Dr Michael Webberley, her husband and co-founder of GenderGP, was struck off the medical register in May 2022.[8] The MPTS found a 'catalogue of failings' in the care he provided to patients between February 2017 and June 2019.[9] In one case, Michael Webberley prescribed puberty blockers to a nine-year-old, following a Skype call lasting 20 minutes, with him 'actually having spoken to Patient V (the child) for only ten minutes'.[10] Patient V had sought the services of GenderGP after being referred to GIDS and being told there would be a five-month wait.[11] In a statement, GenderGP said that the two 'contradictory findings of the Drs. Webberley's cases' demonstrated the 'lack of key expertise… in the provision of trans care within the UK'.[12]

Having transitioned, and now detransitioned, Harriet says her thoughts on GIDS and the pathway towards gender-affirming treatment for young people have changed. 'I thought the whole argument would just be about blockers,' she says, but there are other things to consider. In her case, the 'biggest issue is the transition to adult services'. She says she feels that both GIDS and Nottingham GIC were completely accepting and conducted only a tick-box exercise. 'GIDS didn't really care too much, didn't go into depth; and then Nottingham didn't verify it at all,' she summarises. 'They were just like, "Do you still feel that way?" And I was like, yeah. "Okay."'

She says GIDS clinicians were, and are, right to be concerned that an assessment from them would hold weight in adult services. At Nottingham, she says, the assumption was that she had already been assessed. And all adult gender identity clinics would likely behave in the same way. NHS England guidelines for adult gender identity services are explicit about those who transfer from GIDS to services for over 18s: 'Young people who have completed a diagnostic assessment in the young person's service *will not be re-assessed for diagnosis* [emphasis added] in the adult service.'[13] However, for those who have a 'diagnosis for gender dysphoria' but don't have an existing treatment plan, 'either because they are wanting to explore options more fully, or have related very complex or psychosocial issues that mean physical interventions are not yet appropriate', the guidance states that then the process of transferring 'may be likely to take longer and will require ongoing collaboration and planning between the young person's service and the adult service focused on the needs of the individual'. Harriet had her diagnosis, and while she had not started hormonal treatment, her assessment report made clear her wish to do so. It didn't refer to any complex issues.

Nottingham, no doubt, thought they were helping. Harriet had been waiting a long time to be seen, they acknowledged – why make her wait any longer by doing further exploration? But, she insists, 'I wasn't being assessed in the waiting period.' And she doesn't see this waiting time as a chance for anyone to change their mind about their identity anyway. 'Even if you haven't had any medical anything, once you've said something publicly, and, you know, you've asked everyone to change what they call you… That's a lot of pressure to put on everyone around you. And if you start to have doubts about that, there is that pressure. And then there's also the immense stigma against desisting, or detransitioning. It's like, well, you're just an idiot, you know? You made a mistake, let's get on with it. Leave. And there is no compassion towards it at all.'

The problem with adult services relying on GIDS to assess people is, in Harriet's opinion, that the assessments aren't always very good. 'This is the report from GIDS,' she says, holding a five-page document in her hand. 'It's just so – not incoherent – but it's so disjointed. This wasn't someone who sat down and thought, "I need to craft this report, and… make this a good document, because someone is going to use this as the basis of the next stage."'

She points out various typos along the way – understandable perhaps for a clinician who may have had a caseload of 100 – and raises an eyebrow when the diagnostic criteria for gender dysphoria are discussed. Harriet takes issue with the requirement that a young person must have felt distress for at least six months. 'I know it's relative when you're on about kids, six months is a greater proportion of their lives. But it's still just six months for a decision that [will last] however many years.'

The assessment report, sent to Harriet's GP and Nottingham Centre for Transgender Health, also recommended that CAMHS offer her an appointment for 'low mood and fluctuations with mood' as a 'matter of urgency'. She never received a referral to CAMHS.

Harriet believes her GIDS assessment failed to explore many things that, looking back, she thinks were obvious. Autism. Sexuality. Eating difficulties and mental health problems.

Harriet says she displayed many autistic traits and has since been diagnosed with ADHD, a process that she says, incidentally, was far more thorough than an assessment by a gender clinic. Plus, when it comes to the medication to manage it, she says, you can just stop, unlike with testosterone, which has 'more long-term, permanent effects'.

It's clear, she thinks now, that her trans identity was 'a coping strategy – escapism', coming as it did immediately after a same-sex relationship where she'd been made to feel ashamed, and significant mental health difficulties. But nothing was discussed in much, if any, detail, she tells me. Not the proliferation of eating disorders among her friends, and her own 'heavily disordered eating'; not the fact that many of her friends identified as non-binary and 'that it was becoming somewhat trendy to be non-binary, especially in a single-sex school'; and not the relationship she'd had with another girl at around the age of 13, where her girlfriend had been so terrified about others finding out that she wouldn't even talk to Harriet in front of others. She now believes this relationship was 'a pretty formative event', but 'the clinicians seemed more interested in whether I was non-binary at the time than the obvious internalised lesbophobia I was experiencing'. She said that it was 'not seen as relevant'. Instead, it was simply noted in Harriet's assessment report that she experienced 'sexuality crises' aged between ten and 13.

These 'crises' weren't explored. Nor were her ideas around her all-girls' school, known locally as 'the lesbian school'. 'I think I needed a much deeper examination of just why I felt so disgusted with myself at age 15, that I was convinced I needed to be replaced by this new male persona for the rest of my life. My gender dysphoria diagnosis was based on, essentially, two years of my life.' Harriet says her trans identity provided 'an easy answer' to her poor self-esteem and mental health problems. 'I think sexuality was my big trigger for it at the time, where I started freaking out. I was a repressed lesbian at a girls' school. And then I was quite a heavy Tumblr user. And it was like, you can jump ship and be this other thing.'

'I'm a lesbian,' Harriet tells me. 'I'd repressed my same-sex attraction for most of the time I identified as trans. Though I called myself gay, I only ever dated another trans man and was pretty terrified of men in any romantic encounter. I justified that part to myself by writing it off as worrying about not passing or something. I guess the "revelation" came to me as I was reflecting on things in the process of early detransition.'

Even though it was clear that Harriet's gender-related distress had begun after puberty, she says that those carrying out her assessment at GIDS would 'find things' to indicate it went back to childhood. It's unclear why: distress only needs to be present for six months to meet a clinical diagnosis of gender dysphoria. 'I'm very into computers, and always have been,' she explains, and this was portrayed as being interested in 'male' pursuits. Reflecting on those conversations now, Harriet says many were symptoms of autism. Or just being a teenage girl.

When it comes to sex, like many other aspects of her life, Harriet says the GIDS assessment was 'not intrusive enough'. She laughs remembering the only vague mention of it. 'My clinician, I think, was trying to ask me about sex in a really roundabout way.' Harriet was 16 or 17 at the time. 'I suppose it's difficult because, you know, it's children, they don't want to overstep mark,' she acknowledged, 'but, you know, the age of consent is 16. Some of these people are going to be having sex and that's going to be relevant to how they see themselves.' Having had no proper conversation about sex at GIDS, it was completely different at Nottingham. Within ten minutes of their meeting, Bauman was explicit about the effects of testosterone. 'And the guy goes, "Do you know how to masturbate? Because it's a problem that some people have – because they don't do it. And then testosterone makes you do it all the time."' It was a bit of a shock and felt 'intense', given that this was within a few minutes of being introduced to a new clinician.

It's often argued that even though some will go through the process of transitioning only to regret it or simply change their minds, there is nothing that could have been done differently to have prevented it. At the time they transitioned, the young people were sure it was what they wanted. What could clinicians have done that would have helped while still respecting how the young person saw themselves? Some trans adults I have spoken to say that it's only by going through the process of medical transitioning that someone might realise that it is not for them, but they would never have seen differently beforehand.

Not so, says Harriet.

Although she explains that it did feel 'like the right path at the time', Harriet believes that with more discussion of her sexuality, and the fact that she was a heavy social-media user, she may well have decided not to go through with medical and surgical transition. 'I would have liked to be challenged on why I thought certain things were signs of gender dysphoria, such as not liking skirts or not liking my voice. They could have questioned why I changed identities so rapidly through non-binary to trans boy to whatever else.'

Some of those who transition and later detransition, or no longer identify as trans, do not regret the changes they've undergone. They feel that they made the right decision for them at the time, and that it was a worthwhile process. Some detransition for health reasons, some because they feel they can't 'pass' as another gender, and some because of lack of support from friends, family and society more generally. Others who may regret their choice choose not to detransition because it simply isn't possible as a result of the changes their body has undergone.

Harriet regrets her transition.

'I feel stuck at the moment. I feel like I'm waiting for things to happen. The regret, I think, is the voice and the chest – the big ones – and helpfully also the ones that can't really be changed,' she says. Physically, she is healthy. Regarding her surgery, she says she has 'quite ideal results, which is really weird for me to think about', and while she still experiences 'random aches' in her chest sometimes, it is nothing she is worried about. 'I suppose there is anger,' Harriet says softly. 'I'm not a very angry person. But I suppose it's frustration that there are obvious things that should have been picked up but weren't, and the thought of how things could be different. And also, I think the thing I'm most angry about is how much this affected other parts of my life, like my education, my relationships, everything, because it touches everything.'

'I'm not sure how to move forward, but I can at least take comfort in the fact I'm no longer fighting an uphill battle against my own biology.'

20

WHEN IN DOUBT, DO THE RIGHT THING

It would be false to think that all GIDS safeguarding concerns preceded the review into the service.

New staff joined GIDS and shared the unease that their predecessors had expressed years earlier. Those working in the service as late as 2021 have told me that while small teams were 'supportive and open to questions being asked', larger team meetings could be 'intimidating'. A small group of clinicians 'more in favour of medication' would robustly challenge concerns, believing they 'might be considered transphobic', family therapist Liam McDonnell claims. And, he says, the GIDS Executive could also be 'very defensive' when staff raised concerns.

Concerns around fabricated or induced illness (FII) continued to exercise GIDS clinicians too, as did the idea they might be helping young people transition who were same-sex attracted. Some staff still felt pressured to refer young people for puberty blockers when they did not think it appropriate. Safeguarding concerns, as well as the way they were handled, were raised – and investigated – again.

The response of the Trust to concerns raised by two women highlights how, despite a damning report from Dr David Bell, advice to pause and reconsider referral criteria by an external consultant, and the worrying testimony provided during the GIDS Review, whistle-blowers continued to be treated poorly.

One took her case to a public employment tribunal; the details of the other woman's case have not been disclosed until now.

In 2021 an investigation was completed into safeguarding concerns raised by GIDS clinician, Helen Roberts.[1] Roberts, an experienced nurse who had held safeguarding positions prior to joining GIDS, does not describe herself as a 'whistle-blower' in any of the correspondence I have seen. She simply relayed her concerns to Ailsa Swarbrick, divisional director of gender services at the Tavistock, when asked to. When Swarbrick alerted the Tavistock's director of HR, Craig de Sousa, he ordered an investigation. Incidentally, NHS insiders describe Swarbrick as 'the most constructive person' they have dealt with when it comes to GIDS. She left the Tavistock in January 2022.

Roberts described in private emails a culture at GIDS which, at times, discouraged the airing of concerns and the seeking of safeguarding advice, and where not all of its practices appeared to be safe. Just as others had found years earlier, so Roberts judged that 'anything that could be perceived as a criticism was not well received'.[2] Roberts was concerned about how telephone enquiries to GIDS were handled, fearing this wasn't always safe, and claimed that GIDS Executive member and consultant psychiatrist Rebecca McLaren had suggested that she was too 'thorough' when it came to safeguarding and that Roberts should 'rein it in a bit'.[*] Roberts claimed she had been admonished by McLaren on another occasion for raising a serious safety incident involving a young person on the GIDS waiting list, allegedly being told that she 'could have delayed' submitting the incident form to allow GIDS the chance 'to get things sorted out before [central safeguarding] became involved'.[3] Roberts also claimed she had been advised against taking cases to the Trust's central safeguarding team by GIDS's safeguarding lead, Garry Richardson.[4]

The investigation that followed looked at each of Roberts's concerns and allegations, but the resulting report makes for interesting reading. As with the GIDS Review report before it, at times it is difficult to see how conclusions have been arrived at from the evidence heard.[5]

Extraordinarily, Rebecca McLaren was not interviewed even though it was claimed that McLaren had told Roberts that it had been 'noticed' that she was 'very thorough – particularly with things

---

[*] The author's attempt to contact Dr McLaren for comment was unsuccessful.

like safeguarding and liaising with CAMHS'. McLaren provided several examples of this alleged 'thoroughness', Roberts explained in an email to her supervisors, including a case involving an 'attempted self-castration', another involving a young person injured jumping from their mother's car, but where no medical advice had been sought, and a third where a young person was hallucinating and hearing voices.[6] Just as clinicians had claimed before, it seemed that GIDS staff who spoke too loudly about their fears for the safety of young people in their care were accused of not quite being up to the job.

Neither of Roberts's managers was interviewed by the investigator either. Yet emails show that both seemed genuinely shocked at the treatment of their colleague, and relayed that Polly Carmichael had confirmed to them that there were no problems with Helen Roberts's work.[7]

The investigation heard how Roberts had discovered that a young person on the waiting list had written a letter to GIDS expressing suicidal thoughts in the summer of 2020. It had been sent several months earlier, but not picked up. Roberts felt this was 'so serious' that raising a formal report was the appropriate thing to do.[8] The Tavistock medical director agreed that the concern was valid, but the investigator was unable to clarify 'what, if anything', was said to Helen Roberts by Rebecca McLaren because he did not speak to McLaren. Roberts's view of the risk posed by the unattended suicide note was supported by GIDS's service manager too, however. This is the most senior administrative role in GIDS, and was one of only five people interviewed for the investigation (Roberts, Polly Carmichael, Garry Richardson and Ailsa Swarbrick being the other four). 'The matter of administrators making decisions about appropriate clinical interventions on the basis of information they received from young people was not safe or appropriate,' the investigation heard.[9]

Roberts had explained to Swarbrick that she 'repeatedly raised concerns to the senior exec team about the complexity and urgency of safeguarding issues when working on enquiries'.[10] Calls to 'enquiries' could come from anyone: GPs, those working in CAMHS, young people on the waiting list or even a worried parent wanting advice. And GIDS clinicians took it in turns to answer them. It was stressful. 'Young people are calling in saying they feel suicidal, that they're not under CAMHS,' one GIDS clinician tells me. 'They're on this long GIDS waiting list. They're desperate. And a lot of healthcare professionals call in, a lot of very desperate GPs.' Polly Carmichael acknowledged the work was 'emotionally draining and intellectually complex'.[11]

Often, Roberts explained, 'it felt far more like an urgent duty rota than an enquiry line.'[12] The young people concerned often appeared to be at serious risk of harm. And yet, she says, GIDS staff were instructed to deal with such calls in ten minutes, pushing callers back to the GIDS website and any risk issues 'back to the referrer if possible'.[13] This was 'often impossible' to do safely, Helen Roberts explained. She had sought advice on some of these cases from the Tavistock's central safeguarding team, but 'became increasingly aware of how this process... was perhaps not making me very popular with senior exec in GIDS'.[14]

Answering these calls, and the time spent dealing with them after-wards, did not count towards GIDS's activity targets. In short, the service wasn't paid to deal with them and they didn't help get the waiting list down. 'However... my priority as a clinical nurse specialist is always the patient or inquiry in front of me, rather than the commissioning arrangements,' Roberts explained to Swarbrick.[15]

Carmichael told the investigation into Roberts's concerns that Roberts 'had done excellent work' and often went 'beyond the call of duty'.[16] But, Carmichael is reported to have said, 'trying to make things better oneself leads to a blurring of the lines'.[17] While Roberts was 'an assiduous and thoughtful clinician', Carmichael said, she 'may have set up expectations that can't be met across the service'.[18]

Ailsa Swarbrick, one of the most senior figures in the Trust, told the investigation she had witnessed 'behaviours which might be considered micro-aggression or bullying'.[19] GIDS's service manager described 'what could be considered a closed GIDS management team and a defensiveness', explaining that the 'GIDS executive team don't like it when staff raise concerns inappropriately about GIDS patients'.[20] Just as staff had told the Tavistock Trust's medical director during the GIDS Review several years earlier, there appeared to be an admission that senior figures in GIDS still did not welcome clinicians raising concerns about patient safety. Little appeared to have changed in the GIDS culture.

The investigation report accepted that Helen Roberts 'clearly raised concerns to GIDS management' about the care it was providing to young people, but did not agree that they were 'raised in a whistle-blowing context that highlight a risk of harm'.[21] A reminder: these cases involved attempted self-castration, hallucination and threats of suicide. Roberts's concerns do not appear to reflect an idealised view of what a service struggling for resources should be offering, but rather an underlying fear that not all young people either being seen by GIDS or on the waiting list were safe.

The investigation found that Roberts had not been told to refrain from raising concerns with the central safeguarding team, but goes on to note that a 'dynamic' existed between the GIDS Executive and others that 'could lead to a prevailing sense of protectionism of the GIDS service and, if not explicitly stated, could leave people with the impression not to raise things that reflect badly on the GIDS service outside of the GIDS service'.[22] In other words, staff *perceived* at least that they should not take concerns outside of GIDS.

The investigation suggested that significant tensions remained at GIDS. And Helen Roberts was not a lone voice.

'When in doubt, do the right thing.'

Consultant social worker Sonia Appleby tried to impress this message upon everyone attending her training sessions on safeguarding children.

And it's a principle she's lived by. She has stuck her head above the parapet to stand up for what she believes is right on three occasions in a faultless forty-year career dedicated to keeping children safe. Even when this has made her own life very difficult.

Bringing legal proceedings against the Tavistock and Portman NHS Foundation Trust, whom Appleby joined in 2004, was the third and final time.

Appleby first lodged a whistle-blowing claim against the Trust in November 2019 at the Central London Employment Tribunal.[23] She had become the Tavistock's safeguarding lead for children in 2009 and was responsible for protecting children and young people from risk of maltreatment and preventing impairment of their health or development.[24] But in her tribunal claim, Appleby argued that because she had raised the concerns of GIDS staff – 'that the health or safety of patients was being, had been or was likely to be endangered'[25] – she was punished and prevented from doing her job properly.

Because she raised concerns, Appleby said that the Tavistock had 'misused its own procedures' to 'besmirch' her and 'therefore jeopardize the role of safeguarding within the Trust'.[26] Her line manager – Tavistock medical director Dinesh Sinha – had unfairly subjected her to unofficial disciplinary proceedings because of the concerns she had raised about GIDS. And, as BBC *Newsnight* had publicly revealed, Appleby claimed that 'there was an unwritten but mandated directive' from the Tavistock management that safeguarding concerns should not be brought to her attention and that GIDS clinicians were 'discouraged from reporting safeguarding concerns' to her.[27]

Sonia Appleby won her case in September 2021.*[28] Employment judge Goodman concluded:

> The fact that she questioned not just record-keeping, but the lack of rigour in the service model for making judgements about whether there was background abuse requiring consideration of Safeguarding, meant that she was seen as hostile to a service already under external pressure from politicised groups, and the internal pressure of sometimes acrimonious splits between clinicians. In our view these cannot be separated from the fact that the claimant had made disclosures about concerns on young people needing more consideration of whether there were Safeguarding issues, and staff being too overworked to deal with them properly... Dr Sinha's quasi-disciplinary treatment of her can only be explained as materially influenced by her disclosures, which were viewed by him (and others) as unwarranted interference, overstepping her proper role.[29]

The judgment was highly critical of several Tavistock Trust staff.

GIDS director Polly Carmichael was found to have been 'long suspicious' that Sonia Appleby 'was undermining her and her work',

* Anna Hutchinson, David Bell, Matt Bristow, Kirsty Entwistle and Anastassis Spiliadis were witnesses for Sonia Appleby.

and to have placed Appleby in 'the hostile camp'. Carmichael believed Appleby to be 'against the [GIDS] service model, not just concerned that Safeguarding was weak'. Above all, the tribunal found there *had* been a 'message being communicated to GIDS staff by Dr Carmichael, at the time of the Sinha review, that they should not take Safeguarding issues to the claimant, not because she was not a clinician familiar with the complexities... but because she was hostile to GIDS.'[30] When Helen Roberts had suggested that she had been given a similar message by GIDS's safeguarding lead, the investigation set up by the Trust had not upheld it. That investigation was carried out by DAC Beachcroft LLC – the same legal firm that defended the Tavistock in its claim against Sonia Appleby.

The tribunal found that 'both in emails, and in answers to questions in the tribunal, Dr Carmichael was often both verbose and imprecise'. Carmichael and others GIDS staff doubted Sonia Appleby's 'good faith and neutrality in what GIDS were doing', the judgment stated. When Appleby had first brought staff concerns to Polly Carmichael in 2017, she was said to have had an 'agenda'. And it was plain, said Judge Goodman, that GIDS safeguarding lead Garry Richardson 'resented the claimant, as far back as September 2017'. His actions indicated that his managers in GIDS saw Sonia Appleby 'as a hostile outsider, and [that he] probably held this view himself'.[31]

Tavistock medical director Dinesh Sinha also came in for significant criticism. His handling of allegations made against Sonia Appleby was found to reflect his 'unsympathetic, almost hostile, relationship' with her. (Sinha is criticised for his treatment of Appleby upon her return from a period of ill health, seemingly having 'viewed her approach to reporting sick leave as insubordination'.) Appleby had been accused of comparing GIDS to a 'Jimmy Savile type situation'.[32]* The implication, it was argued, was that the service and Trust were 'turning a blind eye to what was in front of them'; that somehow

---

* After the DJ and BBC presenter Jimmy Savile died in 2011, he was found to have committed sexual abuse, mainly of children, on a grand scale. It is possible that Savile's relationship with certain institutions, including children's hospitals, allowed the abuse to continue. Staff in the institutions he aligned himself with were seemingly unwilling, or unable, to acknowledge the abuse that was occurring.

'GIDS were aware children were not safe and wilfully ignoring it'. Sonia Appleby vehemently denied this, explaining that she routinely referenced Jimmy Savile during training.[33]

Sinha was described as 'judgemental and punitive' towards Sonia Appleby, placing a note on her file which she could not challenge. Had he investigated the claims made, he would have learnt that referencing Jimmy Savile 'was indeed part of her standard training'. The employment tribunal saw only one explanation for Sinha's 'stern, arm's-length approach to' Sonia Appleby – he believed her to be acting in 'bad faith'.[34]

> He therefore banned her from continuing the work getting accurate records for statistics on Safeguarding because he suspected she was digging for dirt to attack the service, when, as far as we can see, her actions were dedicated to finding out why the level of referrals from GIDS was so low, which might have been thought a legitimate activity on the part of the Safeguarding lead for children.[35]

Sonia Appleby herself is found to have acted without fault.

As well as personal vindication for Appleby, the employment tribunal proceedings again highlighted how, rather than tackle the safeguarding concerns being raised about GIDS, the Tavistock Trust had instead attempted to penalise the person raising them.[36] Appleby described a 'full blown organisational assault' against her in response to the concerns she had raised.[37] In her witness statement to the tribunal, Appleby explained how the Trust used the allegations against her 'effectively to silence and intimidate me, and to diminish me and the role I was attempting to carry out in good faith'.[38] 'As I plead this was to prevent a repeat of bad publicity in retaliation for my [protected disclosures],' she said.[39]

The employment-tribunal hearing revealed how Sonia Appleby had listened to GIDS staff and acted. She raised their concerns, and her own, repeatedly, over several years. And she was punished for doing so.

Taking the Tavistock to court was 'brutal' for Sonia Appleby.[40] So why did she do it? It was 'doing the right thing'. 'My job is to keep staff and patients safe and ultimately to keep the organisation safe,' she tells me. 'And, you know, I've got to blooming well be able to stand up for myself. It was as simple as that.'

———

Appleby appeared unflappable when facing two days of aggressive questioning from the Tavistock's legal team during the employment tribunal. When we speak in early 2022, I encounter the same calm, thoughtful woman. Appleby speaks slowly, as if considering each word carefully. She thinks before each answer. She's a details person, who seems able to recall every element of the thousands of pages of evidence in her case: the date and contents of every email, every meeting.

Initially, Appleby's colleague, Dr Rob Senior, the Trust's then medical director, had tended to be more involved with GIDS than her. When there was an 'explosion of cases' in 2016 and staff started approaching her too, she became more hands-on.

The issue initially preoccupying GIDS staff was the involvement of a private GP with the care of some their patients. Dr Helen Webberley was issuing private prescriptions for puberty-blocking drugs and cross-sex hormones to young people being assessed by GIDS, or who were on the waiting list.[41] Staff didn't know how to deal with this and were worried that it was risky for the children involved. Webberley would provide medications faster than GIDS, and at a younger age.[*] The number seeking advice from Sonia Appleby on this grew.[42]

———

[*] Having not been dealt with adequately at the time it was first raised, the issue of GIDS service users also seeing private providers never went away for GIDS clinicians. They say NHS England did not help with this matter either; a very senior figure told the author that NHS England simply 'didn't want to know' about the problem. Indeed, the service specification underpinning GIDS's practices says that while the service would 'not offer shared care with private clinicians', it would 'still provide holistic psychosocial support with input from mental health professionals' to young people who are accessing puberty blockers or hormones elsewhere. GIDS should make the young person and their family aware of the risks involved, and make clear that it could not monitor the impact of any medication provided outside the service, but the young person could continue to be seen. This made things exceptionally difficult for GIDS staff. On occasion, GIDS would allow a young person who had started on puberty blockers or cross-sex hormones privately to remain on them, even if GIDS itself would not have approved that decision, simply because it felt safer for the young person to be under the care of the NHS. Dr Alex Morris explained that this was seen as the lesser of two evils, and 'not that we thought it was particularly the right thing for them to have done in the first place'. Staff felt stuck – they didn't want to hold the clinical risk but also thought these children were vulnerable.

More GIDS staff went to see Sonia Appleby that autumn: three in October and another clinician in November 2017. This time they had far more worries. 'You begin to think, hang on a minute. There is something very significant happening. And we have to do something about this,' Appleby tells me. She sent an email to her line manager, Tavistock medical director Rob Senior, telling him that GIDS staff were concerned: 'Predictably, there are challenges regarding Mermaids, rogue medics and the political expectations of the national service,' she wrote. But 'perhaps more worrying', she continued, was the fact that staff 'feel they are coerced into not reporting safeguarding issues, and to do so is "transphobic"'. There was a 'lack of confidence in Children's Social Care', Appleby relayed, and she was 'most concerned' hearing that there was a 'lack of a team position regarding the clinical management of gender issues and what to do when there are safeguarding concerns whatever the genesis'. Appleby said that she had been invited to talk to some of the staff as a group and suggested that she and Senior have a meeting to follow up on the conversation they had with Polly Carmichael that summer.[43]

Ms Appleby wrote to her manager again a fortnight later, after the fourth member of GIDS staff approached her. All four, she explained, were saying the same thing. It was difficult for GIDS staff to 'raise safeguarding concerns', she said, made even more so 'by staff being referred to as being transphobic'. Clinicians had said the GIDS model did not properly take into account the troubled backgrounds of some children and it seemed that 'some young children are being actively encouraged to be transgender without effective scrutiny of their circumstances'. GIDS was 'bound to be seeing some children' who saw being transgender 'as a less oppressive option than acknowledging they are gay', the staff had told her. And, they said, Polly Carmichael was unwilling to listen to these concerns. Appleby reminded Senior that he had said he would speak to Dr Sally Hodges, the head of the children, young adults and families directorate, which GIDS formed part of at that the time.[44]

Senior did not reply to either email. It is difficult for Appleby to imagine why the Trust's medical director would not respond to correspondence raising such serious concerns, especially when children are involved. The Central London Employment Tribunal remarked that it was 'regrettable'. 'The sense that I made of it was that there was something seriously wrong. My difficulty was what was I going to do about it?' Appleby says. 'In a word, I was saying, "Look, there's an absence of governance here. And therefore, an absence of clinical oversight."' Appleby needed to manage the situation. Be robust. Unless she put in writing what she was doing and hearing, she was sitting on a huge problem.

Appleby was concerned for the safety of GIDS staff, too. They were frightened of speaking up, not only about their patients, but about their own safety. There was a 'level of malignancy' that needed to be dealt with, Appleby felt. The question was how. 'I was concerned about the children. But my access to those children was about actually bringing to the attention of the Trust that we had a service that was providing a *poor* service.'

Appleby fully understood that 'it would have been very difficult for the service to appreciate that this is what its own clinicians thought about it', and, indeed, when GIDS director Polly Carmichael *did* find out, the meeting with Sonia Appleby that followed was 'uncomfortable'.[45] Appleby told Carmichael that some staff did not feel safe but apologised for the fact that no one had made her aware of the concerns at the time.[46] She'd assumed that, given that she'd raised concerns with Rob Senior three times, these would have been passed on.

Appleby says she was left in a difficult position. She was aware that the staff who'd approached her 'felt the children were being conveyed down a medical pathway', who were unable to give informed consent. And she relayed this information to Sally Hodges. But, explains Appleby, she only had the testimony of four people. What she needed was data. And that's what she set out to get. 'First of all, I wanted to see the safeguarding data,' she says. 'The next step would have been to see the data about how they are managing these children clinically.' Data were hard to come by, and when she did get some, she said in her witness statement that she was 'quite surprised' by what she saw.[47]

Appleby undertook a quick audit of safeguarding referrals from different services within the Trust, using records from the patient records system. She compared numbers of referrals accepted by five Trust services – GIDS and four others – and the numbers referred to other agencies by each in 2017/18. GIDS had vastly more referrals to it than any other service, but a far lower rate of referrals to other services.[48] As a percentage, GIDS had only referred 0.6 per cent of its service users to social care, compared to 8.1 per cent for Camden CAMHS.[49] 'It was very concerning to me that we, as the Trust safeguarding team, could not obtain any accurate safeguarding data from GIDS,' Appleby said in her witness statement.[50]

It became clear that one explanation for the lower numbers was that GIDS were not recording events in the same way as any other part of the Tavistock Trust. They were a national service, not using the standard Trust forms for reporting, and, consequently, 'we could have no idea what they were doing,' Appleby says. 'I think it was calculated subterfuge, supported by the Trust,' she says. At the tribunal the Tavistock pointed out that GIDS staff had not been copied into an email about the electronic notes system being used by the rest of the Trust.[51] 'I was beginning to sniff that there were things that they did not want us to know,' Appleby says, and as far as she was aware, nobody else in the Tavistock and Portman NHS Foundation Trust was asking to see safeguarding data relating to GIDS. 'Nobody was asking for the data about consent either,' Appleby says, as far as she knew. And that seemed extraordinary.

Throughout spring and summer 2018, Sonia Appleby was in regular contact with Polly Carmichael and senior figures in the Trust. She raised serious safeguarding concerns and set out suggestions for what should happen next to help the GIDS service and team. Each time she copied in Polly Carmichael, medical director Rob Senior, Sally Hodges, Louise Lyon and Gill Rusbridger.

And there were some significant concessions. Sally Hodges told Appleby she 'completely agree[d]' that there were some children referred to GIDS 'where the gender identity issue is only a small part of the wider family and emotional difficulties'.[52] She is also reported to have said that 'the GID service is not a clinical service'.[53] Rob Senior is recorded as acknowledging the high caseloads of GIDS staff, a need to change the GIDS service model, a need to consider the leadership of

GIDS, and 'the conflictual nature of providing medication to children, who paradoxically cannot be regarded as giving consent'.[54]

Dr David Bell was also privy to some emails. He had heard similar concerns from GIDS staff, and his intention to write a report was clear. Sonia Appleby was given permission to help Bell with 'safeguarding issues' and providing him with some data.[55] She was 'mindful to avoid a potential narrative that the Safeguarding Team had failed to listen and support the Staff Governor'.[56] Others were 'not as helpful as they could have been to assist him', Appleby tells me, and what Bell was asking for was 'basic data'. It wasn't particularly sensitive, and plenty of others had it.

The Gender Identity Development Service was in a 'febrile state' following Bell's report, Appleby says. 'And suddenly, it felt as though the very senior managers were extremely hostile towards me.' She was seen to have been more involved with David Bell's report than in fact she had been, because of a 'misleading' remark made in the introduction to the document.*[57]

Reflecting in 2022, Appleby says Bell's report seemed to her to operate as 'a kind of clarion call for GIDS staff' and the wider Trust to 'make allegations' against her, branding her 'transphobic'.[58] 'What am I transphobic about?' she asks. 'Is it transphobic that I'm trying to determine and ensure children that are in the service actually have a safe service?'

As a result, when the time came for her to speak to her now boss – new Tavistock medical director Dinesh Sinha – for the Trust's review into GIDS, she was 'extremely apprehensive'. The interview that followed was 'very provocative', Appleby says. 'I don't think he [Dinesh Sinha] was prepared to listen to me,' she adds. 'I was determined that I wasn't going to allow the experiences other people had trusted me with, to some extent, to be airbrushed. And, in fact, they were.'

Sonia Appleby relayed the concerns that GIDS clinicians had shared with her to Sinha. While there 'is a plethora of opportunities

---

* David Bell writes in his introduction that 'this report is signed by David Bell but Sonia Appleby has been closely involved throughout its preparation and has read and discussed with me this final version to which she has made a number of very important contributions'.

where staff can talk about the work', attempts to think about difficulties in GIDS had been 'stifled', she said. It had not been possible for others to work properly with GIDS either, Appleby explained, because of the 'level of anxiety' felt by its personnel. 'It is so difficult to have those kind of ordinary safeguarding conversations in a service that is so paranoid.' She had 'never been able to have a fruitful conversation with Polly about tackling what is happening in the Service' around safeguarding.[59]

Sinha chose to follow up all that he was told during the course of the GIDS Review by placing a letter on Appleby's file reminding her to be 'respectful' over an alleged remark which he neither investigated nor provided Appleby with any information about. It appeared that the feelings of some GIDS staff were being prioritised over questions about the safety of the GIDS service, even though these were being raised by the safeguarding lead herself.

'If you look at how the Trust justified how it treated me during that so-called informal meeting,' says Sonia Appleby, it was because the Trust had said she had been 'accusatory'. The Trust 'never actually defined' what she had done that was alleged to have been accusatory, she adds, but she presumes it related to the complaint that she had linked GIDS with Jimmy Savile. The Tavistock 'found themselves in a situation where their case against me was that because I had allegedly been accusatory, that was causal for them to basically do something unlawful – in terms of employment law'.

'We know when institutions fail to follow their own procedures, there will be difficulties,' Appleby explains. 'And it's not just the whole process of the employment tribunal. Of course, there are other issues, more important, in terms of how are we managing this really important group of patients and clients? We weren't collecting data. We didn't have any consent protocols. They were very, very averse to any questions being asked about what was actually happening in their service. And if you asked those questions, before you knew it, there were managers telling you, "Please stay away, and don't do your job."'

Dinesh Sinha did *not* investigate the claim that GIDS staff were being discouraged from seeking advice from the Trust's central safeguarding team. Instead, it emerged at the employment tribunal between the Tavistock and Portman NHS Foundation Trust and Sonia Appleby that he sought advice from HR.[60] Emails presented to the tribunal by Sinha confirm that 'reported comments' made by Carmichael would be subject to a 'fact finding pre investigation',[61] but the contents are sparse and it is not wholly clear what these 'comments' related to.[*] Sinha was challenged about this approach – these were safeguarding concerns, not HR issues, Appleby's counsel argued. Sinha was the Trust's executive with responsibility for safeguarding, as well as being medical director. Appleby's legal team suggested that Sinha had been presented with a systemic problem that was worthy of inclusion in his report.[62] Sinha said the claims were coming only from a minority of the people he spoke to, and insisted that he did not give GIDS 'a clean bill of health'.[63] He said he had found many areas of concern and rejected the accusation that the GIDS Review had been a 'clean up report'.[64]

Nor did Dinesh Sinha inform Sonia Appleby – the woman with a statutory responsibility for safeguarding children across all of the Tavistock's services – of any of the safeguarding concerns raised by GIDS clinicians during the course of his review.[65] Appleby did not learn of what had been said until hearing some of the claims aired on BBC *Newsnight*, and then reading some of the transcripts that the Trust had to disclose as part of her employment tribunal claim. 'I can tell you unequivocally that none of the issues were passed to me,' she tells me. When she did get the opportunity to see the material, Appleby was 'completely overcome'. The transcripts, she says, 'represented a tragedy' for some of the patients involved and 'some of the staff who were telling these stories'. But, she says, they were also a 'tragedy for the organisation – that so many of these narratives had been muzzled, and the people who had raised these concerns were demonised'.

---

* The emails presented to the tribunal are dated July 2019, five months after Sinha completed his review. In late June 2019, Anastassis Spiliadis met with the director of gender services, Ailsa Swarbrick, and made several allegations about Carmichael. These were not formally investigated as Spiliadis chose not to pursue his complaint when he left the Tavistock and Portman NHS Foundation Trust later in 2019.

Appleby says in her witness statement that, in spring 2018, Hodges told her not all clinicians were suitable for GIDS work. 'She said the work is very complex and not suitable for everyone.'[66] Although Hodges did not qualify what she meant, Appleby thought she was talking about the clinicians who had taken their concerns about the service to Appleby in Autumn 2017. It is a line that has allegedly been levelled repeatedly by others in the Trust – that the work isn't for everyone, the implication being that they are not up to the job.[67]

To Sonia Appleby, someone with close to four decades of experience working with children, this suggestion couldn't be further from the truth. The clinicians who have spoken out are not weak, she insists. Those who stand up are, generally, those with 'emotional intelligence' and a 'sense of where the boundaries are', she says. 'I've always been really worried not about the people who speak up, but about the people who are silent. When there's really difficult things happening, and everybody knows what's happening. And there's silence…' Appleby doesn't finish the thought.

Sonia Appleby did not receive an apology from the Tavistock in the immediate aftermath of her victory at the Central London Employment Tribunal. Instead, 'the chief exec wrote to the whole Trust, and said that the outcome of the employment tribunal must have disappointed staff, patients and families,' Appleby says. Statements to the press expressed similar sentiments. The Trust was 'disappointed' by the verdict, but seemingly not sorry.[68] Appleby did later receive both a written and a verbal apology from Tavistock chief executive Paul Jenkins, 'not only for that email, but also for the circumstances that were upheld at the employment tribunal'. This was accepted, but Appleby also asked what lessons would be learnt from the episode and all that had been revealed. 'I left in December [2021], and I didn't get a sniffle of what lessons have been learnt,' she says. 'I can't judge what state [GIDS] was in because the propaganda about the service was spread far and wide throughout the Trust, so it was really difficult to know what was happening.' Appleby says she would regularly ask her former safeguarding colleague for updates, but they didn't know either. 'And it got to a point one day and I said to them, "Look, if you don't know, then we really are in trouble."'

The employment tribunal had found that the director of GIDS had instructed her staff not to seek advice from the named professional for child safeguarding in the Tavistock Trust; that the medical director of the Trust punished that named professional because she had raised concerns – repeatedly and through the right channels – about the standard of safeguarding in GIDS, as well as stating that several staff were extremely concerned and did not feel safe; that the Trust's director of HR failed to intervene when that same individual was subjected to 'quasi-disciplinary' proceedings and a permanent note was left on her file without any means to challenge it; and that the chief executive, in charge of overseeing the management of this Trust, was either unaware of all that was taking place or not willing to prevent it and make sure proper processes were followed.

No one resigned.

21

AN UNCERTAIN FUTURE

It is undoubtedly the case that some GIDS clinicians became much more cautious over time. I've spoken to clinicians who referred only two or three children for puberty blockers from a caseload of around a hundred, and others who would extend assessments, perhaps to dozens of sessions, or keep patients on the books and check in with them a few times a year to see how they were doing. 'I saw kids for years and years,' explains one senior clinician. This wasn't a sustainable way to run the service though, they concede. GIDS was not commissioned to provide ongoing talking therapy. While many young people seen at GIDS were very distressed, not all were. But they still needed some help and there was nowhere else for them to go. 'Some of the children didn't experience high levels of distress, but they really valued coming to a place and just talking with someone who understands. They would never get into CAMHS,' the clinician explained.

One mum, Laura,* whose teenage daughter, Alannah, was seen by GIDS until summer 2021, tells me that they had 12 sessions in their first year – one per month – and then one every eight weeks or so the year after. Alannah had come out as trans, 'overnight', at 13. And within a matter of months, she was presenting as a boy. She was referred to CAMHS, who celebrated Alannah's trans identity, but Alannah's mental health was poor and going downhill quickly, Laura

---

* Not their real name.

explains. Alannah was suffering with severe anxiety and depression, and was having suicidal thoughts. She was prescribed antidepressants, which Laura was not overly keen on her child taking. But they helped.

CAMHS suggested referring to the Tavistock, but Laura was sceptical about what they could offer her daughter. She says a GIDS clinician told her the assessment would be 'quite a fast thing' and that there would be big gaps between appointments. Laura didn't believe a medical pathway was right for her child. But under pressure from both Alannah and CAMHS, Laura reluctantly agreed to the GIDS referral. Laura turned down a GIDS appointment when it was initially offered, worried they'd refer her daughter for puberty blockers. She claims GIDS said they didn't know the legal implications of this, and that they wanted to speak to the GP and might have to contact Alannah directly. That didn't happen, but it left Laura apprehensive. Once Alannah turned 16, Laura could not prevent her taking up the referral. But when the family were seen, she was pleasantly surprised. These clinicians seemed very different to the ones she'd been in contact with previously. They assured her they wouldn't be recommending puberty blockers, suggested Alannah be assessed for autism, and gave the family a chance to talk. Laura does not sing GIDS's praises, but she is glad it provided a space for her daughter that CAMHS seemed unable to. 'They were nice people,' Laura says of the GIDS clinicians they saw. 'They were understanding. They were compassionate – all those things. They didn't push.' The two years at GIDS, Laura says, were really about 'trying to keep the peace, trying to get us to communicate, how can we work together as a family, it wasn't about what happens next, or what to expect. It wasn't about medication.'

Despite having identified as a trans boy for five years, and changing her name at school, with her doctors and on bank accounts, Alannah never proceeded down a medical pathway. Within three months of leaving GIDS she no longer identified as male.

Whether GIDS as a *service* became more cautious is much harder to assess. I am told, for example, there were instances where senior clinicians would override junior clinicians' decisions to suggest puberty blockers. And some clinicians stress that they were supported in saying no to physical interventions – by Dr Polly Carmichael and by others. Total prescriptions for puberty blockers issued by UCLH halved between

2019 and 2020 (young people will typically receive blockers for more than one year), from 226 to 109, and as we saw in Chapter 19 far fewer *new* prescriptions appear to have been made from 2020.[1] It's possible, too, that the fact that more prescriptions were issued to males from 2020 onwards is indicative of a more cautious approach.[2]

Did GIDS become more cautious about referring – perhaps because of the scrutiny it was now under from the media and others – or is the reduction in prescriptions issued to GIDS patients, in part, a by-product of the lengthy waiting list for the service? By the time many arrived at GIDS they might have been too far into puberty and chosen not to take blockers. No one saw the waiting list as a good thing, but GIDS psychologist Alex Morris says that because young people were by and large well into their teens by the time they were seen, it provided clinicians with greater opportunity to talk, rather than refer quickly for puberty blockers.

Or it might simply be down to the Covid pandemic, which saw non-emergency NHS services grind to a halt for much of 2020. Judicial review proceedings had also been issued in 2020, perhaps prompting more caution on behalf of GIDS clinicians, and then – from 2021 – there was the additional oversight of the referral process. One, none or a combination of these reasons may explain the fall in puberty-blocker prescriptions.

Like most things in the story of GIDS, it is more complicated than simply saying that the service became more cautious as time went on. It's clear that some clinicians did, and others did not. One clinician who worked at GIDS's Leeds site reflects that, when she started, 'it felt like a paediatric service'. Years later, she says, 'I felt like I was working in a mental health service.' That meant 'assessments were extended, and we had to offer more. But I wouldn't say that it meant that somebody couldn't be trans or they couldn't then progress down that path. But I just think things took longer and it was more complicated.'

Another former senior clinician explains that the work of the service can be broken down into three loose time periods spanning the last decade or so. Pre-2014, there was 'more time, more space to think', they explain. There was a 'genuine, cautious' attitude, and the work wasn't so 'politically fraught'. It was more acceptable to postulate *why* someone might be feeling gender-related distress. 'Then the explosion starts.' An explosion not just in terms of the numbers referred, but in society's attitudes and in 'trans activism'. This began the 'lack-of-thinking period, panic, where probably lots of very inappropriate decisions were made clinically', they say, and where 'there was intense pressure to make decisions and see the volume of children being referred with very little system change or thinking'. Out of this came, 'a kind of mishmash of lots of things'. This latest period began, they say, after David Bell's report in summer 2018. 'There was recognition that it was all very, very difficult and problematic, and that there were many questions about the nature of what we were dealing with.' And that's where they still see GIDS as being in 2022: with some cautious clinicians, and some who are 'activated by affirmation'. What the service still lacks, they say, is consistency. Clinical practice 'became hugely discrepant between the regional teams', they explain.

Breaking GIDS up into regional teams had been raised as a potential medium-term action by organisational development consultant Dr Femi Nzegwu in her 2015 report into GIDS. Her primary recommendation of 'capping the number of referrals immediately', along with changing referral criteria was not taken up.[3] But by spring 2017 GIDS had 'been re-organised and split into 4 teams'.[4] Each led by an executive, these teams, the senior clinician explains, then operated as 'Darwinian islands' with their own distinct cultures. It provided the mechanism, they say, where 'much more disparate practice' and 'bubbles of thought' began to emerge.

There is some evidence, too, that the once-close relationship between GIDS and trans support group Mermaids began to cool. In conversations with a director of the Big Lottery Fund, which had agreed to grant Mermaids £500,000 in December 2018, GIDS director Polly Carmichael was asked for the service's views on the charity.[5] The Lottery was reviewing the decision after concerns were raised.[6] Carmichael explained that 'it is important and valuable to have localised support groups for families', and that GIDS tried to attend all the residential sessions run by Mermaids.[7] But Carmichael is also reported to have told the Lottery that 'she felt like Mermaids had challenged the Tavistock in the past by suggesting different approaches and that if this is not done in a constructive manner then there is a risk that this can result in the potential of parents losing trust in the services provided by the Tavistock and that this could be unhelpful'. Carmichael explained that in the United States, surgeons advocated 'early surgery and much earlier sex hormones' – something contrary to the Tavistock approach. 'Polly feels it could be argued that the Mermaids approach is more aligned to the American model,' the Lottery director noted. 'Polly finished by saying that Mermaids are an important group with an important view but they have a particular view and that other groups out there offer something else.'[8]

It's understood that more senior figures in the wider Tavistock Trust took a stronger position. Some at board level believed by the middle of 2019 that GIDS should not be engaging with Mermaids at all – including attending any of their events. Mermaids was a lobbying group, they believed, and it was vital for GIDS to have boundaries and retain its patient focus. This message was relayed to Carmichael.

Around the same time, mentions of GIDS or the Tavistock on the Mermaids parents' online forum began falling, and mentions of private providers increased. In 2020, private providers were talked about more often by parents being supported by Mermaids than the NHS's sole provider in England.*

---

* While GIDS has constantly said that it holds the middle ground between two opposite poles – those who call for physical interventions quickly and at younger ages, and those who do not want them at all for under-18s – its treatment of different support groups calls this into question. Mermaids have been allowed to have their information leaflets within GIDS and have had regular ongoing dialogue with the service for many years. The GIDS website has provided links to both GIRES and Gendered Intelligence, too. However, the Bayswater Support Group, which represents around 400 families and describes itself as 'wary of medical solutions to gender dysphoria', particularly as a first-line treatment, had its dialogue with the Trust terminated after just a year. In 2021, Tavistock chief executive Paul Jenkins told them that their 'gender-critical' views would make it difficult for GIDS to work with them. Tavistock chair Paul Burstow repeated similar sentiments, telling the group that they were 'not neutral' and that its website 'makes it more difficult to have a constructive dialogue'. None of the groups supporting gender non-conforming or gender-diverse young people and their families – Mermaids, GIRES, Gendered Intelligence or Bayswater – are neutral. That GIDS and the Tavistock Trust were only willing to engage with those supportive of paediatric medical transition is worthy of note. The author has seen the correspondence cited here.

———

The GIDS Review, undertaken by Tavistock medical director Dinesh Sinha and published in 2019, brought *some* change to the daily workings of GIDS clinicians, too. New standard operating procedures were introduced for gaining informed consent for medical interventions and for safeguarding. But both documents were found wanting by outsiders assessing the service.[9] What these changes *didn't* do, say some former staff, is address the fundamental difficulties GIDS faced. The Tavistock had chosen to go for the 'easy wins', to tinker at the edges, because to address the underlying problems would have been too difficult. GIDS needed to close its waiting list, or certainly insist on much tougher referral criteria, staff argue. It needed to address the complexity of the cases it was seeing and introduce different pathways for different presentations.

'Something absolutely massive had to happen,' says one clinician who hoped they could make things better. The Trust had implemented procedural change at GIDS but hadn't tackled how the service was thinking or how it could better serve its patients, they say. 'Ultimately, what many of us were saying the whole time was you're not fundamentally changing how this issue in children is being conceptualised.' What matters, this clinician explains, is how clinicians thought about the young people in front of them. Were children 'born' with something, possibly genetic, that 'rarely changes' and predicts they will be happily trans forever? Or could it be that sometimes other life events might contribute to gender-related distress in a child – for whom the best solution might not be to transition? 'I think over time GIDS has moved to this much more fundamentalist position whereby… the more that cautious and concerned clinicians left, the more others [who were affirmative] remained, took hold and got more senior.'

It is not that this clinician did not put young people forward for physical interventions – they did. And they, like so many others who were worried about their work at GIDS, believe that puberty blockers 'can be helpful for extremely distressed young people'. But they should be the last resort in children, not a first-line treatment. The treatment exists, this clinician says. It would be foolish to pretend otherwise. The key is how to try to make it as safe as possible, and really explore whom it will benefit most. This, they say, is an approach that the Tavistock did not even attempt.

Real change had to come from external pressure.

The combination of the original judicial review judgment, finding that under-16s were unlikely to be able to provide consent to puberty blockers when used to treat gender dysphoria, and the CQC's rating of GIDS as inadequate, dealt a hammer blow to both the service and the Tavistock Trust. Board minutes across the following year – 2021 – show that morale among GIDS staff was low, and that the service was struggling to both retain and recruit clinicians.[10]

At the very top, there appeared to be almost a reluctance to accept the verdict of independent outsiders on one of the Trust's most prized services. CEO Paul Jenkins believed both judgments – from the High Court and the CQC – treated GIDS harshly.

Nonetheless, they prompted action. Tavistock board minutes from January 2021 reveal that the Trust 'formally requested' a change to the existing GIDS referral criteria from NHS England, acknowledging that 'one cannot simply scale up the service to manage the dramatically increased referral numbers'.[11] Requests from GIDS clinicians to tighten up referrals go back to at least 2014. It is unclear who is responsible for it not happening sooner. Sources in NHS England and senior figures at GIDS each blame the other. One senior GIDS worker recalls being told several times by the service's leaders that they had consistently asked for change, but 'the line was that NHS England was saying that we had to keep the doors wide open'.

A 'different approach to management' was also needed. And there was an acknowledgement that the response to the GIDS Review had not done enough to bring about change in the service. GIDS's 'practices, structures and governance' had 'not kept pace' with the changes that had occurred, the same board minutes note.[12] It's understood that in spring 2021, Tavistock chief executive Paul Jenkins asked NHS England for the GIDS waiting list to be closed – for no new referrals to be accepted – but that NHS England turned down the request.[13] However, it did not take long for NHS England to take over a significant part of the referrals process.

From August 2021 the information provided by those referring to GIDS has had to be far more detailed, with the service introducing a new, comprehensive referral form.[14] This makes clear at the beginning that young people are 'optimally supported' when GIDS and CAMHS work together. The form asks for plenty of information, including how much gender identity is impacting on day-to-day life, a detailed gender history, what associated difficulties the young person may have and how these are being addressed, any risky behaviour and history of bullying, low mood or anxiety, and whether the young person has a child-protection plan or is otherwise known to or supported by social care. Referrers are also asked to provide information on any 'significant family events', which might include miscarriages, separations, bereavements or trauma.[15] Gone are the days where a referral might simply be a scrappy piece of paper from a GP saying little other than 'Please see this patient'. GIDS itself concedes that, historically, the service 'has received a high volume of referrals with scant information'.[16] In a little under half of cases, 'clinicians have had to go back to our referrers to get further information' to assess whether GIDS is appropriate for the young person 'and whether risks exist which need to be addressed'.[17] For referrals coming from anyone other than CAMHS, a separate risk-assessment form is also required.[18] But referrals are still accepted from a wide range of sources. Schools, voluntary organisations and others are able to refer children and young people directly into a national specialist health service.

Other than those made by CAMHS, at the time of writing GIDS no longer processes its own referrals. A 'National Referral Management Service' established by NHS England performs this role. These measures – the improved form and external handling of referrals – appear to have quickly made an impact. By the start of 2022, GIDS had experienced 'the most significant drop' in referrals of any Tavistock and Portman service in the previous quarter. They fell from 1,088 to 695 – a fall of more than a third.[19] The Trust attributed this to the 'new NHSE GIDS referral management service'.[20] But the change was short-lived. Referrals in 2021/22 exploded again, doubling from the previous year to more than 5,000.[21]

———

As we have seen, following several court cases, an attempt to make the process of referring young people under sixteen for medical interventions safer and more robust was also imposed upon GIDS by NHS England.

Since August 2021, all cases where GIDS clinicians have wanted to refer their patients who are under 16 for puberty blockers have had to be reviewed by an independent panel – the Multi-Professional Review Group (MPRG).[22] The panel's job is neither to endorse nor to refuse medical treatment to young people, but instead to check that 'all of the necessary steps have been taken, and all relevant information has been provided to the patient and their parents/carers'.[23]

Cases are only presented to the group after an 'in-depth clinical review' conducted by GIDS itself.[24] This appears to have reduced the numbers being referred for puberty blockers significantly. However, despite everything, the MPRG has still found the service's processes wanting. In the first six months of its operation – August 2021 to 28 February 2022 – the group considered 32 cases of young people under 16 whom GIDS deemed suitable for puberty blockers.[25] Only 26 submissions 'demonstrated the appropriate process has been followed and assurance given on all counts'[26] – even now, one in five cases referred to the MPRG is not being approved at all, even with an extra layer of scrutiny from within GIDS itself. Of those it did approve, half (13) had to be considered twice by the panel. Fifty per cent of all submissions demonstrated 'insufficient information' when they were first submitted. This could have been for a variety of reasons, but in a number of cases the MPRG had 'specific safeguarding concerns'.[27] The group told Hilary Cass and her review team that they were 'particularly concerned about safeguarding shortfalls' in GIDS assessments, with no consistent processes appearing to be in place 'to work with other agencies to identify children and young people and families who may be vulnerable, at risk and require safeguarding'.[28]

At the time of writing, the use of a Multi-Professional Review Group in all Tavistock GIDS referrals for puberty blockers for children under 16 is being challenged in judicial review proceedings brought by the Good Law Project, trans-led organisation Gendered Intelligence and others.[29] It is scheduled to be heard at the end of November 2022.

The claimants argue that the GIDS service specification and MPRG requirement are unlawful and discriminatory.[30] However, the notice granting permission for legal proceedings accepts that NHS England 'makes a powerful case' that, 'far from being discriminatory against or disadvantageous for GID[S] patients', the MPRG mechanism 'is actually about safeguarding'.[31]

In March 2022, the interim review by Dr Hilary Cass, one of the most experienced paediatricians in the country, said that GIDS's 'single specialist provider model is not a safe or viable long-term option' for the care of young people experiencing gender incongruence or gender-related distress.[32]

Commissioned in September 2020, Cass's findings acknowledged many of the concerns raised by GIDS clinicians over many years.[33] She described how there were 'significant gaps in the research and evidence base'.[34] And how the existing weak evidence base did not apply to many of the young people, particularly 'birth-registered females first presenting in early teen years', being seen at GIDS – something clinicians had been raising concerns about since 2015.[35]

GIDS's 'clinical approach has not been subjected to some of the usual control measures that are typically applied when new or innovative treatments are introduced', Cass concluded, nor had the service undertaken 'routine and consistent data collection'.[36]

Cass acknowledged a significant issue of 'diagnostic overshadowing' too – whereby even though many of the children and young people presenting to GIDS had complex needs, once they were identified as having *gender*-related distress, those other important healthcare issues were sometimes overlooked.

The lack of an agreed approach and wide variation in practice between GIDS clinicians was noted several times. 'There were different views held within the staff group about the appropriate clinical approach, with some more strongly affirmative and some more cautious and concerned about the use of physical intervention,' the report said.[37]

At all levels of the NHS – not just at GIDS – Cass found a fundamental lack of agreement and discussion 'about the extent to which gender incongruence in childhood and adolescence can be an inherent and immutable phenomenon for which transition is the best option for the individual'.[38]

Despite the lack of agreement, Hilary Cass and her review team found that GIDS offered 'predominantly an affirmative, non-exploratory approach, often driven by child and parent expectations and the extent of social transition that has developed due to the delay in service provision'. Cass acknowledged the 'strong efforts' made by the Tavistock and Portman Trust following the GIDS Review 'to make practice within GIDS more consistent', but, like those I have spoken to, found that 'although this has resulted in better documentation, variations and inconsistencies in clinical decision making remain'.[39]

And although there were opportunities for staff to discuss difficult individual cases, 'it is still difficult for staff to raise concerns about the clinical approach.'[40]

All these points had been raised by staff during the GIDS Review years earlier.

The report acknowledged the difficulties faced by both GIDS clinicians and young people and their families in the current system. Some children learnt from others what they should and shouldn't say at GIDS in order to access hormone treatment: 'for example, that they are advised not to admit to previous abuse or trauma, or uncertainty about their sexual orientation'.[41] Young people faced long waits, and often experienced the GIDS system as 'gatekeeping'; most of those attending GIDS didn't see themselves as having a psychological or medical condition, Cass wrote, and yet they had to face 'what can seem like intrusive, repetitive and unnecessary questioning' to achieve the medical intervention they wanted. The process could add to, rather than alleviate, their distress. 'However, where a clinical intervention is given, the same ethical, professional and scientific standards have to be applied as to any other clinical condition.'[42]

The Cass Review considered GIDS's approach to differ substantially from the Dutch Model it purported to be following. 'Although GIDS initially reported its approach to early endocrine intervention as being based on the Dutch Approach', there were 'significant differences', the review noted. Unlike the Dutch, GIDS did not appear to require young people who were neurodiverse or who had complex mental health problems to have 'accessed therapeutic support prior to starting hormone blocking treatment'.[43] Unlike the Dutch Model, 'in the NHS, once young people are started on hormone treatment, the frequency of appointments drops off rather than intensifies.' And, unlike the Dutch, the young people presenting at GIDS seemed to be experiencing significant associated difficulties, making it 'difficult to extrapolate from older literature to this current group'. It seemed likely, Cass noted, that 'different subgroups may have quite different needs and outcomes'.[44] Former GIDS psychotherapist Melissa Midgen had suggested a different pathway for 'post-pubescent natal females' in the summer of 2015. Nearly seven years later an independent review agreed: different people required different pathways.

GIDS, Hilary Cass said, was unable to do all that was required of it. 'A fundamentally different service model is needed,' for this group of young people, she insisted. 'It is essential that they can access the same level of psychological and social support as any other child or young person in distress, from their first encounter with the NHS and at every level within the service.'[45]

Cass prefaced her report with a letter to young people. 'I have heard that young service users are particularly worried that I will suggest that services should be reduced or stopped. I want to assure you that this is absolutely not the case – the reverse is true. I think that more services are needed for you, closer to where you live,' she wrote. Cass envisaged a model whereby care would be delivered by regional hubs across the country and by a broader range of health professionals.[46]

But this would take time. In the immediate term, she called on GIDS – and any future gender services for young people – to start collecting standardised data to help inform assessment and treatment. Cass argued for further strengthening of the consent process. And the review addressed an issue that has been largely ignored by media coverage – my own included: the role of the endocrinologists prescribing the puberty blockers and cross-sex hormones (referred to in the report as masculinising or feminising hormones) to those GIDS had identified as needing them.

Paediatric endocrinologists – currently based at either UCLH or Leeds General Infirmary – should take on additional medical responsibility for that diagnosis and become 'active partners' in the decision-making process leading up to referral for hormone treatment, Cass said. She noted that, unlike in the Dutch model, 'NHS endocrinologists do not systematically attend the multi-disciplinary meetings where the complex cases that may be referred to them are discussed, and until very recently did not routinely have direct contact with the clinical staff member who had assessed the child or young person.' It was not the norm for doctors to prescribe powerful medication to people – especially children – they themselves had not diagnosed. In the future, Cass wrote, paediatric endocrinologists treating young people with gender dysphoria should also be responsible for the 'differential diagnosis leading up to the treatment decision', especially 'where a lifechanging intervention is given'. This will support them in 'carrying out their legal responsibility for consent to treatment and the prescription of hormones'.[47]

UCLH paediatric endocrinologist Gary Butler has previously told the High Court that

> the decisions at UCLH and Leeds do not automatically follow on from those made at the GIDS Tavistock. They are a reassessment of physical maturity and cognitive capacity in their own right. They may be at odds with the Tavistock formulation (an infrequent event) and thus would be returned to the Tavistock MDT for reconsideration.[48]

However, when asked by the court for the number of young people who had been assessed to be suitable for puberty blockers by GIDS but then not prescribed them because they were considered not to be competent to make the decision, the Tavistock's legal team 'could not produce any statistics on whether this situation had ever arisen'.[49] A July 2022 academic paper from the UCLH and Leeds endocrinologists revealed that one young person, out of 1,089, was judged to lack capacity to consent to treatment. They were 16 years old.[50]

All GIDS clinicians attended the endocrine clinics as part of a rota, regardless of which patients were attending. This made patients like Jacob deeply uncomfortable, as he was forced to discuss personal medical issues in front of a new set of strangers each time, but some clinicians felt the same. 'You would be expected to sign off someone else's work,' explains one former therapist. 'And you'd be looking and thinking, "Hang on, this kid's got X, Y, Z. There are so many things wrong.' I've been told of examples where young trans men – those born with a female body and sex organs – have asked whether they will start producing sperm once on synthetic testosterone. Despite this worrying lack of understanding, the young person was still prescribed the hormones.*

The Cass Review's interim report said many things. But it did not make a judgement on the best and most appropriate use of puberty blockers and cross-sex hormones. Or whether they should be used at all in the treatment of children and young people with gender-related distress. In her letter to young people at the start of her interim report, Hilary Cass acknowledged their worry that she would suggest hormones treatments be stopped. 'On this issue, I have to share my thoughts as a doctor,' she wrote. 'We know quite a bit about hormone treatments, but there is still a lot we don't know about the long-term effects.' As things stood, she was unable to make a judgement, so she and her team would be 'trying to make sense of all the information that is available, as well as seeing if we can plug any of the gaps in the research'. Plugging the necessary gaps in the evidence base will be a difficult task. The nature of those gaps seems different, too, depending

---

* Neither GIDS nor the Tavistock Trust issued a formal public response to the Cass interim report. The only comments are those contained in a letter by GIDS director Polly Carmichael and Trust CEO Paul Jenkins to the *Observer* newspaper, complaining about an editorial it had written on the topic. The pair took issue with GIDS being characterised as 'affirmative' – a judgement arrived at by Hilary Cass – arguing that 'being respectful of someone's identity does not preclude exploration'. Their letter can be found here: 'Letters: Britain should knuckle down and embrace the boring', *Guardian* (27 March 2022), https://www.theguardian.com/theobserver/commentisfree/2022/mar/27/letters-britain-should-knuckle-down-embrace-boring; and the original editorial here: 'The *Observer* view on gender identity services for children', *Observer* (20 March 2022), https://www.theguardian.com/commentisfree/2022/mar/20/observer-view-cass-review-gender-identity-services-young-people.

on whether one is talking about cross-sex hormones or puberty blockers. Cass pointed out that hormones have been prescribed to transgender adults for decades and the long-terms physical risks and side effects are 'well understood'. 'These include increased cardiovascular risk, osteoporosis, and hormone-dependent cancers.' Much more difficulty 'centres on the decision to proceed to physical transition', Cass said. 'Decisions need to be informed by long-term data on the range of outcomes, from satisfaction with transition, through a range of positive and negative mental health outcomes, through to regret and/or a decision to detransition. The NICE evidence review demonstrates the poor quality of these data, both nationally and internationally.' Some young people would 'remain fluid in their gender identity up to early to mid-20s', Cass noted, 'so there is a limit as to how much certainty one can achieve in late teens'. This is a risk that needs to be understood, she stated.[51]

The challenges surrounding the use of puberty blockers are different. There is a lack of clarity about their intended outcome: do they provide time and space to think? Or are they intended to improve mental health and stop potentially irreversible pubertal changes that make it more difficult to 'pass' as a trans adult? The 'most difficult question', in this regard, 'is whether puberty blockers do indeed provide valuable time for children and young people to consider their options, or whether they effectively "lock in" children and young people to a treatment pathway which culminates in progression to feminising/masculinising hormones by impeding the usual process of sexual orientation and gender identity development', the review argued. Existing data from both GIDS and the Netherlands showed 'almost all' children who are put on blockers go on to cross-sex hormones, but 'the reasons for this need to be better understood'. The long-term impact on bone density is unknown, Cass noted, and there were unknown impacts 'on development, maturation and cognition if a child or young person is not exposed to the physical, psychological, physiological, neurochemical and sexual changes that accompany adolescent hormone surges'. The developing brain may be affected.[52]

In July 2022, Cass repeated these concerns, and went further. She called for the 'rapid establishment of the necessary research infrastructure' to allow 'young people being considered for hormone treatment' to be enrolled into a 'formal research programme with adequate follow up into adulthood'.[53] In future, young people receiving puberty blockers should do so only as part of research, and where they are closely monitored. This is what GIDS's Early Intervention Study set out to do more than a decade earlier, only for that approach to be abandoned in favour of rolling out physical interventions to younger children whom the service did not take it upon themselves to follow up. What the conditions of being part of this research will be is unclear at the time of writing. But, Cass explained, without further research 'the outstanding questions will remain unanswered and the evidence gap will continue to be filled with polarised opinion and conjecture, which does little to help the children and young people, and their families and carers, who need support and information on which to make decisions'.[54] NHS England is now working 'to design and commission the necessary research infrastructure'.[55]

A growing number of European countries agree with Hilary Cass and think it sensible to proceed with caution when there is a limited evidence base. In February 2022, a month before Cass published her interim report, Sweden's National Board of Health and Welfare decided to limit access to puberty blockers for those under 18 to only 'exceptional cases' and in research settings. It too had asked for a review of the evidence base to be undertaken, and found it wanting. The board deemed that 'the risks of puberty suppressing treatment with GnRH-analogues and gender-affirming hormonal treatment currently outweigh the possible benefits'. The judgment was based on the lack of reliable scientific evidence concerning the efficacy of the treatments, 'the new knowledge that detransition occurs among young adults' and the 'uncertainty that follows from the yet unexplained increase' in the numbers coming forward for treatment, particularly among 'adolescents registered as females at birth'.[56]

This followed the example of Finland, whose Council for Choices in Health Care issued new guidelines in 2020 stating that psychotherapy, rather than puberty blockers and cross-sex hormones, should be the first-line treatment for gender-dysphoric youth. Again, a systematic evidence review was completed, leading to the conclusions that 'gender reassignment of minors is an experimental practice'.[57] Medical transition for young people is still allowed, but mostly for those whose gender dysphoria began in early childhood and for those with no co-occurring mental health conditions.

And in France, in March 2022, the National Academy of Medicine called for 'great medical caution' regarding treatment for young people with gender-related distress,[58] saying that

> if France allows the use of puberty blockers or cross-sex hormones with parental authorization and no age limitations, the greatest caution is needed in their use, taking into account the side-effects such as the impact on growth, bone weakening, risk of sterility, emotional and intellectual consequences and, for girls, menopause-like symptoms.[59]

Children and young people wanting to transition should receive 'extended psychological support' first.

In the United States too, there are affirmative clinicians, some who are trans themselves, calling for youth gender clinics to conduct more thorough assessments and not block children's puberty at an early stage. In October 2021, two top transgender doctors shared their concerns with American journalist Abigail Shrier. Clinical psychologist Erica Anderson lamented that some colleagues were carrying out 'sloppy healthcare work' and that she was 'worried that decisions will be made that will later be regretted by those making them'. She feared more young people would choose to detransition and believed there was 'abject failure' on the part of some clinicians 'to evaluate the mental health of someone historically in current time, and to prepare them for making such a life-changing decision'.[60]

Reconstructive surgeon and 'world-renowned vaginoplasty specialist' Marci Bowers voiced concerns over blocking puberty too early in those born male. Not only can surgery be more difficult because of lack of penile tissue to use (a warning that GIDS clinicians had been issued in 2016 and the Dutch team have discussed[61]), but those children would not be able to achieve orgasm as adults. 'If you've never had an orgasm pre-surgery, and then your puberty's blocked, it's very difficult to achieve that afterwards,' Bowers told Shrier. 'I consider that a big problem, actually. It's kind of an overlooked problem that in our "informed consent" of children undergoing puberty blockers, we've in some respects overlooked that a little bit.'[62]

Bowers has subsequently repeated these remarks to students at Duke University, North Carolina, suggesting that perhaps puberty blockers should be delayed until later in puberty.* She said that others – including one of the most well-known affirmative clinicians, Johanna Olson-Kennedy – have told her they've 'changed their approach a little bit' because of these two difficulties.[63] A month after speaking to Shrier, Anderson and the founding psychologist of the first children's gender clinic in the United States, Laura Edwards-Leeper, published an opinion essay in the *Washington Post*. They warned that, while the WPATH standards of care recommend 'comprehensive assessment for all dysphoric youth before starting medical interventions' some clinicians in the United States were 'hastily dispensing medicine or recommending medical doctors prescribe it' without following these guidelines and without proper assessment. As a result, 'we may be harming some of the young people we strive to support – people who may not be prepared for the gender transitions they are being rushed into,' they wrote.[64]

The updated WPATH standards of care (version 8) were published in September 2022. The new chapter on adolescent care suggests that children should show 'gender incongruence' that is 'marked and sustained over time' before embarking on medical interventions (though this waters down the suggestions in the draft chapter, which called for evidence of persistent gender incongruence or gender diversity for 'several years' before being able to access medication).[65] The new chapter says that young people should undergo a comprehensive diagnostic assessment prior to accessing medical interventions, stating that

---

* As part of the symposium 'Trans & gender diverse policies, care, practices, and wellbeing' (21 March 2022), Marci Bowers said: 'Every single child, or adolescent, who was truly blocked at Tanner stage 2 has never experienced orgasm. I mean, it's really about zero.' See https://twitter.com/DonovanCleckley/status/1521625518394773505. Details of the event can be found at https://globalhealth.duke.edu/events/trans-gender-diverse-policies-care-practices-and-wellbeing.

without such an assessment, treatment 'has no empirical support and therefore carries the risk that the decision to start gender-affirming medical interventions may not be in the long-term best interest of the young person at that time'.[66]

However, whereas in draft form and when initially published the new standards of care recommended lowering the recommended age for treatment with cross-sex hormones from 16 to 14 and set a minimum recommended age of 15 for breast-removal surgery, shortly after publication all but one of the stipulated lower-age limits for hormonal and surgical interventions were removed altogether.[67] The only one that remains is for phalloplasty – the surgical creation of a penis using skin taken from another part of the body. 'Given the complexity of phalloplasty, and current high rates of complications in comparison to other gender-affirming surgical treatments, it is not recommended this surgery be considered in youth under 18 at this time,' the standards of care state.[68]

Dutch psychiatrist Annelou de Vries was co-leader for the chapter. But de Vries, part of the Dutch team who pioneered the approach to the medical treatment of young people with gender-related distress now followed (albeit adapted) around the world, has also acknowledged how different the current cohort of young people presenting at gender clinics is from the those upon whom their protocol was based. More data are needed for 'transgender adolescents' to allow clinicians to offer an 'individualized approach' that 'differentiates who will benefit from medical gender affirmation and for whom (additional) mental health support might be more appropriate', she wrote in 2020.[69] Her colleague Thomas Steensma issued similar words of caution a year later, reportedly saying that 'we do not know whether studies that we have done in the past are still applicable to this time' – when more adolescent girls are coming forward for treatment. He also chastised other clinicians for their lack of research. 'In the Netherlands, we conduct structural research,' he said. 'But the rest of the world is taking over our research indiscriminately.'[70]

All of these professionals want what is best for these young people. They aim for an approach with enough caution to allow those who will thrive as transgender adults to benefit, but also to protect those who would be better off on a different, non-medical path. Many trans adults say that, in retrospect, puberty blockers were helpful, life-saving even. Both Hannah and Phoebe, each of whom has her own chapter in this book, have made this point when speaking to me. But these drugs have not been helpful for everyone – both for those who continue to identify as trans, like Jacob, and for those who do not.

Anna Hutchinson says she no longer makes decisions on physical interventions for her patients, 'because I know that I don't know'. She believes that with the knowledge we currently have, each decision to start a gender-questioning child on puberty blockers is a gamble. If blockers are to be used, she says, the system requires a complete overhaul. Physical interventions should be used as 'part of a proper therapeutic intervention', where exploratory work goes alongside it, and where outcomes for these young people are systematically recorded over the longer term, she suggests.

There is ongoing discussion about how best to help children and adolescents with gender dysphoria, and whether it will ever be possible to know in advance whether medical transition will help or harm any given child. Former GIDS staff have started these conversations. It is time for a broader spectrum of mental health professionals, those in the medical profession, those working with children, the trans community and society at large to continue them.

Conclusion

Summer 2022

Whatever the future of care for young people questioning their gender identity looks like, they will not be seen by the Tavistock's Gender Identity Development Service. On 28 July 2022, NHS England announced that it planned to close GIDS by spring 2023.[1]

The service will be replaced, initially, by two 'Early Adopter services' – one in London, the other in north-west England.* These will 'take over clinical responsibility for and management of all GIDS patients – including those on the waiting list – as part of a managed transition'.[2] These services, it is hoped, will offer more holistic treatment to this group of young people. There will be mental health support, and Cass has said that they must be able to provide 'essential related services' including those which cater to children and young people with autism. For those 'for whom medical treatment may be considered appropriate, access to endocrinology services and fertility services', must also be provided.[3] Staff should be experienced in

---

* The London Early Adopter service will be led by a partnership between Great Ormond Street Hospital and Evelina London Children's Hospital, with South London and Maudsley NHS Foundation Trust providing specialist mental health support to children and young people. In the north-west, there will be a partnership between Alder Hey Children's NHS Foundation Trust and the Royal Manchester Children's Hospital. Both trusts will also provide specialist mental health services. GIDS staff and the endocrine teams based at University College London Hospitals NHS Foundation Trust and Leeds Teaching Hospitals NHS Trust will, according to NHS England, 'play a vital role in supporting' the new services.

safeguarding and the 'support of looked-after children and children who have experienced trauma', Cass has advised.[4] This represents the first step in establishing more regional services for young people with gender identity difficulties over the next few years. It is anticipated that there may end up being seven or eight regional centres. With more centres offering better and broader care, it's hoped that young people can be seen closer to home, and more quickly.

The proposed NHS England service specification that the 'Early Adopter services' will follow was put out for consultation in October 2022.[5] At the time of writing the final version has not been published, but the draft marks a significant change in direction for the care of children and young people with gender dysphoria. The primary intervention is 'psychosocial' and 'psychological support', it says – not medical.[6] Clinicians should be 'mindful' that gender incongruence can be 'a transient phase' for young people, particularly prepubescent children, it adds, and therefore caution is advised over social transition, especially for younger children.[7] 'The clinical approach has to be mindful of the risks of an inappropriate gender transition and the difficulties that the child may experience in returning to the original gender role upon entering puberty if the gender incongruence does not persist into adolescence,' the document says. Gone is any mention of the four-to-six-session assessment model, or indeed any time-limited assessment. Instead, the document calls for 'a range of pathways to support these children and young people', something GIDS clinicians had urged years previously. Only GPs and NHS professionals will be able to refer children and young people.

The new services must be led by a consultant medical doctor (compared with consultant psychologists at GIDS), who will head up a team with a wide range of expertise. This will include experts in 'paediatric medicine, autism, neurodisability and mental health'.[8] NHS England argues that 'oversight of the service by a medical doctor is appropriate given that the service may provide medical interventions to some children and young people'.[9] It is proposed that access to those medical interventions – puberty blockers – will only be permitted as part of a 'formal research programme'. The new services will also aim 'to maintain a therapeutic relationship' with those who are prescribed blockers.[10]

The document also places greater emphasis on identifying and addressing any co-occurring difficulties a young person may have and working with other local professional networks. Clinicians are encouraged to 'remain open and explore' the young person's experience, with the overall aim being to 'reduce distress'.[11] It is proposed that the services 'will take part in continuous data collection... to support the NHS in developing a better understanding of the relevant patient cohorts'.[12] The draft specification also tackles a long-standing issue for GIDS – the interaction with private providers. NHS England 'strongly discourages' young people and their families from buying puberty blockers or hormones from private clinicians or online, and will not accept clinical responsibility for the treatment of those who have done so. Where the provider is not regulated by UK regulatory bodies, the new services 'will advise the GP to initiate local safeguarding protocols'.[13] This draft specification is only designed to be interim. A new national service specification will be introduced following Dr Hilary Cass's final recommendations.[14]

At the time of writing, there are more than 7,500 children on the GIDS waiting list and some young people are waiting close to four years to be seen.[15] Lawyers are hoping to bring a class-action clinical-negligence case against the Tavistock and Portman Trust and NHS England, having been prompted by the findings of Hilary Cass's interim report. There is a huge challenge ahead.

Those who have led and worked at GIDS undoubtedly care about the young people they are treating. But it is clear that the service has been unable to cope. To use the word chosen by one of those responsible for GIDS's leadership for a decade, Dr Bernadette Wren, it 'buckled'.[16] There are many reasons for this, not all of which have been in GIDS's control, or even that of the wider Tavistock and Portman Trust which houses it. Young people in the UK have been let down by a lack of adequate funding for youth mental health services. It seems clear that many of the young people attending GIDS might have been better supported if seen closer to home by local CAMHS, which would have treated the young person's difficulties in the round, rather than siphon off gender. But CAMHS provision is patchy, to say the least, and they too have been overwhelmed with demand for their services. There has been a lack of resources to see these children, but also a lack of willingness to engage once the word 'gender' has been mentioned. A false, perhaps even lazy, assumption was made: while local services languished, a well-funded national service like GIDS could somehow fill the void and help thousands of young people, many of whom with complex difficulties, feel better with medication used off-label and without a robust evidence base.

But many of the mistakes made cannot be blamed on others. What has occurred over the last decade or so is quite exceptional. Facing sustained pressure to provide interventions that would halt puberty in those struggling with their gender identity, GIDS rightfully embarked on a research study. The evidence base was poor and so they needed to proceed with caution, evaluating the impact of blocking puberty earlier in young peoples' development. But the service, together with colleagues at UCLH, rejected suggestions for a study design that would allow them to draw more robust conclusions, and chose not to wait for data to emerge before rolling out early puberty blockade as standard practice. The service proceeded over the next eight years to refer more than a thousand young people for puberty blockers – without any data of their own to support this. It's unclear whether anyone – GIDS, UCLH or Leeds General Infirmary – knows precisely how many young people have been started on puberty blockers. If they do know, they do not want to release the information publicly. Having embarked on this innovative approach, GIDS then did nothing to follow up these patients to see how they fared. Nor did it try to find out what happened to those it did not refer for physical interventions, or those who dropped out of their care.

The service faced an exponential increase in referrals during the same period, from 97 in 2009/10 to 2,748 in 2019/20 – a 2,800 per cent increase.[17] Even more pronounced was the rise in girls – a 4,700 per cent increase from 40 to 1,892 during the same period[18] – many of whom only started to experience gender-related distress in adolescence. Yet faced with these numbers and a fundamental shift in the type of young people requesting their help, GIDS simply ploughed on, neither reflecting on the fact that the existing poor evidence base was designed for a different cohort of young people altogether, nor considering that perhaps an alternative to the medical pathway needed to be considered and offered to at least some of these children.

GIDS has had opportunities to change direction, but it has not taken them. It has been advised to pause referrals, and to change referral criteria, but has done neither.* The Trust as a whole did not help to implement change when GIDS clinicians brought their concerns out of the service and to those in senior positions in the Tavistock. Instead, clinicians who spoke out, and those who helped them and amplified their concerns, had to leave the service or Trust one way or another. Those who were gay were told they were 'too close' to the work, and, according to one former senior clinician, *anyone* who spoke out was 'made to feel hysterical' in some way. 'The more anxious and worried you became, the more it was framed that you weren't really someone who could handle it.' It was 'a brilliant way to divert it away from what we're actually doing, which was changing children's bodies', they say. It is not credible to explain away the concerns of so many experienced clinicians either by accusations of transphobia or allegations that they are simply not up to the task at hand.

Important information that came to light during the course of GIDS's day-to-day work was not routinely passed on – whether this was the observation that almost everyone who started on puberty blockers went on to cross-sex hormones, or the potential surgical risk for those born male who'd had their puberty blocked early.† Why this was the case is unclear. Some suggest there was a lack of willingness to

---

* Dr Polly Carmichael did not wish to be interviewed for this book. She told the author GIDS worked on a 'case-by-case basis' and that 'every young person is treated as an individual, with their needs holistically explored and full consideration given to their personal situation and any co-occurring difficulties or complexities that may be present'. She said that she did not accept that GIDS had power over its referral criteria, as these were stipulated by NHS England. 'While we report to our commissioners on the referrals made to us, and what might help make our work more manageable, neither I, nor GIDS, nor the Trust set the criteria for referral,' she said.

† Dr Carmichael said she did not believe this was 'a fair or accurate criticism'. Information about the effects of any physical intervention (including what is not known) were, she claimed, shared with all young people and their families during sessions.

put anything on paper in case it might offend trans support groups like Mermaids or others. The truth should not be offensive, though some clinicians have told me how it felt 'risky' to have honest conversations with young people about the reality of what transition entails. Some clinicians say that their colleagues expressed discomfort at even talking about the biological reality of their young patients' bodies – something important when discussing the implications of the treatments. With concerns listened to but not acted upon, and a reluctance to commit pen to paper, nothing changed. 'It's a service that can't learn,' says former GIDS psychologist Dr Natasha Prescott. As the service grew quickly, its 'organisational memory' was lost, adds her colleague Andrew Oldfield.

GIDS has not been well led.[19] Those at the very top were all highly experienced clinicians, with impressive credentials. And they did not have an easy task. They faced criticism from all quarters, and their work became increasingly politicised. But what should have been professional became personal. Indeed, staff were encouraged to think this way – that they were a family. Director of GIDS Polly Carmichael confirmed this to the Tavistock's medical director in 2018, telling him that the GIDS team was 'very close knit, very committed... it has been like a family'.[20] And it did feel like that to many. When people did challenge, it was taken very badly, Matt Bristow says, 'as a personal affront rather than people raising legitimate professional concerns'. He and others recount how executive members of staff would become tearful when criticisms of the service were raised. It would then be made known among the team that 'this has made Polly cry', Bristow says. 'I don't think that's appropriate as a management style.'

The enormous sense of personal loyalty that members of the GIDS leadership garner among their former colleagues is striking. It's what explains why some clinicians remained in the service for so long, even when they felt concerned. Not only did they like their colleagues and bosses, they felt reassured that such experienced clinicians were on board. It lessened the doubt. It is apparent that different clinicians turned to the member of the Executive team they admired or related to the most when they were struggling with the work the service was doing. And the original three members – Dr Polly Carmichael, Dr Bernadette Wren and Dr Sarah Davidson – had different personalities and qualities that appealed to their staff. Carmichael cared greatly for her staff – she reassured them. Wren was highly respected for her intellect, and for her ability to help others think through the thorniest ethical elements of the work. And Davidson was a pragmatist: impressive with her ability to see a way through the difficulties GIDS was facing and try to solve problems. 'We are all quite strong characters in our different ways,' Polly Carmichael says of the GIDS Executive, 'but you know we probably all like to be liked as well so I think that inadvertently perhaps we have got caught up in some splits.'[21]

Even some of those fiercely critical of GIDS seem to be desperately uncomfortable admitting the weaknesses of management. And this helps explain why change was so hard to force through. It was difficult to voice legitimate concerns when these were construed as a personal attack on people you cared for and admired. Clinicians have told me how defensive some members of the Executive would be whenever the service was criticised. It's understandable, perhaps, given how long all of them had worked there. As Anna Hutchinson explained during the GIDS Review, it would be 'quite intolerable to think about' any potential harm if you have been putting children on to a 'medical pathway' which might include infertility and 'significant surgery' for more than a decade. 'A lot of people would struggle to say, "I was wrong or maybe that was not [the] best thing for all of those kids."'[22] Nonetheless, this defensiveness was not conducive to either the airing of or acting upon concerns. It was not always the leadership who would be defensive: other members of staff would 'jump in' because they wouldn't want to see the Executive upset, I'm told. Some clinicians also say this sense of family explains why they stayed so long at GIDS. It made it much harder to leave.

The sense of GIDS being a family went alongside a feeling of being separate to, or even isolated from, the rest of the organisation that housed it: the Tavistock Trust. It had always been this way. From its early days, GIDS was made to feel like it did not fit in. Staff at the Portman Clinic, where it was first located, had made clear that the service was not welcome. Indeed, when, as the then medical director of the Tavistock, Dr David Taylor undertook a review of the Gender Identity Development Service/Unit in 2005, he noted immediately how it needed be brought within the Trust's structures in order to function well. Taylor noted how a 'tendency towards isolation' and its 'orphan' status had contributed to the problems GIDS was facing, problems that have endured until the present day.[23]

But GIDS was never properly integrated into the wider Trust. It became more isolated over time. Clinicians who worked in GIDS under the directorship of Polly Carmichael say that as external criticism grew, the service developed a 'siege mentality'.[24] When staff expressed their worries about how the service was operating, they'd be told that they needed to 'keep things together or the service will be broken up', says Matt Bristow. If that happened, it would no longer be highly specialised and the work could be undertaken by 'regional services or private providers who do even less of an assessment and, therefore, you know, you shouldn't rock the boat too much', he says. Even if GIDS *was* struggling, it was doing a better job than others would. 'I used to say to Polly, "But that's a race to the bottom,"' says Anna Hutchinson. It may well be the case that others might carry out worse assessments, she would say, 'but that doesn't mean that the NHS should be offering a substandard service'.

It is understandable that the GIDS Executive 'saw part of its role to protect its patients from being stigmatised or pathologized, both by people who didn't understand dysphoric children and those who were actively transphobic', said Hutchinson. 'Some in GIDS seemed to think that there was a risk of being open with colleagues in the wider trust for the same reasons.'[25] But this was a 'dangerous mind-set when it comes to protecting young people', argued Matt Bristow, because it meant the service was 'less likely to seek support and help from outside if it is needed'.[26] Indeed, this is precisely what happened, with extraordinary consequences. The fear of external safeguarding scrutiny on GIDS, for example, led to staff being discouraged from seeking advice from those outside the service, such as the Tavistock's safeguarding lead for children, Sonia Appleby. Appleby herself was all too aware that GIDS felt under 'constant threat', but the inability to have transparent conversations about 'ordinary trust business' like safeguarding referrals was problematic.[27] She told Dinesh Sinha that 'the ordinary process of learning and doing has been affected by a process that has been to create a level of insulation and isolation around the Service that in fact accentuates not only their isolation but their ability to be incorporated into the life of the Trust'.[28]

The feeling of being different from the rest of the Trust – or 'semi-detached', as David Bell puts it – was also a product of GIDS's unique funding arrangement and structure. Although part of the Tavistock and Portman NHS Foundation Trust, its work was commissioned and paid for by NHS England. Bell suggests that Polly Carmichael 'has referred to herself as not seeing herself as answerable to the Trust but only to NHSE (who commission the service)'.[29] Others have made a similar observation. While, in fact, GIDS and its staff were accountable to the Trust, Bell told me it was clear that this 'semi-detachedness' meant that they saw their primary connection as being with NHS England, 'and saw their connection to the Tavistock is kind of secondary'. This 'made it much more possible for the service to function in a way that was very much at odds with the core values of the Tavistock'.

The shutters really came down following David Bell's report, highlighting the concerns of ten GIDS clinicians. 'I suppose it was just a climate of we are under attack, and everybody outside is against us. And no one is to speak or talk to anyone,' says one former senior GIDS clinician. They say that this attitude went so far that staff were advised not to use social media, and not to read what was being said about GIDS and the wider debate on the medical transition of children. Indeed, says this clinician, this was the strategy impressed upon them by the Tavistock communications team: do not speak to anyone. 'They just literally held on to this idea that it's better to say as little as possible to the world outside the clinic. And we'd be saying, "No, we think it's actually better for you to tell our story, say some things that we're doing; get in front of this."' With the benefit of hindsight, this clinician now questions the decision not to engage with public debate or criticism, and brands it a 'disaster'. What was the purpose, they ask? To hope that by saying nothing the attention would disappear? When the Tavistock director of communications learnt that I was approaching former GIDS staff members for this book, I was asked to 'refrain from unsolicited approaches to our staff and former colleagues' and reminded to ask the press office for any comment on GIDS. I was told that (the standard journalistic practice of) contacting people through publicly available information on their own professional websites or social media was 'unpleasant'. It struck me as remarkable that a press team would seek to control what former members of staff who had no employment obligations to the Trust were saying.*

GIDS clinicians also felt that they were isolated within the Trust. They were told that no one else understood what they were doing, that no one was interested in helping the team. This was not the case, but they did not know it. When the Trust's most senior clinicians learnt of some of the difficulties GIDS was experiencing through David Bell's report, they were concerned. And they wanted to help. Yet they were not given permission to do so. Instead of taking their intervention in the spirit in which it was intended, Tavistock clinicians say they too had their concerns shut down by the Trust's chief executive. It appeared, they say, as though any criticism of GIDS, however constructive, was not welcome, and would not be tolerated. These were professionals at the top of their field, with expertise that could be of great assistance to GIDS, but they were given short shrift by CEO Paul Jenkins.

So many former GIDS clinicians I have spoken with have used the same word to describe the service and their time there: mad.

But how can this 'madness' be explained? Dr Will Crouch, a highly experienced psychologist and psychotherapist who worked at GIDS between 2011 and 2013, has given it plenty of thought. 'I'm pretty confident that most people would say what I've said – you know, they were working with well-meaning, well-trained, thoughtful, intelligent colleagues,' Crouch says. 'So what happens then?' he asks. GIDS's struggles cannot simply be explained by 'just pressure of numbers', he says. It's 'much more than that'. GIDS, Crouch says, appears to be part of a wider phenomenon, whereby 'organisations helping a certain group of people will develop symptoms that are related to the work that they do'.[30] 'My reflection is if you're dealing with this

---

* For the record, the author called people where she could find a number or where one had been passed on to her, and otherwise sent a polite email setting out the scope of the book and explaining that she had started looking at GIDS for BBC *Newsnight*. The author asked clinicians if they would be willing to spare some time to talk. The author does not believe it would have been distressing to receive such a message and people were free to ignore it. Some did.

sort of population [of young people], that have such a – what I would call – deeply entrenched and concrete solution to a problem, then that's going to be reflected in the organisation.' Why didn't anyone stop and think? 'Well, this is exactly what the young people don't do, isn't it?' His hypothesis is that exposure to concrete thinking in the young people GIDS was trying to help became embedded in the service itself. 'Everybody sort of gets carried along in this world,' Crouch explains. Whereas GIDS founder Domenico Di Ceglie had always sought for GIDS to navigate a middle path between two extremes, the service became too close to one side, says Crouch: the side demanding physical interventions over and above anything and everything else.

To understand what has happened at GIDS and why, we have to look not just within the service itself, but to the wider Tavistock Trust and its leadership, to those who commissioned the service – NHS England – and to wider society.

'I don't think GIDS could have prospered without the Tavistock functioning differently,' Dr David Taylor tells me, adding pointedly, 'in a good way.' For GIDS to be successful and stand up to challenge from outside groups and interests, it required a strong Trust to support it. And it never had that, says Taylor. Following the publication of his report into the Gender Identity Development Service/Unit in January 2006, he wanted to see the Trust invest in research, to develop partnerships with others, to acknowledge that the NHS internal market required it to diversify if it were to succeed. This needed to happen long before Paul Jenkins took over the reins as chief executive, Taylor explains. Although Taylor speaks very highly of Jenkins's predecessor, saying he had 'kept the Tavistock alive and he kept it afloat', he says that the Trust did not do enough to adapt to the changes in society and the NHS structures it was operating in. The Tavistock did not provide what the external market for healthcare wanted.

Although the need for change in the Trust itself predates Paul Jenkins's tenure as CEO, the Trust's standing has declined under his watch.

The Tavistock Trust, which has housed GIDS since the mid 1990s, is in poor health. In January 2022, board papers revealed how an independent review of the Trust's governance had found it wanting. The report's authors say 'the scale of the corporate governance issues we have identified across the Trust are multiple'. The report argues that while the board has strengths, there is a 'lack of challenge and effective scrutiny of the executives by NEDs [non-executive directors]'. NEDs were 'often very ready to accept positive assurances without always fully testing and probing'. The review team also observed 'a heavy reliance on verbal assurance, lack of oversight and scrutiny, lack of focus on risk', and behaviour that was 'not consistent with governance good practice' elsewhere in the NHS.[31]

The review found that children's safeguarding lead Sonia Appleby's employment tribunal against the Trust 'has impacted the ability of staff to be able speak up if they have concerns' and the authors encouraged a(nother) review of whistle-blowing and raising-concerns procedures. The Trust was also found to have 'deep seated cultural issues'. The review recommended that the Trust recruit non-executive directors with higher-education skills and clinical experience, but the Tavistock's later attempt to do so was also mired in controversy.[32]

When experienced former NHS chief executive Kate Grimes submitted her interest in one of the roles she was told not to 'waste time' applying. Grimes had explained that while she fully respected 'trans peoples [*sic*] right to live their lives free from discrimination', she did not believe 'that they can literally change sex'.[33] The recruitment agency tasked with finding suitable candidates for the Tavistock responded by saying,

> I have to say that your view on sex being immutable is not a view point that the Trust would wish any of their non-executives to hold and as such I would not recommend that you waste time making an application for this – it will be one of the questions I will be asking candidates at first stage interview.[34]

The note ended with a smiley face emoji. When the correspondence was made public NHS England stepped in.[35] In an email, the Department for Health and Social Care confirmed to Grimes's MP that while NHS England and NHS Improvement had 'no formal involvement in the recruitment of chairs and non-executive directors for foundation trusts', on this occasion the Tavistock 'has agreed for

NHSE&I to be involved in the process and sit on the recruitment panel for the Chair role'. Although the appointment of the chair remained the ultimate responsibility of Trust's board, the Tavistock was no longer fully trusted to make its own appointments.

In April 2022, the Tavistock and Portman NHS Foundation Trust became subject to enhanced oversight from the NHS.[36] Whereas it had previously been subject to the lowest possible oversight, it moved to a category ('segment 3') which requires a 'coordinated support package and enhanced oversight'.[37] CEO Paul Jenkins told the Tavistock board that the change reflected a number of challenges the Trust was facing, including its financial performance, its leadership and governance, and issues surrounding GIDS.[38]

By June, the once world-famous mental health institution had vacancies for the posts of medical director, director of nursing, director of HR and chief executive officer. Paul Jenkins, the man who had been at the helm for eight years, overseeing the rapid expansion of GIDS, retired in September 2022. His counterpart through much of that period, Paul Burstow, stepped down as chair in April 2022, a few months before his term was due to end. Those who led GIDS through much of this time have also largely left. At the time of writing, only GIDS director Polly Carmichael remains.

The decline of the Tavistock is notable. In 2015, the Tavistock and Portman was listed in the top one hundred (out of 219 in England) NHS trusts to work for. Eighty-four per cent of staff recommended it as a place to receive treatment and 73 per cent recommended it as a place to work.[39] Just six years later, fewer than half (47.2 per cent) would recommend it as an employer and 59.7 per cent said they'd be happy with the standard of care it provided.[40] In May 2022, the Tavistock was revealed to have the worst scores in the country for answers to questions on raising concerns contained in the NHS Annual Staff Survey.[41] Fewer than half (48 per cent) of staff felt confident the Trust would address their concerns if they raised them or felt safe to speak up about them; only two-thirds felt comfortable raising concerns about 'unsafe clinical practice'; and a little over a third (34.3 per cent) agreed with the statement 'If I spoke up about something that concerned me I am confident my organisation would address my concern'.[42]

The Trust also recorded the worst scores on questions relating to staff morale and whether employees were considering leaving in the next year.[43]

There has also been an increase in concerns brought to the Tavistock's current Freedom to Speak Up Guardian, Sarah Stenlake. These include three cases where staff say they felt mistreated or punished for having spoken up, and 20 cases of bullying or harassment. Speaking-up cases, we are told, have occurred from staff members across the Trust and from each directorate, including GIDS. Stenlake noted that 'a frequent theme of concerns raised was that people had already tried to speak with a manager, supervisor, or senior person within the Trust, but that no further action had been taken and no further communication had occurred'. It's a point which bears striking similarity to the experience of many of the GIDS clinicians featured in this book. This 'significant problem with bullying and harassment in this Trust' affected 'worker safety, patient care, and staff retention', Stenlake concluded.[44]

It is impossible to say how much of this wider cultural malaise at the Tavistock Trust can be attributed to the way its leaders' handled concerns about GIDS. Health-service insiders tell me that the whole Trust has been poorly run. Its 'weak management' has been a major factor in its decline. But it cannot be disputed that the inability to manage the concerns about GIDS in particular has played a significant role. 'It's gone from being a place where I'm proud to say I work, to being embarrassed,' one very senior Tavistock clinician – who does not work in GIDS – tells me. They say there is difficulty recruiting at all levels as a result of the 'damning reputation the Trust now has' – in large part down to 'the GIDS debacle', they add. They do not blame the GIDS leadership for that. It is 'all down to Paul Jenkins', they say. And other (non-GIDS) Tavistock clinicians have made similar remarks when we have spoken. The way the concerns of GIDS staff – via David Bell's report – was handled, this clinician says, created 'wider anxiety' in the Trust. It sent a message to everyone that if you spoke out, you would be vilified, they say, referencing the public statement issued by the Tavistock suggesting that Dr Bell was not qualified to speak on these matters and making the false claim that his report 'presented hypothetical vignettes rather than actual case studies'.[45] Senior Tavistock staff tell me there was no longer a feeling that the Tavistock would protect staff if they too had concerns about clinical safety in their own services. Paul Jenkins does not accept this, but agreed that recent years 'have been a difficult time for the Trust'. He says: 'As the only provider of this kind of service, we have found ourselves at the centre of a polarised public debate and the subject of constant media coverage. It has been very challenging for the organisation and its staff.'

When, in 2018 and 2019, senior Tavistock clinicians outside GIDS had tried to voice their worries about the service and, importantly, offer help, Tavistock CEO Paul Jenkins rebuffed them. He accused them of criticising a group of 'hard-working, conscientious colleagues', it's claimed, though they were doing nothing of the sort. 'This really was the beginning of the relationship between Paul Jenkins and really the adult service as a whole, I think, becoming quite sour,' explains one of the group of senior staff who spoke with the CEO. The Tavistock as it was once known, they say, has already gone. 'My point of view is that the problem started with a highly defensive chief executive officer who wouldn't let us think about it and discuss things, which is what the Tavistock has historically done best; it's been able to reflect on its own processes and be thoughtful, and that that culture has disappeared.'

Those on the council of governors faced a similar experience, being told that it was not their job to ask questions about GIDS. Their job was to 'hold the board to account', chairman Paul Burstow would remind them 'fairly frequently'. But that didn't make sense to Dr Juliet Singer, one of very few Tavistock governors who asked questions and raised concerns about clinical practice. 'All I could think was… we're in the middle of what a lot of people consider potentially a massive medical scandal,' she says, 'we're seeing detransitioners talk about how let down they've been, how irreversible the interventions are, how angry they are that nobody paid any attention to anything else that was going on in their lives… And I'm sitting in this governors' meeting, and I'm being told that our role is to hold the board to account. And I think that's what we're doing. We're expressing our serious concerns. And I'm speaking not just as a child psychiatrist: I was elected as public governor for Camden, as a parent, as a member of the local community… it's not a tiny minority of people who have concerns. It's a huge number of people who have concerns.'

'I'm feeling guilty as a voice at a small insignificant table, but nonetheless, at a table,' Singer reflects. 'But then there's the board of directors, there's the regulators, the government.' Everybody saw what was happening, but nobody said 'stop', she says. 'Concerns raised are dismissed, complainants attacked. There's something powerful and disturbing at play.'

Some senior Tavistock figures have remarked that it seemed to them that this was a Trust that appeared to want to protect its Gender Identity Development Service at all costs. Any concern was both unwelcome and framed as an attack on those who worked in the service. 'There were lots of comms about how distressed GIDS staff were, and how we had to be mindful of them and their service users and their families. And of course, that seems to be absolutely appropriate,' one tells me. 'But it got to the point where I certainly was beginning to feel and think that what seemed to be being conveyed was a subliminal message never to question GIDS.'

Indeed, the response provided by the Trust's leadership each time it heard clinical concerns over GIDS appears to have been to criticise the *way* those concerns have been voiced – the tone of them – or to argue that such remarks are upsetting to other GIDS staff. What seems to have been lacking is a willingness to grapple with the substance of concerns, and put patients first and foremost.*

---

* Tavistock chief executive Paul Jenkins declined to be interviewed for this book. He was given the opportunity to respond to a number of points via email, and told the author that there was 'ample evidence to show that there is no substance' to claims that concerns about GIDS were shut down or that he presided over a culture where criticism of the service was not tolerated. Mr Jenkins cited the GIDS review and 'the Trust's implementation of its recommendations' as evidence of this. 'I am a firm believer that policies and practices within the Trust in general, and the GIDS service in particular, should be under constant review. As part of this, concerns which have been raised have been debated in Board meetings and at the Council of Governors,' he said. 'I have also encouraged clinical experience to be shared between GIDS staff and clinical staff in other parts of the Trust.' Mr Jenkins said that he was 'aware that there are some former Trust employees who disagree with the way the Trust provides the GIDS service and who have been dissatisfied with the outcome of their complaints and concerns'. He believes the Trust 'always sought to deal fairly and appropriately with such concerns'.

Why would this be so? It is certainly the case that Paul Jenkins was genuinely moved by the personal testimonies of some of the young people who had been helped by GIDS. He saw a vulnerable group who needed help and viewed the work of the service as 'ground breaking'. It was a service he was committed to 'nurturing'.[46] But, for many I have spoken to, this does not explain the way in which the Tavistock Trust responded to years of serious concerns being raised about GIDS. 'The senior management regarded it as a star in our crown,' says David Bell, 'because they saw it as a way of showing that we weren't crusty old conservatives; that we were up with the game and cutting-edge. That was very important to the management to show we were like that. And they really seemed to believe in it.'

One explanation has been raised by countless people I have spoken to – both those who have worked at GIDS itself, and those who have worked in the wider Tavistock: money. Financially, GIDS was 'propping us up', says a senior Tavistock clinician who tried to speak out. 'That to my mind is the elephant in the room. You know that the reason Paul Jenkins did not want [David Bell's] report to be circulated was he didn't want to jeopardise the budget that came from this enormous number of referrals.' Jenkins does 'not accept this allegation' and says that the Trust 'always sought to take concerns and complaints seriously and investigate them appropriately'.

It is no secret that GIDS brought in a substantial amount of money for the Trust, but, as David Bell points out, 'the economic considerations have to be housed within an understanding of how the health service works, because the Trust can't be blamed for the economic problem.' In England, all NHS trusts have to function as businesses. The Tavistock, like other health providers, faced an 'external culture of cuts', Bell says, which brought great anxiety about money for years. The Trust, given its small size, had never been awash with cash, but 'one of the great advantages of the gender work is that once we had a national contract, that's guaranteed income', Bell explains.

In a market-driven approach, there was less money for the Tavistock's 'long tradition of psychodynamic (and latterly systemic) practice and training', former GIDS associate director Bernadette Wren explained. 'As some departments attracted fewer commissions for explicitly psychoanalytic services, they found it harder to cover the costs of the very senior staff on whom the international reputation of the trust depended,' she said.

> On top of this, the usual practice of departmental cross-subsidy was frowned on by NHS accountants, so some sections were left languishing, at least for a time, while other new and rapidly growing services, including GIDS, with its disconcerting client group and eclectic model of practice, played a larger and larger role in trust finances.[47]

GIDS went from being a supporting actor, at best, to the leading lady. And it was a strategic objective of the Trust to bring this about. GIDS's contribution to the Tavistock Trust's income increased from 5.9 per cent in 2015/16 to 13.1 per cent in 2020/21. When income from the Charing Cross Gender Identity Clinic is added, gender services accounted for a quarter (24.4 per cent) of the Tavistock's income in 2020/21.[48] This figure has potentially been as high as 28 per cent, with the Trust noting that there is 'added value of having the children's and adults gender services in the same trust.'[49] With gender services contributing around a quarter of the Tavistock's income, 'that must have an influence,' says David Bell. Neither he nor anybody else implies any malice. Instead, he says it allowed the Trust to be 'blinkered'. It had 'become so overcommitted to something that you can't allow yourself to see something that puts the whole thing into question'.

Just how important GIDS's income is, or was, to the Tavistock is borne out by a look at its current predicament. In 2022, the Trust is in financial disarray. In the space of a few years the Tavistock has gone from operating a small surplus to a deficit of £12.3 million in 2021/22.[50] Based on assumptions in a slightly more favourable forecast, the council of governors was told that 'at the current level of deficit, the Trust would run out of cash during 2022/23 and would therefore need to seek support from NHSE/I [NHS England and NHS Improvement]'.[51] The Trust's budget for the current financial year – 2022/23 – shows the Trust making a deficit of £3.7 million on an income of £65.1 million.[52] This was revised up from an initial estimated deficit of £6 million. It bears repeating: the Tavistock may run out of money in 2022/23 and will need help to survive.

But the lack of willingness to tackle the fundamental problems at GIDS cannot be explained by money alone. 'It's not just the money,' insists David Bell. To have responded adequately to the concerns raised with him by GIDS staff, it would have required 'a complete structural rethink', he says. 'You can't take what these clinicians are saying and put some Band-Aids on.' It required a fundamental change of belief. The Tavistock as an institution had become so committed to GIDS it could not allow itself 'to see something that puts the whole thing into question', Dr Bell argues. 'They've swallowed the ideology that it's edgy; it's seen as being the greatest thing we have.' GIDS, he says, came to have 'such a driving power within the Trust that no doubt could be allowed in'. And where the Tavistock had once been world-famous for its thoughtful psychoanalytic approach, it is now synonymous with gender, Bell believes. Even the Tavistock telephone switchboard reflects this. Options 1 and 2 are reserved for the adult gender identity clinic and for GIDS.

I have not found GIDS staff to be 'in the grip of an ideology'.[53] It has not, or was not, generally been staffed by ideologues. But, as former GIDS associate director Bernadette Wren said, what is true is that 'GIDS, from its modest start, was a justice project as well as a therapeutic project'.[54] She said that the service 'aspired to widen the circle of people whose experience of the self is listened to with respect'. For some, she explained, 'this justice-based approach extends to the demand that all gender-diverse people, including the young, should have the unquestionable right to make fully autonomous treatment decisions – the full freedom, we might say, to make their own mis-takes'.[55] Wren added: 'This has never been GIDS's position.' But I have spoken with clinicians who at least sympathise strongly with this view, and have heard from others that this was an argument not infrequently made by some senior clinicians at GIDS.

It seems that ideology and feelings have been allowed to trump traditional medical evidence in the work of GIDS. And where ideology impacted GIDS so strongly was in the service's inability to keep an appropriate distance from charities and support groups like Gendered

Intelligence and Mermaids. That the bosses of both organisations saw themselves as entitled to write to GIDS director Polly Carmichael directly and demand clinicians be reprimanded, or switched, or that the service go further and faster with physical interventions, is telling. Presumably, they believed their words would be heeded. GIDS put itself in a position which made it difficult to say no to these groups. Carmichael for one had attended Mermaids meetings since at least the mid 2000s, and had fostered a friendly relationship with its chief, Susie Green, who left the charity in November 2022.[56] It appeared from emails that Carmichael had responded sympathetically when Green asked for changes to GIDS's practices. GIDS Executive member Sarah Davidson was listed by the Gendered Intelligence website as one of its 'team members'.[57] She has spoken publicly about working closely with them and delivered professional training and education events alongside them.[58] It was pressure, in part, from lobby groups that took the service initially down a path of providing physical interventions to younger children without a strong evidence base. And some argue that the fear of a backlash from these same groups prevented GIDS changing direction when it should have.

While GIDS itself and the Tavistock Trust must bear responsibility for much of what has occurred, so too must GIDS's commissioners – NHS England. The pressure that GIDS was under in terms of increasing referrals was impossible not to notice, and it was clear that simply increasing staff numbers was not helping. The suggestion that these highly complex cases and vulnerable young people be seen by a service predominantly staffed with junior clinicians seems foolish. It is difficult to understand why NHS England did not suggest an alternative when it was clear that GIDS was struggling, and waiting times were growing.

The argument that GIDS was helpless to challenge the contractual obligations it had signed up to does not withstand scrutiny. GIDS helped design the contract with NHS England; its own staff had warned that the contract was undeliverable; and GIDS itself had significant bargaining power. While it is *possible* that NHS England would have threatened to take its business elsewhere if GIDS had said it could not provide the standard of service it wanted to, it is unlikely. There simply was no other provider to award the national contract to.

But several GIDS staff have told me that they found little support from their commissioners, especially when it came to how to respond to families who were also receiving treatment privately.

While GIDS was not a victim of having an undeliverable contract forced upon it, there has been an astonishing lack of oversight from NHS England. Why did they allow the early blocking of puberty to be rolled out as routine practice without demanding to see some data supporting this radical shift? Why didn't it insist on seeing any data at all? One can only assume that NHS England did not, given that GIDS was unable to supply any long-term data to the High Court when asked. Why too did NHS England seemingly not act when it read David Bell's report, or even the findings of the GIDS Review?

Health sources have acknowledged to me that NHS England was slow to act – that it 'could have moved faster'. They concede that GIDS was allowed to 'develop in a vacuum without scrutiny'. They acted when the Tavistock appeared to be 'losing control of any chance to improve things', I'm told. I have seen no evidence of any conspiracy to explain the lack of intervention from NHS England, but this does not mean they are off the hook. I'm told that there has been no one else willing to take on the contract for gender-diverse young people. But, again, this does not explain the failure to step in years earlier.

Writing this book has been an extraordinary experience. Frustrating and difficult at times, overwhelming even. I have been struck by how conflicted many former GIDS staff feel about the service, in some cases many years after they have left. There is a sense that by reflecting truthfully on their own experiences and airing their genuinely held concerns, they feel they are betraying both the personal relationships they made at GIDS and the deep-seated affection they feel for the Tavistock as an institution. One put it this way: 'It's just the key dilemma, isn't it? Do I screw over my colleagues to try and help these patients, or do I protect my colleagues and inadvertently screw over the patients? You can't win.'

'The Tavistock', I've learnt, represents a set of values to many mental health professionals. It has made significant mistakes in the past – not least its controversial history of 'treating homosexuality' (which some believe helps explain why GIDS was so concerned about not being seen as transphobic) and its involvement in the so-called 'satanic panic' of the 1990s – but it has also done great good.[59] As cognitive behavioural therapy (CBT) became increasingly seen as the way the NHS could fix people's mental health, the Tavistock pushed back. Sometimes people's difficulties were more complicated, it insisted. And this required slower and more in-depth exploration than CBT allowed. But these alternatives are expensive. CBT can be hugely effective in many situations, but it's not a panacea for all mental health problems, clinicians say. Even faced with this shift, somehow the Tavistock managed to hang on to a different approach, while, on the whole, the NHS did not. Some professionals saw this as standing up for patients: pushing back against quick fixes and treating people as complex individuals. 'We loved the Tavi for saying, "Hang on, these are people's lives we are talking about here,"' explains Anna Hutchinson. Many of the professionals who agreed to talk to me wanted their experiences at GIDS to be known, and for lessons to be learnt. But I was left with a strong sense that they felt torn: they did not want to bring down the Tavistock in the process.

It is impossible to overstate the impact that working at GIDS has had on some clinicians. It's not normal for psychologists and therapists to speak to journalists. Those who spoke to me for films broadcast by *Newsnight* or for BBC articles did so as a last resort, having exhausted all the official channels open to them for raising concerns. Speaking to many, many more for this book, it has been clear that some find talking about their experiences upsetting, unsettling and difficult. They've remarked at the end of our conversations that it has felt like a therapy session. For some, their time at GIDS was life-altering and they've been unable to let go of what they witnessed and, at times, participated in. There's guilt. Some are angry at being dismissed. Persecuted. Others have had recurring nightmares and been traumatised. And some can't bring themselves to talk about it at all.

'It's now three and a half years since I left GIDS, so I don't think about the service every day,' Matt Bristow says. 'But sometimes I do wonder what happened to some of those young people. In both ways. I sometimes think, there's someone who I thought was on a really good path, and I hope that things have worked out well, and continue to go well for them. And there are others where I think I really wasn't sure about that one, and I hope they're okay. But there's kind of a fear there that they're not. I'll never know.' Family therapist Anastassis Spiliadis explains that he only realised he had been traumatised by the experience once he had left. He speaks with astonishing honesty, acknowledging that there is some guilt about 'how ignorant' he was when he joined GIDS, 'and how I could have done things differently'. He questions whether he did 'enough in terms of speaking up and challenging things'. And he recalls talking with colleagues, comparing their experience to the East German athletics doping scandal of the 1970s and 1980s. 'We're like, "Oh my God, will we look back in ten, 20 years and be like, what did we do?" And I just started realising that I'm doing a really complex and complicated piece of work without it being in a safe context.' Spiliadis says he was unable to 'practice ethically'.

'I felt morally violated,' Anna Hutchinson reflects. 'I feel like so many of my core values have been challenged by my knowledge of what happened in GIDS and what is happening in GIDS that I couldn't walk away and just forget about it.'

Not everyone feels this way, by any means. Some I've spoken to look back on their time at GIDS fondly. They're proud of the work they've done, under difficult circumstances. And they left the service simply because of other career opportunities or life and family circumstances. But I've been struck by the fact that no one speaking favourably of GIDS has been willing to put their name to their comments, a fact that some have put down to the toxicity of public debate about young gender non-conforming people and how anyone who speaks out, from whatever viewpoint, faces attacks.

But even those defending GIDS have, in many ways, remarkably similar reflections to those who are critical of the service and believe it to have been clinically unsafe. It's just that they interpret what they have seen differently. For example, junior psychologist David Burrows tells me he 'loved' working at GIDS – that it was the perfect role for him at the time. Yet, he also explains how his 'brilliant' supervisor, who encouraged him to be 'thoughtful and question everything', left the service 'because she was too concerned about everything'. He also reflects that 'the whole thing sometimes felt like madness', and, like almost everyone I've spoken to, acknowledges differences of approach within the GIDS team. The so-called 'clinician lottery'.[60]

Burrows saw himself as holding a 'middle-ground position', being neither pro-physical intervention nor very against it. But he tells me he only referred two young people for puberty blockers from a caseload of 100. Both had long-standing, persistent gender dysphoria from childhood. 'My experience was that the assessments were really rigorous,' he says, 'and it was a really big decision to put anyone on blockers. And I think that's where the split is – as in some clinicians... they put [young people] on much easier, much quicker.' A minority of clinicians were 'very pro-physical interventions', he says. 'I'd say they were a handful who made you feel transphobic, but the majority were careful.' Burrows tells me that physical interventions did not seem appropriate for the majority of the young people attending GIDS, so how does he square *his* practice with that of colleagues who, he says, would refer quickly and in almost all cases? 'I was newly qualified,' he says, 'so maybe my cautiousness was part of that, whereas really experienced clinicians might have had greater confidence in making those decisions earlier.' Maybe those clinicians were able to spot those for whom physical interventions would work, where he couldn't. I probe a little a harder: did he feel uncomfortable that, given *he* deemed puberty blockers unsuitable for so many young people (he tells me many were gay and struggling with their sexuality), other more affirmative clinicians were referring so many to endocrinology? 'Yes,' he replies. Were there aspects of the service he wasn't totally comfortable with, I ask? 'Yeah, but they were always being discussed. It wasn't like it was happening and it wasn't being discussed.'

For some, as long as difficulties were acknowledged, it was enough. For others, the fact that problems were acknowledged but then not actually tackled forced them to leave and speak out. Why clinicians have reached such different conclusions is not something I can answer definitively, but there are some features which may perhaps help to explain. On the whole, it is those who worked at GIDS for a shorter period of time – a year or two – who are less concerned. 'Until you've been there for a while you don't see the impact of the decisions you're making,' one former GIDS psychologist explains. 'For those clinicians who only maybe stay a year, those are the ones who maybe think the interventions are safe because they don't see how the child changes over time and that perhaps things don't get better. Over time the anxiety about the decisions you have been part of becomes huge and overwhelming when children don't seem to benefit from medical interventions.' For those who stayed longer, in some instances they would see that their patients did not flourish on puberty blockers; their mental and physical health may have deteriorated, and cross-sex hormones did not appear to help either. They also saw that the blocker did not herald the beginning of an exploratory phase; rather, it seemed to shut down thinking. Junior staff appear to be less worried, generally, than those with more clinical experience, especially those who held posts in other NHS mental health services prior to joining GIDS. Burrows is honest about this, saying that it was maybe because he was junior that he was protected from some of what was going on and that perhaps he didn't think 'too much' about it.

Some GIDS clinicians did not see it as *their* responsibility to know if medical transition was right for any given young person. 'Once we have gotten to a point where we think this is the right thing to do with the family,' one former GIDS psychologist said, 'often we are putting responsibility back on the family because we don't have the evidence base to say it's these kids and not these kids [who will benefit].' They explain that 'this is a massively under-researched and quite an experimental area especially in terms of young people.'[61] Their former colleague Dr Alex Morris tells me she cannot think of a single instance in which she signed off a recommendation for puberty blockers 'with a real sense that this is 100 per cent the right thing to do. Because how could you?' She says that it was impossible to be sure, and anyone who says otherwise is not being honest.

I asked Morris whether, once she'd seen the first data from the Early Intervention Study showing that everyone who had started on puberty blockers went on to cross-sex hormones, she felt the need to be 'more sure' when assessing for puberty blockers. 'I didn't really see it as my job to know or to be sure,' she answers, honestly. 'Because how could I? And how could anybody? I know that sounds really extraordinary, but what's the nature of expertise in this field? Given the state of research, nobody's got a clue really about what the life course of any of this is. So I tend to think more in terms of how can I feel sure that the people involved in making the decision have done so skilfully and in the best way that they can for them?' Did she consider herself and her GIDS colleagues responsible for these decisions? In part, Morris says. 'We hold some [responsibility]. I don't think we hold all of it.' Who holds the rest? 'I think the child to a certain extent, obviously more so as they're older… I think parents to some significant extent, and medical teams as well.'

Morris believes it will take decades to achieve anything like a level of certainty that will allow clinicians to know who is most likely to benefit from early medical transition and who will not. She agrees that what evidence GIDS did have applied 'largely to a very different cohort to the one which was presenting', and that she 'wouldn't have much confidence in cross-reading any of that evidence to the current demographic'. But, she says, there are lots of areas in medicine, 'especially in paediatrics, where we've got no idea at all about the long-term follow-up'. Like what, I ask? But she could not think of an example.

This same argument has been advanced by Bernadette Wren, who added that 'many paediatric medical interventions… depend on confidence in the existing, broader knowledge base (often from studies on adults) and are justified by the concern to relieve suffering'.[62] The difficulty here is that while there is no doubt that GIDS clinicians wanted to relieve the suffering of the young people in their care, there was little persuasive evidence that the physical interventions they were referring them for were having such an effect. The clinical experience of many I have spoken to does not support this idea. Nor does GIDS's own limited data, which found 'no evidence of change in psychological function' with puberty-blocker treatment. GIDS said that 'the majority' of participants in its Early Intervention Study found the experience of puberty-blocking treatment 'positive', and that none wanted to stop. But even this subjective measure is 'mixed', the research team acknowledged. At six to 15 months on puberty blockers, 'the majority reported mood to be improved (49%)', but 24 per cent reported 'negative changes in mood'.[63] It is stated that findings were similar for the second period studied, between 15 and 24 months, but this does not appear to be the case.[64] Those experiencing positive changes in mood decreases to just below 30 per cent, while those experiencing negative mood *increases* to the same figure – around 30 per cent.[65] It is difficult to draw any meaningful conclusion from these data. Or, to put it another way, the argument for *not* beginning physical interventions is just as persuasive as that in favour.

I have heard it said several times throughout writing this book that staff who left GIDS because they were concerned about what they were witnessing and taking part in could not manage the uncertainty that the work necessarily entails. It is not possible to know for sure that physical interventions are the best path for any child, because there is no magic test that can show who will grow up to be a trans adult and who will not. I think that this is a mischaracterisation of the position of these worried staff. In fact, the opposite is true. These clinicians saw uncertainty everywhere in the work of GIDS and acknowledged it: uncertainty in not being able to predict which of their patients would benefit from puberty blockers; uncertainty in the evidence base underpinning paediatric transition as an approach; and even more uncertainty surrounding that approach for a new cohort of young people. But they also saw this uncertainty not being managed, and instead being responded to with certainty: a referral in many cases – indeed, to 'anyone who wants it'[66] – for physical interventions, or on to adult services who would provide them.

What these clinicians wanted was for the uncertainty and risk in what they were doing to be properly acknowledged, and for GIDS as a service to act accordingly. They wanted their clinical actions to be as safe and as evidence-based as possible. What would that have looked like? For Anna Hutchinson it meant being more honest, 'telling young people that not every single one of them was going to benefit, talking with them in detail in advance about what could happen if they didn't benefit – what that might look like'. By the end of her time at GIDS this is what Hutchinson did with patients. So did some of her colleagues who are quoted on these pages. But it 'wasn't something that was being consistently done'. Properly acknowledging risk meant 'beginning to collect data and do proper research to see if there was any way we could differentiate between those who would benefit and those who wouldn't and keeping these ethical conversations on the table.

Because as a society we may at some point have decided that the risks were too high for the potential benefits with children.' Hutchinson does not claim to have the answers. 'But what I'm saying is that we needed to have the conversations and we needed to acknowledge the truth of the risks we were taking.'

Would this approach really have made a difference? Some clinicians say that many of the young people attending GIDS just would not entertain these types of conversations, and could not have been dissuaded from the desire to transition by anything that was said. As responsible clinicians, 'We had a duty to try,' says Hutchinson. It may well have given pause for thought with some young people, she says. Harriet, who features in this book, for one, is explicit that further exploration of her sexuality and mental health issues may well have prevented her from embarking on a course of testosterone and a double mastectomy. 'We don't know, because we never tried,' Hutchinson says bluntly. 'Had somebody sat there and said, "Look, here are the stats. Here's a trans man telling us about their experience. Here's a detransitioned woman telling us about their experience. Here's the whole plethora of potential outcomes. Here's what we do know about the meds. Here's what we don't know, here are the risks in true detail in terms of how they would apply to your life. What would it be like to have an enlarged clitoris? You know, how will that affect your sex life? What would it be like to have an increased risk of cardiovascular disease? What does that mean? What might that mean for you at 30, 40, 50 years of age?" Really talking it through in a way that might feel real to a young person.'

Could all the young people coming through GIDS's doors deal with those kinds of conversations, I ask, knowing that other clinicians say that providing that level of detail felt necessary, but also risky? 'No,' Anna Hutchinson says. They couldn't. 'In which case, could they consent?' If the fear of the truth is so great it cannot be handled, 'One has to address the treatment and whether it's appropriate, because the truth will out. The child will live that truth… It's also cruel to not inform children of what's going to actually happen to them.'

The pioneers of the Dutch protocol were well aware that the pathway they had devised – puberty blockers, followed by cross-sex hormones and surgery – would not work for all. They acknowledged that by lowering the age at which puberty was blocked, it might 'increase the incidence of "false positives".'[67] It is this group, the group for whom this pathway will not be of benefit, say Hutchinson and others, that has been ignored by gender clinics across the Western world, including GIDS. 'Everyone who's worked in that service knows, and anyone who's read the research knows, that in every single piece of research since the 70s onwards, children who identify as trans, some persist and some don't,' Hutchinson says. There is 'huge diversity' within them, but there are fundamentally two groups, she goes on. GIDS, she argues, was 'only really considering those that would persist – those that would identify as trans for life'. Speaking in 2016, GIDS director Polly Carmichael posed the question of why 'none stop once they've started on the blocker', pondering whether it was possible that the blocker 'in and of itself may have an impact and set people on a path'.[68] 'That's what I mean,' Hutchinson responds, when hearing this comment. 'The other group, the "non-trans-for-life group" are just not given a second thought.' They are treated as 'collateral damage', she says. 'Because everybody is so geared up around meeting the needs of those who identify as trans for life, the second group got totally, totally ignored… We weren't able to see both and work with both. And that's where the harm was coming in.'

This is a story that is yet to end. For the 10,000 or so young people who have been seen by GIDS over its 30-plus-year history, it is a story that may never end.

Some will be like Jack or Pheobe, living happy lives, having transitioned and feeling finally that they are accepted for the person they are. Some, like Ellie, will have come through a period of questioning their gender identity and be comfortable in the body they were born with. And some will be less fortunate. It is impossible to know how many might feel like Harriet: unhappy with what they say was a lack of rigour and curiosity in exploring *why* they might be feeling the way they did about their gender identity and now living with the consequences of cross-sex hormones and surgery that they now wish they had not had. We do not know the number of young people who may feel like Jacob: still identifying as trans, but who have not benefited after years of puberty blockade, and who are living with a sense of not knowing what harm might have been done to their bodies in the process. The Gender Identity Development Service has undoubtedly helped some people. It has unquestionably harmed others.

Dr Anna Hutchinson now works with people on a variety of issues. Gender is a small part of her private practice, but she continues to see questioning teenagers, happy trans adults and those who are struggling or have detransitioned. But since leaving GIDS she has worked constantly and quietly trying to raise the standard of care for young people with gender-related distress. She has spoken with governments and many mental health professionals about the need for a more explorative approach. 'I work with trans people... and help them thrive in their lives,' she says. But GIDS was different. 'We were talking about very, very young children here and they weren't being given any alternative explanation for their distress. And they were very quickly, in some cases, being put on to a medical pathway that will have totally altered their life.' Others do not share her assessment, or at least not yet. 'I really hope I haven't come across as blasé about risk, or harm,' Alex Morris says to me, 'because I really don't feel like I am. I think maybe, though, I don't see yet the harm that I think some of my colleagues see, or worry about, for whatever reason. It could be that it is there, and we don't know about it yet.'

Hutchinson believes that the true nature of what has happened will unfold over the next decade or so. But she fears that she and her colleagues have had front-row seats on a medical scandal. One that, despite their efforts, they were unable to stop. 'I genuinely believe that some of those kids would not have ended up identifying as trans had they not been put on the medical pathway,' she says. 'And, of course, that doesn't mean to say that identifying as trans is a bad outcome. But what is a bad outcome is creating a cohort of people who are medically dependent who'd never needed to be. And not only medically dependent, but perhaps – we don't yet know – medically damaged.'

'Are we hurting children?' Anna Hutchinson asked her GIDS supervisor in 2017.

'Yes,' she now knows. Some. But today we are left with a new question. How many?

ACKNOWLEDGEMENTS

This book would never have been written without the endless support of my husband, Pat, who has kept our family on track while allowing me to research, conduct interviews, write and rewrite. Enormous thanks are also due to my parents and step-parents for their love, and for their help with looking after their amazing grandchildren.

To all those who shared their experience of GIDS as service users or as their family members, thank you for telling your stories. Ellie, Jack, Phoebe, Hannah, 'Jacob', 'Michelle', 'Diana', 'Harriet' – thank you for trusting with me with such personal accounts, and, in some cases, highly sensitive information.

I owe a huge debt a of gratitude to all of the GIDS clinicians who have given me their time, shared their thoughts – whatever they may be – and who met or spoke with me, even if they did not feel comfortable being interviewed. To Anna Hutchinson, who patiently shared her experiences over many hours, to Matt Bristow, Will Crouch, Kirsty Entwistle, Sue Evans, Az Hakeem, Melissa Midgen, Natasha Prescott, Anastassis Spiliadis, and to the many, many others who have spoken on condition of anonymity – thank you. For some, I am aware it has been a difficult experience, and I do not take lightly how daunting it might have been to share your views – for a variety of reasons. There are also further, unnamed clinicians who have spoken out over several years, and who have tried to bring about change away from the public eye.

Thanks too to all who have spoken with me who work or worked in the Tavistock and Portman NHS Foundation Trust, or were charged with its governance: Sonia Appleby, Juliet Singer, David Bell, Marcus

Evans, Stanley Ruszczynski, David Taylor, Marilyn Miller and those who do not wish to be named.

Paul Moran, Donal O'Shea, Russell Viner, David Freedman and Stephanie Davies-Arai also deserve my thanks, as do Lucy Bannerman, Susan Matthews and Richard Stephens.

My first, and exceptionally brilliant, reader was my uncle, Robert Barnes, and I thank him for his many thoughtful, wise suggestions and feedback. My second was Julia Murphy, who managed to squeeze in reading alongside work and family life. Thank you.

This book would also not have been written without the encouragement of Innes Bowen, who convinced me that I had it in me. Nor would it have been possible without my agent Toby Mundy, who took it – and me – on, and who has been a consistent voice of calm when I have needed it. And to Mark Richards and Diana Broccardo at Swift Press, who were brave enough to publish it. For bringing coherence to the many, many references, thank you to the ever-patient Alex Middleton.

The seeds were sown at BBC *Newsnight*, and there would have been no book without the original backing and courage of my former editor, Esmé Wren, and my friend and former colleague Deborah Cohen, as well as support from deputy editors Dan Clarke, Verity Murphy and Stewart Maclean.

Finally, thank you to everyone who has sent me source material or shared information, and to those whose names I don't know who have had the wisdom to archive hundreds of webpages. I am indebted to you all.

NOTES

1. 'Are we hurting children?'

1 For 50 young people each year, see Domenico Di Ceglie, 'The use of metaphors in understanding atypical gender identity development and its psychosocial impact', *Journal of Child Psychotherapy* 44/1 (2018), 5–28, doi: 10.1080/0075417X.2018.1443151. For thousands, see 'Referrals to GIDS, financial years 2010–11 to 2021–22', GIDS [website] (7 June 2022), https://gids.nhs.uk/number-referrals, archived at https://web.archive.org/web/20221006112951/https://gids.nhs.uk/about-us/number-of-referrals/.
2 Di Ceglie, 'The use of metaphors'.
3 Sarah Davidson to Anna Hutchinson [email], 14 December 2016.
4 Anna Hutchinson, 'Confidential: statement for the review of the GIDS service, October 2018'.
5 'About us', GIDS [website], https://gids.nhs.uk/about-us.
6 'Early or delayed puberty', NHS [website], https://www.nhs.uk/conditions/early-or-delayed-puberty/.
7 'Gonadotropin releasing hormone (GnRH) analogues', National Library of Medicine [website] (20 March 2018), https://www.ncbi.nlm.nih.gov/books/NBK547863/; Rizwan Saleem et al., 'Clinical experience of the use of triptorelin as an antilibidinal medication in a high-security hospital', *Journal of Forensic Psychiatry & Psychology* 22/2 (2011), 243–51, doi: 10.1080/14789949.2011.552621.
8 Annelou L. C. de Vries et al., 'Puberty suppression in adolescents with gender identity disorder: a prospective follow-up study', *Journal of Sexual Medicine* 8/8 (August 2011; published online July 2010), 2276–83, doi: 10.1111/j.1743-6109.2010.01943.x; Chantal M. Wiepjes et al., 'The Amsterdam cohort of gender dysphoria study (1972–2015): trends in prevalence, treatment, and regrets', *Journal of Sexual Medicine* 15/4 (2018), 582–90, doi: 10.1016/j.jsxm.2018.01.016; Tessa Brik et al., 'Trajectories of adolescents treated with gonadotropin-releasing hormone analogues for gender dysphoria', *Archives of Sexual Behavior* 49/7 (2020), 2611–18, doi: 10.1007/s10508-020-01660-8; Polly Carmichael et al., 'Short-term outcomes of pubertal suppression in a selected cohort of 12 to 15 year old young people with persistent gender dysphoria in the UK', *PLoS ONE* 16/2 (2021), e0243894, doi: 10.1371/journal.pone.0243894.
9 Peter Russell, '£1.3 million research award into child gender dysphoria',

Medscape UK [website] (25 February 2019), https://www.medscape.com/viewarticle/909478.

10 Bernadette Wren, 'Debate: you can't take politics out of the debate on gender-diverse children', *Child and Adolescent Mental Health* 25 (2020), 40–2, doi: 10.1111/camh.12350.

11 Bernadette Wren, 'Early physical intervention for young people with atypical gender identity development', *Clinical Child Psychology and Psychiatry* 5/2 (2000), 220–31, doi: 10.1177/1359104500005002007.

12 For high satisfaction and improved mental health, see de Vries et al., 'Puberty suppression in adolescents with gender identity disorder' and Jack L. Turban et al., 'Pubertal suppression for transgender youth and risk of suicidal ideation', *Pediatrics* 145/2 (February 2020), e20191725, doi: 10.1542/peds.2019-1725 (erratum in *Pediatrics* 147/4 (April 2021), e2020049767, doi: 10.1542/peds.2020-049767). For changes in sexuality, see Talia N. Shirazi et al., 'Pubertal timing predicts adult psychosexuality: evidence from typically developing adults and adults with isolated GnRH deficiency', *Psychoneuroendocrinology* 119/104733 (September 2020), doi: 10.1016/j.psyneuen.2020.104733. For changes in sexual function, see Mauro E. Kerckhof et al., 'Prevalence of sexual dysfunctions in transgender persons: results from the ENIGI follow-up study', *Journal of Sexual Medicine* 16/12 (December 2019), 2018–29, doi: 10.1016/j.jsxm.2019.09.003. For poor bone health, see Sebastian E. E. Schagen et al., 'Bone development in transgender adolescents treated with GnRH analogues and subsequent gender-affirming hormones', *Journal of Clinical Endocrinology & Metabolism* 105/12 (December 2020), e4252–e4263, doi: 10.1210/clinem/dgaa604. For stunted height, see Carmichael et al., 'Short-term outcomes of pubertal suppression'. For tumour-like masses in the brain, see 'Risk of pseudotumor cerebri added to labeling for gonadotropin-releasing hormone agonists', AAP News [website] (1 July 2022), https://publications.aap.org/aapnews/news/20636/Risk-of-pseudotumor-cerebri-added-to-labeling-for. For infertility, see Philip J. Cheng et al., 'Fertility concerns of the transgender patient', *Translational Andrology and Urology* 8/3 (June 2019), 209–18, doi: 10.21037/tau.2019.05.09 and Wylie C. Hembree, 'Guidelines for pubertal suspension and gender reassignment for transgender adolescents' *Child and Adolescent Psychiatric Clinics of North America* 20/4 (2011), 725–32, doi: 10.1016/j.chc.2011.08.004.

13 For blood clots, see Milou Cecilia Madsen et al., 'Erythrocytosis in a large cohort of trans men using testosterone: a long-term follow-up study on prevalence, determinants, and exposure years', *Journal of Clinical Endocrinology & Metabolism* 106/6 (June 2021), 1710–17, doi: 10.1210/clinem/dgab089. For cardiovascular disease, see Paul J. Connelly and Christian Delles, 'Cardiovascular disease in transgender people: recent research and emerging evidence', *Cardiovascular Research* 117/14 (1 December 2021), e174–e176, doi: 10.1093/cvr/cvab288.

14 National Institute for Health and Care Excellence, 'Evidence review: gonadotrophin releasing hormone analogues for children and adolescents with gender dysphoria' [PDF], Cass Review [website] (2020), https://cass.independent-review.uk/wp-content/uploads/2022/09/20220726_Evidence-review_GnRH-analogues_For-upload_Final.pdf, archived at https://web.archive.

org/web/20220414202655/https://arms.nice.org.uk/resources/hub/1070905/attachment.

15 For studies claiming to show the benefits, see Diana M. Tordoff et al., 'Mental health outcomes in transgender and nonbinary youths receiving gender-affirming care', *JAMA Network Open* 5/2 (2022), e220978, doi: 10.1001/jamanetworkopen.2022.0978 and Turban et al., 'Pubertal suppression for transgender youth and risk of suicidal ideation'. For critiques, see Jesse Singal, 'Researchers found puberty blockers and hormones didn't improve trans kids' mental health at their clinic. Then they published a study claiming the opposite', Singal-Minded [blog] (6 April 2022), https://jessesingal.substack.com/p/researchers-found-puberty-blockers?s=r; Jason Rantz, 'Rantz: despite "concerning" transgender study, UW kept quiet because of positive coverage', Mynorthwest [website] (23 August 2022), https://mynorthwest.com/3602854/rantz-despite-concerning-trans-study-uw-kept-quiet-because-of-positive-coverage/; Michael Biggs, 'Puberty blockers and suicidality in adolescents suffering from gender dysphoria', *Archives of Sexual Behavior* 49 (2020), 2227–9, doi: 10.1007/s10508-020-01743-6.

16 Deborah Cohen and Hannah Barnes, 'Evidence for puberty blockers use very low, says NICE', BBC News [website] (1 April 2021), https://www.bbc.co.uk/news/health-56601386.

17 National Institute for Health and Care Excellence, 'Evidence review: gonadotrophin releasing hormone analogues for children and adolescents with gender dysphoria'.

18 National Institute for Health and Care Excellence, 'Evidence review: gender-affirming hormones for children and adolescents with gender dysphoria' [PDF], Cass Review [website] (2020), https://cass.independent-review.uk/wp-content/uploads/2022/09/20220726_Evidence-review_Gender-affirming-hormones_For-upload_Final.pdf, archived at https://web.archive.org/web/20220215111922/https://arms.nice.org.uk/resources/hub/1070871/attachment.

19 Ibid.

20 For Sweden, see 'Care of children and adolescents with gender dysphoria' [PDF], National Board of Health and Welfare (Sweden) [website] (February 2022), https://www.socialstyrelsen.se/globalassets/sharepoint-dokument/artikelkatalog/kunskapsstod/2022-3-7799.pdf. For France, see National Academy of Medicine, France, 'Press release: medical care of children and adolescents with transgender identity' [PDF; unofficial English translation of 'Communiqué: la médecine face à la transidentité de genre chez les enfants et les adolescents'], Society for Evidence Based Gender Medicine [website] (2 March 2022), https://segm.org/sites/default/files/English%20Translation_22.2.25-Communique-PCRA-19-Medecine-et-transidentite-genre.pdf and 'National Academy of Medicine in France advises caution in pediatric gender transition', Society for Evidence Based Gender Medicine [website] (3 March 2022), https://segm.org/France-cautions-regarding-puberty-blockers-and-cross-sex-hormones-for-youth. For Finland, see 'Recommendation of the Council for Choices in Health Care in Finland (PALKO / COHERE Finland): medical treatment methods for dysphoria related to gender variance in minors' [PDF; unofficial English translation], Society for

Evidence Based Gender Medicine [website] (June 2020), https://segm.org/sites/default/files/Finnish_Guidelines_2020_Minors_Unofficial%20Translation.pdf and 'One year since Finland broke with WPATH "Standards of Care"', Society for Evidence Based Gender Medicine [website] (2 July 2021), https://segm.org/Finland_deviates_from_WPATH_prioritizing_psychotherapy_no_surgery_for_minors.

21 Cecilia Dhejne et al., 'Long-term follow-up of transsexual persons undergoing sex reassignment surgery: cohort study in Sweden', *PLoS ONE* 6/2 (22 February 2011), e16885, doi: 10.1371/journal.pone.0016885.

22 For complex mental health problems, see Nastasja M. de Graaf et al., 'Psychological functioning in adolescents referred to specialist gender identity clinics across Europe: a clinical comparison study between four clinics', *European Child & Adolescent Psychiatry* 27/7 (2017), 909–19, doi:10.1007/s00787-017-1098-4 and Nastasja M. de Graaf and Polly Carmichael, 'Reflections on emerging trends in clinical work with gender diverse children and adolescents', *Clinical Child Psychology and Psychiatry* 24/2 (April 2019), 353–64, doi: 10.1177/1359104518812924. For self-harm, see Elin Skagerberg, Rachel Parkinson and Polly Carmichael, 'Self-harming thoughts and behaviors in a group of children and adolescents with gender dysphoria', *International Journal of Transgenderism* 14/2 (2013), 86–92, doi: 10.1080/15532739.2013.817321 and Vicky Holt, Elin Skagerberg and Michael Dunsford, 'Young people with features of gender dysphoria: demographics and associated difficulties', *Clinical Child Psychology and Psychiatry* 21/1 (January 2016), 108–18, doi: 10.1177/1359104514558431.

23 Kasia Kozlowska et al., 'Australian children and adolescents with gender dysphoria: clinical presentations and challenges experienced by a multidisciplinary team and gender service', *Human Systems* 1/1 (2021), 70–95, doi: 10.1177/26344041211010777.

24 Dawn DeLay et al., 'The influence of peers during adolescence: does homophobic name calling by peers change gender identity?' *Journal of Youth and Adolescence* 47/3 (March 2018), 636–49, doi: 10.1007/s10964-017-0749-6.

25 For gay children, see Holt, Skagerberg and Dunsford, 'Young people with features of gender dysphoria'. For children on the autistic spectrum, see Elin Skagerberg, Domenico Di Ceglie and Polly Carmichael, 'Brief report: autistic features in children and adolescents with gender dysphoria', *Journal of Autism and Developmental Disorders* 45/8 (August 2015), 2628–32, doi: 10.1007/s10803-015-2413-x; Holt, Skagerberg and Dunsford, 'Young people with features of gender dysphoria'; and Tavistock and Portman NHS Foundation Trust FOI 18-19354 ('Subject: GIDS Referrals with autism traits 2017–18'), https://tavistockandportman.nhs.uk/documents/1435/FOI_18-19354_GIDS_Referrals_with_Autism_Traits_2017-18.pdf.

26 'NHS standard contract for Gender Identity Development Service for children and adolescents, service specification E13/S(HSS)/e' [PDF], NHS England [website] (April 2016), https://www.england.nhs.uk/wp-content/uploads/2017/04/gender-development-service-children-adolescents.pdf. On methodological flaws, see Kenneth J. Zucker, 'The myth of persistence: response to "A critical commentary on follow-up studies and 'desistance' theories about transgender and gender non-conforming children" by Temple Newhook et al.', *International Journal of Transgenderism* 19/2 (2018), 231–45, doi: 10.1080/15532739.2018.1468293.

27 'NHS standard contract for Gender Identity Development Service for children and adolescents, service specification E13/S(HSS)/e' (April 2016) and American Psychiatric Association, *Diagnostic and Statistical Manual of Mental Disorders* (5th edn; Washington DC: American Psychiatric Publishing, 2013), 302.85:455.

2. The Vision

1 'Italian, obviously': 'Dr Polly Carmichael – developments and dilemmas' [recording of talk at ACAMH conference 'Gender in 2017: meeting the needs of gender diverse children and young people with mental health difficulties', Bristol, 12 October 2017], https://soundcloud.com/user-664361280/dr-polly-carmichael-developments-and-dilemmas; 'for children [...]': Domenico Di Ceglie, 'Castaway's corner', *Clinical Child Psychology and Psychiatry* 7/3 (2002), 487–91, doi: 10.1177/1359104502007003.

2 Ibid.

3 Ibid.

4 R. J. Stoller, 'A contribution to the study of gender identity', *International Journal of Psychoanalysis* 45 (1964), 220–6.

5 Di Ceglie, 'Castaway's corner'.

6 Ibid.

7 Ibid.

8 Domenico Di Ceglie, 'Primary therapeutic aims', in Domenico Di Ceglie and David Freedman (eds), *A Stranger in My Own Body: Atypical Gender Identity Development and Mental Health* (London: Karnac, 1998).

9 Ibid.

10 Glenn Gossling, 'Bernadette Wren: on change', Tavistock and Portman NHS Foundation Trust [website] (2020), https://100years.tavistockandportman.nhs.uk/bernadette-wren-on-change/.

11 Domenico Di Ceglie, 'The use of metaphors in understanding atypical gender identity development and its psychosocial impact' [video of conference held by the Site for Contemporary Psychoanalysis at the Freud Museum, March 2017], YouTube (21 June 2020), https://www.youtube.com/watch?v=nJr0kFe257s.

12 L. Rogers, 'Boys may be girls', *Sunday Times* (4 July 1993).

13 James Cantor, 'Do trans kids stay trans when they grow up?', Sexology Today! [blog] (11 January 2016), http://www.sexologytoday.org/2016/01/do-trans-kids-stay-trans-when-they-grow_99.html.

14 Di Ceglie, 'Castaway's corner'.

15 P. T. Cohen-Kettenis and S. H. van Goozen, 'Sex reassignment of adolescent transsexuals: a follow-up study', *Journal of the American Academy of Child and Adolescent Psychiatry* 36/2 (1997), 263–71, doi: 10.1097/00004583-199702000-00017.

16 D. Di Ceglie, C. Sturge and A. Sutton, *Gender Identity Disorders in Children and Adolescents: Guidelines for Management*, council report CR63 (London: Royal College of Psychiatrists, 1998).

17 For the doubling in referrals, see Domenico Di Ceglie, 'The use of metaphors in understanding atypical gender identity development and its psychosocial impact', *Journal of Child Psychotherapy* 44/1 (2018), 5–28, doi: 10.1080/0075417X.2018.1443151.

18 Di Ceglie and Freedman (eds), *A Stranger in My Own Body*.

19 Di Ceglie, 'The use of metaphors'.

20 Domenico Di Ceglie at al., 'Children and adolescents referred to a specialist gender identity development service: clinical features and demographic characteristics', *International Journal of Transgenderism* 6/1 (2002).

21 Ibid.

22 Ibid.

23 Ibid.

24 Domenico Di Ceglie, 'Gender identity disorder in young people', *Advances in Psychiatric Treatment* 6/6 (2000), 458–66, doi: 10.1192/apt.6.6.458.

25 Di Ceglie at al., 'Children and adolescents referred to a specialist gender identity development service'.

26 'Transgender issues in the light of the High Court ruling', Health Matters [website] (9 December 2020), archived at https://web.archive.org/web/20210515041519/http:/www.healthmatters.org.uk/era-3/transgender-issues-in-the-light-of-the-high-court-ruling/.

27 For psychotherapy, see 'Families and beyond: an introduction to systemic thinking (eCPD94)', Tavistock and Portman NHS Foundation Trust [website], https://tavistockandportman.ac.uk/courses/families-and-beyond-an-introduction-to-systemic-thinking-ecpd94/ and 'Family therapy and systemic research centre', Tavistock and Portman NHS Foundation Trust [website], https://tavistockandportman.nhs.uk/research-and-innovation/research-centres/family-therapy-systemic-research-centre/. For psychoanalytic (or psychodynamic) psychotherapy, see 'Psychoanalytic psychotherapy', Tavistock and Portman NHS Foundation Trust [website], https://tavistockandportman.nhs.uk/care-and-treatment/treatments/psychoanalytic-psychotherapy/.

28 'Portman clinic', Tavistock and Portman NHS Foundation Trust [website], https://tavistockandportman.nhs.uk/care-and-treatment/our-clinical-services/portman-clinic/.

29 David Taylor, 'Report on GIDU review (May–Oct. 2005)' [PDF] (January 2006), https://tavistockandportman.nhs.uk/documents/2248/FOI_20-21117_2005_David_Taylor_Report.pdf.

30 Gossling, 'Bernadette Wren: on change'.

31 Ibid.

32 'An interview with Dr Az Hakeem', Transgender Trend [website] (1 September 2021), https://www.transgendertrend.com/interview-az-hakeem/.

33 Gossling, 'Bernadette Wren: on change'.

34 Clare Dyer, 'Landmark ruling for transsexuals forces Britain to change law', *Guardian* (12 July 2002), https://www.theguardian.com/uk/2002/jul/12/claredyer.

35 Ruth Berkowitz et al., 'Fantasy of transsexuals' [letter], *Guardian* (16 July 2002), https://www.theguardian.com/theguardian/2002/jul/16/guardianletters; Sira Dermen et al., 'The psychiatry of transsexuality' [letter], *Telegraph* (15 July 2002), https://www.telegraph.co.uk/comment/letters/3579186/The-psychiatry-of-transsexuality.html.

36 Ibid.

37 Domenico Di Ceglie, 'Working at the edge', *Neuropsychiatrie de l'enfance et de l'adolescence* 56/6 (2008), 403–6, doi: 10.1016/j.neurenf.2008.06.005 and National Clinical Group meeting, 4 June 2008 (NCG(08/09)47), agenda item 4.3: 'Child and Adolescent Gender Identity Development Service'.

38 Di Ceglie, 'Castaway's corner'.

39 Domenico Di Ceglie and Elizabeth Coates Thümmel, 'An experience of group work with parents of children and adolescents with gender identity disorder', *Clinical Child Psychology and Psychiatry* 11/3 (2006), 387–96, doi: 10.1177/1359104506064983.

40 Di Ceglie, 'Castaway's corner'.

41 'Gender identity issues in children and adolescents', Mermaids [website], archived at https://web.archive.org/web/20000622035655/http:/www.mermaids.freeuk.com/gidca.html.

42 National Clinical Group meeting, 4 June 2008 (NCG(08/09)47), agenda item 4.3: 'Child and Adolescent Gender Identity Development Service'.

43 Berkowitz et al., 'Fantasy of transsexuals'.

44 'Tavistock adult depression study (TADS)', Tavistock and Portman NHS Foundation Trust [website], https://tavistockandportman.nhs.uk/research-and-innovation/our-research/research-projects/tavistock-adult-depression-study-tads/.

45 'Freedom of Information Act 2000 (FOIA) decision notice [ref. FS50881691]' [PDF], Information Commissioner's Office [website] (4 August 2020), https://ico.org.uk/media/action-weve-taken/decision-notices/2020/2618201/fs50881691.pdf. See also Hannah Barnes, 'Children's gender identity clinic concerns go back 15 years', BBC News [website] (1 October 2020), https://www.bbc.co.uk/news/uk-54374165.

46 Taylor, 'Report on GIDU review (May–Oct. 2005)'.

47 Ibid.

48 Ibid.

49 Ibid.

50 Ibid.

51 Ibid.

52 Ibid.

Ellie

1 For phalloplasty and metoidioplasty, see West of England Specialist Gender Identity Clinic, 'Trans man fact sheet', Devon Partnership NHS Trust [website], https://www.dpt.nhs.uk/download/9YvnBWlk62.

3. The Push for Puberty Blockers

1 Jenny Bryan, 'What are little girls made of?', *Independent* (4 February 1996), https://www.independent.co.uk/life-style/what-are-little-girls-made-of-1317192.html.

2 L. Rogers, 'Children of 14 get sex change treatment on NHS', *Sunday Times* (12 October 1997).

3 Bryan, 'What are little girls made of?'

4 Ibid.

5 Rogers, 'Children of 14 get sex change treatment on NHS'.

6 'Dr Domenico Di Ceglie: an interview', Mermaids [website], archived at https://web.archive.org/web/20090926091059/http:/www.mermaidsuk.org.uk/dicegli.html.

7 Terry Reed, 'It's still not easy being a trans child. This is what schools can do to help', *Guardian* (5 June 2017), https://www.theguardian.com/profile/terry-reed; 'Meet the parents who've dedicated their lives to fighting for transgender rights', *Attitude* (8 August 2017), https://attitude.co.uk/article/meet-the-parents-whove-dedicated-their-lives-to-fighting-for-transgender-rights/15580/.

8 Viv Groskop, 'My body is wrong', *Guardian* (14 August 2008), https://www.theguardian.com/society/2008/aug/14/children.youngpeople.

9 Ibid.

10 Annelou L. C. de Vries and Peggy T. Cohen-Kettenis, 'Clinical management of gender dysphoria in children and adolescents: the Dutch approach', *Journal of Homosexuality* 59/3 (2012), 301–20, doi: 10.1080/00918369.2012.653300.

11 P. T. Cohen-Kettenis and S. H. M. van Goozen, 'Pubertal delay as an aid in diagnosis and treatment of a transsexual adolescent', *European Child and Adolescent Psychiatry* 7/4 (December 1998), 246–8, doi: 10.1007/s007870050073.

12 Peggy T. Cohen-Kettenis, Henriette A. Delemarre-van de Waal and Louis J. G. Gooren, 'The treatment of adolescent transsexuals: changing insights', *Journal of Sexual Medicine* 5/8 (2008), 1892–97, doi: 10.1111/j.1743-6109.2008.00870.x.

13 Ibid.

14 Cohen-Kettenis and van Goozen, 'Pubertal delay as an aid in diagnosis and treatment of a transsexual adolescent'.

15 M. W. Ross and J. A. Need, 'Effects of adequacy of gender reassignment surgery on psychological adjustment: a follow-up of fourteen male-to-female patients', *Archives of Sexual Behavior* 18/2 (1989), 145–53, doi: 10.1007/BF01543120.

16 Cohen-Kettenis and van Goozen, 'Pubertal delay as an aid in diagnosis and treatment of a transsexual adolescent'.

17 Ibid.

18 Henriette A. Delemarre-van de Waal and Peggy T. Cohen-Kettenis, 'Clinical management of gender identity disorder in adolescents: a protocol on psychological and paediatric endocrinology aspects', *European Journal of Endocrinology* 155/supp.1 (2006), S131–S137, doi: 10.1530/eje.1.02231.

19 Ibid.

20 'Guidelines for the management of Gender Identity Disorder (GID) in adolescents and children: specific endocrinological recommendations approved by the British Society of Paediatric Endocrinology & Diabetes', BSPED [website] (2005), archived at https://web.archive.org/web/20051214002955/bsped.org.uk/professional/guidelines/docs/BSPEDGIDguidelines.pdf.

21 Ibid.

22 'BSPED "Guidelines for the management of gender identity disorder (GID) in adolescents and children" – a commentary', Gender Identity Research and Education Society [website] (4 October 2014), https://www.gires.org.uk/bsped-guidelines-for-the-management-of-gender-identity-disorder-gid-in-adolescents-and-children-a-commentary/; Catherine Bruton, 'Should I help my 12 year old get a sex change?', *Times* (21 July 2008), https://www.thetimes.co.uk/article/should-i-help-my-12-year-old-get-a-sex-change-rjdp9dhnxqf; Simona Giordano, 'Gender atypical organisation in children and adolescents: ethico-legal issues and a proposal for new guidelines', *International Journal of Children's Rights* 15/3 (2007), 365–90, doi: 10.1163/092755607X262793.

23 Bruton, 'Should I help my 12 year old get a sex change?'

24 Linda Geddes, 'Delaying puberty could help gender-confused teens', *New Scientist* (5 December 2008), https://www.newscientist.com/article/dn16211-delaying-puberty-could-help-gender-confused-teens/#ixzz7IcIcMB4F.

25 R. M. Viner et al., 'Sex on the brain: dilemmas in the endocrine management of children and adolescents with gender identity disorder', *Archives of Disease in Childhood* 90 (2005), A77–A81, doi: 10.1136/adc.2003.039412.

26 'Consensus report on symposium in May 2005', Gender Identity Research and Education Society [website] (1 October 2014), https://www.gires.org.uk/consensus-report-on-symposium-in-may-2005/.

27 'GIRES final report to the Nuffield Foundation', Gender Identity Research and Education Society [website] (1 October 2014), https://www.gires.org.uk/gires-final-report-to-the-nuffield-foundation/.

28 Susie Green, 'Transgender: a mother's story | Susie Green | TEDxTruro', via https://www.youtube.com/watch?v=2ZiVPh12RQY

29 Nikki Murfitt, 'At 16, this girl became the youngest in the world to have a life-changing operation… can you guess what it was?', *Mail Online* (3 November 2012), https://www.dailymail.co.uk/health/article-2227381/At-16-girl-youngest-world-life-changing-operation-guess-was.html.

30 For the early data from the Dutch team, see Delemarre-van de Waal and Cohen-Kettenis, 'Clinical management of gender identity disorder in adolescents'.

31 Ibid.

32 Ibid.

33 Domenico Di Ceglie, 'Working at the edge', *Neuropsychiatrie de l'enfance et de l'adolescence* 56/6 (2008), 403–6, doi: 10.1016/j.neurenf.2008.06.005.

34 Domenico Di Ceglie, 'The use of metaphors in understanding atypical gender identity development and its psychosocial impact', *Journal of Child Psychotherapy* 44/1 (2018), 5–28, doi: 10.1080/0075417X.2018.1443151.

35 Di Ceglie, 'Working at the edge'.

36 Ibid.

37 Di Ceglie, 'The use of metaphors'.

38 Ibid.

39 For the UK's 'unethical' position, see S. Giordano, 'Lives in a chiaroscuro. Should we suspend the puberty of children with gender identity disorder?', *Journal of Medical Ethics* 34/8 (2008), 580–4, doi: 10.1136/jme.2007.021097. For illegitimate arguments about consent, see Giordano, 'Gender atypical organisation in children and adolescents'.

40 'The early intervention study', GIDS [website], https://gids.nhs.uk/our-early-intervention-study, archived at http://web.archive.org/web/20200206071156/https://gids.nhs.uk/our-early-intervention-study.

41 Richard Green, 'Young transsexuals should be allowed to put puberty on hold', *Guardian* (28 August 2008), https://www.theguardian.com/commentisfree/2008/aug/28/sexeducation.gayrights.

42 'The early intervention study', GIDS [website].

43 Groskop, 'My body is wrong'.

44 For the review of the 2005 guidelines, see Fionnuala Bourke, 'Youngsters tried to commit suicide when denied sex change drugs by Brit doctors', *Sunday Mercury* [Birmingham newspaper] (27 January 2008).

45 British Society of Paediatric Endocrinology and Diabetes, 'Statement on the management of gender identity disorder (GID) in children and adolescents' [PDF] (2009), archived at http://web.archive.org/web/20100525095817_if/http://www.bsped.org.uk:80/professional/guidelines/docs/BSPEDStatementOnTheManagementOfGID.pdf.

46 Di Ceglie, 'The use of metaphors'.

4. Early Intervention

1 Russell Viner, 'Early pubertal suppression in a carefully selected group of adolescents with gender identity disorder' [proposal submitted to Central London Research Ethics Committee (REC) 1, 14 July 2010; no. 10/H0718/62].

2 Ibid.

3 Minutes of the meeting of Central London Research Ethics Committee (REC) 1 held on 25 August 2010 at the Association of Anaesthetists.

4 'The early intervention study', GIDS [website], https://gids.nhs.uk/our-early-intervention-study, archived at http://web.archive.org/web/20200206071156/https://gids.nhs.uk/our-early-intervention-study.

5 Viner, 'Early pubertal suppression in a carefully selected group of adolescents with gender identity disorder' [proposal, 14 July 2010].

6 Letter from chair of Central London REC 1 to researchers based at UCL Institute of Child Health, 6 September 2010, accessed via Health Research Authority FOI response 1819/FOI/070, 3 April 2019 (not available online).

7 D. Mul et al., 'Psychological assessments before and after treatment of early puberty in adopted children', *Acta Pædiatrica* 90/9 (2001), 965–71, doi: 10.1111/j.1651-2227.2001.tb01349.x.

8 Viner, 'Early pubertal suppression in a carefully selected group of adolescents with gender identity disorder' [proposal, 14 July 2010].

9 Ibid. Viner later wrote that 'we know of three or four cases, but there might be more' (letter from Russell Viner to chair of Central London Research Ethics Committee (REC) 2, November 2010).

10 Dominic Wilkinson and Julian Savulescu, 'Puberty-blocking drugs: the difficulties of conducting ethical research', The Conversation [website] (25 July 2019), https://theconversation.com/puberty-blocking-drugs-the-difficulties-of-conducting-ethical-research-120906.

11 Minutes of the meeting of Central London Research Ethics Committee (REC) 1 held on 25 August 2010 at the Association of Anaesthetists.

12 Letter from chair of Central London REC 1 to researchers based at UCL Institute of Child Health, 6 September 2010, accessed via Health Research Authority FOI response 1819/FOI/070, 3 April 2019 (not available online).

13 Ibid.

14 Deborah Cohen and Hannah Barnes, 'Gender dysphoria in children: puberty blockers study draws further criticism', *BMJ* 366/l5647 (20 September 2019), doi: 10.1136/bmj.l5647. For the unaltered research application, see Russell Viner, 'Early pubertal suppression in a carefully selected group of adolescents with gender identity disorder' [proposal submitted to Central London Research Ethics Committee (REC) 2, 5 November 2010; no. 10/H0713/79].

15 Letter from Russell Viner to chair of Central London Research Ethics Committee (REC) 2, November 2010.

16 Ibid. See also Carl Heneghan and Tom Jefferson, 'Gender-affirming hormone in children and adolescents', BMJ EBM Spotlight [blog] (25 February 2019), https://blogs.bmj.com/bmjebmspotlight/2019/02/25/gender-affirming-hormone-in-children-and-adolescents-evidence-review/, archived at http://web.archive.org/web/20220820092837/https://blogs.bmj.com/bmjebmspotlight/2019/02/25/gender-affirming-hormone-in-children-and-adolescents-evidence-review/; National Institute for Health and Care Excellence, 'Evidence review: gonadotrophin releasing hormone analogues for children and adolescents with gender dysphoria' [PDF], Cass Review [website] (2020), https://cass.independent-review.uk/wp-content/uploads/2022/09/20220726_Evidence-review_GnRH-analogues_For-upload_Final.pdf, archived at https://web.archive.org/web/20220414202655/https://arms.nice.org.uk/resources/hub/1070905/attachment.

17 Cohen and Barnes, 'Gender dysphoria in children'.

18 Ibid.

19 Russell Viner et al., 'Research protocol: an evaluation of early pubertal suppression in a carefully selected group of adolescents with Gender Identity Disorder (version 1.2)' (3 July 2012).

20 Ibid.

21 Henriette A. Delemarre-van de Waal and Peggy T. Cohen-Kettenis, 'Clinical management of gender identity disorder in adolescents: a protocol on psychological and paediatric endocrinology aspects', *European Journal of Endocrinology* 155/supp.1 (2006), S131–S137, doi: 10.1530/eje.1.02231.

22 Viner et al., 'Research protocol'.

23 Ibid.

24 Ibid.

25 Delemarre-van de Waal and Cohen-Kettenis, 'Clinical management of gender identity disorder in adolescents'.

26 Ibid.

27 Annelou L. C. de Vries et al., 'Puberty suppression in adolescents with gender identity disorder: a prospective follow-up study', *Journal of Sexual Medicine* 8/8 (August 2011; published online July 2010), 2276–83, doi: 10.1111/j.1743-6109.2010.01943.x.

28 Deborah Cohen and Hannah Barnes, 'Transgender treatment: puberty blockers study under investigation', BBC News [website] (22 July 2019), https://www.bbc.co.uk/news/health-49036145; 'Transgender treatment: Puberty blockers study under investigation' [video], *Newsnight*, BBC (23 July 2019), https://www.youtube.com/watch?v=1bIt5MQIozc.

29 Cohen and Barnes, 'Gender dysphoria in children'.

30 Michael Biggs, 'The Tavistock's experiment with puberty blockers' [PDF] (29 July 2019), https://users.ox.ac.uk/~sfos0060/Biggs_ExperimentPubertyBlockers.pdf; 'it is argued that [...]': Viner, 'Early pubertal suppression in a carefully selected group of adolescents with gender identity disorder' [proposal, 5 November 2010].

31 'Consensus report on symposium in May 2005', Gender Identity Research and Education Society [website] (1 October 2014), https://www.gires.org.uk/consensus-report-on-symposium-in-may-2005/.

32 'Investigation into the study "Early pubertal suppression in a carefully selected group of adolescents with gender identity disorders"', Health Research Authority [website] (14 October 2019), https://www.hra.nhs.uk/about-us/governance/feedback-raising-concerns/investigation-study-early-pubertal-suppression-carefully-selected-group-adolescents-gender-identity-disorders/.

33 Deborah Cohen and Hannah Barnes, 'Questions remain over puberty-blockers, as review clears study', BBC News [website] (15 October 2019), via https://www.bbc.co.uk/news/health-50046579.

34 Peggy T. Cohen-Kettenis et al., 'Puberty suppression in a gender-dysphoric adolescent: a 22-year follow-up', *Archives of Sexual Behavior* 40/4 (August 2011), 843–7, doi: 10.1007/s10508-011-9758-9.

35 'The early intervention study', GIDS [website]. Professor Russell Viner explained to the author that he wrote this document.

36 Cohen-Kettenis et al., 'Puberty suppression in a gender-dysphoric adolescent'.

37 The Dutch team have indicated that they will be publishing more long-term follow-up data in the years ahead. See Annelou L. C. de Vries, 'Ensuring care for transgender adolescents who need it: response to "reconsidering informed consent for trans-identified children, adolescents and young adults"', *Journal of Sex and Marital Therapy* (2022), doi: 10.1080/0092623X.2022.2084479.

38 de Vries et al., 'Puberty suppression in adolescents with gender identity disorder'.

39 Ibid.

5. A New Era

1 Russell Viner, 'Early pubertal suppression in a carefully selected group of adolescents with gender identity disorder' [proposal submitted to Central London Research Ethics Committee (REC) 2, 5 November 2010; no. 10/H0713/79].

2 National Clinical Group meeting, 4 June 2008 (NCG(08/09)47), agenda item 4.3: 'Child and Adolescent Gender Identity Development Service'.

3 Psychiatrists can prescribe medication and psychologists cannot. Psychiatrists are also medically trained, and – generally speaking – the use of medication is more fundamental to their work. However, the child and adolescent psychiatrist's function at GIDS was not to prescribe. The author has been unable to answer definitively why there was always one present on the team.

4 Natasha Prescott, exit interview with GIDS, 7 February 2018.

5 According to Michael First, co-chair of the 'revision subcommittee' and DSM-5-TR editor, and others, the text revision reflected the 'evolving terminology in the area of gender dysphoria. "Desired gender" is replaced with "experienced gender"; "natal male/natal female" with "individual assigned male at birth" or "individual assigned female at birth"; and "cross-sex treatment regimen" with "gender-affirming treatment regimen".' See Michael B. First et al., 'DSM-5-TR: overview of what's new and what's changed', *World Psychiatry* 21 (2022), 218–19, doi: 10.1002/wps.20989.

6 Kenneth J. Zucker, 'The DSM-5 diagnostic criteria for gender dysphoria', in Carlo Trombetta, Giovanni Liguori and Michele Bertolotto (eds), *Management of Gender Dysphoria* (Milan: Springer, 2015), 33–37, doi: 10.1007/978-88-470-5696-1_4.

7 Ibid.

8 For outdated gender stereotypes, see ibid.

9 Brandé Flamez, Jason H. King and Joshua D. Francis, 'Conceptualizing DSM-5 disorders in children and adolescents', in Brandé Flamez and Carl J. Sheperis (eds), *Diagnosing and Treating Children and Adolescents: A Guide for Mental Health Professionals* (Hoboken, NJ: John Wiley, 2016), 3–27.

10 Zucker, 'The DSM-5 diagnostic criteria for gender dysphoria'.

6. All Change

1 Niccie Le Roux, 'Gender variance in childhood/adolescence: gender identity journeys not involving physical intervention' [prof. doc. thesis, University of East London School of Psychology] (2013), doi: 10.15123/PUB.3493.

2 'Puberty', NHS 111 Wales [website], https://111.wales.nhs.uk/Puberty/.

3 Sanchez Manning and Stephen Adams, 'NHS to give sex change drugs to nine-year-olds: clinic accused of "playing God" with treatment that stops puberty', *Daily Mail* (18 May 2014), https://www.dailymail.co.uk/news/article-2631472/NHS-sex-change-drugs-nine-year-olds-Clinic-accused-playing-God-treatment-stops-puberty.html.

4 'NHS standard contract for Gender Identity Development Service for children and adolescents, service specification E13/S(HSS)/e' [PDF], NHS England [website] (April 2016), https://www.england.nhs.uk/wp-content/uploads/2017/04/gender-development-service-children-adolescents.pdf.

5 Deborah Cohen and Hannah Barnes, 'Transgender treatment: puberty blockers study under investigation', BBC News [website] (22 July 2019), https://www.bbc.co.uk/news/health-49036145

6 For the date of April 2014, see 'Investigation into the study "Early pubertal suppression in a carefully selected group of adolescents with gender identity disorders"', Health Research Authority [website] (14 October 2019), https://www.hra.nhs.uk/about-us/governance/feedback-raising-concerns/investigation-study-early-pubertal-suppression-carefully-selected-group-adolescents-gender-identity-disorders/.

7 Tavistock and Portman NHS Foundation Trust FOI 19-20108 (not published but shared via private correspondence).

8 Tavistock and Portman NHS Foundation Trust FOI 19-20155 ('Subject: GIDS ethical approval protocol'), https://tavistockandportman.nhs.uk/documents/1691/FOI_19-20155_GIDS_Ethical_Approval_Protocol-2.pdf.

9 NHS England FOI-059870 (shared via private correspondence).

10 'Standards of care for the health of transsexual, transgender, and gender-nonconforming people [version 7]' [PDF], WPATH [website], https://www.wpath.org/media/cms/Documents/SOC%20v7/SOC%20V7_English2012.pdf?_t=1613669341.

11 Jonathan Leake, 'NHS helps children choose their sex', *Sunday Times* (17 November 2013), https://www.thetimes.co.uk/article/nhs-helps-children-choose-their-sex-r3vw0fx9r38.

12 Annelou L. C. de Vries et al., 'Young adult psychological outcome after puberty suppression and gender reassignment', *Pediatrics* 134/4 (October 2014), 696–704, doi: 10.1542/peds.2013-2958.

13 Russell Viner et al., 'Research protocol: an evaluation of early pubertal suppression in a carefully selected group of adolescents with Gender Identity Disorder (version 1.2)' (3 July 2012).

14 de Vries et al., 'Young adult psychological outcome after puberty suppression and gender reassignment'.

15 T. D. Steensma et al., 'The Utrecht gender dysphoria scale: a validation study', in T. D. Steensma (ed.), *From Gender Variance to Gender Dysphoria: Psychosexual Development of Gender Atypical Children and Adolescents* (Amsterdam: Ridderprint, 2013), 41–56.

16 Annelou L. C. de Vries et al., 'Puberty suppression in adolescents with gender identity disorder: a prospective follow-up study', *Journal of Sexual Medicine* 8/8 (August 2011; published online July 2010), 2276–83, doi: 10.1111/j.1743-6109.2010.01943.x.

17 Stephen B. Levine, E. Abbruzzese and Julia W. Mason, 'Reconsidering informed consent for trans-identified children, adolescents, and young adults', *Journal of Sex and Marital Therapy* (17 March 2022), 1–22, doi: 10.1080/0092623X.2022.2046221. For the positive results, see de Vries et al., 'Young adult psychological outcome after puberty suppression and gender reassignment'.

18 Annelou L. C. de Vries, 'Ensuring care for transgender adolescents who need it: response to "reconsidering informed consent for trans-identified children, adolescents and young adults"', *Journal of Sex and Marital Therapy* (2022), doi: 10.1080/0092623X.2022.2084479.

19 'Board of directors (part one): agenda and papers of a meeting to be held in public 2.00 p.m.–4.20 p.m. Tuesday 24th February 2015' [PDF], Tavistock and Portman NHS Foundation Trust [website], https://tavistockandportman.nhs.uk/documents/190/board-papers-2015-02.pdf.

20 Domenico Di Ceglie, 'The use of metaphors in understanding atypical gender identity development and its psychosocial impact', *Journal of Child Psychotherapy* 44/1 (2018), 5–28, doi: 10.1080/0075417X.2018.1443151.

21 'Written evidence submitted by Polly Carmichael to the Transgender Equality Inquiry' [PDF], Parliament.uk [website] (21 August 2015), http://data.parliament.uk/writtenevidence/committeeevidence.svc/evidencedocument/women-and-equalities-committee/transgender-equality/written/19794.pdf.

22 Domenico Di Ceglie at al., 'Children and adolescents referred to a specialist gender identity development service: clinical features and demographic characteristics', *International Journal of Transgenderism* 6/1 (2002).

23 Tavistock and Portman NHS Foundation Trust FOI 16-17147 and 16-17126 ('Subject: GIDS referrals April 2011 to March 2016'), https://tavistockandportman.nhs.uk/documents/876/FOI_16-17147_GIDS_Referrals_Stats_04.2011_to_03.2016_V9U0I6Q.pdf.

24 'Referrals to GIDS, financial years 2015–16 to 2019–20', GIDS [website] (20 April 2020), archived at https://web.archive.org/web/20200701000226/https://gids.nhs.uk/number-referrals.

25 'Referrals to GIDS, financial years 2010–11 to 2021–22', GIDS [website] (7 June 2022), https://gids.nhs.uk/about-us/number-of-referrals/, archived at https://web.archive.org/web/20221002200800/https://gids.nhs.uk/about-us/number-of-referrals/.

26 'Referrals to GIDS, financial years 2010–11 to 2021–22', GIDS [website] (3 May 2021), https://gids.nhs.uk/professionals/number-of-referrals/, captured April 2022 and archived at http://web.archive.org/web/20220415225720/https:/gids.nhs.uk/professionals/number-of-referrals/.

27 Di Ceglie et al., 'Children and adolescents referred to a specialist gender identity development service'.

28 Vicky Holt, Elin Skagerberg and Michael Dunsford, 'Young people with features of gender dysphoria: demographics and associated difficulties', *Clinical Child Psychology and Psychiatry* 21/1 (January 2016), 108–18, doi: 10.1177/1359104514558431.

29 'Main findings: children's social care in England 2021', Gov.uk [website] (30 March 2022), https://www.gov.uk/government/statistics/childrens-social-care-data-in-england-2021/main-findings-childrens-social-care-in-england-2021.

30 Ibid.

31 Jos Twist and Nastasja M. de Graaf, 'Gender diversity and non-binary presentations in young people attending the United Kingdom's National Gender

Identity Development Service', *Clinical Child Psychology and Psychiatry* 24/2 (April 2019), 277–90, doi: 10.1177/1359104518804311.

32 'Dr Polly Carmichael – developments and dilemmas' [recording of talk at ACAMH conference 'Gender in 2017: meeting the needs of gender diverse children and young people with mental health difficulties', Bristol, 12 October 2017], https://soundcloud.com/user-664361280/dr-polly-carmichael-developments-and-dilemmas.

33 Thomas D. Steensma, 'Desisting and persisting gender dysphoria after childhood: a qualitative follow-up study', *Clinical Child Psychology and Psychiatry* 16/4 (October 2011), 499–516, doi: 10.1177/1359104510378303.

34 Jenny Kleeman, 'Transgender children: "This is who he is – I have to respect that"', *Guardian* (12 September 2015), https://www.theguardian.com/society/2015/sep/12/transgender-children-have-to-respect-who-he-is.

35 Ben Machell, 'The transgender kids', *Times* (13 May 2016), https://www.thetimes.co.uk/article/the-transgender-kids-9wr82hhng.

36 Ibid.

37 For the study, see Kristina R. Olson et al., 'Gender identity 5 years after social transition', *Pediatrics* 150/2 (2022), e2021056082, doi: 10.1542/peds.2021-056082.

38 'The Cass Review: independent review of gender identity services for children and young people: interim report' [PDF], Cass Review [website] (February 2022), https://cass.independent-review.uk/wp-content/uploads/2022/03/Cass-Review-Interim-Report-Final-Web-Accessible.pdf.

39 de Vries et al., 'Young adult psychological outcome after puberty suppression and gender reassignment'.

40 Bernadette Wren, in Women and Equalities Committee, 'Oral evidence: Transgender Equality Inquiry, HC 390' [PDF], Parliament.uk [website] (15 September 2015), http://data.parliament.uk/writtenevidence/committeeevidence.svc/evidencedocument/women-and-equalities-committee/transgender-equality/oral/21638.pdf.

41 'Written evidence submitted by Polly Carmichael to the Transgender Equality Inquiry'.

42 Ibid.

43 Bernadette Wren, in Women and Equalities Committee, 'Oral evidence: Transgender Equality Inquiry, HC 390'.

44 'Written evidence submitted by Polly Carmichael to the Transgender Equality Inquiry'.

45 'Board of directors (part one): agenda and papers of a meeting to be held in public 2.00 p.m.–4.40 p.m. Tuesday 23rd June 2015' [PDF], Tavistock and Portman NHS Foundation Trust [website], https://tavistockandportman.nhs.uk/documents/142/board-papers-2015-06.pdf.

46 'Board of directors (part one): agenda and papers of a meeting to be held in public 2.00 p.m.–4.30 p.m. Tuesday 28th July 2015' [PDF], Tavistock and Portman NHS Foundation Trust [website], https://tavistockandportman.nhs.uk/documents/143/board-papers-2015-07.pdf.

47 Madison Aitken et al., 'Evidence for an altered sex ratio in clinic-referred adolescents with gender dysphoria', *Journal of Sexual Medicine* 12/3 (2015),

756–63, doi: 10.1111/jsm.12817; Kenneth J. Zucker, 'Epidemiology of gender dysphoria and transgender identity', *Sex Health* 14/5 (October 2017), 404–11, doi: 10.1071/SH17067.

48 Riittakerttu Kaltiala-Heino et al., 'Two years of gender identity service for minors: overrepresentation of natal girls with severe problems in adolescent development', *Child and Adolescent Psychiatry and Mental Health* 9/9 (2015), doi: 10.1186/s13034-015-0042-y.

49 Ibid. For the Dutch study, see Annelou L. C. de Vries, 'Psychiatric comorbidity in gender dysphoric adolescents', *Journal of Child Psychology and Psychiatry* 52/11 (2011), 1195–202, doi: 10.1111/j.1469-7610.2011.02426.x.

50 Ibid.

51 Melissa Midgen to Polly Carmichael [email], July 2015.

52 Tavistock and Portman NHS Foundation Trust FOI 19-20154 ('Subject: the number of people working at the Charring Cross GIC and the GIDS 2012–19'), https://tavistockandportman.nhs.uk/documents/1690/FOI_19-20154_The_Number_of_People_Working_at_GIC__GIDS_2012-19.pdf.

53 Tavistock and Portman NHS Foundation Trust FOI 20-21180 ('Subject: GIDS funding & referrals to 17 December 2020'), https://tavistockandportman.nhs.uk/documents/2219/FOI_20-21180_GIDS_Funding__Referrals_to_17.12.20.pdf; 'Tavistock and Portman NHS Foundation Trust annual report and accounts 2015/16' [PDF], Tavistock and Portman NHS Foundation Trust [website], https://tavistockandportman.nhs.uk/documents/409/tavistock-portman-annual-report-2015-16.pdf; 'Tavistock and Portman NHS Foundation Trust annual report and accounts 2016/17' [PDF], Tavistock and Portman NHS Foundation Trust [website], https://tavistockandportman.nhs.uk/documents/707/tavistock-portman-annual-report-2016-17.pdf.

54 'I am Leo', Tavistock and Portman NHS Foundation Trust [website] (21 November 2014), https://tavistockandportman.nhs.uk/about-us/news/stories/i-am-leo/; 'Kids on the edge: the gender clinic', Tavistock and Portman NHS Foundation Trust [website], https://tavistockandportman.nhs.uk/about-us/kids-edge-channel-4-documentary/kids-edge-gender-clinic/.

55 'Board of directors (part one): agenda and papers of a meeting to be held in public 2.00 p.m.–4.00 p.m. Tuesday 25th October 2016' [PDF], Tavistock and Portman NHS Foundation Trust [website], https://tavistockandportman.nhs.uk/documents/439/board-papers-october-2016.pdf; 'Board of directors (part one): agenda and papers of a meeting to be held in public 2.00 p.m.–4.30 p.m. Tuesday 29th November 2016' [PDF], Tavistock and Portman NHS Foundation Trust [website], https://tavistockandportman.nhs.uk/documents/454/board-papers-november-2016.pdf; 'Board of directors (part one): agenda and papers of a meeting to be held in public 2.00 p.m.–4.30 p.m. Tuesday 23rd May 2017' [PDF], Tavistock and Portman NHS Foundation Trust [website], https://tavistockandportman.nhs.uk/documents/705/May_2017_Boardpack_Part_1.pdf.

56 'Letter in response to *The Observer* editorial on the Cass Review', Tavistock and Portman NHS Foundation Trust [website] (28 March 2022), https://tavistockandportman.nhs.uk/about-us/news/stories/letter-in-response-to-theobserver-editorial-on-the-cass-review/; 'Letters: Britain should knuckle down and embrace the boring', *Guardian* (27 March 2022), https://www.theguardian.com/theobserver/commentisfree/2022/mar/27/letters-britain-should-knuckle-down-embrace-boring.

57 'The Cass Review: independent review of gender identity services for children and young people: interim report'.

58 Trilby Langton, Bernadette Wren and Polly Carmichael, 'Seeing the child in context: supporting gender diverse children and their families in multiple ways – an introduction to this special edition', *Clinical Child Psychology and Psychiatry* 24/2 (April 2019), 199–202, doi: 10.1177/1359104518800143.

59 Cal Horton, '"It felt like they were trying to destabilise us": parent assessment in UK children's gender services', *International Journal of Transgender Health* (2021), doi: 10.1080/26895269.2021.2004569.

60 Cal Horton, '"Of course, I'm intimidated by them. They could take my human rights away": trans children's experiences with UK gender clinics', *Bulletin of Applied Transgender Studies* 1/1–2 (2022), 47–70, doi: 10.57814/20hf-7n94; Anna Carlile, 'The experiences of transgender and non-binary children and young people and their parents in healthcare settings in England, UK: interviews with members of a family support group', *International Journal of Transgender Health* 21/1 (2020), 16–32, doi: 10.1080/15532739.2019.1693472; Anna Carlile, Ethan Butteriss and Annie Pullen Sansfaçon, '"It's like my kid came back overnight": experiences of trans and non-binary young people and their families seeking, finding and engaging with clinical care in England', *International Journal of Transgender Health* 22/4 (2021), 412–24, doi: 10.1080/26895269.2020.1870188.

61 Bernadette Wren in Women and Equalities Committee, 'Oral evidence: Transgender Equality Inquiry, HC 390'.

62 Ibid.

63 Ibid.

64 Ibid.

65 Tavistock and Portman NHS Foundation Trust FOI 16-17200 ('Subject: Gender Identify Development Service (GIDS) waiting times and treatments'), https://tavistockandportman.nhs.uk/documents/736/FOI_16-17200_Gender_Identity_Development_Service_-_GIDS_-_Waiting_Times__Treatments.pdf.

66 Originally reported in Andrew Gilligan, 'Parents' anger as child sex change charity Mermaids puts private emails online', *Sunday Times* (16 June 2019), https://www.thetimes.co.uk/article/parents-anger-as-child-sex-change-charity-puts-private-emails-online-3tntlwqln.

67 'NHS standard contract for Gender Identity Development Service for children and adolescents, service specification E13/S(HSS)/e' (April 2016).

68 'NHS standard contract for Gender Identity Development Service for children and adolescents, service specification E13/S(HSS)/e' [PDF], Gender Identity Research and Education Society [website] (2013), https://www.gires.org.uk/wp-content/uploads/2015/01/Existing-GID-Service-for-Children-and-Adolescents-Service-Specification.pdf.

69 Transcript of Dinesh Sinha's interview with Anastassis Spiliadis ('BD007') (7 January 2019).

70 Transcript of Dinesh Sinha's interview with Matt Bristow ('BD016') (7 January 2019).

71 Ibid.

72 Transcript of Dinesh Sinha's interview with Anastassis Spiliadis ('BD007') (7 January 2019).

73 Ibid.

74 Dinesh Sinha, 'A review in to [*sic*] concerns raised about the Gender Identity Development Service' ['Annex A' of *GIDS Review Action Plan*, 26 March 2019] (February 2019), https://tavistockandportman.nhs.uk/documents/1376/GIDS_Action_plan_review.pdf.

75 'Gender Identity Development Service leaflet (GIDS): information for parents' [leaflet still being provided in April 2015], available via Tavistock and Portman NHS Foundation Trust FOI 21-22046 ('Subject: patient information leaflet 2015'), https://tavistockandportman.nhs.uk/documents/2585/21-22046_Patient_information_leaflet_2015.pdf.

76 For the service specification, see 'NHS standard contract for Gender Identity Development Service for children and adolescents, service specification E13/S(HSS)/e' (April 2016).

77 Kleeman, 'Transgender children: "This is who he is – I have to respect that"'.

7. The Bombshell

1 Hannah Barnes, 'The crisis at the Tavistock's child gender clinic', BBC News [website] (30 March 2021), via https://www.bbc.co.uk/news/uk-56539466.

2 Femi Nzegwu, 'GIDS report on sustainable working' (2015). Supplied to the author privately.

3 Tavistock and Portman NHS Foundation Trust FOI 19-20154 ('Subject: the number of people working at the Charring Cross GIC and the GIDS 2012–19'), https://tavistockandportman.nhs.uk/documents/1690/FOI_19-20154_The_Number_of_People_Working_at_GIC__GIDS_2012-19.pdf.

4 Ibid.

5 Ibid.

6 Bernadette Wren, 'Epistemic injustice', *London Review of Books* 43/23 (2 December 2021), https://www.lrb.co.uk/the-paper/v43/n23/bernadette-wren/diary.

7 Ibid.

8 Barnes, 'The crisis at the Tavistock's child gender clinic'.

9 'NHS standard contract for Gender Identity Development Service for children and adolescents, service specification E13/S(HSS)/e' [PDF], NHS England [website] (April 2016), https://www.england.nhs.uk/wp-content/uploads/2017/04/gender-development-service-children-adolescents.pdf.

10 'Board of directors (part one): agenda and papers of a meeting to be held in public 2.00 p.m.–4.30 p.m. Tuesday 23rd May 2017' [PDF], Tavistock and Portman NHS Foundation Trust [website], https://tavistockandportman.nhs.uk/documents/705/May_2017_Boardpack_Part_1.pdf.

11 Ibid.

12 Polly Carmichael, 'Time to reflect: gender dysphoria in children and adolescents, defining best practice in a fast changing context' [conference paper presented at WPATH symposium, Amsterdam, 18 June 2016], https://av-media.vu.nl/mediasite/Play/581e58c338984dafb455c72c56c0bfa31d?.

13 Ibid.

14 'Board of directors (part one): agenda and papers of a meeting to be held in public 2.00 p.m.–4.40 p.m. Tuesday 23rd June 2015' [PDF], Tavistock and Portman NHS Foundation Trust [website], https://tavistockandportman.nhs.uk/documents/142/board-papers-2015-06.pdf.

15 For the significant increase in those answering the statement 'I deliberately try to hurt or kill myself', see Deborah Cohen and Hannah Barnes, 'Transgender treatment: puberty blockers study under investigation', BBC News [website] (22 July 2019), https://www.bbc.co.uk/news/health-49036145; Michael Biggs, 'The Tavistock's experiment with puberty blockers' [PDF] (29 July 2019), https://users.ox.ac.uk/~sfos0060/Biggs_ExperimentPubertyBlockers.pdf.

16 'Board of directors (part one): agenda and papers of a meeting to be held in public 2.00 p.m.–4.40 p.m. Tuesday 23rd June 2015'.

17 Cohen and Barnes, 'Transgender treatment: puberty blockers study under investigation'.

18 Carmichael, 'Time to reflect' [slide 28].

19 Ibid.

20 Harriet Gunn et al., 'G470 early medical treatment of gender dysphoria: baseline characteristics of a UK cohort beginning early intervention', *Archives of Disease in Childhood* 100/supp.3 (2015), A198–A198, doi: 10.1136/archdischild-2015-308599.424.

21 Rosalia Costa, 'Psychological support, puberty suppression, and psychosocial functioning in adolescents with gender dysphoria', *Journal of Sexual Medicine* 12/11 (November 2015), 2206–14, doi: 10.1111/jsm.13034.

22 Carmichael, 'Time to reflect' [slide 28].

23 Ibid.

24 'NHS standard contract for Gender Identity Development Service for children and adolescents, service specification E13/S(HSS)/e' (April 2016).

25 Hannah Barnes and Deborah Cohen, 'Tavistock puberty blocker study published after nine years', BBC News [website] (11 December 2020), https://www.bbc.co.uk/news/uk-55282113.

26 *Bell v Tavistock* [2020] EWHC 3274 (Admin) [PDF] (1 December 2020), https://www.judiciary.uk/wp-content/uploads/2020/12/Bell-v-Tavistock-Judgment.pdf.

27 Polly Carmichael et al., 'Short-term outcomes of pubertal suppression in a selected cohort of 12 to 15 year old young people with persistent gender dysphoria in the UK', *PLoS ONE* 16/2 (2021), e0243894, doi: 10.1371/journal.pone.0243894.

28 *Bell v Tavistock* [2020] EWHC 3274 (Admin).

29 For the High Court's rejection of the first assertion, see ibid. For the Court of Appeal ruling, see *Bell & Anor v The Tavistock and Portman NHS Foundation*

Trust [2021] EWCA Civ 1363 (17 September 2021), https://www.bailii.org/ew/cases/EWCA/Civ/2021/1363.html.

30 Laura E. Kuper, 'Body dissatisfaction and mental health outcomes of youth on gender-affirming hormone therapy', *Pediatrics* 145/4 (2020), e20193006, doi: 10.1542/peds.2019-3006; Tessa Brik et al., 'Trajectories of adolescents treated with gonadotropin-releasing hormone analogues for gender dysphoria', *Archives of Sexual Behavior* 49/7 (2020), 2611–18, doi: 10.1007/s10508-020-01660-8.

31 Barnes and Cohen, 'Tavistock puberty blocker study published after nine years'.

32 The GIDS/UCLH researchers found no psychological benefit when using quantitative measures, which are more generalisable than qualitative measures based on individual experience. Both approaches have their merits, but here they appeared to be pulling in opposite directions. The quantitative data do not support the qualitative data.

33 Carmichael et al., 'Short-term outcomes of pubertal suppression'.

34 For the earlier findings presented to the board, see 'Board of directors (part one): agenda and papers of a meeting to be held in public 2.00 p.m.–4.40 p.m. Tuesday 23rd June 2015'.

35 Carmichael et al., 'Short-term outcomes of pubertal suppression'.

36 'Our research and staff publications', GIDS [website] (May 2022), https://gids.nhs.uk/research/, archived at https://web.archive.org/web/20220526120551/https://gids.nhs.uk/research/.

37 James Bellringer personal website: GenderXchange [website], http://www.genderxchange.com/styled/index.html.

38 'Consensus report on symposium in May 2005', Gender Identity Research and Education Society [website] (1 October 2014), https://www.gires.org.uk/consensus-report-on-symposium-in-may-2005/.

39 Melissa Midgen, 'The problem with early hormonal intervention and feminising genital reconstruction in natal males' [proposed information leaflet].

40 Ibid.

41 Ibid.

42 Internal personal email.

8. How to Cope

1 Anna Hutchinson, contemporaneous handwritten note.

2 Melissa Midgen to senior team [email; subject: 're Tuesday meeting aftermath…'], 9 February 2016.

3 Polly Carmichael [email; subject: 're Tuesday meeting aftermath…'], 9 February 2016.

4 Sarah Davidson and Helen Eracleous, 'The gender identity development service: examples of multi-agency working', *Clinical Psychology Forum* 201 (2009), 46–50.

5 Bernadette Wren, 'Making up people: understanding gender non-conformity of childhood as both biologically grounded and socially constructed' [talk presented at the first biennial conference of the European Professional Association For Transgender Health: 'Transgender health care in Europe', Ghent, Belgium, 14 March 2015].

6 'Evidence base', GIDS [website], https://gids.nhs.uk/evidence-base.

7 Tavistock and Portman NHS Foundation Trust FOI 18-19180 ('Subject: Gender Identity Development Service (GIDS) patients suicide data'), https://tavistockandportman.nhs.uk/documents/1253/FOI_18-19180_GIDS_Patients_Suicide_Data.pdf, archived at https://web.archive.org/web/20220419161833/https://trustsrv-io-tavistock-tenant-mediabucket-jxlat5oi107p.s3.amazonaws.com/media/documents/FOI_18-19180_GIDS_Patients_Suicide_Data.pdf?X-Amz-Algorithm=AWS4-HMAC-SHA256&X-Amz-Credential=AKIASPFGSFA5MV75PZDY%2F20220419%2Feu-west-2%2Fs3%2Faws4_request&X-Amz-Date=20220419T161833Z&X-Amz-Expires=3600&X-Amz-SignedHeaders=host&X-Amz-Signature=6543e34d0cbcdd920388ddf71a3ce883a9810c28e0b3806673b9c88fd7a0027d and Tavistock and Portman NHS Foundation Trust FOI 19-20375 ('Subject: GIDS suicide rate 2018/19 & 2019/20'), https://tavistockandportman.nhs.uk/documents/2741/FOI_19-20375_GIDS_suicide_rate_2018-19__2019-20.pdf.

8 'Board of directors (part one): agenda and papers of a meeting to be held in public Tuesday 30th March 2021' [PDF], Tavistock and Portman NHS Foundation Trust [website], https://tavistockandportman.nhs.uk/documents/2251/Part_1_-_March_21_Board_of_Directors_-_final_boardpack_e-version.pdf.

9 Michael Biggs, 'Suicide by clinic-referred transgender adolescents in the United Kingdom', *Archives of Sexual Behavior* 51 (2022), 685–90, doi: 10.1007/s10508-022-02287-7.

10 'Evidence base', GIDS [website].

11 Bernadette Wren, 'Epistemic injustice', *London Review of Books* 43/23 (2 December 2021), https://www.lrb.co.uk/the-paper/v43/n23/bernadette-wren/diary.

12 'NHS standard contract for Gender Identity Development Service for children and adolescents, service specification E13/S(HSS)/e' [PDF], Gender Identity Research and Education Society [website] (2013), https://www.gires.org.uk/wp-content/uploads/2015/01/Existing-GID-Service-for-Children-and-Adolescents-Service-Specification.pdf.

13 'NHS standard contract for Gender Identity Development Service for children and adolescents, service specification E13/S(HSS)/e' [PDF], NHS England [website] (April 2016), https://www.england.nhs.uk/wp-content/uploads/2017/04/gender-development-service-children-adolescents.pdf.

14 'Stafford Hospital scandal: the real story behind Channel 4's *The Cure* published', BBC News [website] (19 December 2019), https://www.bbc.co.uk/news/uk-england-stoke-staffordshire-50836324.

15 'Independent inquiry into care provided by Mid Staffordshire NHS Foundation Trust January 2005–March 2009, volume I, chaired by Robert Francis QC' [PDF], Gov.uk [website] (24 February 2010), https://assets.publishing.service.gov.uk/government/uploads/system/uploads/attachment_data/file/279109/0375_i.pdf; Denis Campbell, 'Mid Staffs hospital scandal: the essential guide', *Guardian* (6

February 2013), https://www.theguardian.com/society/2013/feb/06/mid-staffs-hospital-scandal-guide.

9. Speed in Leeds

1 Tavistock and Portman NHS Foundation Trust FOI 19-20050 ('Subject: GIDS referrals from Ireland'), https://tavistockandportman.nhs.uk/documents/1561/FOI_19-20050_GIDS_Referrals_from_Ireland.pdf.
2 Laura Charlton and Jo Charsley, 'Service pathway for older adolescents in the Gender Identity Development Service (GIDS)' [presentation delivered at second EPATH conference: 'Contemporary Trans Health in Europe: Focus on Challenges and Improvements', 7 April 2017; the author has a copy of the presentation slides; 'Book of abstracts' for conference available at https://epath.eu/wp-content/uploads/2014/02/AbstractbookEPATH2017.pdf].
3 Laura Charlton and Jo Charsley, 'Service pathway for older adolescents in the Gender Identity Development Service (GIDS)' [abstract of presentation contained in 'Book of abstracts' for second EPATH conference: 'Contemporary Trans Health in Europe: Focus on Challenges and Improvements', 6–8 April 2017], https://epath.eu/wp-content/uploads/2014/02/AbstractbookEPATH2017.pdf.
4 Ibid.
5 Ibid.
6 Charlton and Charsley, 'Service pathway for older adolescents in the Gender Identity Development Service (GIDS)' [presentation].
7 Ibid.
8 Charlton and Charsley, 'Service pathway for older adolescents in the Gender Identity Development Service (GIDS)' [abstract of presentation].
9 Theo's words are direct quotations taken from a series of four videos posted on YouTube. These videos are no longer available online, but the author has copies.
10 Charlton and Charsley, 'Service pathway for older adolescents in the Gender Identity Development Service (GIDS)' [presentation].
11 'Treating gender dysphoria in adolescents and young adults at Tavistock GIDS and the GIC' [email], 14 September 2018.
12 Paul Jenkins [email], 2 October 2018.
13 Jamie Doward, 'Gender identity clinic accused of fast-tracking young adults', *Observer* (3 November 2018), https://www.theguardian.com/society/2018/nov/03/tavistock-centre-gender-identity-clinic-accused-fast-tracking-young-adults.
14 *Victoria Derbyshire* [television programme], BBC (5 November 2018).

Hannah

1 This was later reduced to three to six sessions.
2 See Hannah Philips's YouTube channel: https://www.youtube.com/c/HannahPhillipsReal.

3 Hannah Phillips, 'I wish I knew this before starting hormone blockers!!!' [video], YouTube (4 September 2017), https://www.youtube.com/watch?v=C6UGVdzeh18.

4 'Hannah's story', GIDS [website], https://gids.nhs.uk/young-people/hannahs-story. Deleted during the writing of this book but archived at https://web.archive.org/web/20211127215057/https://gids.nhs.uk/young-people/hannahs-story.

5 For the GIDS stakeholder group, see 'Patient and public involvement', Tavistock and Portman NHS Foundation Trust [website], https://tavistockandportman.nhs.uk/about-us/get-involved/patient-and-public-involvement/.

6 Ibid.

7 'Involving people in their own health and care: statutory guidance for clinical commissioning groups and NHS England' [PDF], NHS England [website], https://www.england.nhs.uk/wp-content/uploads/2017/04/ppp-involving-people-health-care-guidance.pdf.

10. Raising Concerns

1 Melissa Midgen [email], October 2016.

2 'Notes from 5th Tuesday meeting – July 31st 2018' [notes taken by Bernadette Wren, typed up 21 August 2018 and circulated to the GIDS team via email].

3 'Council of governors (part one): agenda and papers of a meeting to be held in public 3.00 p.m.–6.00 p.m. Tuesday 5th June 2018' [PDF], Tavistock and Portman NHS Foundation Trust [website], https://tavistockandportman.nhs.uk/documents/985/council-of-governors-boardpack-20180605.pdf.

4 Originally reported in Andrew Gilligan, 'Parents' anger as child sex change charity Mermaids puts private emails online', *Sunday Times* (16 June 2019), https://www.thetimes.co.uk/article/parents-anger-as-child-sex-change-charity-puts-private-emails-online-3tntlwqln. The author has seen the text of several of the emails that were available as part of the breach, but none containing any personally identifying information. However, the whole group of emails did contain such information, and Mermaids was fined and heavily criticised by the Information Commissioner's Office (ICO) in 2021. See 'ICO fines transgender charity for data protection breach exposing sensitive personal data', Information Commissioner's Office [website] (8 July 2021), https://ico.org.uk/about-the-ico/news-and-events/news-and-blogs/2021/07/ico-fines-transgender-charity-for-data-protection-breach-exposing-sensitive-personal-data/.

5 American Psychiatric Association, 'Anxiety disorders', in *Diagnostic and Statistical Manual of Mental Disorders* (5th edn; Washington DC: American Psychiatric Association, 2013), doi: 10.1176/appi.books.9780890425596.

6 Andres Roman-Urrestarazu et al., 'Association of race/ethnicity and social disadvantage with autism prevalence in 7 million school children in England', *JAMA Pediatrics* 175/6 (29 March 2021), e210054, doi: 10.1001/jamapediatrics.2021.0054.

7 Gary Butler et al., 'Assessment and support of children and adolescents with gender dysphoria', *Archives of Disease in Childhood* 103/7 (July 2018), 631–6, doi: 10.1136/archdischild-2018-314992.

8 Transcript of Dinesh Sinha's interview with Anastassis Spiliadis ('BD007') (7 January 2019).

9 'GIDS safeguarding operating procedure', version 1.0 (November 2019), contained in Tavistock and Portman NHS Foundation Trust FOI 21-22103 ('Subject: Request for GIDS safeguarding SOP'), https://tavistockandportman. nhs.uk/documents/2607/21-22103_Request_for_GIDS_Safeguarding_SOP.pdf.

10 'Safeguarding children and child protection', NSPCC [website], https:// learning.nspcc.org.uk/safeguarding-child-protection.

11 'About NHS England safeguarding', NHS England [website], https://www. england.nhs.uk/safeguarding/about/#:~:text=Safeguarding%20means%20 protecting%20a%20citizen's,providing%20high%2Dquality%20health%20care; 'Safeguarding Policy' [PDF], NHS [website], https://www.england.nhs.uk/ wp-content/uploads/2019/09/safeguarding-policy.pdf.

12 Gu Li, Karson T. F. Kung and Melissa Hines, 'Childhood gender-typed behavior and adolescent sexual orientation: a longitudinal population-based study', *Developmental Psychology* 53/4 (2017), 764–77, doi: 10.1037/dev0000281.

13 Matt Bristow, exit interview with GIDS, 22 May 2018.

14 Lucy Bannerman, 'It feels like conversion therapy for gay children, say clinicians', *Times* (8 April 2019), https://www.thetimes.co.uk/article/it-feels-like-conversion-therapy-for-gay-children-say-clinicians-pvsckdvq2.

15 Vicky Holt, Elin Skagerberg and Michael Dunsford, 'Young people with features of gender dysphoria: demographics and associated difficulties', *Clinical Child Psychology and Psychiatry* 21/1 (January 2016), 108–18, doi: 10.1177/1359104514558431.

16 'Current debates', GIDS [website], https://gids.nhs.uk/gender-identity-and-sexuality/, archived at https://archive.ph/Yuln2.

17 Ibid.

18 Annelou L. C. de Vries et al., 'Puberty suppression in adolescents with gender identity disorder: a prospective follow-up study', *Journal of Sexual Medicine* 8/8 (August 2011; published online July 2010), 2276–83, doi: 10.1111/j.1743-6109.2010.01943.x.

19 Julia Temple Newhook et al, 'A critical commentary on follow-up studies and "desistance" theories about transgender and gender-nonconforming children', *International Journal of Transgenderism* 19/2 (2018), 212–24, doi: 10.1080/15532739.2018.1456390.

20 Matt Bristow, exit interview with GIDS, 22 May 2018 (as amended by Matt Bristow, 8 October 2018).

21 Emily Dugan and Sian Griffiths, 'Tavistock gender clinic "converting" gay children', *Sunday Times* (20 June 2021), https://www.thetimes.co.uk/article/ tavistock-gender-clinic-converting-gay-children-tz8cs77p3.

22 Kimberley Bond, '"These children need love and care": why it's vital to support children questioning their gender identity', *Metro* (31 March 2022), https:// metro.co.uk/2022/03/31/why-its-vital-to-support-children-questioning-their-gender-identity-16378164/.

23 Gary Butler et al., 'Discharge outcome analysis of 1089 transgender young people referred to paediatric endocrine clinics in England 2008–2021', *Archives of Disease in Childhood* (18 July 2022), doi: 10.1136/archdischild-2022-324302.

11. Scapegoats and Troublemakers

1 David Bell, 'Serious concerns regarding the Gender Identity Service (GIDS), of the Tavistock and Portman NHS Foundation Trust' [report] (2018).
2 Glenn Gossling, 'Bernadette Wren: on change', Tavistock and Portman NHS Foundation Trust [website] (2020), https://100years.tavistockandportman.nhs.uk/bernadette-wren-on-change/.
3 Ibid.
4 Marina Bonfatto and Eva Crasnow, 'Gender/ed identities: an overview of our current work as child psychotherapists in the Gender Identity Development Service', *Journal of Child Psychotherapy* 44/1 (2018), doi: 10.1080/0075417X.2018.1443150.
5 'Notes from 5th Tuesday meeting – July 31st 2018' [notes taken by Bernadette Wren, typed up 21 August 2018 and circulated to the GIDS team via email].
6 These sentiments are repeated in Matt Bristow, exit interview with GIDS, 22 May 2018.
7 Matt Bristow, exit interview with GIDS, 22 May 2018.
8 Melissa Midgen to Polly Carmichael, Sarah Davidson and Bernadette Wren [email], October 2017.
9 'Patients put at risk by "aggressive" treatment at Great Ormond Street', *Observer* (14 April 2018), https://www.theguardian.com/uk-news/2018/apr/14/patients-at-risk-aggressive-treatment-great-ormond-street.
10 'Freedom to speak up guardian job description' [PDF], CQC [website] (March 2018), https://www.cqc.org.uk/sites/default/files/20180213_ngo_freedom_to_speak_up_guardian_jd_march2018_v5.pdf; 'About us', National Guardian [website], https://nationalguardian.org.uk/about-us/.
11 'National freedom to speak up guardian visits Tavistock Centre', Tavistock and Portman NHS Foundation Trust [website] (6 March 2017), https://tavistockandportman.nhs.uk/about-us/news/stories/national-freedom-speak-guardian-visits-tavistock-centre/.
12 *Ms S. Appleby v Tavistock and Portman NHS Foundation Trust* [case no. 2204772/2019] [PDF], https://assets.publishing.service.gov.uk/media/6149eb48d3bf7f05ac396f79/Ms_S_Appleby__vs___Tavistock_and_Portman_NHS_Foundation_Trust.pdf and Sonia Appleby to Rob Senior [email; subject: 're GIDS'], 30 October 2017.
13 *Ms S. Appleby v Tavistock and Portman NHS Foundation Trust* and Sonia Appleby to Rob Senior [email; subject: 're GIDS'], 13 November 2017.
14 'being actively encouraged […]': *Ms S. Appleby v Tavistock and Portman NHS Foundation Trust*; 'lack of a team position […]': Sonia Appleby to Rob Senior [email; subject: 're GIDS'], 30 October 2017.
15 Sonia Appleby to Rob Senior [email; subject: 're GIDS'], 13 November 2017.

16 An archived webpage lists GIDS staff at this point in time. The author is not providing a link to protect the privacy of those who have worked at the service.
17 Hutchinson also read this contemporaneous note verbatim in 2018 when she was interviewed by the Tavistock's medical director as part of the GIDS Review.
18 Natasha Prescott, exit interview with GIDS, 7 February 2018.
19 Ibid.
20 Ibid.
21 Ibid.
22 Ibid.
23 Midgen's article is Melissa Midgen, 'Transgender children and young people: born in your own body', *Journal of Child Psychotherapy* 44/1 (2018), 140–42, doi: 10.1080/0075417X.2018.1435707. The quotation 'central contention […]' is taken from the first chapter of the book Midgen was reviewing. See Heather Brunskell Evans and Michele Moore, 'The fabrication of "the transgender child"', in Heather Brunskell-Evans and Michele Moore (eds), *Transgender Children and Young People: Born in Your Own Body* (Newcastle upon Tyne: Cambridge Scholars Publishing, 2018).
24 Midgen, 'Transgender children and young people: born in your own body'.
25 'Written evidence submitted by Mermaids (HSC0068)', Parliament.uk [website] (October 2018), http://data.parliament.uk/writtenevidence/committeeevidence.svc/evidencedocument/women-and-equalities-committee/health-and-social-care-and-lgbt-communities/written/91159.html.
26 For the inquiry, see Women and Equalities Committee, 'Health and social care and LGBT communities: first report of session 2019' [PDF], Parliament.uk [website] (16 October 2019), https://publications.parliament.uk/pa/cm201919/cmselect/cmwomeq/94/94.pdf.

12. The Bell Report

1 'Governor guidance document and message from George Wilkinson, lead governor' [PDF], Tavistock and Portman NHS Foundation Trust [website] (November 2021), https://tavistockandportman.nhs.uk/documents/2366/Governor_guidance_document_Nov_2021.pdf.
2 Bell, 'Serious concerns regarding the Gender Identity Service'.
3 Ibid.
4 Ibid.
5 The Tavistock has confirmed that 15 members of staff left GIDS in 2017, though would not agree this was largely down to ethical concerns with the work. Five had left in 2016. This was confirmed in the following FOI request: Tavistock and Portman NHS Foundation Trust FOI 18-19060 ('Subject: GIDS clinician resignations since 2017'), https://tavistockandportman.nhs.uk/documents/1205/FOI_18-19060_GIDS_Clinician_Resignations_since_2017.pdf. However, the Tavistock Trust gives inconsistent figures for the number of resignations from GIDS, providing different answers when asked the same question. For example, while one answer says 20 staff left GIDS in 2016 and 2017, another – answered

eight months later – puts the figure at 11. See Tavistock and Portman NHS Foundation Trust FOI 18-19304 ('Subject: GIDS clinician resignations since 2017'), https://tavistockandportman.nhs.uk/documents/1360/FOI_18-19304_GIDS_Clinician_Resignations_Since_2017.pdf.

6 Bell, 'Serious concerns regarding the Gender Identity Service'.
7 Ibid.
8 Ibid.
9 Ibid.
10 Ibid.
11 GIDS income is provided in Tavistock and Portman NHS Foundation Trust FOI 20-21180 ('Subject: GIDS funding & referrals to 17 December 2020'), https://tavistockandportman.nhs.uk/documents/2219/FOI_20-21180_GIDS_Funding__Referrals_to_17.12.20.pdf. Total income is provided in the Tavistock and Portman's annual reports and accounts. 2015/16 is here: 'Tavistock and Portman NHS Foundation Trust annual report and accounts 2015/16' [PDF], Tavistock and Portman NHS Foundation Trust [website], https://tavistockandportman.nhs.uk/documents/409/tavistock-portman-annual-report-2015-16.pdf. My calculation for 2018/19 excludes Provider Sustainability Fund (PSF) income, as this is treated differently in different sets of accounts. Including this, GIDS's income was 13 per cent of the Trust's total. The 2018/19 accounts are here: 'The Tavistock and Portman NHS Foundation Trust annual report and accounts 2018/19' [PDF], Tavistock and Portman NHS Foundation Trust [website], https://tavistockandportman.nhs.uk/documents/1647/Tavistock_and_Portman_annual_report_2018-19.pdf. The income received from Charing Cross GIC is from FOI 19-20386 ('Subject: trust Funding 2017–19, apportionment to gender services'), https://tavistockandportman.nhs.uk/documents/1884/FOI_19-20386_Trust_Funding_2017-19_apportionment_to_Gender_Services.pdf. The author has used the figures provided for GIDS in the most recent FOI, as stated.
12 'Tavistock and Portman awarded Charing Cross Adult Gender Clinic contract', Tavistock and Portman NHS Foundation Trust [website] (9 December 2016), https://tavistockandportman.nhs.uk/about-us/news/stories/tavistock-and-portman-awarded-charing-cross-adult-gender-clinic-contract/.
13 Bell, 'Serious concerns regarding the Gender Identity Service'.
14 Ibid.
15 Ibid.

13. Bell: The Aftermath

1 Fiona Fernandez to all GIDS teams [email; subject: 're: GIDS Review ("Sent for and on behalf of Dr Dinesh Sinha, Medical Director")'], 16 October 2018.
2 Michele Moore and Heather Brunskell-Evans (eds), *Inventing Transgender Children and Young People* (Newcastle upon Tyne: Cambridge Scholars Publishing, 2019).
3 'not a neutral sounding board': Caitlin Moscatello, 'Blocked: a U.K. teen caught up in the battle over trans health care', *New York* (30 March 2022), https://

nymag.com/intelligencer/article/bell-v-tavistock-transgender-health-care.html. For the suggestion that Bell was sceptical and did not believe that young people should transition, see Bernadette Wren, 'Letters', *London Review of Books* 43/24 (16 December 2021), https://www.lrb.co.uk/the-paper/v43/n24/letters.

4 Moscatello, 'Blocked'.

5 Polly Carmichael to GIDS Executive and seniors [email; subject: 're GIDS FINAL SENT TO PB'] (29 August 2018).

6 *Ms S. Appleby v Tavistock and Portman NHS Foundation Trust* [case no. 2204772/2019] [PDF], https://assets.publishing.service.gov.uk/media/6149eb48d3bf7f05ac396f79/Ms_S_Appleby__vs___Tavistock_and_Portman_NHS_Foundation_Trust.pdf.

7 'First witness statement of Polly Carmichael' [official document from employment tribunal *Ms Sonia Appleby vs the Tavistock and Portman NHS Foundation Trust*; case no. 2204772/2019].

8 For the *Observer* article, see Jamie Doward, 'Gender identity clinic accused of fast-tracking young adults', *Observer* (3 November 2018), https://www.theguardian.com/society/2018/nov/03/tavistock-centre-gender-identity-clinic-accused-fast-tracking-young-adults.

9 'Our gender identity development service', Tavistock and Portman NHS Foundation Trust [website] (4 November 2018), https://tavistockandportman.nhs.uk/about-us/news/stories/our-gender-identity-development-service/. Archived version here: http://web.archive.org/web/20211027184406/https://tavistockandportman.nhs.uk/about-us/news/stories/our-gender-identity-development-service/.

10 *Ms S. Appleby v Tavistock and Portman NHS Foundation Trust*. For the *Sunday Times* article, see Andrew Gilligan, 'Tavistock trans clinic fears damage to children as activists harass staff', *Sunday Times* (17 February 2019), https://www.thetimes.co.uk/article/tavistock-trans-clinic-fears-damage-to-children-as-activists-harass-staff-xf5sxg3pp.

11 'GIDS Review', NHS [website], https://gids.nhs.uk/news-events/2019-02-17/gids-review, archived at http://web.archive.org/web/20211127230458/https://gids.nhs.uk/news-events/2019-02-17/gids-review.

12 Dinesh Sinha, 'A review in to [*sic*] concerns raised about the Gender Identity Development Service' ['Annex A' of *GIDS Review Action Plan*, 26 March 2019] (February 2019), https://tavistockandportman.nhs.uk/documents/1376/GIDS_Action_plan_review.pdf.

13 Ibid.

14 Ibid.

15 Ibid.

16 Ibid.

17 Ibid.

18 Ibid.

19 Ibid.

20 'GIDS Review', NHS [website].

21 Paul Jenkins, introduction to *GIDS Review Action Plan* [PDF] (26 March 2019), https://tavistockandportman.nhs.uk/documents/1376/GIDS_Action_plan_review.pdf.

22 For the *Sunday Times* article, see Gilligan, 'Tavistock trans clinic fears damage to children as activists harass staff'.

23 For the action plan, see *GIDS Review Action Plan* [PDF] (26 March 2019), https://tavistockandportman.nhs.uk/documents/1376/GIDS_Action_plan_review.pdf.

24 Gary Butler et al., 'Assessment and support of children and adolescents with gender dysphoria', *Archives of Disease in Childhood* 103/7 (July 2018), 631–6, doi: 10.1136/archdischild-2018-314992.

25 Ibid.

26 'Detransitioning: "How do I go back to the Debbie I was?"' [video interview with Dr Elizabeth van Horn], *Newsnight*, BBC (26 November 2019), https://www.bbc.co.uk/programmes/p07w3f1q.

27 A. Hutchinson and M. Midgen, 'The "natal female" question', Woman's Place UK [website] (17 February 2020), https://womansplaceuk.org/2020/02/17/the-natal-female-question/.

28 Ibid.

29 'Our gender identity development service', Tavistock and Portman NHS Foundation Trust [website].

30 'Our clinical services', Tavistock and Portman NHS Foundation Trust [website], https://tavistockandportman.nhs.uk/care-and-treatment/our-clinical-services/.

31 'Outcomes of 2018/19 strategic plan and annual operational plan May 2019', contained in 'Council of governors (part one): agenda and papers of a meeting to be held in public Thursday 13th June 2019' [PDF], Tavistock and Portman NHS Foundation Trust [website], https://tavistockandportman.nhs.uk/documents/1494/Council-of-Governors-papers-june2019.pdf.

32 'Annual operational plan 2019/20, 4 April 2019 submission to NHSi', contained in 'Council of governors (part one): agenda and papers of a meeting to be held in public Thursday 13th June 2019' [PDF], Tavistock and Portman NHS Foundation Trust [website], https://tavistockandportman.nhs.uk/documents/1494/Council-of-Governors-papers-june2019.pdf.

33 Ibid.

34 Ibid.

35 'Annual operational plan 2020/21' [draft], contained in 'Council of governors (part one): agenda and papers of a meeting to be held in public Tuesday 12th March 2020' [PDF], Tavistock and Portman NHS Foundation Trust [website], https://tavistockandportman.nhs.uk/documents/1869/March_2020_-_Part_1_Council_of_Governors.pdf.

36 'GIDS Review', NHS [website].

37 For the Newsnight report, see 'NHS child gender clinic: staff welfare concerns "shut down"' [video], *Newsnight*, BBC (18 June 2020), https://www.youtube.com/watch?v=zTRnrp9pXHY. For the Trust's assertion, see 'GIDS Review Action Plan', Tavistock and Portman NHS Foundation Trust [website] (29 March 2019), https://tavistockandportman.nhs.uk/about-us/news/stories/gids-action-plan/.

14. First Fears

1 'First do no harm: the ethics of transgender healthcare, House of Lords', Transgender Trend [website] (22 May 2019), https://www.transgendertrend.com/first-do-no-harm-ethics-transgender-healthcare-house-of-lords/.

2 'Transphobia guidelines "contrary to freedom of expression", court hears', BBC News [website] (20 November 2019), https://www.bbc.co.uk/news/uk-england-lincolnshire-50490311; 'Harry Miller: legal victory after alleged transphobic tweet', BBC News [website] (20 December 2021), https://www.bbc.co.uk/news/uk-england-lincolnshire-59727118.

3 Johanna Olson-Kennedy et al., 'Chest reconstruction and chest dysphoria in transmasculine minors and young adults: comparisons of nonsurgical and postsurgical cohorts', *JAMA Pediatrics* 172/5 (1 May 2018), 431–6, doi: 10.1001/jamapediatrics.2017.5440.

4 Greg Hurst, 'Mother sues Tavistock child gender clinic over treatments', *Times* (12 October 2019), https://www.thetimes.co.uk/article/mother-sues-tavistock-child-gender-clinic-over-treatments-r9df8m987; Greg Hurst, 'Therapist raised alert at troubling practices at Tavistock clinic', *Times* (12 October 2019), https://www.thetimes.co.uk/article/therapist-raised-alert-at-troubling-practices-at-tavistock-clinic-nfhsbb76n; Greg Hurst, 'Tavistock clinic: my daughter can't understand the risk, says mother', *Times* (12 October 2019), https://www.thetimes.co.uk/article/tavistock-clinic-my-daughter-cant-understand-the-risk-says-mother-jr59vz0ck.

5 'Freedom of Information Act 2000 (FOIA) decision notice [ref. FS50881691]' [PDF], Information Commissioner's Office [website] (4 August 2020), https://ico.org.uk/media/action-weve-taken/decision-notices/2020/2618201/fs50881691.pdf. See also 'NHS child gender clinic: staff concerns date back more than a decade' [video], *Newsnight*, BBC (1 October 2020), via https://www.youtube.com/watch?v=8MYWT1Cfp1g.

6 Ibid.

7 David Taylor, 'Report on GIDU review (May–Oct. 2005)' [PDF] (January 2006), https://tavistockandportman.nhs.uk/documents/2248/FOI_20-21117_2005_David_Taylor_Report.pdf.

8 Ibid.

9 'NHS child gender clinic: staff concerns date back more than a decade'.

10 Hannah Barnes, 'Children's gender identity clinic concerns go back 15 years', BBC News [website] (1 October 2020), https://www.bbc.co.uk/news/uk-54374165.

Jacob

1 For the study, see Polly Carmichael et al., 'Short-term outcomes of pubertal suppression in a selected cohort of 12 to 15 year old young people with persistent gender dysphoria in the UK', *PLoS ONE* 16/2 (2021), e0243894, doi: 10.1371/journal.pone.0243894.

2 For Sarah Davidson, see 'The Gendered Intelligence team', Gendered Intelligence [website], archived at http://web.archive.org/web/20190118080159/http:/genderedintelligence.co.uk/about-us/the-team.

3 Women and Equalities Committee, 'Oral evidence: Transgender Equality Inquiry, HC 390' [PDF], Parliament.uk [website] (15 September 2015), http://data.parliament.uk/writtenevidence/committeeevidence.svc/evidencedocument/women-and-equalities-committee/transgender-equality/oral/21638.pdf.

4 'Information for young people', GIDS [website], https://gids.nhs.uk/young-people/; 'Puberty and physical intervention', GIDS [website], https://gids.nhs.uk/young-people/puberty-and-physical-intervention/.

5 'Beta blockers', NHS [website], https://www.nhs.uk/conditions/beta-blockers/.

6 'The use of GnRH agonists in central precocious puberty (CPP)' [PDF], NHS Berkshire West Clinical Commissioning Group [website], https://www.berkshirewestccg.nhs.uk/media/2512/apc-pg-030-the-use-of-gnrh-agonists-in-central-precocious-puberty-cpp.pdf.

15. 200 Miles up the M1…

1 Kirsty Entwistle, 'An open letter to Dr Polly Carmichael from a former GIDS clinician' (18 July 2019), https://medium.com/@kirstyentwistle/an-open-letter-to-dr-polly-carmichael-from-a-former-gids-clinician-53c541276b8d.

2 Ibid.

3 Ibid.

4 Tavistock and Portman NHS Foundation Trust FOI 18-19262 ('Subject: hormone blocking treatments'), https://tavistockandportman.nhs.uk/documents/1427/FOI_18-19262_Hormone_Blocking_Referrals_2014-18.pdf.

5 Kirsty Entwistle to Gill Rusbridger [letter], 29 July 2019.

6 Ibid.

7 Entwistle, 'An open letter to Dr Polly Carmichael from a former GIDS clinician'.

8 Kirsty Entwistle to Gill Rusbridger [letter], 29 July 2019.

9 Ibid.

10 Ibid.

11 Ibid.

12 Ibid.

13 Ibid.

14 'Multi-agency public protection arrangements: annual report 2017/18' [PDF], Gov.uk [website] (25 October 2018), https://assets.publishing.service.gov.uk/government/uploads/system/uploads/attachment_data/file/751006/mappa-annual-report-2017-18.pdf.

15 'Population estimates for the UK, England and Wales, Scotland and Northern Ireland: mid-2018', ONS [website] (26 June 2019), https://www.ons.gov.uk/peoplepopulationandcommunity/populationandmigration/populationestimates/bulletins/annualmidyearpopulationestimates/mid2018.

16 Kirsty Entwistle, 'Letters', *London Review of Books* 43/24 (16 December 2021), https://www.lrb.co.uk/the-paper/v43/n24/letters.

17 Ibid.

18 For Rochdale, see Rochdale Borough Safeguarding Children Board, 'Overview report of the serious case review in respect of young people 1, 2, 3, 4, 5 & 6' [PDF] (20 December 2013), https://www.scribd.com/document/192690414/Rochdale-Safeguarding-Children-Board-Serious-Case-Review-1. For Rotherham, see Alexis Jay OBE, 'Independent inquiry into child sexual exploitation in Rotherham 1997–2013' [PDF] (August 2014), https://www.rotherham.gov.uk/downloads/file/279/independent-inquiry-into-child-sexual-exploitation-in-rotherham.

19 Helen Carter and Haroon Siddique, 'Rochdale gang jailed for total of 77 years for sexually exploiting young girls', *Guardian* (9 May 2012), https://www.theguardian.com/uk/2012/may/09/rochdale-gang-jailed-sexually-exploiting; Helen Pidd and Vikram Dodd, 'Police errors may have let abusers of up to 52 children escape justice', *Guardian* (14 January 2020), https://www.theguardian.com/uk-news/2020/jan/14/police-errors-may-have-let-abusers-of-up-to-52-children-escape-justice.

16. Across the Sea

1 Paul Moran [email], 25 April 2019.

2 Ibid.

3 Tavistock and Portman NHS Foundation Trust FOI 19-20050 ('Subject: GIDS referrals from Ireland'), https://tavistockandportman.nhs.uk/documents/1561/FOI_19-20050_GIDS_Referrals_from_Ireland.pdf.

4 'About the scheme', HSE [website] (8 November 2018), https://www2.hse.ie/services/treatment-abroad-scheme/treatment-abroad-scheme.html.

5 Tavistock and Portman NHS Foundation Trust FOI 16-17147 and 16-17126 ('Subject: GIDS referrals April 2011 to March 2016'), https://tavistockandportman.nhs.uk/documents/876/FOI_16-17147_GIDS_Referrals_Stats_04.2011_to_03.2016_V9U0I6Q.pdf.

6 Ibid.

7 'Ireland recruiting psychiatrist to head youth gender clinic', GenderGP [website] (24 May 2021), https://www.gendergp.com/irish-youth-gender-clinic-seeks-psychiatrist-lead/; Vic Parsons, 'Ireland's sole gender clinic is so short-staffed it can't even deal with 300 patients a year', Pink News [website] (4 January 2022), https://www.pinknews.co.uk/2022/01/04/ireland-trans-healthcare-gender-clinic/.

8 Aidan Kelly, 'Working with gender difficulties in adolescence' [video of talk at the Independent Guardian ad Litem Agency (TIGALA) conference 'Getting it right – caring for LGBT+ children in care', February 2018], https://www.tigala.ie/conferences/getting-it-right-caring-for-lgbt-children-in-care.

9 Tavistock and Portman NHS Foundation Trust FOI 19-20335 ('Subject: GIDS referrals from Ireland'), https://tavistockandportman.nhs.uk/documents/1875/FOI_19-20335_GIDS_Referrals_from_Ireland.pdf.

10 Anne Sheridan, 'Irish teenagers are "fast-tracked to sex change treatment in London clinic"', *Irish Mail on Sunday* (18 November 2018).

11 Vic Parsons, 'Ireland's sole gender clinic is so short-staffed it can't even deal with 300 patients a year', Pink News [website] (4 January 2022), https://www.pinknews.co.uk/2022/01/04/ireland-trans-healthcare-gender-clinic/.

12 Paul Moran [email], 25 April 2019.

13 Ibid.

14 Shane Phelan, 'Doctors in row with HSE over claims children's transgender care is "unsafe"', *Irish Independent* (3 February 2020), https://www.independent.ie/irish-news/health/doctors-in-row-with-hse-over-claims-childrens-transgender-care-is-unsafe-38920159.html.

15 Paul Oslizlok [email; subject: 'FW: Transgender Service Meeting Minutes 20th March 2019'], 25 April 2019.

16 Paul Moran to Paul Oslizlok [email; subject: 'RE: Transgender Service Meeting Minutes 20th March 2019'], 26 April 2019.

17 Transgender service meeting notes, boardroom, Children's Health Ireland at Crumlin, 20 March 2019.

18 Wayne O'Connor, 'HSE spends €50,000 to send children to gender treatment clinics', *Irish Independent* (1 May 2022), https://www.independent.ie/irish-news/health/hse-spends-50000-to-send-children-to-gender-treatment-clinics-41604443.html.

19 Aisling Kenny, 'HSE defends patient referrals to UK's Tavistock clinic', RTE [website] (9 August 2022), https://www.rte.ie/news/ireland/2022/0809/1314785-hse-tavistock-clinic/.

20 O'Connor, 'HSE spends €50,000 to send children to gender treatment clinics'.

17. The GIDS Review and Outside Scrutiny

1 Tavistock and Portman NHS Foundation Trust FOI 19-20380 ('Subject: GIDS staff resignations since 2016'), https://tavistockandportman.nhs.uk/documents/1857/FOI_19-20380_GIDS_Staff_Resignations_since_2016_.pdf.

2 This descriptor is attributed to Polly Carmichael in contemporaneous notes made by Andrew Hodge of Woodbury Hodge Ltd during their meeting in either later 2019 or early 2020, as part of an investigation into concerns raised by the Trust's children's safeguarding lead Sonia Appleby. A solicitor by training, Hodge was asked by the Tavistock and Portman NHS Foundation Trust to conduct an investigation in October 2019. His final report was dated 7 February 2020.

3 Anna Hutchinson, 'Confidential: statement for the review of the GIDS service, October 2018'.

4 Ibid.

5 Ibid.

6 Ibid.

7 Hannah Barnes live-tweeting of employment tribunal proceeding between Sonia Appleby and the Tavistock and Portman NHS Foundation Trust (21 June 2021), https://twitter.com/hannahsbee/status/1407063838223126530.

8 Transcript of Dinesh Sinha's interview with Anastassis Spiliadis ('BD007') (7 January 2019).

9 Transcript of Dinesh Sinha's interview with Matt Bristow ('BD016') (7 January 2019).

10 Transcript of Dinesh Sinha's interview with Anastassis Spiliadis ('BD007') (7 January 2019).

11 Transcript of Dinesh Sinha's interview with Anna Hutchinson ('BD005') (14 December 2018).

12 Transcript of Dinesh Sinha's interview with Anastassis Spiliadis ('BD007') (7 January 2019).

13 Transcript of Dinesh Sinha's interview with Matt Bristow ('BD016') (7 January 2019).

14 Transcript of Dinesh Sinha's interview with Anna Hutchinson ('BD005') (14 December 2018).

15 Ibid.

16 Transcript of Dinesh Sinha's interview with Anastassis Spiliadis ('BD007') (7 January 2019).

17 Transcript of Dinesh Sinha's interview with Anna Hutchinson ('BD005') (14 December 2018).

18 'First witness statement of Polly Carmichael' [official document from employment tribunal *Ms Sonia Appleby vs the Tavistock and Portman NHS Foundation Trust*; case no. 2204772/2019].

19 Ibid.

20 Transcript of Dinesh Sinha's interview with Matt Bristow ('BD016') (7 January 2019).

21 Ibid.

22 Transcript of Dinesh Sinha's interview with Anastassis Spiliadis ('BD007') (7 January 2019).

23 'NHS child gender clinic: staff welfare concerns "shut down"' [video], *Newsnight*, BBC (18 June 2020), https://www.youtube.com/watch?v=zTRnrp9pXHY.

24 Transcript of Dinesh Sinha's interview with 'BD004' (12 December 2018).

25 Transcript of Dinesh Sinha's interview with Anastassis Spiliadis ('BD007') (7 January 2019).

26 Ibid.

27 Ibid.

28 Transcript of Dinesh Sinha's interview with 'M002' (8 October 2018).

29 Transcript of Dinesh Sinha's interview with Polly Carmichael ('M003') (19 October 2018).

30 Transcript of Dinesh Sinha's interviews with 'BD015' (28 November 2018), 'BD017' (17 December 2018) and 'BD018' (17 December 2018).

31 Paul Jenkins, introduction to *GIDS Review Action Plan* [PDF] (26 March 2019), https://tavistockandportman.nhs.uk/documents/1376/GIDS_Action_plan_review.pdf.

32 Dinesh Sinha, 'A review in to [*sic*] concerns raised about the Gender Identity Development Service' ['Annex A' of *GIDS Review Action Plan*, 26 March 2019]

(February 2019), https://tavistockandportman.nhs.uk/documents/1376/GIDS_ Action_plan_review.pdf.

33 Ibid.

34 Anna Hutchinson to Paul Jenkins, Paul Burstow and Gill Rusbridger [email; subject: 're: GIDS Concerns'], 22 May 2019.

35 Paul Burstow to Anna Hutchinson, Paul Jenkins and Gill Rusbridger [email; subject: 're: GIDS Concerns'], 22 May 2019.

36 Ibid.

37 Paul Jenkins to Anna Hutchinson, Paul Burstow and Gill Rusbridger [email; subject: 're: GIDS Concerns'], 29 May 2019.

38 Anna Hutchinson to Paul Jenkins, Paul Burstow and Gill Rusbridger [email; subject: 're: GIDS Concerns'], 15 July 2019.

39 Ibid.

40 *Today*, BBC Radio 4 (22 July 2019).

41 Matt Bristow, 'Very surprised to hear @PaulJThinks say on @BBCr4today that hormone blockers are "fully reversible". The #GIDS website itself says that some long-term health risks are still unknown' [Twitter thread] (22 July 2019), via https://twitter.com/psychomologist/status/1153301937565130753.

42 Sally Hodges to Melissa Midgen and Anna Hutchinson [email; subject: 're Meeting'], 30 September 2019.

43 Ibid.

44 Anna Hutchinson to Sally Hodges [email; subject: 're Meeting'], 1 October 2019.

45 'NHS child gender clinic: staff welfare concerns "shut down"'.

46 Hannah Barnes and Deborah Cohen, 'NHS child gender clinic: staff concerns "shut down"', BBC News [website] (19 June 2020), https://www.bbc.co.uk/news/ health-51806962.

47 'NHS child gender clinic: staff welfare concerns "shut down"'.

48 'Response to questions on GIDS' [document setting out Jenkins's answers to a series of questions raised by governors, attached to email to all governors and Paul Burstow, subject: 're: "Amended Agenda and additional Papers for CoG"', 9 December 2020].

49 Ibid.

50 Ibid.

51 'Response' [document responding to Jenkins's answers to questions raised by governors, attached to an email to all governors and Paul Burstow, subject: 're: "Amended Agenda and additional Papers for CoG"', 9 December 2020].

52 For the earlier wording, see 'Treatment: gender dysphoria', NHS [website], archived at https://web.archive.org/web/20200214042527/https://www.nhs. uk/conditions/gender-dysphoria/treatment/. For the more recent version, see 'Treatment: gender dysphoria', NHS [website], https://www.nhs.uk/conditions/ gender-dysphoria/treatment/.

53 James Kirkup, 'The NHS has quietly changed its trans guidance to reflect reality', *Spectator* (4 June 2020), https://www.spectator.co.uk/article/the-nhs-has-quietly-changed-its-trans-guidance-to-reflect-reality; *Woman's Hour* [radio programme], BBC Radio 4 (30 June 2020), https://www.bbc.co.uk/programmes/m000kgsj.

54 'Minutes of the meeting held on 11 June 2020', in 'Council of governors (part one): agenda and papers of a meeting to be held in public Thursday 10th September 2020' [PDF], Tavistock and Portman NHS Foundation Trust [website], https://tavistockandportman.nhs.uk/documents/2139/Part_1_Council_of_Governors_Sept20_-_e-version.pdf.

55 'Puberty and physical intervention', GIDS [website], https://gids.nhs.uk/young-people/puberty-and-physical-intervention/, archived at https://web.archive.org/web/20220412184019/https://gids.nhs.uk/young-people/puberty-and-physical-intervention/.

56 'NHS announces independent review into gender identity services for children and young people', NHS England [website] (22 September 2020), https://www.england.nhs.uk/2020/09/nhs-announces-independent-review-into-gender-identity-services-for-children-and-young-people/. For the review's wide-ranging remit, see 'Terms of reference for review of Gender Identity Development Service for children and adolescents' [PDF], NHS England [website], https://www.england.nhs.uk/wp-content/uploads/2020/09/GIDS_independent_review_ToR.pdf.

57 'Care Quality Commission demands improved waiting times at Tavistock and Portman NHS Foundation Trust' [press release], CQC [website] (20 January 2021), https://www.cqc.org.uk/news/releases/care-quality-commission-demands-improved-waiting-times-tavistock-portman-nhs.

58 'Ratings', CQC [website], https://www.cqc.org.uk/what-we-do/how-we-do-our-job/ratings.

59 'Tavistock and Portman NHS Foundation Trust: gender identity services inspection report' [PDF], CQC [website] (20 January 2021), https://api.cqc.org.uk/public/v1/reports/7ecf93b7-2b14-45ea-a317-53b6f4804c24.

60 Ibid.
61 Ibid.
62 Ibid.
63 Ibid.
64 Ibid.
65 Ibid.
66 Ibid.
67 Ibid.
68 Ibid.
69 Ibid.

70 'Statement in response to the January 2021 CQC report on GIDS', Tavistock and Portman NHS Foundation Trust [website] (20 January 2021), https://tavistockandportman.nhs.uk/about-us/news/stories/statement-response-january-2021-cqc-report-gids/.

71 'Board of directors (part one): agenda and papers of a meeting to be held in public Tuesday 26th January 2021' [PDF], Tavistock and Portman NHS Foundation Trust [website], https://tavistockandportman.nhs.uk/documents/2162/Part_1_January_2021_Board_of_Directors_Meeting_final_e-version.pdf.

72 Ibid.
73 Ibid.

18. Regret and Redress

1 'Going back: the people reversing their gender transition' [radio programme], *File on Four*, BBC Radio 4 (1 December 2019), https://www.bbc.co.uk/programmes/m000bmy9; 'Detransitioning: "how do I go back to the Debbie I was?"' [video interview with Dr Elizabeth van Horn], *Newsnight*, BBC (26 November 2019), https://www.bbc.co.uk/programmes/p07w3f1q; Hannah Barnes and Deborah Cohen, 'How do I go back to the Debbie I was?', BBC News [website] (26 November 2019), https://www.bbc.co.uk/news/health-50548473.

2 Transcript of Dinesh Sinha's interview with Anna Hutchinson ('BD005') (14 December 2018).

3 'Detransition: the elephant in the room part two' [video of panel hosted by Make More Noise to launch the Detransition Advocacy Network, held in Manchester on 30 November 2019], YouTube [website] (12 December 2019), https://www.youtube.com/watch?v=stBt7_NTT3o.

4 Transcript of 'Detransition: the elephant in the room' [PDF] [panel hosted by Make More Noise to launch the Detransition Advocacy Network, held in Manchester on 30 November 2019], https://08e98b5f-7b7a-40c9-a93b-8195d9b9a854.filesusr.com/ugd/305c8f_34b673d3097c4df88bf9b9e8f6ed1006.pdf.

5 Ibid.

6 Ibid.

7 Greg Hurst, 'Woman who halted gender transition sues child clinic', *Times* (23 January 2020), https://www.thetimes.co.uk/article/woman-who-halted-gender-transition-sues-child-clinic-q3cmlgzpt.

8 Keira Bell, 'Keira Bell: my story', Persuasion [website] (7 April 2021), https://www.persuasion.community/p/keira-bell-my-story.

9 Ibid.

10 Ibid.

11 Anna Churcher Clarke and Anastassis Spiliadis, '"Taking the lid off the box": the value of extended clinical assessment for adolescents presenting with gender identity difficulties', *Clinical Child Psychology and Psychiatry* 24/2 (April 2019), 338–52, doi: 10.1177/1359104518825288.

12 Transcript of Dinesh Sinha's interview with Anastassis Spiliadis ('BD007') (7 January 2019).

13 Ibid.

14 Tavistock and Portman NHS Foundation Trust FOI 16-17254 ('Subject: gender dysphoria treatment'), https://tavistockandportman.nhs.uk/documents/641/FOI_16-17254_Gender_Dysphoria_Treatment.pdf.

15 Tavistock and Portman NHS Foundation Trust FOI 17-18124 ('Subject: Gender Identity Development Service (GIDS) questionnaires and treatment cessation'), https://tavistockandportman.nhs.uk/documents/771/FOI_17-18124_GIDS_Questionnaires_and_Treatment_Cessation.pdf.

16 Tavistock and Portman NHS Foundation Trust FOI 19-20192 ('Subject: GIDS update on (closed) FOI case 16-17254 interventions & treatments cessations'), https://tavistockandportman.nhs.uk/documents/1699/FOI_19-20192_GIDS_Update_16-17254_Interventions__Treatments_Cessations.pdf.

17 Ibid.

18 Ibid.

19 Ibid.

20 'Notes from 5th Tuesday meeting – July 31st 2018' [notes taken by Bernadette Wren, typed up 21 August 2018 and circulated to the GIDS team via email].

21 'Council of governors (part one): agenda and papers of a meeting to be held in public Tuesday 12th March 2020' [PDF], Tavistock and Portman NHS Foundation Trust [website], https://tavistockandportman.nhs.uk/documents/1869/March_2020_-_Part_1_Council_of_Governors.pdf.

22 'Council of governors (part one): agenda and papers of a meeting to be held in public Thursday 9th September 2021' [PDF], Tavistock and Portman NHS Foundation Trust [website], https://tavistockandportman.nhs.uk/documents/2338/Part_1_September_2021_Council_of_Governors_final_pack_e-version.pdf.

23 'Response to questions on GIDS' [document setting out Jenkins's answers to a series of questions raised by governors, attached to email to all governors and Paul Burstow, subject: 're: "Amended Agenda and additional Papers for CoG"', 9 December 2020].

24 For the argument that detransition is very rare, see Kirrin Medcalf, 'Dispelling myths around detransition', Stonewall [website] (7 October 2019), https://www.stonewall.org.uk/about-us/news/dispelling-myths-around-detransition. For the claim that fewer than 1 per cent change their minds or regret transition, see 'Evidenced research on detransition "regret"', for *Newsnight*, GenderGP [website] (26 November 2019), https://www.gendergp.com/research-on-detransition-regret/.

25 Skye Davies, Stephen McIntyre and Craig Rypma, 'Detransition rates in a national UK gender identity clinic' [talk delivered at third biennial EPATH conference: 'Inside matters: on law, ethics and religion', 11 April 2019], https://epath.eu/wp-content/uploads/2019/04/Boof-of-abstracts-EPATH2019.pdf; C. Richards and J. Doyle, 'Detransition rates in a large national gender-identity clinic in the UK', *Counselling Psychology Review* 34 (2019), 60–6.

26 Lisa Littman, 'Individuals treated for gender dysphoria with medical and/or surgical transition who subsequently detransitioned: a survey of 100 detransitioners', *Archives of Sexual Behavior* 50/8 (November 2021), 3353–69, doi: 10.1007/s10508-021-02163-w.

27 Yolanda L. S. Smith et al., 'Sex reassignment: outcomes and predictors of treatment for adolescent and adult transsexuals', *Psychological Medicine* 35/1 (2005), 89–99, doi: 10.1017/S0033291704002776.

28 Anne A. Lawrence, 'Factors associated with satisfaction or regret following male-to-female sex reassignment surgery', *Archives of Sexual Behavior* 32 (2003), 299–315, doi: 10.1023/A:1024086814364.

29 Cecilia Dhejne et al., 'An analysis of all applications for sex reassignment surgery in Sweden, 1960–2010: prevalence, incidence, and regrets', *Archives of Sexual Behavior* 43/8 (November 2014), 1535–45, doi: 10.1007/s10508-014-0300-8.

30 Gary Butler et al., 'Discharge outcome analysis of 1089 transgender young people referred to paediatric endocrine clinics in England 2008–2021', *Archives of Disease in Childhood* (18 July 2022), doi: 10.1136/archdischild-2022-324302.
31 R. Hall, L. Mitchell and J. Sachdeva, 'Access to care and frequency of detransition among a cohort discharged by a UK national adult gender identity clinic: retrospective case-note review', *BJPsych Open* 7/6 (2021), e184, doi: 10.1192/bjo.2021.1022.
32 Isabel Boyd, Thomas Hackett and Susan Bewley, 'Care of transgender patients: a general practice quality improvement approach', *Healthcare (Basel)* 10/1 (7 January 2022), 121, doi: 10.3390/healthcare10010121.
33 Elie Vandenbussche, 'Detransition-related needs and support: a cross-sectional online survey', *Journal of Homosexuality* 69/9 (2021), 1602–20, doi: 10.1080/00918369.2021.1919479.
34 Littman, 'Individuals treated for gender dysphoria with medical and/or surgical transition who subsequently detransitioned'.
35 Ibid.
36 Vandenbussche, 'Detransition-related needs and support'; Littman, 'Individuals treated for gender dysphoria with medical and/or surgical transition who subsequently detransitioned'.
37 'Going back: the people reversing their gender transition'.
38 'Awards for BD22' [PDF], Gov.uk [website], https://assets.publishing.service.gov.uk/government/uploads/system/uploads/attachment_data/file/1079895/birthday-honours-2022.pdf.
39 Gabriella Swerling, 'Gender clinic offers "fairytale" promises to children over transitioning, court hears', *Telegraph* (7 October 2020), https://www.telegraph.co.uk/news/2020/10/07/gender-clinic-offers-fairytale-promises-children-transitioning/.
40 'Skeleton argument on behalf of the defendant' [official document in *Bell v Tavistock*; claim No CO/60/2020].
41 'a radical proposition': 'Children not able to give "proper" consent to puberty blockers, court told', BBC News [website] (7 October 2020), https://www.bbc.co.uk/news/uk-54450273. For Gillick competency, see 'GP mythbuster 8: Gillick competency and Fraser guidelines', CQC [website], https://www.cqc.org.uk/guidance-providers/gps/gp-mythbuster-8-gillick-competency-fraser-guidelines.
42 'Skeleton argument on behalf of the defendant'.
43 Janice Turner, 'Can life-changing decisions be left to children?', *Times* (10 October 2020), https://www.thetimes.co.uk/article/can-life-changing-decisions-be-left-to-children-ng8rs9kmr; Hannah Barnes, 'Tavistock barrister says that one of the criteria for puberty blockers is that tanner stage 2 is reached, so can speculate that there is the beginning of sexual feelings. Fact remains that some people remain uninterested in sex throughout their lives' [Twitter post] (7 October 2020), https://twitter.com/hannahsbee/status/1313861890951520256.
44 Hannah Barnes, 'Judge says you can't assume a given 10 year old will be one of those people. Tavi barrister says that's why there's ongoing dialogue. Also, while convening for claimant to focus on younger patients, most are 15' [Twitter post] (7 October 2020), https://twitter.com/hannahsbee/status/1313861893669429254.

45 *Bell v Tavistock* [2020] EWHC 3274 (Admin) [PDF] (1 December 2020), https://www.judiciary.uk/wp-content/uploads/2020/12/Bell-v-Tavistock-Judgment.pdf.

46 Ibid.

47 Ibid.

48 Ibid.

49 'Amendments to service specification for Gender Identity Development Service for children and adolescents (E13/S(HSS)/e), effective 1 December 2020' [PDF], NHS England [website]', archived at http://web.archive.org/web/20201201211148/https://www.england.nhs.uk/wp-content/uploads/2020/12/Amendment-to-Gender-Identity-Development-Service-Specification-for-Children-and-Adolescents.pdf.

50 Ibid.

51 Ibid.

52 *AB v CD & Ors* [2021] EWHC 741 (Fam) [PDF] (26 March 2021), http://web.archive.org/web/20211023132832/https://www.judiciary.uk/wp-content/uploads/2021/03/AB-v-CD-and-ors-judgment.pdf.

53 Ibid.

54 Ibid.

55 Ibid.

56 *Bell & Anor v The Tavistock and Portman NHS Foundation Trust* [2021] EWCA Civ 1363 (17 September 2021), https://www.bailii.org/ew/cases/EWCA/Civ/2021/1363.html.

57 'Treatment: gender dysphoria', NHS [website], https://www.nhs.uk/conditions/gender-dysphoria/treatment/.

58 *Bell & Anor v The Tavistock and Portman NHS Foundation Trust.*

59 Ibid.

60 Ibid.

61 Ibid.

62 Ibid.

63 Ibid. For the CQC's findings, see 'Tavistock and Portman NHS Foundation Trust: gender identity services inspection report' [PDF], CQC [website] (20 January 2021), https://api.cqc.org.uk/public/v1/reports/7ecf93b7-2b14-45ea-a317-53b6f4804c24.

64 'Implementing advice from the Cass Review', NHS England [website], https://www.england.nhs.uk/commissioning/spec-services/npc-crg/gender-dysphoria-clinical-programme/implementing-advice-from-the-cass-review/.

19. Data and 'Disproportionate effort'

1 On the lack of knowledge about long-term side effects of puberty blockers, see 'Treatment: gender dysphoria', NHS [website], https://www.nhs.uk/conditions/gender-dysphoria/treatment/.

2 *Bell v Tavistock* [2020] EWHC 3274 (Admin) [PDF] (1 December 2020), https://www.judiciary.uk/wp-content/uploads/2020/12/Bell-v-Tavistock-Judgment.pdf.

3 Ibid.

4 Ibid.

5 Hannah Barnes and Deborah Cohen, 'Tavistock puberty blocker study published after nine years', BBC News [website] (11 December 2020), https://www.bbc.co.uk/news/uk-55282113. For the study, see Polly Carmichael et al., 'Short-term outcomes of pubertal suppression in a selected cohort of 12 to 15 year old young people with persistent gender dysphoria in the UK' [preprint], medRxiv [website] (2 December 2020), doi: 10.1101/2020.12.01.20241653, https://www.medrxiv.org/content/10.1101/2020.12.01.20241653v1.

6 'Letter to Paul Jenkins re GIDS' [document attached to email to all governors and Paul Burstow, subject: 're: "Amended Agenda and additional Papers for CoG"', 9 December 2020].

7 'Response to questions on GIDS' [document setting out Jenkins's answers to a series of questions raised by governors, attached to email to all governors and Paul Burstow, subject: 're: "Amended Agenda and additional Papers for CoG"', 9 December 2020].

8 Ibid.

9 For the research, see 'About the study', The Logic Study [website], https://logicstudy.uk/about/ and E. Kennedy et al, 'Longitudinal outcomes of gender identity in children (LOGIC): study protocol for a retrospective analysis of the characteristics and outcomes of children referred to specialist gender services in the UK and the Netherlands', *BMJ Open* 11 (2021), e054895, doi: 10.1136/bmjopen-2021-054895. For the £1.3 million, see 'Funding and awards', NIHR [website], https://fundingawards.nihr.ac.uk/award/17/51/19.

10 *Bell v Tavistock [2020] EWHC 3274 (Admin)*.

11 The full breakdown provided was as follows: three were ten or 11 years old at the time of referral. Thirteen were 12 years old; ten were 13 years old; 24 were 14 years old; 45 were 15 years old; 51 were 16 years old; and 15 were 17 or 18 years old.

12 'Skeleton argument on behalf of the defendant' [official document in *Bell v Tavistock*; claim No CO/60/2020].

13 *Bell v Tavistock [2020] EWHC 3274 (Admin)*.

14 'Pathways through our service', Tavistock and Portman NHS Foundation Trust [website], https://gids.nhs.uk/research/pathways-through-our-service/.

15 Ibid.

16 'Tavistock and Portman NHS Foundation Trust: gender identity services inspection report' [PDF], CQC [website] (20 January 2021), https://api.cqc.org.uk/public/v1/reports/7ecf93b7-2b14-45ea-a317-53b6f4804c24.

17 'Our gender identity development service', Tavistock and Portman NHS Foundation Trust [website] (4 November 2018), https://tavistockandportman.nhs.uk/about-us/news/stories/our-gender-identity-development-service/. Archived version here: http://web.archive.org/web/20211027184406/https://tavistockandportman.nhs.uk/about-us/news/stories/our-gender-identity-development-service/; Jamie Doward, '"Take these children seriously": NHS clinic in the eye of trans rights storm', *Guardian* (19 November 2017), https://www.theguardian.com/society/2017/nov/19/nhs-clinic-trans-rights-storm-

gender-identity-specialist-centre-transgender; Gary Butler et al., 'Assessment and support of children and adolescents with gender dysphoria', *Archives of Disease in Childhood* 103/7 (July 2018), 631–6, doi: 10.1136/archdischild-2018-314992; Henry Bodkin, 'Encouraging children to "socially transition" gender risks long-term harm, say NHS experts', *Telegraph* (17 July 2019), https://www.telegraph. co.uk/news/2019/07/17/encouraging-children-socially-transition-gender-risks-long-term/; 'Dr Polly Carmichael – developments and dilemmas' [recording of talk at ACAMH conference 'Gender in 2017: meeting the needs of gender diverse children and young people with mental health difficulties', Bristol, 12 October 2017], https://soundcloud.com/user-664361280/dr-polly-carmichael-developments-and-dilemmas; Tavistock and Portman NHS Foundation Trust FOI 17-18326 ('Subject: GIDS referrals and outcomes'), https://tavistockandportman. nhs.uk/documents/1131/FOI_17-18326_GIDS_Referrals_and_Outcomes.pdf.
18 'minority': 'Trust defence of GIDS', Tavistock and Portman NHS Foundation Trust [website], https://tavistockandportman.nhs.uk/about-us/news/stories/trust-defence-gids/.
19 Butler et al., 'Assessment and support of children and adolescents with gender dysphoria'.
20 Ibid.
21 Ibid.
22 Tavistock and Portman NHS Foundation Trust FOI 21-22169 (copy shared with the author, but not published online by the Trust).
23 University College London Hospitals NHS Foundation Trust FOI/2022/0028 (copy shared with the author, but not published online by the Trust).
24 Tavistock and Portman NHS Foundation Trust internal investigation into FOI 21-22169.
25 As the data relates to those referred between 2010 and 2013, these young people will have been seen within 18 weeks of referral. GIDS did not breach this target until 2015.
26 'Dr Polly Carmichael – developments and dilemmas'.
27 Polly Carmichael and Claudia Zitz, 'Diverging models of care for children and adolescents' [workshop held as part of British Association of Gender Identity Specialists (BAGIS) Scientific Symposium for 2019, Durham, 4 October 2019], https://bagis.co.uk/wp-content/uploads/2020/08/Draft-Program-Symposium-2019-Ver-12-27.9.pdf.
28 If 40 per cent is the overall average of all patients and 20 per cent is the rate for those referred prepubertally, the rate for others must be 60 per cent: 20 + 60 / 2 = 40.
29 University College London Hospitals NHS Foundation Trust FOI/2022/0016 (author's own request; not published by the Trust in its FOI Disclosure List).
30 Matt Bristow, 'Very surprised to hear @PaulJThinks say on @BBCr4today that hormone blockers are "fully reversible". The #GIDS website itself says that some long-term health risks are still unknown' [Twitter thread] (22 July 2019), https://twitter.com/psychomologist/status/1153301937565130753.
31 'Board of directors (part one): agenda and papers of a meeting to be held in public Tuesday 30th March 2021' [PDF], Tavistock and Portman NHS Foundation

Trust [website], https://tavistockandportman.nhs.uk/documents/2251/Part_1_-_March_21_Board_of_Directors_-_final_boardpack_e-version.pdf.

32 For the claim that they do not hold the data, see Tavistock and Portman NHS Foundation Trust FOI 18-19063 ('Subject: use of puberty blockers'), https://tavistockandportman.nhs.uk/documents/1206/FOI_18-19063_Use_of_Puberty_Blockers.pdf and Tavistock and Portman NHS Foundation Trust FOI 16-17282 ('Subject: GIDS (Gender Identity Development Service) under 18's service users analysis'), https://tavistockandportman.nhs.uk/documents/627/FOI_16-17282_GIDS_under_18s_Service_Users_Analysis.pdf. For the claim that they do not hold it in a way that is easily searchable, see Tavistock and Portman NHS Foundation Trust FOI 18-19243 ('Subject: FOI 18-19243 GIDS patients by CCG, age, prescription of puberty blockers'), https://tavistockandportman.nhs.uk/documents/1280/FOI_18-19243_GIDS_Patients_by_CCG_Age_Prescription_of_Puberty_Blockers.pdf.

33 Tavistock and Portman NHS Foundation Trust FOI 17-18189 ('Subject: referrals involving puberty blockers'), https://tavistockandportman.nhs.uk/documents/1060/FOI_17-18189_Referrals_Involving_Puberty_Blockers.pdf.

34 Tavistock and Portman NHS Foundation Trust FOI 18-19262 ('Subject: hormone blocking treatments'), https://tavistockandportman.nhs.uk/documents/1427/FOI_18-19262_Hormone_Blocking_Referrals_2014-18.pdf.

35 Tavistock and Portman NHS Foundation Trust FOI 19-20426 ('Subject: GIDS referrals to endocrinology clinics 2019 & consent for hormone blockers'), https://tavistockandportman.nhs.uk/documents/1990/FOI_19-20426_GIDS_Referrals_to_Endo_Clinics_-2019_Consent_for_Hormone_Blockers_QL1jP7U.pdf.

36 Tavistock and Portman NHS Foundation Trust FOI 22-23027 ('Subject: GIDS: 1st appts and prescriptions'), https://tavistockandportman.nhs.uk/documents/2727/FOI_22-23027_GIDS1stApptsPrescripns.pdf.

37 University College London Hospitals NHS Foundation Trust FOI/2022/0016 (author's own request; not published by the Trust in its FOI Disclosure List).

38 University College London Hospitals NHS Foundation Trust FOI-0016-22, internal review response (author's own request; not published by the Trust in its FOI Disclosure List).

39 University College London Hospitals NHS Foundation Trust FOI/2022/0359 (author's own request; not published by the Trust in its FOI Disclosure List).

40 Data for January to May 2022 only.

41 University College London Hospitals NHS Foundation Trust FOI/2022/0655 (author's own copy; not published by the Trust in its FOI Disclosure List).

42 Butler et al., 'Discharge outcome analysis of 1089 transgender young people'.

43 Leeds Teaching Hospitals NHS Trust FOI Ref; 2022–0280 (author's own request; not available online).

44 Leeds Teaching Hospitals NHS Trust FOI Ref; 2022–0280a (author's own request; not available online).

45 For the data published in July 2022, see Butler et al., 'Discharge outcome analysis of 1089 transgender young people'.

46 Domenico Di Ceglie, 'Castaway's corner', *Clinical Child Psychology and Psychiatry* 7/3 (2002), 487–91, doi: 10.1177/1359104502007003

47 Ibid.

48 Hitomi Nakamura, 'Follow-up study of children and adolescents with gender identity development issues who attended the specialist Gender Identity Development Unit (GIDU) and who are now 18 or older' [thesis submitted for the degree of doctorate in counselling psychology, Department of Health and Human Sciences, University of Essex] (5 June 2007).

49 Lorna Hobbs, 'What happens to gender diverse young people who are referred to an adult gender identity service from a child and adolescent service? A cross-sectional look at intervention choices and outcomes' [prof. doc. thesis, University of East London School of Psychology] (2018), doi: 10.15123/uel.874y5.

50 Ibid.

51 Ibid.

52 Butler et al., 'Discharge outcome analysis of 1089 transgender young people'.

53 Ibid.

54 On the issue of fertility preservation, see Tavistock and Portman NHS Foundation Trust FOI 19-20360 ('Subject: GIDS talking therapy and prescription'), https://tavistockandportman.nhs.uk/documents/1878/FOI_19-20360__GID_Talking_Therapy_and_Prescription.pdf. On the issue of how many patients go on to adult gender services, and how many leave GIDS after receiving talking therapies only, see Tavistock and Portman NHS Foundation Trust FOI 19-20418 ('Subject: GIDS referrals, discharges transfers, rejections'), https://tavistockandportman.nhs.uk/documents/1933/FOI_19-20418_GIDS_Referrals_-Discharges_-Transfers_-Rejections.pdf.

55 Tobin Joseph, Joanna Ting and Gary Butler, 'The effect of GnRH analogue treatment on bone mineral density in young adolescents with gender dysphoria: findings from a large national cohort', *Journal of Pediatric Endocrinology and Metabolism* 32/10 (2019), 1077–81, doi: 10.1515/jpem-2019-0046.

56 Ibid. The information about the resumption of bone mass accrual is from Peggy T. Cohen-Kettenis and Daniel Klink, 'Adolescents with gender dysphoria', *Best Practice and Research Clinical Endocrinology and Metabolism* 29/3 (2015), 485–95, doi: 10.1016/j.beem.2015.01.004.

57 Deborah Cohen and Hannah Barnes, 'Gender dysphoria in children: puberty blockers study draws further criticism', *BMJ* 366/l5647 (20 September 2019), doi: 10.1136/bmj.l5647

58 Joseph, Ting and Butler, 'The effect of GnRH analogue treatment on bone mineral density'.

59 Michael Biggs, 'Revisiting the effect of GnRH analogue treatment on bone mineral density in young adolescents with gender dysphoria' *Journal of Pediatric Endocrinology and Metabolism* 34/7 (2021), 937–9, doi: 10.1515/jpem-2021-0180.

60 David Taylor, 'Report on GIDU review (May–Oct. 2005)' [PDF] (January 2006), https://tavistockandportman.nhs.uk/documents/2248/FOI_20-21117_2005_David_Taylor_Report.pdf.

Harriet

1 For the respective guidelines, see 'Service specification: gender identity services for adults (surgical interventions)' [PDF], NHS England [website], https://www.england.nhs.uk/wp-content/uploads/2019/12/nhs-england-service-specification-gender-identity-surgical-services.pdf and 'Standards of care for the health of transsexual, transgender, and gender-nonconforming people [version 7]' [PDF], WPATH [website], https://www.wpath.org/media/cms/Documents/SOC%20v7/SOC%20V7_English2012.pdf?_t=1613669341. The eighth version was published in September 2022 and is available here: https://www.tandfonline.com/doi/pdf/10.1080/26895269.2022.2100644.
2 'Information about atrophic vaginitis' [PDF], Royal United Hospitals Bath NHS Foundation Trust [website], https://www.ruh.nhs.uk/patients/Urology/documents/patient_leaflets/Atrophic_Vaginitis.pdf.
3 'Apply for a Gender Recognition Certificate', Gov.uk [website], https://www.gov.uk/apply-gender-recognition-certificate.
4 Women and Equalities Committee, 'Reform of the Gender Recognition Act: third report of session 2021–22', Parliament.uk [website] (15 December 2021), https://committees.parliament.uk/publications/8329/documents/84728/default/.
5 'Dr Helen Webberley', Medical Practitioners Tribunal Service [website], https://www.mpts-uk.org/hearings-and-decisions/medical-practitioners-tribunals/dr-helen-webberley-jul-21.
6 Ibid.
7 Helen Webberley, '11/ My firm belief is that I did not fail Patient C in any way, and that my care was correct and timely and potentially life-saving. I believe that I discussed fertility options with his Mum until she was happy, and that she had discussed this with him' [Twitter post] (4 August 2022), https://twitter.com/MyWebDoctorUK/status/1555230954515488770?s=20&t=HpuysE150PAFbhyYsyt4g.
8 Michael Webberley's 'Record of determinations' from the Medical Practitioners Tribunal Service, https://www.mpts-uk.org/-/media/mpts-rod-files/dr-michael-webberley-25-may-22.pdf.
9 Ibid. See also Ewan Somerville, '"Reckless" doctor struck off after giving puberty blockers to nine-year-old', *Telegraph* (25 May 2022), https://www.telegraph.co.uk/news/2022/05/25/reckless-doctor-struck-giving-puberty-blockers-nine-year-old/.
10 Michael Webberley's 'Record of determinations'.
11 Ibid.
12 'GenderGP comment on Dr. Michael Webberley's MPTS hearing', GenderGP [website] (19 May 2022), https://www.gendergp.com/gendergp-comment-on-dr-michael-webberleys-mpts-hearing/.
13 'Appendix D: transfers from the Gender Identity Development Service for children and young people', contained in 'Gender identity services for adults (non-surgical interventions)' [PDF], NHS England [website], https://www.england.nhs.uk/wp-content/uploads/2019/07/service-specification-gender-dysphoria-services-non-surgical-june-2019.pdf.

20. When in Doubt, Do the Right Thing

1 Mark Hudson, 'Investigation report into concerns raised under the Trust's freedom to speak up: raising concerns and whistleblowing procedure about the culture and practice within the Trust's Gender Identity Development Service (GIDS)' (January 2021).

2 Ibid.

3 Helen Roberts to Ailsa Swarbrick, c.c. Sonia Appleby and Caroline McKenna [email containing forwarded thread between Helen Roberts and others, begun on 20 March 2020; subject: 'Strictly Private and Confidential'], 10 October 2020.

4 Helen Roberts to Ailsa Swarbrick, c.c. Sonia Appleby and Caroline McKenna [email containing forwarded thread between Helen Roberts and Garry Richardson, 11–12 December 2019; subject: 'FW: 22164'], 10 October 2020.

5 For the GIDS Review report, see Dinesh Sinha, 'A review in to [*sic*] concerns raised about the Gender Identity Development Service' ['Annex A' of *GIDS Review Action Plan*, 26 March 2019] (February 2019), https://tavistockandportman.nhs.uk/documents/1376/GIDS_Action_plan_review.pdf.

6 Helen Roberts to Ailsa Swarbrick, c.c. Sonia Appleby and Caroline McKenna [email containing forwarded thread between Helen Roberts and others, begun on 20 March 2020; subject: 're: Strictly Private and Confidential'], 10 October 2020.

7 Ibid.

8 Hudson, 'Investigation report into concerns raised under the Trust's freedom to speak up'; 'Report a patient safety incident', NHS England [website], https://www.england.nhs.uk/patient-safety/report-patient-safety-incident/.

9 Hudson, 'Investigation report into concerns raised under the Trust's freedom to speak up'.

10 Helen Roberts, Ailsa Swarbrick, Sonia Appleby and C. McKenna [email; subject: 're: Strictly Private and Confidential'], 10 October 2020.

11 Hudson, 'Investigation report into concerns raised under the Trust's freedom to speak up'.

12 Helen Roberts, Ailsa Swarbrick, Sonia Appleby and C. McKenna [email; subject: 're: Strictly Private and Confidential'], 10 October 2020.

13 Ibid.

14 Ibid.

15 Ibid.

16 Hudson, 'Investigation report into concerns raised under the Trust's freedom to speak up'.

17 Ibid.

18 Ibid.

19 Ibid.

20 Ibid.

21 Ibid.

22 Ibid.

23 Sonia Appleby, 'Safeguarding concerns at GIDS', Crowd Justice [website], https://www.crowdjustice.com/case/gids-concerns/ and 'Particulars of claim' [official document from employment tribunal *Ms Sonia Appleby vs the Tavistock and Portman NHS Foundation Trust*; case no. 2204772/2019].

24 Appleby, 'Safeguarding concerns at GIDS'.

25 Ibid.

26 Ibid.

27 'NHS child gender clinic: staff welfare concerns "shut down"' [video], *Newsnight*, BBC (18 June 2020), https://www.youtube.com/watch?v=zTRnrp9pXHY.

28 *Ms S. Appleby v Tavistock and Portman NHS Foundation Trust* [case no. 2204772/2019] [PDF], https://assets.publishing.service.gov.uk/media/6149eb48d3bf7f05ac396f79/Ms_S_Appleby__vs___Tavistock_and_Portman_NHS_Foundation_Trust.pdf.

29 Ibid.

30 Ibid.

31 Ibid.

32 'Extract from transcript of interview with Garry Richardson', in *Ms S. Appleby v Tavistock and Portman NHS Foundation Trust*.

33 *Ms S. Appleby v Tavistock and Portman NHS Foundation Trust*.

34 Ibid.

35 Ibid.

36 Ibid.

37 'First witness statement of Sonia Appleby' [official document from employment tribunal *Ms Sonia Appleby vs the Tavistock and Portman NHS Foundation Trust*; case no. 2204772/2019] (24 May 2021).

38 Ibid.

39 Ibid.

40 Sonia Appleby, 'Many thanks to you all' [update on Appleby's 'Safeguarding concerns at GIDS' crowdfunding webpage hosted by the website CrowdJustice, 6 September 2021], https://www.crowdjustice.com/case/gids-concerns/.

41 *Ms S. Appleby v Tavistock and Portman NHS Foundation Trust*.

42 Henry Martin, 'Whistleblower is suing NHS child gender clinic for freezing her out after she raised concerns about doctor prescribing puberty blockers to young patients, tribunal hears', *Daily Mail* (16 June 2021), https://www.dailymail.co.uk/news/article-9693535/Whistleblower-suing-NHSs-child-gender-clinic-freezing-out.html; Hannah Barnes, 'He determined that we should have a meeting with Dr Carmichael. It started as drizzle, then a trickle and then a stream of staff coming to me about Dr Webberley – a private GP who were prescribing puberty blockers and CSH to children on the waiting list' [Twitter post] (16 June 2021), https://twitter.com/hannahsbee/status/1405124538392797184?.

43 *Ms S. Appleby v Tavistock and Portman NHS Foundation Trust*.

44 Ibid.

45 'First witness statement of Sonia Appleby'.

46 *Ms S. Appleby v Tavistock and Portman NHS Foundation Trust* and Sonia Appleby to Polly Carmichael, c.c. Sally Hodges and Rob Senior [email; subject: 're Monday's Meeting: 5 February 2018'], 8 February 2018.

47 'First witness statement of Sonia Appleby'.

48 *Ms S. Appleby v Tavistock and Portman NHS Foundation Trust.*

49 'First witness statement of Sonia Appleby'.

50 Ibid.

51 Hannah Barnes, 'YG – were you aware that for some time GIDS had been missed off an all-trust email circulation list re: updates to care notes? SA – yes. I believe it was a matter that the patient safety officer uncovered' [Twitter post] (17 June 2021), https://twitter.com/hannahsbee/status/1405517396345966592.

52 Sally Hodges to all [email; subject: 'Re Service Matter'], 24 May 2018.

53 Sonia Appleby to Sally Hodges, c.c. Rob Senior [email; subject: 're: Further to our brief meeting on Friday'], 18 June 2018.

54 Sonia Appleby to David Bell and Rob Senior [email; subject: 're: GIDS'], 21 June 2018.

55 *Ms S. Appleby v Tavistock and Portman NHS Foundation Trust.*

56 From a statement Sonia Appleby prepared prior to her interview for the GIDS Review. It set out the history of her involvement with GIDS, the concerns she had raised and conversations she had held with others in the Trust. The document is dated 24 October 2018. Appleby was one of ten individuals it was originally stipulated that Tavistock medical director Dinesh Sinha speak to as part of his review. Their meeting took place the following day, 25 October 2018.

57 Ibid.

58 The word 'transphobic' is taken from the transcript of Dinesh Sinha's interview with 'M010' (26 November 2018).

59 Transcript of Dinesh Sinha's interview with Sonia Appleby ('M009') (25 October 2018).

60 Hannah Barnes, 'AP – Did you do anything about that allegation – that there is a particular child being damaged by stunted growth and PC did not want to refer it? DS – i can't remember exact detail of that concern but when things came up thematically i took to HR' [Twitter thread] (21 June 2021), https://twitter.com/hannahsbee/status/1407069064485298181.

61 Dinesh Sinha, Sally Hodges, Craig de Sousa [emails; subject: 're GIDS issues'], 2 July 2019.

62 Hannah Barnes, 'An allegation that Polly Carmichael guided staff not to seek advice from central s/g falls squarely in your remit doesn't it? DS – Yes AP takes DS to his findings. You've had three people tell you that PC has instructed staff not to take safeguarding concerns to SA...' [Twitter post] (22 June 2021), https://twitter.com/hannahsbee/status/1407299028115656708; Hannah Barnes, 'AP – But I'm questioning your approach These three people are all making the same allegations; it's serious; it's about the director of GIDS; and it has ramifications for other people; even if you did take it to HR that's not an appropriate way of dealing with is it?' [Twitter post] (22 June 2021), https://twitter.com/hannahsbee/status/1407299035761975298.

63 Hannah Barnes, 'DS – I don't think so... Actually I find lots of areas of concerns and my action plan was to deal with those... I was not giving a clean bill of health to the service' [Twitter post] (22 June 2021), https://twitter.com/hannahsbee/status/1407299802233253897.

64 Hannah Barnes, 'AP – well that's how it comes across – you receive the same serious allegation about the director of the service and you don't mention it – that's exactly what it does look like – "a clean up report"' [Twitter post] (22 June 2021), https://twitter.com/hannahsbee/status/1407299805735534595?; Hannah Barnes, 'AP – if anything that suggests that you saw concerns from AH, AS, MB as a management issue that needed to be contained rather than a s/g issue that needed to be addressed' [Twitter post] (22 June 2021), https://twitter.com/hannahsbee/status/1407301176245243908.

65 Statutory guidance makes it clear that 'everyone who works with children has a responsibility for keeping them safe'. In addition, all NHS Trusts are required by law to have named or designated professionals for safeguarding children. See 'Working together to safeguard children' [PDF], Gov.uk [website] (July 2018), https://assets.publishing.service.gov.uk/government/uploads/system/uploads/attachment_data/file/942454/Working_together_to_safeguard_children_inter_agency_guidance.pdf. See also 'Safeguarding children and young people: roles and competencies for healthcare staff', Royal College of Nursing [website] (30 January 2019), https://www.rcn.org.uk/professional-development/publications/pub-007366 and 'London safeguarding children procedures and practice guidance', London Safeguarding Children Procedures [website], https://www.londonsafeguardingchildrenprocedures.co.uk/.

66 'First witness statement of Sonia Appleby'.

67 'First witness statement of Dr Matt Bristow' [official document from employment tribunal *Ms Sonia Appleby vs the Tavistock and Portman NHS Foundation Trust*; case no. 2204772/2019] (23 May 2021); 'First witness statement of Dr Anna Hutchinson' [official document from employment tribunal *Ms Sonia Appleby vs the Tavistock and Portman NHS Foundation Trust*; case no. 2204772/2019] (24 May 2021); transcript of Dinesh Sinha's interview with Anastassis Spiliadis ('BD007') (7 January 2019).

68 'NHS child gender identity clinic whistleblower wins tribunal', BBC News [website] (5 September 2021), https://www.bbc.co.uk/news/uk-58453250; David Connett, 'NHS gender identity clinic whistleblower wins damages', *Guardian* (4 September 2021), https://www.theguardian.com/society/2021/sep/04/gender-identity-clinic-whistleblower-wins-damages.

21. An Uncertain Future

1 University College London Hospitals NHS Foundation Trust FOI/2022/0016 (author's own request; not published by the Trust in its FOI Disclosure List).

2 The increase prescriptions issued to males is recorded in University College London Hospitals NHS Foundation Trust FOI/2022/0359 (author's own request; not published by the Trust in its FOI Disclosure List at the time of writing).

3 Femi Nzegwu, 'GIDS report on sustainable working' (2015). Supplied to the author privately.

4 'Board of directors (part one): agenda and papers of a meeting to be held in public 2.00 p.m.–4.30 p.m. Tuesday 23rd May 2017' [PDF], Tavistock and

Portman NHS Foundation Trust [website], https://tavistockandportman.nhs.
uk/documents/705/May_2017_Boardpack_Part_1.pdf.

5 Notes from two telephone conversations between Martin Cawley and Polly
Carmichael, 16 January 2019, via Tavistock and Portman NHS Foundation Trust
FOI 20-21072 and ICO Complaint IC-64728-M8PO. Original request provided
to the author in private correspondence and not available online. The Information
Commissioner's Office decision notice can be found here: https://ico.org.uk/
media/action-weve-taken/decision-notices/2021/2620272/ic-64728-m8p0.pdf.
For the grant, see Andrew Gilligan, 'Child sex-change charity Mermaids handed
£500,000 by national lottery', *Sunday Times* (16 December 2018), https://www.
thetimes.co.uk/article/child-sex-change-charity-handed-500-000-by-national-
lottery-dvbt7t2kb.

6 Aamna Mohdin, 'National Lottery to give grant to transgender children's group',
Guardian (19 February 2019), https://www.theguardian.com/uk-news/2019/
feb/19/national-lottery-to-give-grant-to-transgender-childrens-group.

7 Notes from two telephone conversations between Martin Cawley and Polly
Carmichael, 16 January 2019, via Tavistock and Portman NHS Foundation Trust
FOI 20-21072 and ICO Complaint IC-64728-M8PO.

8 Ibid.

9 'Tavistock and Portman NHS Foundation Trust: gender identity services
inspection report' [PDF], CQC [website] (20 January 2021), https://api.cqc.org.
uk/public/v1/reports/7ecf93b7-2b14-45ea-a317-53b6f4804c24; Mark Hudson,
'Investigation report into concerns raised under the Trust's freedom to speak up:
raising concerns and whistleblowing procedure about the culture and practice
within the Trust's Gender Identity Development Service (GIDS)' (January 2021).

10 On low morale, see 'Board of directors (part one): agenda and papers of
a meeting to be held in public Tuesday 30th March 2021' [PDF], Tavistock
and Portman NHS Foundation Trust [website], https://tavistockandportman.
nhs.uk/documents/2251/Part_1_-_March_21_Board_of_Directors_-_final_
boardpack_e-version.pdf and 'Board of directors (part one): agenda and papers
of a meeting to be held in public Tuesday 18th May 2021' [PDF], Tavistock
and Portman NHS Foundation Trust [website], https://tavistockandportman.
nhs.uk/documents/2290/Part_1_May_Board_of_Directors_final_boardpack_e-
version_-_Updated_June_2021.pdf. On staff retention and recruitment, see
'Board of directors (part one): agenda and papers of a meeting to be held in public
Tuesday 29th March 2022' [PDF], Tavistock and Portman NHS Foundation
Trust [website], https://tavistockandportman.nhs.uk/documents/2455/Part_1_
Board_of_Directors_e-version_final_pack.pdf.

11 'Board of directors (part one): agenda and papers of a meeting to be held in public
Tuesday 26th January 2021' [PDF], Tavistock and Portman NHS Foundation
Trust [website], https://tavistockandportman.nhs.uk/documents/2162/Part_1_
January_2021_Board_of_Directors_Meeting_final_e-version.pdf.

12 Ibid.

13 A Freedom of Information request to NHS England seeking further detail
on this request from the Trust has not been answered at the time of writing. It
is five months overdue.

14 For referral information, see 'Make a referral to GIDS', GIDS [website], https://gids.nhs.uk/referrals/. For the form, see 'GIDS smart form version 4.1(1)' [spreadsheet], downloadable at https://tavistockandportman.nhs.uk/documents/2334/GIDS_smart_form_version_5_-_updated_29-11-2021.xlsx.

15 Ibid.

16 'Make a referral to GIDS', GIDS [website].

17 Ibid.

18 'Addendum to referral form: service users with identified risk' [Word document], Tavistock and Portman NHS Foundation Trust [website], https://tavistockandportman.nhs.uk/documents/2333/GIDS_referral_addendum_risk_assessment_form_-_updated_29-11-2021.docx.

19 'Board of directors (part one): agenda and papers of a meeting to be held in public Tuesday 25th January 2022' [PDF], Tavistock and Portman NHS Foundation Trust [website], https://tavistockandportman.nhs.uk/documents/2407/Board_papers_-_January_2022.pdf.

20 Ibid.

21 'Regional model for gender care announced for children and young people', Tavistock and Portman NHS Foundation Trust [website] (28 July 2022), https://tavistockandportman.nhs.uk/about-us/news/stories/regional-model-for-gender-care-announced-for-children-and-young-people/; 'Implementing advice from the Cass Review', NHS England [website], https://www.england.nhs.uk/commissioning/spec-services/npc-crg/gender-dysphoria-clinical-programme/implementing-advice-from-the-cass-review/.

22 'Update following recent court rulings on hormone blockers,' NHS England [website], https://www.england.nhs.uk/commissioning/spec-services/npc-crg/gender-dysphoria-clinical-programme/update-following-recent-court-rulings-on-hormone-blockers/, archived at http://web.archive.org/web/20220617131256/https://www.england.nhs.uk/commissioning/spec-services/npc-crg/gender-dysphoria-clinical-programme/update-following-recent-court-rulings-on-hormone-blockers/.

23 Ibid.

24 'Accessing hormone suppressants', Tavistock and Portman NHS Foundation Trust [website], https://gids.nhs.uk/accessing-hormone-suppressants/, archived at http://web.archive.org/web/20220617130932/https://gids.nhs.uk/accessing-hormone-suppressants/.

25 NHS England FOI-2203-1709490 (author's own request; not available online).

26 Ibid.

27 On 'insufficient information', see 'Independent multi-professional review group decision document' [PDF], NHS [website], https://www.england.nhs.uk/wp-content/uploads/2021/10/B1054-independent-multi-professional-review-group-decision-document.pdf, archived at http://web.archive.org/web/20220617131552/https://www.england.nhs.uk/wp-content/uploads/2021/10/B1054-independent-multi-professional-review-group-decision-document.pdf. On 'specific safeguarding concerns', see 'The Cass Review: independent review of gender identity services for children and young people: interim report' [PDF], Cass Review [website] (February 2022), https://cass.independent-review.uk/wp-

content/uploads/2022/03/Cass-Review-Interim-Report-Final-Web-Accessible.
pdf.

28 Ibid.

29 'Four years is too long to wait for healthcare: we're going to court', Good
Law Project [website] (11 May 2022), https://goodlawproject.org/update/
trans-healthcare-court-permission/?utm_source=Twitter&utm_campaign=
TransHealthcareBlog110522&utm_medium=social%20media; Hayley Dixon,
'Campaigners seek to scrap parental consent from NHS trans treatment', *Telegraph*
(11 May 2022), https://www.telegraph.co.uk/news/2022/05/11/campaigners-
bid-scrap-parental-consent-nhs-trans-treatment/.

30 'Statement of facts and grounds' (17 December 2021), https://drive.google.
com/file/d/18mUC9gOF6a1U6XtOQpsoem4TNK6L3tHr/view.

31 'Notification of the judge's decision on the application for permission to
apply for judicial review (CPR 54.11, 54.12)', https://drive.google.com/file/
d/19KmnaKSvWACi9H_MhUdCq_EAk09kCTgk/view.

32 'The Cass Review […] interim report'.

33 For the commissioning in September 2020, see 'NHS announces independent
review into gender identity services for children and young people', NHS England
[website] (22 September 2020), https://www.england.nhs.uk/2020/09/nhs-
announces-independent-review-into-gender-identity-services-for-children-
and-young-people/.

34 'The Cass Review […] interim report'.

35 Ibid.

36 Ibid.

37 Ibid.

38 Ibid.

39 Ibid.

40 Ibid.

41 Ibid.

42 Ibid.

43 Ibid.

44 Ibid.

45 Ibid.

46 Ibid.

47 Ibid.

48 *Bell v Tavistock* [2020] EWHC 3274 (Admin) [PDF] (1 December 2020),
https://www.judiciary.uk/wp-content/uploads/2020/12/Bell-v-Tavistock-
Judgment.pdf.

49 Ibid.

50 Gary Butler et al., 'Discharge outcome analysis of 1089 transgender young
people referred to paediatric endocrine clinics in England 2008–2021', *Archives
of Disease in Childhood* (18 July 2022), doi: 10.1136/archdischild-2022-324302.

51 'The Cass Review […] interim report'.

52 Ibid.

53 Letter from Dr Hilary Cass to John Stewart, national director, specialised
commissioning NHS England, 19 July 2022 [PDF], Cass Review [website],

https://cass.independent-review.uk/wp-content/uploads/2022/07/Cass-Review-Letter-to-NHSE_19-July-2022.pdf.

54 Ibid.

55 'Implementing advice from the Cass Review', NHS England [website], https://www.england.nhs.uk/commissioning/spec-services/npc-crg/gender-dysphoria-clinical-programme/implementing-advice-from-the-cass-review/.

56 'Care of children and adolescents with gender dysphoria' [PDF], National Board of Health and Welfare (Sweden) [website] (February 2022), https://www.socialstyrelsen.se/globalassets/sharepoint-dokument/artikelkatalog/kunskapsstod/2022-3-7799.pdf.

57 'Recommendation of the Council for Choices in Health Care in Finland (PALKO / COHERE Finland): medical treatment methods for dysphoria related to gender variance in minors' [PDF; unofficial English translation], Society for Evidence Based Gender Medicine [website] (June 2020), https://segm.org/sites/default/files/Finnish_Guidelines_2020_Minors_Unofficial%20Translation.pdf and 'One year since Finland broke with WPATH "Standards of Care"', Society for Evidence Based Gender Medicine [website] (2 July 2021), https://segm.org/Finland_deviates_from_WPATH_prioritizing_psychotherapy_no_surgery_for_minors.

58 National Academy of Medicine, France, 'Press release: medical care of children and adolescents with transgender identity' [PDF; unofficial English translation of 'Communiqué: la médecine face à la transidentité de genre chez les enfants et les adolescents'], Society for Evidence Based Gender Medicine [website] (2 March 2022), https://segm.org/sites/default/files/English%20Translation_22.2.25-Communique-PCRA-19-Medecine-et-transidentite-genre.pdf and 'National Academy of Medicine in France advises caution in pediatric gender transition', Society for Evidence Based Gender Medicine [website] (3 March 2022), https://segm.org/France-cautions-regarding-puberty-blockers-and-cross-sex-hormones-for-youth.

59 Ibid.

60 Abigail Shrier, 'Top trans doctors blow the whistle on "sloppy" care', Common Sense [blog] (4 October 2021), https://bariweiss.substack.com/p/top-trans-doctors-blow-the-whistle.

61 Tim C. van de Grift et al., 'Timing of puberty suppression and surgical options for transgender youth', Pediatrics 146/5 (2020), e20193653, doi: 10.1542/peds.2019-3653.

62 Shrier, 'Top trans doctors blow the whistle on "sloppy" care'.

63 Marci Bowers, speaking at 'Trans & gender diverse policies, care, practices, and wellbeing' [symposium held at Duke University, North Carolina, 21 March 2022], https://globalhealth.duke.edu/events/trans-gender-diverse-policies-care-practices-and-wellbeing.

64 Laura Edwards-Leeper and Erica Anderson, 'The mental health establishment is failing trans kids', *Washington Post* (24 November 2021), https://www.washingtonpost.com/outlook/2021/11/24/trans-kids-therapy-psychologist/. For the WPATH standards of care, see 'Standards of care for the health of transsexual, transgender, and gender-nonconforming people [version 7]' [PDF],

WPATH [website], https://www.wpath.org/media/cms/Documents/SOC%20 v7/SOC%20V7_English2012.pdf?_t=1613669341.

65 'gender incongruence'; 'marked and sustained over time': E. Coleman et al., 'Standards of care for the health of transgender and gender diverse people, version 8', *International Journal of Transgender Health* 23/supp.1 (2022), S1–S259, doi: 10.1080/26895269.2022.2100644. For the draft chapter, see 'Adolescent' [PDF], WPATH [website], https://www.wpath.org/media/cms/Documents/SOC%20 v8/SOC8%20Chapters%20for%20Public%20Comment/SOC8%20Chapter%20 Draft%20for%20Public%20Comment%20-%20Adolescent.pdf. See also 'The battle over gender therapy', *New York Times* (15 June 2022), https://www.nytimes. com/2022/06/15/magazine/gender-therapy.html.

66 Coleman et al., 'Standards of care for the health of transgender and gender diverse people, version 8'.

67 'Correction', *International Journal of Transgender Health* 23/supp.1 (2022), S259–S261, doi: 10.1080/26895269.2022.2125695. For the draft chapter, see 'Adolescent' [PDF], WPATH [website] and 'The battle over gender therapy', *New York Times* (15 June 2022), https://www.nytimes.com/2022/06/15/magazine/ gender-therapy.html.

68 Coleman et al., 'Standards of care for the health of transgender and gender diverse people, version 8'.

69 Annelou L. C. de Vries, 'Challenges in timing puberty suppression for gender-nonconforming adolescents', *Pediatrics* 146/4 (2020), e2020010611, doi: 10.1542/ peds.2020-010611.

70 'Dringend meer onderzoek nodig naar transgenderzorg aan jongeren: "Waar komt de grote stroom kinderen vandaan?"' ['Urgently need more research into transgender care for young people: "Where does the large flow of children come from?"'], *Algemeen Dagblad* (27 February 2021), https://www.ad.nl/nijmegen/ dringend-meer-onderzoek-nodig-naar-transgenderzorg-aan-jongeren-waar-komt-de-grote-stroom-kinderen-vandaan~aec79d00/; 'Hormonen geven aan transgenderkinderen is omstreden, maar volgens artsen toch soms nodig: "Het is kiezen uit twee kwaden"' ['Giving hormones to transgender children is controversial, but according to doctors sometimes necessary: "It is choosing between two evils"'], *De Gelderlander* (2 February 2021), https://www.gelderlander. nl/nijmegen/hormonen-geven-aan-transgenderkinderen-is-omstreden-maar-volgens-artsen-toch-soms-nodig-het-is-kiezen-uit-twee-kwaden~ab8da190/.

Conclusion

1 'Implementing advice from the Cass Review', NHS England [website], https://www.england.nhs.uk/commissioning/spec-services/npc-crg/gender-dysphoria-clinical-programme/implementing-advice-from-the-cass-review/; 'Regional model for gender care announced for children and young people', Tavistock and Portman NHS Foundation Trust [website] (28 July 2022), https:// tavistockandportman.nhs.uk/about-us/news/stories/regional-model-for-gender-care-announced-for-children-and-young-people/.

2 'Implementing advice from the Cass Review'.

3 Letter from Dr Hilary Cass to John Stewart, national director, specialised commissioning NHS England, 19 July 2022 [PDF], Cass Review [website], https://cass.independent-review.uk/wp-content/uploads/2022/07/Cass-Review-Letter-to-NHSE_19-July-2022.pdf.

4 Ibid.

5 'Interim service specification for specialist gender dysphoria services for children and young people – public consultation', NHS England [website], https://www.engage.england.nhs.uk/specialised-commissioning/gender-dysphoria-services/.

6 'Interim service specification: specialist service for children and young people with gender dysphoria (phase 1 providers)' [PDF], NHS England [website] (20 October 2022), https://www.engage.england.nhs.uk/specialised-commissioning/gender-dysphoria-services/user_uploads/b1937-ii-specialist-service-for-children-and-young-people-with-gender-dysphoria-1.pdf.

7 Ibid.

8 'Interim service specification for specialised services for children and young people with gender dysphoria (phase 1 services)' [PDF; NHS England: Equality and Health Inequalities Impact Assessment (EHIA) proposal], NHS England [website] (12 October 2022), https://www.engage.england.nhs.uk/specialised-commissioning/gender-dysphoria-services/user_uploads/b1937_iii_equalities-health-impact-assessment-interim-service-specification.pdf.

9 Ibid.

10 'Interim service specification: specialist service for children and young people with gender dysphoria (phase 1 providers)' [PDF], NHS England [website] (20 October 2022), https://www.engage.england.nhs.uk/specialised-commissioning/gender-dysphoria-services/user_uploads/b1937-ii-specialist-service-for-children-and-young-people-with-gender-dysphoria-1.pdf.

11 Ibid.

12 Ibid.

13 Ibid.

14 'Interim service specification for specialised services for children and young people with gender dysphoria (phase 1 services)' [PDF; NHS England: Equality and Health Inequalities Impact Assessment (EHIA) proposal], NHS England [website] (12 October 2022), https://www.engage.england.nhs.uk/specialised-commissioning/gender-dysphoria-services/user_uploads/b1937_iii_equalities-health-impact-assessment-interim-service-specification.pdf.

15 For numbers waiting, see ibid. For length of wait, see 'Board of directors (part one): agenda and papers of a meeting to be held in public Tuesday 26th July 2022' [PDF], Tavistock and Portman NHS Foundation Trust [website], https://tavistockandportman.nhs.uk/documents/2554/Board_of_Directors_meeting_papers_-_26_july_2022.pdf.

16 Bernadette Wren, 'Epistemic injustice', *London Review of Books* 43/23 (2 December 2021), https://www.lrb.co.uk/the-paper/v43/n23/bernadette-wren/diary.

17 For 2009/10, see 'Referral figures for 2016–17', GIDS [website], https://web.archive.org/web/20170511232820/https://gids.nhs.uk/number-referrals. For

2019/20, see 'Referrals to GIDS, financial years 2015–16 to 2019–20', GIDS [website], https://web.archive.org/web/20220304130542/https://gids.nhs.uk/number-referrals.

18 There may well have been more natal females referred in the year 2019/20 than 1,892. There were more than 100 children referred to GIDS during the year whose sex is unknown to GIDS from their records. See 'Referrals to GIDS, financial years 2015–16 to 2019–20', GIDS [website], https://web.archive.org/web/20200826182009/https://gids.nhs.uk/number-referrals.

19 'Tavistock and Portman NHS Foundation Trust: gender identity services inspection report' [PDF], CQC [website] (20 January 2021), https://api.cqc.org.uk/public/v1/reports/7ecf93b7-2b14-45ea-a317-53b6f4804c24.

20 Transcript of Dinesh Sinha's interview with Polly Carmichael ('M003') (19 October 2018).

21 Ibid.

22 Transcript of Dinesh Sinha's interview with Anna Hutchinson ('BD005') (14 December 2018).

23 David Taylor, 'Report on GIDU review (May–Oct. 2005)' [PDF] (January 2006), https://tavistockandportman.nhs.uk/documents/2248/FOI_20-21117_2005_David_Taylor_Report.pdf.

24 'First witness statement of Dr Matt Bristow' [official document from employment tribunal *Ms Sonia Appleby vs the Tavistock and Portman NHS Foundation Trust*; case no. 2204772/2019] (23 May 2021); 'First witness statement of Dr Anna Hutchinson' [official document from employment tribunal *Ms Sonia Appleby vs the Tavistock and Portman NHS Foundation Trust*; case no. 2204772/2019] (24 May 2021); transcript of Dinesh Sinha's interview with Matt Bristow ('BD016') (7 January 2019).

25 'First witness statement of Dr Anna Hutchinson'.

26 Transcript of Dinesh Sinha's interview with Matt Bristow ('BD016') (7 January 2019).

27 Transcript of Dinesh Sinha's interview with Sonia Appleby ('M009') (25 October 2018).

28 Ibid.

29 David Bell, 'Serious concerns regarding the Gender Identity Service (GIDS), of the Tavistock and Portman NHS Foundation Trust' [report] (2018).

30 David Armstrong, 'Bion's work group revisited', in Caroline Garland (ed.), *The Groups Book: Psychoanalytic Group Therapy: Principles and Practice Including The Groups Manual: A Treatment Manual with Clinical Vignettes* (London: Karnac Books, 2010), 139–51.

31 Office of Modern Governance, 'Tavistock and Portman NHS Foundation Trust: well led review final draft report' (3 December 2021), contained in 'Board of directors (part one): agenda and papers of a meeting to be held in public Tuesday 25th January 2022' [PDF], Tavistock and Portman NHS Foundation Trust [website], https://tavistockandportman.nhs.uk/documents/2407/Board_papers_-_January_2022.pdf.

32 Ibid.

33 Kate Grimes to Gatenby Sanderson employee [email], 24 January 2022.

34 Gatenby Sanderson employee to Kate Grimes [email], 11 February 2022.

35 Hayley Dixon, 'Don't bother applying for a job if you think people can't change sex, NHS trust tells health official', *Telegraph* (24 February 2022), https://www.telegraph.co.uk/news/2022/02/24/dont-bother-applying-job-think-people-cant-change-sex-nhs-trust/; Joe Davies, 'Lesbian NHS executive is turned down for top job at controversial Tavistock centre that offers children gender-reassignment treatment because she believes "sex is immutable"', *Daily Mail* (25 February 2022), https://www.dailymail.co.uk/health/article-10551023/NHS-Trust-accused-passing-former-LGBT-role-model-gender-critical-views.html.

36 Hannah Barnes, 'NEW: Tavistock and Portman NHS Foundation Trust is now subject to enhanced oversight from the NHS. It follows its Gender Identity Development Service being rated inadequate by CQC in January 2021 and an independent governance review finding several areas requiring improvement' [Twitter post] (13 April 2022), https://twitter.com/hannahsbee/status/1514182835577438212.

37 'NHS oversight framework segmentation', NHS England [website] (11 November 2021), https://england.nhs.uk/publication/nhs-system-oversight-framework-segmentation/.

38 'Board of directors (part one): agenda and papers of a meeting to be held in public Tuesday 24th May 2022' [PDF], Tavistock and Portman NHS Foundation Trust [website], https://tavistockandportman.nhs.uk/documents/2492/Board_of_Directors_May_2022_meeting_board_pack.pdf.

39 'HSJ reveals the best places to work in 2015', HSJ [website] (7 July 2015), https://www.hsj.co.uk/best-places-to-work/hsj-reveals-the-best-places-to-work-in-2015/5087434.article; 'Best places to work' [PDF], HSJ [website] (22 July 2015), https://www.hsj.co.uk/Uploads/2015/07/28/z/p/o/HSJ-Best-Places-to-Work-2015.pdf.

40 'Tavistock and Portman NHS Foundation Trust 2021 NHS staff survey' [PDF], NHS Staff Survey [website], https://cms.nhsstaffsurveys.com/app/reports/2021/RNK-benchmark-2021.pdf.

41 'NHS staff survey local results', NHS Staff Survey [website], https://www.nhsstaffsurveys.com/results/local-results/; 'Board of directors (part one): agenda and papers of a meeting to be held in public Tuesday 24th May 2022' [PDF], Tavistock and Portman NHS Foundation Trust [website], https://tavistockandportman.nhs.uk/documents/2492/Board_of_Directors_May_2022_meeting_board_pack.pdf; Emily Townsend, 'Three more directors depart top team at trust with "significant bullying problem"' HSJ [website] (26 May 2022), https://www.hsj.co.uk/mental-health/three-more-directors-depart-top-team-at-trust-with-significant-bullying-problem/7032510.article.

42 Sarah Stenlake, 'Report from the Trust's freedom to speak up guardian', contained in 'Board of directors (part one): agenda and papers of a meeting to be held in public Tuesday 24th May 2022'.

43 'Tavistock and Portman NHS Foundation Trust 2021 NHS staff survey'.

44 Sarah Stenlake, 'Report from the Trust's freedom to speak up guardian', contained in 'Board of directors (part one): agenda and papers of a meeting to be held in public Tuesday 24th May 2022'.

45 'GIDS Review', GIDS [website], https://gids.nhs.uk/news-events/2019-02-17/gids-review, archived at http://web.archive.org/web/20211127230458/https://gids.nhs.uk/news-events/2019-02-17/gids-review.
46 'Board of directors (part one): agenda and papers of a meeting to be held in public 2.00 p.m.–4.30 p.m. Tuesday 28th October 2014' [PDF], Tavistock and Portman NHS Foundation Trust [website], https://tavistockandportman.nhs.uk/documents/187/board-papers-2014-10.pdf.
47 Wren, 'Epistemic injustice'.
48 'Tavistock and Portman NHS Foundation Trust annual report and accounts 2020/21' [PDF], Tavistock and Portman NHS Foundation Trust [website], https://tavistockandportman.nhs.uk/documents/2344/tavistock-portman-annual-report-2020-21.pdf.
49 'Tavistock and Portman NHS Foundation Trust annual operational plan 2020/21', contained in 'Council of governors (part one): agenda and papers of a meeting to be held in public Tuesday 12th March 2020' [PDF], Tavistock and Portman NHS Foundation Trust [website], https://tavistockandportman.nhs.uk/documents/1869/March_2020_-_Part_1_Council_of_Governors.pdf.
50 'Council of governors (part one): agenda and papers of a meeting to be held in public Thursday 10th March 2022' [PDF], Tavistock and Portman NHS Foundation Trust [website], https://tavistockandportman.nhs.uk/documents/2438/Part_1_March_22_Council_of_Governors_final_pack_e-version.pdf; '2022/23 trust budget plan', contained in 'Board of directors (part one): agenda and papers of a meeting to be held in public Tuesday 26th July 2022' [PDF], Tavistock and Portman NHS Foundation Trust [website], https://tavistockandportman.nhs.uk/documents/2554/Board_of_Directors_meeting_papers_-_26_july_2022.pdf.
51 'Council of governors (part one): agenda and papers of a meeting to be held in public Thursday 10th March 2022'.
52 'Board of directors (part one): agenda and papers of a meeting to be held in public Tuesday 26th July 2022'.
53 Wren, 'Epistemic injustice'.
54 Ibid.
55 Ibid.
56 See Mermaids [website] https://mermaidsuk.org.uk/news/susie-green-leaves-mermaids/; Amelia Gentleman, 'Head of trans children charity Mermaids resigns after six years', *Guardian* (25 November 2022), https://www.theguardian.com/society/2022/nov/25/head-of-trans-children-charity-mermaids-resigns-after-six-years.
57 'The Gendered Intelligence team', Gendered Intelligence [website], archived at http://web.archive.org/web/20190118080159/http:/genderedintelligence.co.uk/about-us/the-team.
58 For Davidson's speaking publicly about working closely with Gendered Intelligence, see Sarah Davidson and Jon Sutton, 'It's a real critical period around gender', *Psychologist* 32 (2019), 46–9. For professional training and education events, see 'UMO host regular CPD events for specialist mentors and wellbeing staff, hosted at King's College, London', UMO [website], https://umo.services/cpd.shtml.

59 On 'treating homosexuality', see '"Homosexuality" and the history of the Tavistock and Portman', Tavistock and Portman NHS Foundation Trust [website], https://100years.tavistockandportman.nhs.uk/homosexuality-and-the-history-of-the-tavistock-and-portman/. On the 'satanic panic', see 'Portman and Tavistock clinic pilot study on alleged organsied [*sic*] ritual abuse', What Do They Know [website], https://www.whatdotheyknow.com/request/portman_and_tavistock_clinic_pil and Robert Hale and Valerie Sinason, 'Pilot study on alleged organised ritual abuse: final report' [PDF], What Do They Know [website], https://www.whatdotheyknow.com/request/389624/response/969467/attach/4/REDACTED%20REPORT.pdf.

60 'The Cass Review: independent review of gender identity services for children and young people: interim report' [PDF], Cass Review [website] (February 2022), https://cass.independent-review.uk/wp-content/uploads/2022/03/Cass-Review-Interim-Report-Final-Web-Accessible.pdf.

61 'Working with gender difficulties in adolescence' [video of talk by Aidan Kelly at Tigala conference 2018], YouTube (26 March 2018), https://www.youtube.com/watch?v=kPlCGBBcw90.

62 Wren, 'Epistemic injustice'.

63 Polly Carmichael et al., 'Short-term outcomes of pubertal suppression in a selected cohort of 12 to 15 year old young people with persistent gender dysphoria in the UK', *PLoS ONE* 16/2 (2021), e0243894, doi: 10.1371/journal.pone.0243894.

64 Antony Latham, 'Puberty blockers for children: can they consent?', *New Bioethics* 28/3 (2022), 268–91, doi: 10.1080/20502877.2022.2088048.

65 'Fig. 1: Ratings of change in life overall, mood and friendships at 6–15 months (n = 41) and 15–24 months (n = 29)', in Carmichael et al., 'Short-term outcomes of pubertal suppression'.

66 Bernadette Wren, in Women and Equalities Committee, 'Oral evidence: Transgender Equality Inquiry, HC 390' [PDF], Parliament.uk [website] (15 September 2015), http://data.parliament.uk/writtenevidence/committeeevidence.svc/evidencedocument/women-and-equalities-committee/transgender-equality/oral/21638.pdf.

67 P. T. Cohen-Kettenis and S. H. M. van Goozen, 'Pubertal delay as an aid in diagnosis and treatment of a transsexual adolescent', *European Child and Adolescent Psychiatry* 7/4 (December 1998), 246–8, doi: 10.1007/s007870050073.

68 Polly Carmichael, 'Time to reflect: gender dysphoria in children and adolescents, defining best practice in a fast changing context' [conference paper presented at WPATH symposium, Amsterdam, 18 June 2016], https://av-media.vu.nl/mediasite/Play/581e58c338984dafb455c72c56c0bfa31d?.

INDEX

abuse *see* bullying; sexual abuse
adolescence 2, 5, 14, 79–80, 142–6;
   see also girls
adult gender services 19, 67–8,
   144–5, 226, 269
  and Ireland 232, 237–8
  see also Charing Cross Gender
   Identity Clinic (GIC);
   Nottingham Centre for
   Transgender Health
age of consent 14, 305
'Alannah' 325–6
Alder Hey Children's NHS
   Foundation Trust 345
'Alex' 83–9
Anderson, Erica 341, 342
Appleby, Sonia 157, 172–3, 187,
   224, 246
  and Tavistock Trust 352–3
  and tribunal 312–24, 356
As Seen on TV (TV show) 31–2
autism 2, 8, 156, 256–7, 278, 279
'away days' 116, 141, 278

Bayswater Support Group 329
Bell, David 179–84, 185–94, 195,
   197–8, 200
  and Appleby 320
  and Tavistock Trust 353, 358,
   361, 362, 363
Bell, Keira 204, 263–4, 270, 271–3,
   274–5, 276

Bellringer, James 124–5, 126
bereavement 15, 17
beta blockers 214
Big Lottery Fund 328–9
Biggs, Michael 53, 290–1
bisexuality 35, 162
bone density 40–1, 42, 151, 214–15,
   289–91
Bouman, Walter 301, 305
Bowers, Marci 341–2
Bristow, Matt 90, 91, 92, 107–8,
   110, 366–7
  and CAMHS 130
  and concerns 158–9, 166, 169,
   172, 350
  and data 285
  and GIDS Review 241–2, 243,
   245, 246, 248
  and Leeds 141, 142
  and puberty blockers 120–1, 122,
   250
  and referrals 111, 114, 132
  and sexuality 160–1, 163
  and Tavistock Trust 352
BSPED (British Society of
   Paediatric Endocrinology and
   Diabetes) 40, 46
bullying 8, 25, 32, 42, 48, 82,
   83–4, 88, 98, 102, 147, 160, 176,
   187–8, 192, 224, 227, 245, 248,
   265, 279, 311, 332, 358
'Burrows, David' 190, 246–7, 367–9

Burstow, Paul 185–6, 198, 199, 329,
  357
  and data 279
  and detransition 267
  and GIDS Review 249, 252
Butler, Gary 269, 282, 283, 301, 337

CAMHS (Child and Adolescent
  Mental Health Services) 23, 47,
  84–8, 89, 129–30, 131–2, 148,
  208, 325–6, 332, 347–8
care system 17, 65, 229–30
Carmichael, Polly 6, 10, 106, 163,
  196–7, 310, 311, 326, 349
  and adolescent pathway 145, 146
  and affirmative model 105
  and Appleby 313–14, 317, 318,
    319, 322
  and David Bell 183, 185, 187, 190
  and Cass review 338
  and concerns 173, 174–5, 178
  and CQC 259, 260
  and data 282, 284, 285
  and detransition 264
  and Early Intervention Study 53,
    59
  and Entwistle 221, 222, 228
  and GIDS Review 246, 247
  and Hutchinson 76, 77, 78
  and Ireland 236
  and leadership 71, 72
  and media 115
  and Mermaids 23, 156, 328–9,
    364
  and Midgen early hormonal
    intervention leaflet 125, 126,
    127
  and patient groups 80
  and puberty blockers 40, 41,
    42–4, 45, 53, 59, 92, 101, 103,
    105, 106, 110, 117, 119, 125,
    126–7, 157, 222, 282, 284, 326,
    349, 373
  and referrals 101, 108–9, 113, 132
  and Roberts 310, 311
  and Singer 196–7

and social transition 100
and staff recruitment 115
and stage approach 92, 93–4
and Tavistock Trust 352, 353
and team 350–1
Cass, Hilary 255, 292, 345–6, 347
  and Cass Review Interim report
    334–40
CBT (cognitive behavioural therapy)
  130, 366
Charing Cross Gender Identity
  Clinic (GIC) 44, 67, 68, 150,
  184, 199, 232, 267, 286, 288,
  362
  and data 288
  and detransition 267
  and funding 362
Charybdis 74
chemical castration 5
Clarke, Anna Churcher 264
Cohen, Deborah 53, 60
Connelly, Peter 76, 170
Conrathe, Paul 203
control groups 53–4, 55, 123
Court of Appeal 123, 275–6
Covid pandemic 327
CQC (Care Quality Commission)
  112, 252, 255–60
cross-sex hormones 5, 6, 7, 13, 14,
  37–8, 42
  and persistence data 118–19,
    122–3
  and age limits 105–6, 343
  and data 278
  see also oestrogen; testosterone
Crouch, William 72–6, 77, 354–5
Crumlin (Children's Health Ireland)
  231, 232, 234–40

data 277–92; see also Early
  Intervention Study
Davidson, Sarah 2, 3, 4, 72, 77, 173
  and assessment speeds 108
  and Gendered Intelligence
    212–13, 364
  and referrals 113, 133–4

and resignation 259
and team 350–1
Davies-Arai, Stephanie 270–1
De Graaf, Nastasja 282
De Sousa, Craig 309
De Vries, Annelou 343
depression 2, 8, 11, 16, 27, 62,
  65, 83, 98, 107, 117, 129, 144,
  183, 214, 234, 237, 264, 294,
  326
Derbyshire, Victoria 146
detransition 7, 19, 51, 261–3,
  264–70
  and 'Harriet' 298–301, 306–7
Di Ceglie, Domenico 10, 11, 12, 13,
  32–4, 162
  and case note studies 15–16
  and data 287–8
  and goals 74, 355
  and Mermaids 23–4, 26
  and puberty blockers 40, 41,
    42–4, 45
  and Taylor report 205
  and therapy 36
'Diana' 83–9
discharges 280–1
DSM (*Diagnostic and Statistical
  Manual of Mental Disorders*) 9,
  78, 79–80
Dutch Model *see* Netherlands

Early Adopter services 345–7
Early Intervention Study 53–63, 81,
  116–22, 370–1
  and publication 122–4
eating disorders 2, 8, 15, 29, 71, 87,
  98, 99, 129, 167, 237, 263, 296,
  304
Edwards-Leeper, Laura 342
Ellie 31–5, 288, 373
endocrinology 5, 14–15, 44–5; *see
  also* puberty blockers; UCLH
Entwistle, Kirsty 221–30, 250
European Court of Human Rights
  (ECHR) 21
Evans, Marcus 181, 191, 193–4

Evans, Sue 21, 22, 23, 24–7, 40
  and Di Ceglie 42–3
  and House of Lords meeting
    201–4
  and Taylor report 205
Evelina London Children's Hospital
  345

Family Days 213
family relationships 16–18, 32, 34,
  99, 157, 165, 182–3, 208, 226–7
Ferring Pharmaceuticals 42
fertility 6, 42, 50–1, 57–8, 122, 126,
  183, 192, 266, 271, 289, 295–6,
  301, 345, 351
FII (fabricated or induced illness)
  157–8, 308
Finland 7, 102–3, 340–1
France 7, 341
Francis, Sir Robert 137
Freedman, David 15–16, 18
Freedom to Speak Up Guardians
  171–2, 173, 181, 182, 224, 225,
  241, 319, 358
Freud, Sigmund 19

gay *see* bisexuality; homosexuality
Gendered Intelligence 157, 177,
  333–4, 212–13, 363–4
GenderGP 301–2
GIDS (Gender Identity
  Development Service) 1–5, 6,
  7–8, 348–50
  and affirmative model 104–5
  and 'Alex' 86–8, 89
  and Appleby 314–24
  and assessment speeds 105–9, 110
  and David Bell 179–84, 185–94
  and CAMHS 129–30
  and case note studies 16–18
  and Cass review 334–40
  and caution 325, 326–8
  and clinical judgement 154–9
  and closure 345
  and concerns 128–9, 165–78,
    197–9, 366–74

GIDS (*cont.*)
  and contribution to Trust finances
    104, 184, 198, 199, 200, 361–3
  and CQC inspection 255–60
  and creation 10, 11–12
  and data 277–92
  and detransition 263–8
  and Early Intervention Study
    53–63
  and endocrinology 14–15
  and Ellie 32–34
  and Evans 24–7
  and GIDS Review 241–50, 251–4
  and growth plans 199–200
  and Hannah 148–51, 152–3
  and 'Harriet' 294–7, 302–4, 305
  and House of Lords committee
    201–4
  and Hutchinson 76–9
  and Ireland 231–2, 235–40
  and Jack 66–7, 68–9
  and 'Jacob' 208–16, 217–20
  and judicial review 270–6
  and management 350–1
  and Mermaids 328–9, 363–4
  and MPRG 333–4
  and nationwide service 71–2
  and NHS England 364–5
  and older adolescents 142–6
  and organisation 354–5
  and patient groups 80–1
  and Phoebe 47, 48–50, 51
  and Portman Clinic 18–22
  and puberty blockers 42–4, 45, 46
  and referrals 97–102, 111–14,
    131–8, 331–2
  and Roberts 309–12
  and sexuality 159–64
  and Singer 195–7
  and staff recruitment 103–4,
    114–15
  and stage approach 92–4
  and support groups 23–4
  and Tavistock Trust 351–4, 360–2
  and Taylor report 27–30, 204–6
  and teams 75–6
  and therapy 22–3, 73–5
  and trainees 72–3, 90–1
  and working environment 115–16
GIDS Leeds 72, 139–42, 221–30,
  250, 288–9, 290
GIRES (Gender Identity Research
  and Education Society) 37, 40,
  41, 43, 80–1, 130–1
girls 9, 62–3, 97–8, 136, 195, 105
  and 'adolescent trans boy' 109
  and teenage girls 2, 8, 10, 102,
    103, 160, 163, 196, 240, 280,
    305, 325, 343
GMC (General Medical Council)
  301–2
Gonadotropin-releasing hormone
  (GnRH) agonists *see* puberty
  blockers
Good Law Project 333–4
GOSH (Great Ormond Street
  Hospital) 76, 170–1, 345
GRC (Gender Recognition
  Certificate) 292, 300
Green, Richard 44
Green, Susie 41–2, 106, 127, 155–6,
  364
Grimes, Kate 356

Hakeem, Az 20–1, 25–6
Hannah 147–53, 344
'Harriet' 293–301, 302–7, 373
Health and Social Care Act (2012)
  152
Health Research Authority (HRA)
  60
High Court 122, 123, 275, 277–8,
  280
Hobbs, Lorna 288
Hodges, Sally 156, 251, 317, 318,
  323
Holt, Vicky 18
homophobia 8, 84, 140
  and families 165, 182–3
  and GIDS 160, 161, 163
  and GIDS Leeds 224
  and GIDS Review 245–6, 248

homosexuality 8, 9, 12, 13, 35, 36, 90, 120, 140, 146, 159–64, 165, 167, 173, 174, 175, 177, 182, 224, 246, 248, 270, 288, 317, 349, 365, 368
  and 'Alex' 83–4, 85, 88
  and 'Harriet' 297, 304–5
  and 'Jack' 65–6, 68
  and lesbianism 65–6, 68, 160, 162, 174, 177, 224, 270, 297, 304–5
  and Phoebe 48
  and 'treatment' 365–6
House of Lords meeting 201–4, 248
HSE (Health Service Executive) 231, 237, 238, 240
Hunt, Ruth 177
Hutchinson, Anna 1–4, 7–8, 9, 76–9, 374
  and adolescent pathway 143, 145, 146
  and affirmative model 104, 105
  and assessment speeds 107, 108–9
  and David Bell 180, 189–90
  and concerns 165, 167, 168, 170–2, 173–5, 351, 367, 371–3
  and data 278
  and detransition 261–3
  and Early Intervention Study 116-117, 118, 199, 120, 121
  and Entwistle 221, 222–3
  and FII 158
  and GIDS Review 242–4, 245, 246, 248–50, 253
  and Hodges 251
  and House of Lords meeting 201–3
  and increased numbers 96–7
  and patient groups 80–1
  and puberty blockers 81–2, 109–10, 118, 119, 120, 121, 344
  and referrals 112–13, 114, 132–3
  and resignation 241
  and sexuality 159–60, 161, 164
  and Tavistock Trust 352, 366

  and Taylor report 206
  and teenage girls 196
  and working environment 116
Hyam, Jeremy, QC 271

infertility *see* fertility
Ireland 231–40

Jack 64–70, 373
'Jacob' 207–20, 373–4
Jenkins, Paul 114, 145–6, 152, 331
  and Appleby 323
  and David Bell 185–6, 187–8, 193, 194, 197, 198
  and Cass review 338
  and data 279, 281
  and detransition 267, 268
  and GIDS Review 242, 247, 249–50, 252–3
  and Mermaids 155–6
  and NHS guidance 254–5
  and Oversight Committee 260
  and patient support groups 329
  and Rusbridger 171
  and Singer 195, 196
  and Tavistock Trust 354, 355, 357, 358, 359, 360–1

'Laura' 325–6
Leeds *see* GIDS Leeds
lesbianism *see* homosexuality
Littman, Lisa 269–70
Lyon, Louise 172, 173, 182

'McConnell, Liam' 259, 273–4, 308
McLaren, Rebecca 259, 309–10
Make More Noise 261
media see *Newsnight*; *Sunday Times*; *Today*
medical pathway *see* cross-sex hormones; puberty blockers
Mermaids 23–4, 26, 37, 80–1, 130–1
  and cross-sex hormones 105, 106
  and demands 363–4
  and 'Jacob' 213

Mermaids (*cont.*)
  and Leeds 139, 140
  and Lottery Fund 328–9
  and Midgen 178
  and Midgen early hormonal
    intervention leaflet 126–7
  and puberty blockers 41, 43
  and stage approach 94
Mid Staffordshire NHS hospital
  trust 137, 171
Midgen, Melissa 97, 103, 128–9,
  154, 336
  and David Bell 179, 180
  and concerns 169–70, 172, 177–8
  and early hormonal intervention
    leaflet 125–6, 127
  and Hodges 251
  and teenage girls 196
Miller, Marilyn 181, 186–7
Moran, Paul 231, 232–6, 237–40
'Morris, Alex' 127, 129, 130, 163,
  327
  and concerns 369–70, 374
  and judicial review 274
  and referrals 132, 134
Morris, Fenella, QC 272
MPRG (Multi-Professional Review
  Group) 276, 287, 333–4

Nakamura, Hitomi 288
National Institute for Health and
  Care Excellence (NICE) 6, 339
neovagina 59, 95, 125–6
Netherlands 13, 37–40, 41–2,
  335–6
  and the Dutch protocol 39–40
  and Early Intervention Study
    56–7, 58, 61–2
  and pathways 372–3
  and puberty blockers 123
  and screening 100–1
  and sexuality 162
  and stage approach 93, 94
  and surgery 95–6, 126
Newsnight (TV programme) 60,
  92–3, 157, 366

and Appleby 313, 322
and CQC 255
and detransition 266–7
and GIDS Review 251–2, 253
and Taylor 205
non-binary identity 99, 293
Nottingham Centre for Transgender
  Health 144–5
  and 'Harriet' 297–9, 300–1,
    303–4, 305
Nzegwu, Femi 111–12, 113, 114,
  168, 328

OCD (obsessive-compulsive
  disorder) 83, 84, 85, 87–8
oestrogen 5, 13, 14
off-label drugs 5
Older Adolescent Pathway 142–6
'Oldfield, Andrew' 135–6, 350
Olson-Kennedy, Johanna 342
O'Shea, Donal 232–6, 237, 238–9,
  240
osteoporosis 41, 42, 290–1

Patient and Public Involvement
  (PPI) 152
patient support groups *see*
  Mermaids; Gendered
  Intelligence; GIRES
Phillott, Sally 140, 225
Phoebe 47–52, 344, 373
Portman Clinic 15, 18–22
Prescott, Natasha 72, 73, 137, 158
  and concerns 166, 168, 169, 175,
    176–7, 350
  and puberty blockers 121, 122
  and referrals 133–4, 135
  and staff recruitment 115
  and stage approach 93–4
prostrate cancer 5
psychoanalysis 19, 22–3, 72–3,
  179
psychotherapy *see* therapy
puberty blockers 1, 2–4, 5–8
  and assessment speeds 107–8,
    109–10

and Cass review 336–40
and caution 326–7, 330–1
and clinical judgement 156–7
and CQC inspection 256–7, 258
and cross-sex hormones 122–3
and data 277–8, 280–7, 289–91
and Early Adopter services 346
and Early Intervention Study
    53–63, 74, 116–22, 370–1
and early prescribing 12–13
and effectiveness 123–4
and Entwistle 228
and Sue Evans 24–6
and guidelines 13–14, 41–2, 46
and Hannah 149–51
and 'Harriet' 294, 295
and House of Lords meeting
    202–3
and Hutchinson 78–9, 81–2
and Ireland 239
and Jack 67, 68–9
and 'Jacob' 209, 210–12, 213–16,
    217–20
and judicial review 272–6
and Leeds 140
and media 250
and the Netherlands 37–40
and NHS guidance 254–5
and Phoebe 48–9
and push 36–7, 42–5
and referrals 90–2
and risks 40–1
and stage approach 92–4
and surgery 124–6, 341–2
and Taylor 28–30
and Webberleys 301–2
and WPATH 342–3

randomised control trials 55
Reed, Bernard 37, 80
Reed, Terry 37
regret see detransition
Research Ethics Committees
    (RECs) 54–5
Richardson, Garry 309, 310, 314
Roberts, Helen 309–12, 314

Rochdale 229–30
Royal College of Psychiatrists 13
Royal Manchester Children's
    Hospital 345
Royal Society of Medicine (RSM)
    44–5
Rusbridger, Gill 171–2, 173, 182,
    241, 224, 225–6
Ruszczynski, Stanley 18, 19, 21, 22,
    188, 199

safeguarding 102, 158, 192–3, 199,
    200
    and Appleby 172–3, 187–8,
        312–24, 352
    and GIDS Review 246, 247, 252
    and Roberts 308–12
St George's Hospital (London) 11
same-sex attraction 2, 159–63; see
    also homosexuality
Savile, Jimmy 314–15, 321
scapegoating 168–9
Scylla 74
self-harm 2, 8, 17, 26, 41, 43, 69,
    98, 116, 117, 123, 129, 131,
    139, 144, 234, 237, 244, 256,
    294
Senior, Rob 102, 182, 316, 317–18,
    319–20
sexual abuse 2, 3, 8, 11, 15, 17, 24,
    25, 98, 99, 139, 157, 158, 159,
    167, 176, 196, 221, 235, 244,
    279, 313, 314, 335
    and care system 229–30
Shrier, Abigail 341–2
Singer, Juliet 195–7, 252–4, 255,
    267, 278–80, 359–60
Sinha, Dinesh 186, 187, 191–3, 200
    and Appleby 313, 314–15, 320–2,
        352–3
    and GIDS Review 241, 242,
        243–4, 245–6, 247–8, 252
South London and Maudsley NHS
    Foundation Trust 345
Spack, Norman 41
sperm freezing 50–1

Spiliadis, Anastassis 104, 107, 108, 120, 127, 172, 177, 367
and allegations 322
and data 285
and detransition 264–6
and FII 157
and Gendered Intelligence 212
and GIDS Review 243, 244–5, 246
and Midgen early hormonal intervention leaflet 127
and referrals 134
and resignation 241
and second opinions 155–6
and sexuality 160, 163, 164
Steensma, Thomas 343
Stenlake, Sarah 358
Stewart, Jay 178
Stoller, Robert 10, 11
Stonewall 177
suicide 131
Sunday Times (newspaper) 191, 194, 195, 200
surgery 7, 13, 33, 68, 297–8
and minimum age 343
and Netherlands 95–6
and puberty blockers effects 59–60, 124–6, 341–2
and regret 268, 269
Swarbrick, Ailsa 251, 259–60, 309, 310, 311, 322
Sweden 7, 340

Tanner stages 60, 71, 92
Tavistock and Portman NHS Foundation Trust 1–2, 15, 152, 365–6
and Appleby 312–13
and David Bell 185–91, 197–9, 200
and CQC 259
and directorates 29
and finances 184, 362–3
and GIDS 351–4, 360–2
and governance 355–60
and Ireland 231, 234–5, 240
and judicial review 270–3
and Singer 195–7
see also Portman Clinic
Taylor, David 20, 22, 27–9, 204–6, 291
and Tavistock Trust 351–2, 355
team meetings 75–6, 77, 93, 165, 173, 308
teenage girls see girls
testosterone 5, 13, 297, 298–9, 305
and side effects 144–5
therapy 12, 19, 22–3, 26, 72–5
and assessments 91–2
and gender affirmative 176–7
Thomas, Laure 202, 248
Today (radio programme) 250, 281
trans identity
and 'Alannah' 325–6
and 'Alex' 84–8
and families 165, 182–3
and Hannah 147–53
and 'Harriet' 293–4, 304–5
and Jack 65–6, 68, 69
and 'Jacob' 208–9, 216–17, 218–19
and puberty blockers 119–20
transphobia 37, 84, 109, 165, 168, 172, 191, 203, 221–2, 223, 224, 225–6, 265, 308, 317, 320, 349, 352, 366, 368
trauma 2, 8, 11, 15, 17, 18, 25, 27, 44, 73, 88, 90–1, 105, 107, 108, 120, 127, 148, 158, 159, 165, 167, 182, 198, 221, 224, 226, 228, 242, 270, 279, 298, 332, 335, 346, 366
triptorelin 5, 42

UCLH (University College London Hospitals) 27, 29, 46, 213–16
and Cass review 337
and data 283, 286–7, 288–90
and Institute of Child Health 53–4
and puberty blockers 149–50

United States of America (USA) 14–15, 41, 42, 203, 329
and DSM 79
and puberty blockers 341–2

vaginoplasty 59–60, 125–6
Viner, Russell 14–15, 94, 289
and Early Intervention Study 53, 54, 55–6, 57–9, 60–1, 117
and puberty blockers 41, 44, 45, 46, 81

'Walker, Andrea' 94, 139–41
Webb, Justin 250
Webberley, Helen 301–2, 316
Webberley, Michael 302
whistle-blowing 171–3, 312–24
World Professional Association for

Transgender Health (WPATH) 77, 93, 342–3
Wren, Bernadette 6, 12, 20, 21, 72, 347, 363
and David Bell 189
and CAMHS 131–2
and concerns 167, 174, 370
and cross-sex hormones 105–6
and data 282
and detransition 265
and Gendered Intelligence 213
and Mermaids 131
and Midgen early hormonal intervention leaflet 125
and referrals 101, 113, 114
and retirement 259
and Tavistock Trust 361–2
and team 350–1